Hawker's Early Jets

Hawker's Early Jets

Dawn of the Hunter

Christoper Budgen

First published in Great Britain in 2021 by
Pen & Sword Air World
An imprint of
Pen & Sword Books Ltd
Yorkshire – Philadelphia

Copyright © Christoper Budgen 2021

ISBN 978 1 52679 217 4

The right of Christoper Budgen to be identified as Author of this work has been asserted by him in accordance with the Copyright, Designs and Patents Act 1988.

A CIP catalogue record for this book is
available from the British Library.

All rights reserved. No part of this book may be reproduced or transmitted in any form or by any means, electronic or mechanical including photocopying, recording or by any information storage and retrieval system, without permission from the Publisher in writing.

Typeset by Mac Style
Printed and bound by CPI Group (UK) Ltd, Croydon, CR0 4YY

Pen & Sword Books Limited incorporates the imprints of Atlas, Archaeology, Aviation, Discovery, Family History, Fiction, History, Maritime, Military, Military Classics, Politics, Select, Transport,
True Crime, Air World, Frontline Publishing, Leo Cooper, Remember When, Seaforth Publishing, The Praetorian Press, Wharncliffe
Local History, Wharncliffe Transport, Wharncliffe True Crime
and White Owl.

For a complete list of Pen & Sword titles please contact

PEN & SWORD BOOKS LIMITED
47 Church Street, Barnsley, South Yorkshire, S70 2AS, England
E-mail: enquiries@pen-and-sword.co.uk
Website: www.pen-and-sword.co.uk

Or

PEN AND SWORD BOOKS
1950 Lawrence Rd, Havertown, PA 19083, USA
E-mail: Uspen-and-sword@casematepublishers.com
Website: www.penandswordbooks.com

Contents

Acknowledgements vi
Glossary vii
Foreword ix
Introduction xiii

Chapter 1 The Origins of Jet Power 1

Chapter 2 Hawker's Early Jet Designs 18

Chapter 3 P.1040 – Hawker's First Jet 33

Chapter 4 P.1072 – Rocket Propulsion 51

Chapter 5 N7/46 – The Naval Project 66

Chapter 6 P.1052 – Swept Wings 79

Chapter 7 P.1081 – A Clean Sweep 95

Chapter 8 Sea Hawk into Service 112

Chapter 9 P.1067 – Dawn of the Hunter 127

Chapter 10 Early Hunter 159

Chapter 11 Other Companies' Projects 183

Chapter 12 Future Hawker Projects 197

Notes 234
Appendix I: Hawker Pilots Involved in Early Jet Testing 238
Appendix II: Flights Undertaken during Testing of Early Hawker Jets 242
Index 291

Acknowledgements

As with any work of this scope, the number of people and organisations kind enough to assist with my research has been many and varied and inevitably there will be those whose names have slipped through the net.

In particular, I would like to extend my grateful thanks to Peter Amos whose knowledge of aviation is truly encyclopaedic. Similarly Chris Farara, at Brooklands Museum, has been most helpful in answering my queries by drawing on his many years at Hawker Siddeley and British Aerospace. Heinz Frick and Chris Roberts were kind enough to share their experiences of the Hunter during their RAF career and later with British Aerospace.

I would also like to thank Andrew Lewis at Brooklands Museum and Charles Hutcheon at Tangmere Military Aviation Museum and Peter Bedford for their kind assistance with access to documentation.

Finally my thanks to BAE Systems, The National Archives, Brooklands Museum and Tangmere Military Aviation Museum and to my proofers – Sue and Elaine – who have waded through the text seeking out my errors.

Back cover colour image showing Hunter WB188 (actually a GA.11, formally WV256) courtesy of Michael Brazier. Unless otherwise credited, all images BAE Systems, courtesy of Brooklands Museum.

Glossary

AAA	Anti Aircraft Artillery
A&AEE	Aircraft and Armament Experimental Establishment
ACAS/OR	Assistant Chief of the Air Staff/Operational Requirements branch
ACAS/T	Assistant Chief of the Air Staff/Technical branch
ADDL	Aerodrome Dummy Deck Landing
AFDS	Air Fighting Development Squadron
ARC	Aeronautical Research Committee
BTH	British Thomson-Houston
CA	Controller Aircraft
Cat 3, Cat 5 etc	Category of damage to aircraft reflecting its repair status
CEAD	Chief Engineer Armament Development
CFE	Central Fighter Establishment
CG	Centre of Gravity
CNR	Comptroller of Naval Research
CS/A	Controller of Supplies/Air
CTP	Chief Test Pilot
DCNR	Deputy Comptroller of Naval Research
DDARD	Deputy Director Aircraft Research and Development
DGTD	Director General of Technical Development
DMARD	Directorate of Military Aircraft Research and Development
DO	Drawing Office
DOR	Directorate of Operational Requirements
DTD	Directorate of Technical Development
FAW	Fighter, All Weather
FGA	Fighter, Ground Attack
FRU	Fleet Requirements Unit
GA	General Arrangement drawing
GOR	General Operational Requirement
HNLMS	His/Her Netherland Majesty's Ship

IMN	Indicated Mach Number
M	Mach number. Aircraft speed as a factor of Mach unity (Mach 1), the local speed of sound.
MAP	Ministry of Aircraft Production
MCA	Ministry of Civil Aviation
MDAP	Mutual Defence Assistance Programme
MRU	Medical Rehabilitation Unit
MoS	Ministry of Supply
MU	Maintenance Unit
MWDP	Mutual Weapons Development Programme
NATO	North Atlantic Treaty Organisation
RAAF	Royal Australian Air Force
RAE	Royal Aircraft Establishment
RAFVR	Royal Air Force Volunteer Reserve
RARDE	Royal Armament Research and Development Establishment
RATO	Rocket Assisted Take-Off
RATOG	Rocket Assisted Take-Off Gear
RLM	German Ministry of Aviation (Reichsluftfahrtministerium)
RNAS	Royal Navy Air Service/Station
RNVR	Royal Naval Volunteer Reserve
RNZAF	Royal New Zealand Air Force
RTO	Resident Technical Officer
SBAC	Society of British Aircraft Companies
TRE	Telecommunications Research Establishment
USSR	Union of Soviet Socialist Republics
V/STOL	Vertical/Short Take-off and Landing
VTOL	Vertical Take-off and Landing

Foreword

Typical of the pilots who grew up with the Hawker Hunter was Heinz Frick. Recruited to the RAF in 1959 flying Hunters and Lightnings. He attended the Empire Test Pilots' School course no.27 in 1968 and remained at Boscombe Down with A Squadron before moving to Rolls-Royce in 1971 as an engine test pilot. In 1978, Heinz was recruited by BAe, based at Dunsfold, working on Harrier and Hawk programmes. He was promoted to Chief Test Pilot in 1988, retiring from flying in 1990. His memories of the Hunter reveal with what affection the aircraft was held by pilots of the day.

> I wanted to fly from a very early age whilst living in Switzerland. In 1953 I joined my mum and stepfather in London and set about getting my five O-levels, the minimum requirement to join the RAF. I bought Neville Duke's book ' Test Pilot' and started to find out about Hawkers and the Hunter and was privileged to see the Black Arrows loop 22 Hunters at Farnborough in 1958. I was very lucky to join the RAF in 1959 and trained on Jet Provosts and the Vampire T.11. Being a bit of a cartoonist I missed no opportunity to draw myself in a Hunter and was extremely lucky to get a Hunter posting. RAF Chivenor was the Operational Conversion Unit were I first flew a Hunter. What an experience for a young man. The Hunter is without doubt one of the most graceful flying machines and we quickly learned to fire guns air-to-air and air-to-ground. One day I was told to do a practice diversion to Thorney Island near Portsmouth. The aircraft allocated was unbelievably a black Hunter ex-111 Squadron of the Black Arrows (the squadron had converted on to Lightnings) and I well remember thinking that life could not get any better.
>
> On completion of the course I was posted to 20 Squadron in Singapore flying the Hunter FGA.9. This is when I truly started to appreciate the outstanding flying qualities of the Hunter and the reliability of both airframe and the Rolls-Royce Avon engine. The Hunter did however have a few shortcomings thanks to the incompetence of the Ministry of Defence.

Radio and navigational aids were old and substandard, and we used to laugh that a four-ship formation was essential to get to the destination. The four 30mm cannon came in a quick-change pod and were great and accurate; the shells were jettisoned but the links were kept in aerodynamic containers under the front fuselage called Sabrinas. It was not a good idea to use the space for spare clothing on long trips as the internal airflow turned everything into cornflakes. The only other weapon we had was the dreaded 3-inch rocket known as the 'drainpipe', a left over from the Second World War; a lot of drag and not very accurate. Indeed, one of the Hunter pilots in Germany carrying out air-to-ground firing near the German-Dutch border asked the range safety officer how he was doing only to be told that he had missed the country!

One night I was woken up in downtown Singapore and told to pack and report to the Squadron. A quick brief at 4am informed us that four Hunters were off to Kuching in Borneo. I was to be number two for a pairs take off immediately. When I mentioned that it was pitch black, the flight commander said that he knew that (the Hunter never had any lights apart from tiny nav lights). Once in Borneo, border patrols were to be flown to stop the Indonesians encroaching. (Indonesia sought to add North Borneo and other lands to its own.) The maps that were given to us showed the island of Borneo and boundaries with UNCHARTED TERRITORY written everywhere. In the Hunter we were used to navigating with map and stop-watch, now all we had was the stop-watch. In contrast, the USAF who were assisting as part of SEATO were operating F-100, F-101 and F-105s, ground attack aircraft that had radar, inertial systems and the latest weapons. Despite all of that I was proud and happy to be flying the Hunter, a stunning, reliable and safe flying machine.

Most of the flying in the Far East was done with two or four external fuel drop tanks. As with most aircraft it was designed for the day fighter role and ended up a ground attack machine. So all the external stations were used to carry fuel that should have been designed into the airframe. The ministry and indeed the politicians wanted speed above everything else. The weapons were clearly not as important as seeing lots of shiny jets on the line. The problem of not having enough pilots rotating between Thailand and two bases in Borneo was covered with "you will do as you're told". Pilots lived in tents and the aircraft were left outside in the monsoon, not good for the electrics but the Hunter somehow survived.

Having flown the Hunter while in the RAF, Heinz would meet it again at Hawker Siddeley's flight development centre at BAe Dunsfold from where many of the Hunters had originally flown. In the late 1970s, the Sea Harrier FRS.1 was being developed for service in the Royal Navy and several Hunter T.8 trainers were modified to carry the Sea Harrier equipment to assist in development and pilot training, the completed modification making them T.8Ms. One of them, XL602 was based at Dunsfold, Heinz being one of several pilots flying the aircraft. 'I did a fair bit of flying in XL602 but it was mainly navigation and radar trials, very enjoyable and satisfying. We flew the aircraft with four 100 gallon tanks which made the take off quite risky … imagine a bird strike on lift off and both having to eject.'

Also acquainted with this Hunter was the author who spent time on and off in the 1990s, looking after the aircraft as part of the Flight Test Operations staff. XL602 was looked upon with fondness. Although rather long in the tooth by then, it still drew an audience when flying from Dunsfold and rarely gave any trouble. A lady of mature years to be sure, but a beauty none-the-less.

Heinz's fellow Test Pilot (and later Chief Test Pilot) at BAe Dunsfold in the 1980s and '90s was Chris Roberts. Coincidentally, Chris had also been posted to Singapore with 20 Squadron on Hunters. At the end of the tour, a posting to CFS initially as a Gnat QFI, turned into a tour as a Hunter QFI at RAF Valley. What are his abiding impressions of the Hunter?

> Everybody that's flown the Hunter loves it. It had aesthetics, flew very well, and was a very rewarding fast jet for both the novice and the experienced pilot. Conversely, if you examine the flight control characteristics against modern standards and requirements you would conclude that the handling would leave a lot to be desired. And yet on the squadrons pilots achieved good weapons scores but this was perhaps more to do with training standards and the ability of a typical pilot to adapt to their equipment, than being down to the engineering standards that existed when it was designed. Of course the Black Arrows formation aerobatic team (and the famous twenty-two aircraft loop at Farnborough) proved that the handling was more than good enough for the roles.
>
> It was a very enjoyable, easy and safe aeroplane to fly. It had very few bad characteristics so it was forgiving during air combat manoeuvring, and was very effective in the ground attack role despite being designed as an air defence aeroplane. At the end of a hard flight bringing it back to the circuit

to land did not need any exacting techniques, nor was it waiting to catch out the weary or stressed pilot. Simply put, it was brilliant for its time.

I was fortunate to fly the Hunter on and off for nearly thirty years, so I never felt that I had been out of it for very long. Altogether it was about seven times that I needed to re-familiarise myself with it, and each time it felt as though I had never been away. Such was the comfort and confidence that the Hunter gave to the pilot – an old friend that could be relied on. It made you feel very much at home whether you flew it daily or occasionally.

The Hunter fitted well with the pattern of other historic Hawker fighters, the Hurricane and the Harrier. They all had charisma and generated the enthusiasm that pilots have for such legendary aeroplanes. There was that 'X' factor that put the man-and-machine combination ahead of the opposition; between the Hurricane and the Harrier the Hunter followed the Hawker philosophy well.

Heinz Frick and Chris Roberts.
November 2020.

Introduction

The Second World War was the first truly global conflict to envelop mankind, greater even than the First World War in its far-reaching effect on the peoples of so many lands and it was therefore with longing that nations looked to the future, to an end to misery, fear and oppression.

The global population rightly looked to the post-war period as one in which they could turn away from hardship and vicissitude and return to a more normal life. Yet for many, indeed most, it was not to be. The destruction of totalitarianism of one colour was simply replaced by one of another hue. The main protagonists of the war had weathered the storm in very different forms. The United States of America at this time was probably home to the greatest free society ever known but had suffered greatly in the economic decline known as the Great Depression. The logistics of the world war had, however, resulted in the US becoming the greatest economic power of the century so for Americans, it appeared that a rosy future beckoned. In contrast, the UK had ended the war in the state of penury. The pre-war period had been tough economically for the UK as well, but wartime exigencies caused by the requirement to fund the war when the country stood alone, and its Empire trade routes being constantly attacked, meant that the UK was financially exhausted in 1945; a situation that would get worse before it got better.

The third member of the Allied triumvirate, the USSR, had started the war with its economy broadly unaffected by the world-wide depression that had so enfeebled western nations. Its command economy had enabled it to maintain its social fabric on an even keel, though accompanied by appalling oppression and widespread famine, the result of ideological decisions by Stalin rather than economic shortcomings. However, its fight for survival following the invasion by Germany had at first threatened to topple Stalin's dictatorship, but with vast war materiel and economic assistance from the USA and UK, the country had emerged stronger than ever and at the end of the war, its armies straddled a large part of western Europe.

The USA had no plans to remain in Europe once the Zone of Occupation in Germany was calm, indeed its traditionally neutral stance meant that politically, the withdrawal of its troops from Europe could not happen soon enough. Stalin's armies, however, were already in Europe and he had no intention of withdrawing them any time soon. For him, security was paramount: for him, his country and his ideology. Never again would the USSR suffer such a grievous invasion as it had suffered at the hands of Germany; (the invasion and dismantling of its neighbour Poland by the USSR and Germany in 1939 was quietly papered over). To this end, Stalin sought to retain control over most of the territories that his armies occupied at the end of the war. That this included nations other than Germany was but a small concern; these countries would be offered elections which would be free and fair provided governments friendly to continued Soviet influence were elected. If not, then there were other ways of obtaining what was required.

As continuing Soviet coercion and aggression mounted in Europe, disquiet among the Western Allies grew. While the USSR was not yet strong enough to use military force to support its claims, other means were available to encourage the West to see the Soviet 'point of view'. Finally, on 24 June 1948, the land routes that connected West Berlin to the Allied zone of West Germany were severed by the USSR, effectively isolating the Allied sector of the city in the midst of Soviet held East Germany; the intention being to 'encourage' the abandonment of the enclave by the Western Powers. As the first major provocation of the Cold War, Stalin no doubt thought that he held all the cards in this particular stand-off. The USA was desperate to withdraw its remaining troops home, the UK was a spent force and France was still a shattered nation; there could be little point in the West fighting what must have seemed a fait accompli.

Yet, not only would the Allied Powers keep the population of West Berlin fed and clothed with a massive air-lift, the action would awaken any that still needed to see, to the intentions of the Soviet Union and lead in 1949 to the formation of the North Atlantic Treaty Organisation – NATO – which would effectively bind the USA to the nations of Western Europe with economic and military aid, enabling these countries to rebuild their depleted economies and Armed Services and assist in the supply of modern weaponry. Stalin eventually accepted the inevitable and reopened the land corridor but it was too little too late; henceforth the actions of the USSR and indeed NATO, were viewed by the opposition as inevitably aggressive, suspicion replacing what little trust there may once have been.

As a consequence of this new threat, the UK now faced the need to rearm as soon as practicable, though there was the small problem of there being no money to pay for such a strategy. Not only were the coffers alarmingly low, an additional requirement was vying for attention. Throughout the war years, government committees had been tangling with what the future shape of society should be. Led by influential voices schooled in the woolly utopia of a 'New Jerusalem', there were increasing calls for radical social reform including a National Health Service, universal economic support for the unemployed, increases in the scope and extent of pensions, homes for all, extension of schooling and further education and so on. All well and good, but all these schemes would need paying for and as the Chancellor pointed out, once made available, could never be controlled, they would become an endless financial burden on the country. However, with a Labour Government now in power, the schemes HAD to be rolled out, the financial crisis notwithstanding.

So it was that the rapidly reducing pot of money was stretched to breaking point. Military budgets were stripped to the bone to fund the social reforms, squadrons and regiments disbanded; obsolescent equipment not replaced. In a fit of comradely fervour, Rolls-Royce was even allowed to export its latest jet engine technology to the Soviet Union, equipment which was immediately reverse engineered to power a new line of aircraft that NATO would meet a few years hence in battle.

So it was that the British aircraft industry upon which the requirement for new aircraft designs would fall, found themselves facing a vast drop in orders, a critical lack of research funding and an Air Ministry that appeared befuddled as to what, if any, equipment should be ordered for the future.

Hawker Aircraft Ltd and its Project Office sought to define what was in the Air Staff's mind by producing various designs that might answer the need of future aircraft, particularly with the growing threat – real or imagined – of high-speed jet bomber fleets winging their way from the Soviet sphere into southern England and devastating all that they beheld. This book follows the progress at Hawker Aircraft in seeking to provide a viable, successful, jet fighter with which to counter such a threat. That it would take some eight years to produce a successful interceptor reflects the parlous state of research into jet engine technology and high-speed flight, political indifference and vacillation and competing government programmes.

The Hawker Hunter would be the right aircraft at the right time; it was the best that could be produced with the budget available though the supersonic version, that would have given the west a truly world-beating fighter, was considered beyond the time-scale and finance available, even though it was in build when cancelled.

Following the tribulations encountered in bringing the aircraft into service, the Hunter would go on to feature widely in the Royal Air Force inventory as well as that of many overseas nations and remain in service for decades after its contemporaries had faded from memory. It would be remembered with fondness and respect by most who flew it as a benign and forgiving aircraft that packed a powerful punch, surely deserving of its place among the all-time greats of the aviation world. Widely considered to be the best fighter aircraft of its time, the road to perfection was strewn with difficulties and dead ends. This book examines the tortuous path that the company trod before the Hunter entered service and Hawker's continued battle to make it what so many pilots remember with affection.

Chapter 1

The Origins of Jet Power

One fine day in April 1944, a delegation of Rolls-Royce's most illustrious members travelled south from their vast headquarters at Derby to Surrey – to Kingston-upon-Thames – to meet with Sydney Camm and his design team at Hawker Aircraft Ltd. Led by the redoubtable Ernest Hives, General Manager of Rolls-Royce Aero Engines plant at Derby, the group also included W. Lappin, J.E. Ellor (Chief Experimental Engineer), R.N. Dorey (Manager of Installation and Flight Testing at Hucknall) and Stanley Hooker. Hooker had been responsible for doubling the power of the Merlin engine through improvement of the supercharger and Hives had tasked him with development of the new gas turbine engines. Based at Barnoldswick, the former Rover facility in Lancashire, Hooker was the kingpin of Rolls-Royce gas turbine development. Hives realised that at the end of the war, the global market would be awash with unwanted Merlin engines, nearly 150,000 of which had been produced. What was needed in the post-war world would be a game changer that would render the Merlin obsolete and create a new clamour for Rolls-Royce products. The gas turbine would be that engine.

It may be that Hives was also concerned that the profitable relationship with Hawker Aircraft Ltd, which had seen Camm's Hurricane and Hives' Merlin engine combined into a potent weapon, was now in the past; Hawker was now using Napier Sabre engines in their Typhoon fighter, while their Tempest fighter was equipped with either Napier Sabre or Bristol Centaurus radial powerplants and the forthcoming Fury would be based around the Bristol Centaurus engine. At this rate, Rolls-Royce and the country's premier fighter design house would cease to do business with each other.

The assembled worthies from Rolls-Royce met with Hawker's senior staff – Camm himself, Chief Designer for Hawker; Robert Lickley, Head of the Project Office; Roy Chaplin, Camm's deputy; A.N. Spriggs, the Works Manager and 'George' Bulman, Director and former test pilot. The Rolls-Royce group had come to Kingston to discuss with Hawker the potentialities of the new jet engine that they were planning and the possibility of persuading Hawker to design a

2 Hawker's Early Jets

new airframe powered by this. The engine, the RB.40, was to be capable of a thrust of 4,000lb which should be more than adequate for a single engine fighter. Given that Rolls-Royce had broken all records in the production of the Merlin and its follow on, the Griffon, how had they been capable of entering the new field of gas turbine technology and the production of a potentially winning design, seemingly out of thin air in the exigencies of war?

The complex and tortured route by which the UK acquired the gas turbine engine began in the 1920s and was the result of the vision and persistence of two men; one a government civil servant and the other a serving officer in the RAF.

In its simplest form, the gas turbine consists of a compressor drawing air into a chamber where the air is mixed with fuel and ignited, the expanding gas passing through a turbine which drives the compressor, the remaining energy being used as an exhaust jet to drive the vehicle forward. In its basic form there is only one moving part – the rotor assembly consisting of compressor and turbine mounted at each end of a connecting shaft.

The idea of the internal gas turbine had been in circulation in one form or another since the eighteenth century but attempts to use the theory to construct a working model failed due to the inability to obtain sufficient efficiency from

Visit by senior Rolls-Royce Staff to Hawker Aircraft Ltd to 'sell' their new jet engine. Left to right: R.L. Lickley, HAL; Neville Spriggs, HAL; E.W. Hives, RR; R.H. Chaplin, HAL; S.G. Hooker, RR; W. Lappin, RR; J.E. Ellor, RR; R.N. Dorey, RR; P.W.S. Bulman, HAL. April 1944.

the compression stage and because the availability of materials capable of withstanding the high temperatures required by the combustion process did not exist. The matter was summarised in 1920 by Professor William Stern of the Air Ministry Research Laboratory in South Kensington. In his report, he concluded that with the present state of technology, such an engine would be too heavy and require too much fuel; the metallurgy required to withstand the internal stresses was not available and anyway, the difficulty of obtaining sufficiently high compression ratios meant that for the foreseeable future, the gas turbine was 'pie in the sky'. While this summary should have been recognised as a 'snapshot' of the position in 1920, it in fact came to be seen by civil servants as Holy Writ, in turn repeatedly delaying the possibility of early advances in the gas turbine field.[1]

In July 1926, a scientist working at the Royal Aircraft Establishment at Farnborough – Dr Alan Arnold Griffith, then a Senior Scientific Officer – produced a paper wherein he discussed the potentialities of a powerplant based on gas turbine technology rather than the reciprocating engine that had till then been the prime mover for aircraft. His paper was, in effect, a response to Stern's report of 1920. Griffith determined to study compressor and turbine design with a view to improving the efficiency of a gas turbine sufficiently for it to be able to drive a propeller with which to power an aircraft.

Born in June 1893, Griffith studied Mechanical Engineering at the University of Liverpool, obtaining a Doctorate in the subject before entering the Royal Aircraft Factory (from 1918 Royal Aircraft Establishment) at Farnborough in 1915 as a trainee. His early work on stress in materials and crack propagation was original and led in 1920 to his seminal paper, 'The Phenomenon of Rupture and Flow in Solids', which revolutionised the way that engineers understand materials. Having turned his attention to turbines, Griffith realised that existing turbine blade assemblies were woefully inefficient due to their flat cross section and proposed a redesign using an aerofoil section for the blades. Building on this, his 1926 paper, titled 'An Aerodynamic Theory of Turbine Design', argued that the most efficient means of using a gas turbine to drive a propeller would be an engine deriving its power from a turbine driven by a multi-stage axial compressor and this was the design that Griffith presented to a committee comprising Air Ministry and RAE officials in 1926 with a recommendation that development work should begin with a view to eventually producing such an engine.

The Aeronautical Research Committee (ARC) agreed that small scale experimentation should proceed to test Griffith's theory and to that end, a small wind tunnel was constructed in which to test various arrangements of compressor and turbine blades, and also a model of a compressor and axial turbine mounted on a common shaft which could be powered by air drawn through the casing to investigate airflow over the various blade profiles used. The work was broadly complete by 1929 and in a subsequent report, Griffith stated: 'The turbine is superior to existing Service engines … in every aspect examined.' The ARC's report was less than heartening, stating that 'the superiority of the turbine … cannot be predicted … and there is no intention of advocating the expenditure that would be involved in further development of a turbine powerplant by the Air Ministry', but agreeing to further small-scale research of his ideas.[2]

By now, Griffith had left Farnborough to take up a position as Principal Scientific Officer at the Air Ministry Research Laboratory in Kensington where he refined his ideas on axial flow compressors. The results of his thinking led to a complex design for a contra-flow gas turbine arrangement in which the multiple stages featured compressor blades incorporating the turbine blades at their extremity with each stage rotating in the opposite direction to the preceding stage, thereby obviating the requirement for stators. By 1931, he had returned to Farnborough to become head of Engine Research and it was in this capacity that Griffith would be shown Whittle's work on gas turbines and damn it with faint praise.

With the ARC's decision in 1930 that the time was not ripe for the construction of a full-sized gas turbine, Griffith was left to refine his theories while working on other projects, with the result that little was done in the next five years to further the revolutionary concept. However, in 1937, perhaps prompted by Whittle's successful work on gas turbines, the ARC authorised RAE to look again at Griffith's work and investigation began of a gas turbine able to drive a propeller. With Hayne Constant, his deputy in the Engine Research Department, Griffith began construction of an eight-stage axial flow compressor which was completed in 1938. The completed compressor was successfully run and gave much valuable information until destroyed by German bombing in 1940. The decision was now made to manufacture some test engines to further the development process, but since RAE's workshops were not suitable for this, Metropolitan Vickers Electrical (Metrovick) and several other companies were approached to carry out manufacture. By 1939, the various requirements for the engine had resulted in an overly complex compound design comprising a seventeen-stage axial compressor, annular combustion chamber, eight-stage high pressure turbine driving the compressor, and a further five-stage power turbine to actually drive the propeller; RAE was trying to run before it could walk!

Throughout this period, the RAE approach had been one of long-term research into component parts. Eschewing the centrifugal compressor, much work was carried out on various axial compressor designs, turbine airflow characteristics and combustion components and therefore RAE scientists were able to build a comprehensive database of results with which to move forward to full axial compressor designs. However, the insistence on pursuing designs for engines capable of driving a propeller (i.e. turbo-prop designs) was resulting in overly complex and heavy designs, and it was not until 1940 that this approach was abandoned and research reverted to deletion of propellers as the method of propulsion in favour of direct propulsion via the jet exhaust and it was this design that was passed to Metrovick to construct a working engine.

Ultimately, the relationship between RAE and Metrovick would culminate in the F.2 axial flow turbojet upon which Armstrong Siddeley would base their successful Sapphire engine. Griffith had left the Civil Service in 1939 to join Rolls-Royce, while RAE continued, under Hayne Constant, to develop plans for an axial flow engine in collaboration with Metrovick. At Rolls-Royce, Hives allowed Griffith free reign to develop his own designs for a turbojet engine ('just keep thinking' was Hives' instruction), but again, the resulting design was overly complex and never went into production; Griffith's axial flow work was eventually abandoned in 1944, having never produced a working engine. However, as we will see later, his work would be central to the modern gas turbine engine used on most aircraft today. Griffith epitomised the research scientists at Farnborough at that time: highly intelligent, able to assess and understand complex theory and capable of innovative thinking. But this same scientific environment could, and perhaps did, result in Griffith being content to explore the potentialities of gas turbine technology as an abstract concept and therefore tended to ignore simpler solutions that did not perhaps give the result that his pure discipline suggested was possible. If Griffith represented the Scientific Civil Service community's approach to engineering design and development, with its iterative research and committee-led ponderous progress, where time was measured in decades, Frank Whittle represented the more direct 'can-do' approach to the problem.

Born in July 1907 – the son of Moses Whittle, a machine tool factory foreman – Frank Whittle grew up surrounded by the impedimenta of engineering life. His father possessed an inventive turn of mind, but not the education to turn concept into reality. Unlike Griffith, Whittle's early education was strictly working class, but in 1916 his father was able to buy a small engineering concern that allowed Frank an early induction into machine tools and their use. Proving to be an intelligent pupil, Whittle won two scholarships and was able to study physics, chemistry and mathematics and, with an avid interest in aircraft and engineering, applied for an apprenticeship in the RAF at the age of 14.[3]

In September 1923, the young Whittle took his first steps in the service to which he would always look for support, and reported for duty at RAF Cranwell to serve an apprenticeship as a fitter and later as a fitter/rigger with hopes of one day becoming a pilot. Three years later, his dream came a step closer when he was accepted as an Officer Cadet and entered the RAF College, also at Cranwell. While there, his interest in science – particularly physics and mathematics – grew along with aerodynamics and, in 1928, the young Flight Cadet, submitted an essay as part of his educational training titled 'Future Developments in Aircraft Design'. In this, he postulated future aviation trends and in particular, approached the question of how to increase the speed at which aircraft might fly in the future. He realised that flight at great height, where air resistance would be lower, would allow greater speeds to be achieved, but that the contemporary reciprocating engine and propeller combination would be incapable of the heights necessary and therefore some other form of prime mover would be required. He then considered both rocket power and gas turbines driving propellers as alternatives. From this, Whittle later arrived at the realisation that one could eliminate the heavy propeller and reduction gear altogether and use the propulsive thrust of the gas turbine directly.

Convinced of the rightness of his theories and encouraged by colleagues, in 1930 he took out a patent for a gas turbine (utilising a centrifugal compressor) specifically to power an aircraft, which was granted in 1932; prior to this, he had managed to present his ideas to W.L. Tweedie, a Technical Officer in the Directorate of Engine Development at the Air Ministry. Tweedie then arranged for him to meet with A.A. Griffith who, as we have seen, was also interested in gas turbines but used to drive a propeller. Whittle showed his design calculations regarding his proposed engine to Griffith, who was dismissive of the work, telling Whittle that his idea was broadly unrealisable at the present time and would result in an engine of excessive weight and fuel consumption. It is difficult at this remove to understand the reasons for Griffith's attitude; was it concern that Whittle's project might draw what funding was available away from his own work, or perhaps professional jealousy that this lowly officer had produced a design that was competitive with what the combined expertise of the scientific community at RAE had achieved? We will never know; it may just have been that Griffith, so convinced of the rightness of his complex axial flow designs, felt that Whittle's work, utilising a centrifugal flow system, was not the right way to pursue the subject.

However, suffice it to say that Whittle's meetings with various members of the Civil Service were sufficiently discouraging for Whittle to go back over his research and discover at least two mistakes in his calculations, though they tended to cancel each other out in terms of the practicability of his ideas. In 1936, accepting that no funding would be forthcoming from government sources, together with like-minded colleagues, Whittle set up a private company called Power Jets Ltd with which to pursue funding that would enable his gas turbine ideas to become reality. It would be a long hard slog against the disinterest of officialdom, the self-interest of existing engine manufacturers, and the absence of suitable materials able to withstand the high stresses and temperatures represented by the internal forces likely to be met in the gas turbine engine.

Unlike Griffith's designs, Whittle had aimed for the simplest design capable of producing a jet engine in time to influence the performance of future aircraft. With war with Germany now almost a certainty, his desire was to be able to produce the means by which RAF aircraft could fly higher and faster than the enemy's. Against seemingly insuperable odds, Whittle succeeded where all others had failed and was able to produce a working centrifugal engine, the remarkable milestone of firing up the world's first gas turbine engine being achieved on 12 April 1937. This engine, the Whittle WU (manufactured by British Thompson Houston – BTH – to Whittle's drawings), was remarkable in its simplicity, having only one moving part – a shaft assembly with the compressor at one end and turbine at the other. However, although simple in layout, getting the right materials to withstand the enormous forces acting on the compressor and turbine and solving the complicated combustion pressures involved would take Whittle and his Power Jets team several further years of frustrating and ceaseless struggle.

The Air Ministry was of course given access to Power Jets' work and witnessed the first engine running, so that, from total disinterest, the official attitude to gas turbines slowly changed to one of cautious interest and some small funding was made available to facilitate development of a flight engine and a research airframe to carry it. This was achieved and the first flight engine, the Power Jets W.1, took to the air in the Gloster E28/39 aircraft on 15 May 1941.

The act of getting an aircraft into the air driven by this upstart technology did not go unnoticed by the established aero-engine manufacturers. Their previously dismissive attitude to the technology of the internal gas turbine now changed abruptly as a competitive system of powering aircraft threatened to upset their apple cart. As we have seen, early in the war Rolls-Royce had given facilities to Griffith for him to develop his own version of an axial flow gas turbine, but this work failed to achieve fruition in time to influence the war. However, Hives was interested in what Whittle had achieved and instructed Stanley Hooker to keep in touch with Power Jets and their centrifugal compressor approach and also offered Whittle assistance in the manufacture of parts and in the provision of test facilities, thus keeping his options open with the new technology.

In his search for a suitable partner before the war, Whittle had approached the Rover car company with a view to manufacture of the first flight engines and had supplied detailed designs for them to work to. Unfortunately, the working relationship between Whittle and Rover failed, due in large part to Rover attempting to modify Whittle's designs to produce their own version of the engine, causing needless delays. Eventually, with the acquiescence of the Ministry of Aircraft Production (MAP), Rolls-Royce took over Rover's (and therefore Whittle's) concerns in the jet engine business along with the factory at Barnoldswick with Hooker now in charge of all jet engine production. Rolls-Royce took the Power Jets engine design that Rover had modified (the W.2B/23) and applied their tremendous corporate strength to its successful manufacture and development, the engine becoming the Rolls-Royce B.23 Welland I, producing 1,600lb thrust. This engine would become the UK's first operational jet engine, entering service as the powerplant for the Gloster Meteor in 1944.

Rolls-Royce found that development of the gas turbine could be achieved much more quickly than with the traditional reciprocating engine and within a short time, had developed the Welland to become the B.37 Derwent engine increasing the thrust from 1,600lb to 2,000lb. Thus the company was confident that it was well placed to dominate the post-war aero-engine market which could not be long in coming. Rolls-Royce, however, would not have the market all to themselves. In conjunction with RAE, MAP had constituted a committee to manage the new gas turbine technology; this – the ponderously named Gas Turbine Technical Advisory Coordinating Committee – included in its ranks representatives from the main aero-engine manufacturers. With an eye on the post-war market for their own jet engine products, the manufacturers lost no time in lobbying to prevent Power Jets from manufacturing engines in

The Origins of Jet Power 9

The Rolls-Royce Derwent Ser.1 engine, the first Rolls-Royce turbojet to enter series production, heavily based on Frank Whittle's work at Power Jets.

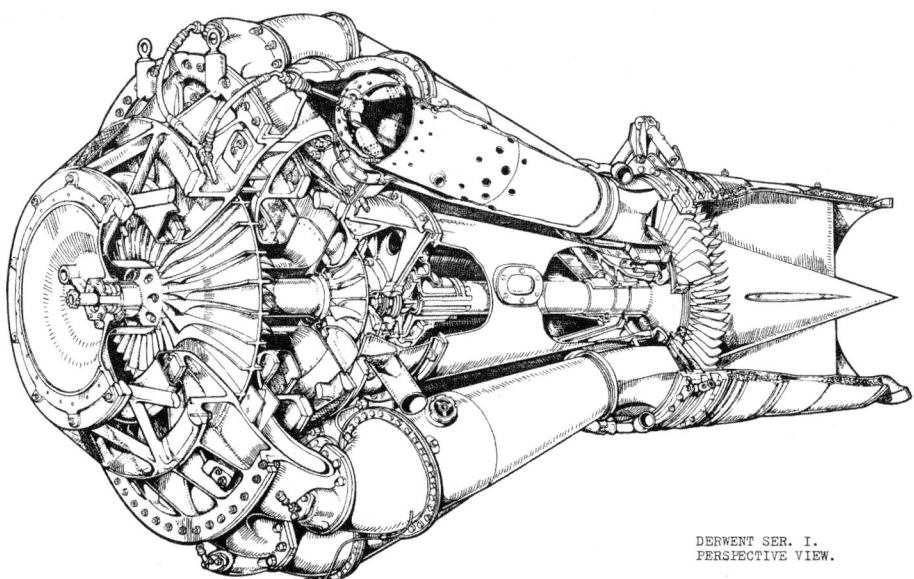

Cutaway view of Rolls-Royce Derwent engine showing the main impeller at the front comprising the axial compressor, the reverse flow combustion chambers and the single turbine at the rear.

competition with the existing companies. In a disgraceful move, not only did the MAP agree to this but in 1944, Minister of Aircraft Production Sir Stafford Cripps nationalised Power Jets, removing its control from the board and from Whittle himself![4]

With the inventor of the UK's first workable jet engine thus neutered, MAP instructed Power Jets to supply to the aero engine companies their technical research results regarding the gas turbine so that they might benefit from all of the research completed thus far by Whittle's team – free! It was in this manner that de Havilland, under the guidance of Major Frank Halford, the company's consulting engineer for engine development, began their work on a centrifugal jet engine. In January 1941, Chairman of the ARC Sir Henry Tizard approached de Havilland with an invitation to design a jet aircraft and the engine to power it. Having thoroughly assessed the Power Jets research, Halford and his team settled on a centrifugal flow engine giving around 3,000lb thrust which was numbered H.1. With the benefit of Power Jet's hard-won technology, de Havilland had their first engine running on the test stand on 13 April 1942, just 248 days from release of drawings. To accommodate the engine, a small single-engined twin boom aircraft was designed largely built of wood, the prototype of what would become the Vampire, flying on 20 September 1943 with an engine delivering 2,300lb thrust. Such was the rapid progress that de Havilland was able to achieve with the H.1 engine that the prototype Meteor, the Gloster F.9/40 first flew with H.1 engines, the Welland engine not being quite ready. De Havilland would follow the H.1 Goblin engine with the larger H.2 Ghost producing initially some 4,400lb thrust, later increased to 5,000lb.[5]

Thus, by 1944, the UK had two jet propelled aircraft in its inventory, one just entering service and the other, the Vampire, just missing the conflict. Both these aircraft utilised the centrifugal flow gas turbine. Although rather thirsty, especially at low level, this engine type was simple in operation, robust and capable of mass production within the aero engine industry.

By contrast, the axial flow engine offered a lower cross section and better fuel consumption as well as greater development potential but was a more complex piece of engineering. The early work on axial compressors carried out for RAE by Metrovick had matured into flight testing of the UK's first axial flow engine; the Metrovick F.2, producing a thrust of approximately 1,800lb. The engine was later tested in the F9/40 Meteor prototype but did not produce the thrust hoped for, though development through 1943 raised this to 2,700lb. Further development resulted in the F.3 – the world's first turbofan engine – and the F.5, another turbofan rated at some 4,710lb. It should be noted that these became the first turbofan engines because Whittle's work at Power Jets on turbofan technology was cancelled by the government in 1944. The F.3 and F.5 engines were development units only and did not progress to commercial examples and Metrovick, with government 'encouragement', made the decision to leave the aero engine business entirely.

As has been seen, the Metrovick development of axial compressors in concert with Hayne Constant at RAE had led, in 1940, to the production of the Metrovick F.2 gas turbine. This featured a nine-stage axial compressor driven by a two-stage turbine and annular combustion chamber and offered a thrust of some 1,800lb. Flight testing commenced in the tail of a Lancaster in June 1943 and later in the prototype F9/40 Meteor. A developed engine, the F.2/2 offered 2,400lb thrust and later, as the F.2/3, 2,700lb. By 1945 the F.2/4 Beryl engine was rated at 3,500lb thrust and was manufactured in small numbers but was quickly superseded by the F.9 which would later be named the Sapphire.[6]

With Metrovick now out of the picture, it fell to Armstrong Siddeley Engines at Coventry to continue the work on axial flow technology. This company had also been used by RAE to manufacture parts for their engine designs and so were recognised as suitably versed in the skills required to pick up Metrovick's F.9 engine design of 1946 and continue with its development. Armstrong Siddeley was part of the Hawker Siddeley Group of companies and, starting work on their first engine design in 1942, had by the following year produced a turbojet engine designated ASX and a turboprop version, the ASP. Due to poor results from the ASX, the ASP was instead developed to become the AS Python turboprop which would later power the Westland Wyvern fighter. Work on developing the ASX version of the engine had continued, but in 1947, with the arrival of the F.9 Sapphire axial engine from Metrovick, work proceeded to develop this engine. Flight testing began in 1950 with the engine, designated Sa.1 fitted into the tail of a Lancaster, producing 6,500lb thrust. Shortly, this engine was superseded by the Sa.2 giving 7,380lb and later by the Sa.3 which was type tested at 8,000lb. The Sa.6 followed offering 8,300lb thrust with lower fuel consumption and this was type tested at 8,200lb, this engine being installed in the third prototype P.1067 Hunter WB202. With the great success of this engine, mass-production began in 1953 at a Hawker Siddeley Group site at Hucclecote in Gloucestershire, the engine being fitted in the Hunter F.2 and F.5 as well as the Gloster Javelin and Handley Page Victor bomber. It was also licensed to the US company Curtiss-Wright as the J-65.

12   Hawker's Early Jets

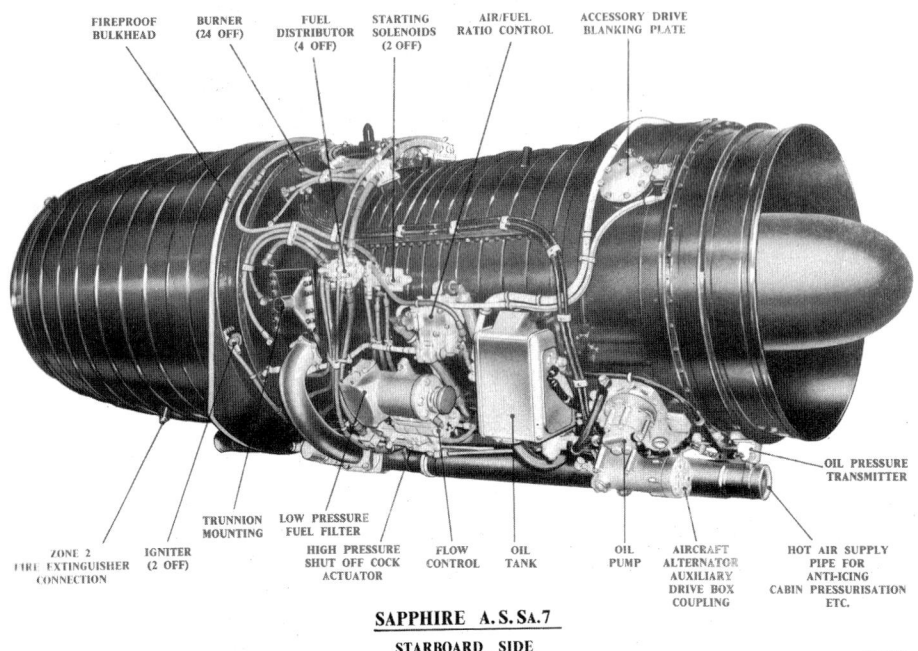

Armstrong Siddeley Sa.7 Sapphire engine, used to power the Hawker Hunter F.2 and F.5 aircraft.

To return to the fortunes of Rolls-Royce: as described above, Rolls-Royce's Derwent engine was to be used to power the new twin jet from Gloster, the Meteor. As the Meteor was developed through various marks, so the Derwent also underwent progressive development, from the Derwent II of 2,200lb thrust up to the Derwent V producing 3,500lb thrust and then 4,000lb. While these engines were excellent for their time, they were all derivatives of Whittle designs, Rolls-Royce had yet to develop a gas turbine to their own design.

In 1944, MAP approached Rolls-Royce with a request for an engine more powerful than the Derwent. Stanley Hooker took this opportunity to put into practice all of the knowledge thus far gained from the Power Jets designs, and proposed an entirely new design, still with a centrifugal flow compressor, which it was hoped would produce a thrust in excess of any so far achieved. The new design, designated RB.40, looked promising but with US engine development already producing similar thrusts, it was decided to redesign the RB.40, which became the RB.41 potentially capable of 5,000lb thrust. This engine, later named the Nene, would become the engine that kick-started jet engine production globally, though not perhaps in the way that Rolls-Royce had hoped.[7]

The Nene utilised a double-sided centrifugal compressor driven by a single stage turbine and nine combustion chambers. Within six months of issue of drawings, on 27 October 1944 the engine was running on the test stand, producing 4,000lb, which was increased the next day to 5,000lb thrust; a quite remarkable achievement and confirmation that Rolls-Royce had fully absorbed the requirements of gas turbine technology, at least in the utilisation of centrifugal compression. It would, however, be an entirely different matter when the company sought to move to axial compressors. The Nene first flew as the prime mover in a de Havilland Vampire in March 1946 with the bulk of testing carried out using Avro Lancastrians with the engines installed in the outer nacelles. Entering production in September 1946 as the Nene 1, the engine produced 4,850lb thrust for a weight of 1,560lb.

Although not widely used in the UK, its technology being overtaken by axial flow designs, the engine was licence-produced in the US as the Pratt & Whitney J-42. It was also extensively produced by the Soviet Union as the Klimov VK-1

Rolls-Royce Nene engine, the first 'clean sheet' design from the company and the engine used to power Hawker Aircraft's first jet aircraft.

following a fateful decision by the post-war Labour administration to sell a number of the engines to the USSR. The engine was immediately reverse engineered and became the main powerplant of the MiG-15 that would be fielded by the Soviet Union in the forthcoming Korean War, the aircraft proving a serious embarrassment for the United Nations Forces fighting for their survival. Needless to say, Rolls-Royce never saw any royalties from these engines.

The last iteration of the centrifugal engine at Rolls-Royce was the RB.44 Tay, a scaled-up Nene producing initially 6,250lb thrust but later licence-built examples raised the output to 7,720lb. While the Tay would be considered for a later Hawker design, for the present it was the RB.41 Nene that Hives and Hooker had come to Hawker to discuss and which they hoped they could persuade Camm and the Hawker board to back with a suitable airframe.

Henceforth, however, the axial flow turbojet would eclipse the centrifugal flow designs of the 1940s. Although simple and robust, the centrifugal compressor design resulted in a large frontal area and indifferent fuel consumption at low level. Further development was fundamentally governed by increases in the diameter of the compressor, leading to greater cross-section. The axial compressor on the other hand, although far more complex, offered a small frontal area, improved fuel consumption and seemingly unlimited development potential and it would be this technology that would dominate the industry in the latter half of the twentieth century.

While Armstrong Siddeley had experienced comparatively few major problems with the axial turbojet, for Rolls-Royce, used to getting things right first time, the experience would prove anything but trouble-free. With A.A. Griffith still on the books as the resident axial compressor expert and development of centrifugal compressor engines coming to an end with the Tay, Rolls-Royce now turned their attention to the design and development of an axial flow turbojet engine. Initial design work to Griffith's calculations for an engine capable of some 6,500lb thrust designated AJ.65 ('axial jet 6,500lb') began in 1945 and when complete, was passed up to the Rolls-Royce jet engine centre at Barnoldswick under Stanley Hooker for detail design, manufacture and development. This was new ground for the company and within days, problems were apparent in that Griffith had seriously underestimated the weight of the engine by as much as 50 per cent. Rolls-Royce was soon mired in the technicalities of the new engine technology, Hooker later explaining that whereas the Nene had been broadly made in seven months, it took seven years to produce a reliable AJ.65 Avon engine![8]

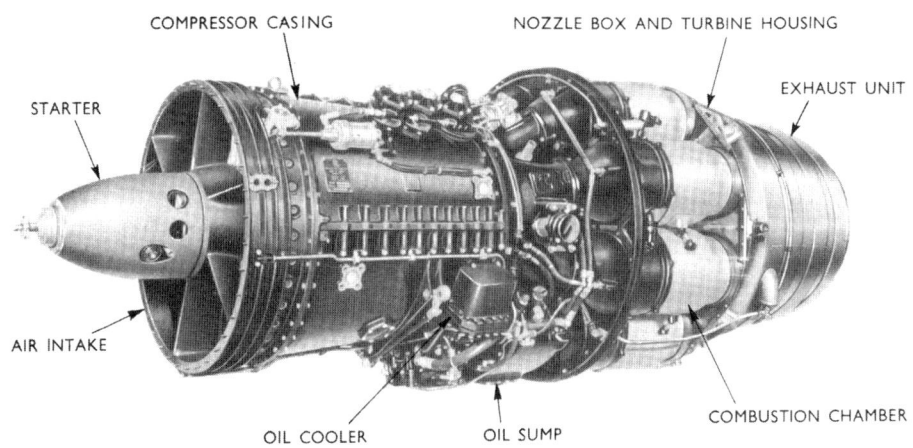

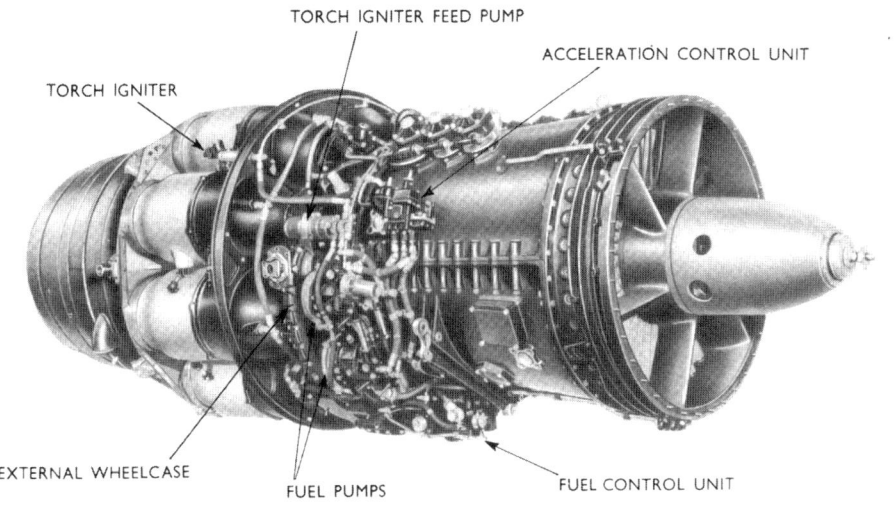

Rolls-Royce Avon engine, the first Rolls-Royce axial flow engine to enter service and which would be the main powerplant for the forthcoming Hawker Hunter. Note the separate combustion 'cans' later changed to an annular combustion chamber.

The first engine, the RA.1, was ready for testing in 1946 and was initially a disaster; it was difficult to start, had poor acceleration and the compressor fan blades regularly snapped off. Following a redesign of the compressor by two of Hooker's proteges, the engine was just capable of producing about 5,000lb thrust, but by March 1947 one run produced a thrust of 6,500lb. Such was the scale of the problem that the Rolls-Royce General Manager Ernest Hives insisted that the engine be taken away from Hooker and the Barnoldswick team and moved to the main works at Derby. Such was the enormity of this decision

16 Hawker's Early Jets

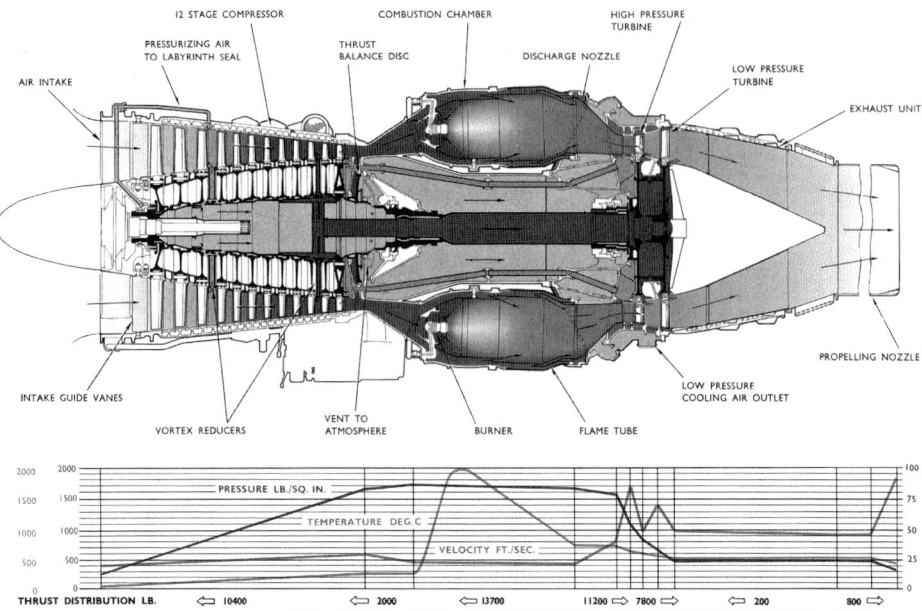

Cutaway view of the Rolls-Royce Avon Mark 1 engine showing the airflow and combustion process.

that Hives and Hooker, up till then so close, parted acrimoniously, with Hooker moving in December 1948 to become Chief Engineer at Bristol Engines.

With the engine now at Derby, improvements resulted in the RA.2 capable of a continuous 5,500–5,800lb, while the RA.3 was now capable of producing 6,500lb thrust regularly. The Canberra bomber was the first aircraft produced that used the Avon engine – the RA.3 – in 1950 but work continued on the engine at Rolls-Royce to upgrade performance, leading to the RA.7, a more powerful engine offering 7,500lb thrust intended for the new generation of fighters represented by the Swift and Hunter. Early RA.7 Avons began delivery in 1950 and, by 1952, now termed the 100 series engine, passed their 150-hour type test and were released for mass production. This would be the engine that the Hunter F.1 would use as its powerplant. However, as will be seen, the engine still had one major shortcoming up its sleeve waiting to bite Rolls-Royce and Hawker Aircraft Ltd.

While all of this effort had been continuing in the UK to produce jet propelled aircraft, the potential (and later actual) enemy – Nazi Germany – had also been busy with the technology. Despite the bold claims of post-war propaganda that the UK had 'invented' the jet engine (and radar for that matter), the truth was rather more complex.

Hans von Ohain had started to take an interest in the concept of a gas turbine to drive an aircraft around 1935. His first proposals involved a centrifugal flow engine and an early model was constructed to test the theory. Unfortunately it was less than a whole-hearted success, but his professor at the University of Gottingen assisted by contacting Ernst Heinkel, the owner of the Heinkel Aircraft Company, and arranging for von Ohain to meet him. Heinkel hired the young student and arranged assistance and facilities for him to continue his work. By September 1937, von Ohain had his first working engine on the test bed and Heinkel moved swiftly to design a small aircraft to be powered by a development of this engine. By 1938, the RLM (the German Ministry of Aviation) was apprised of the work undertaken by Heinkel and was actively encouraging other companies to explore the new technology. Ultimately, however, it would be Heinkel who achieved the flight of the world's first jet propelled aircraft, the He 178, on 27 August 1939. The design of von Ohain's engine would not be continued in development, other more efficient designs being used in Germany, particularly the axial flow design.

These axial flow engines would be developed by several German companies. Junkers, BMW and Daimler Benz in addition to Heinkel would produce engines that were used to place into service aircraft such as the Messerschmitt Me 262, Arado Ar 234, and Heinkel He 162 in limited numbers. Both production and development of these engines and aircraft were restricted by Allied offensive operations.[9]

It will be seen, then, that the prize for being the first person to successfully run an internal gas turbine engine fell to Frank Whittle, and that for the first flight fell to von Ohain's engine in the He.178. In yet another twist to the story, it would be the UK that would field jet-propelled aircraft in service, ahead of the German effort by some months. It should be noted here that although von Ohain always denied that he was influenced by Whittle's work, Whittle's engine patents were printed and distributed around the various interested parties in Germany in the early 1930s and his work was thus available to German scientists before anyone in the UK government realised or cared that secrecy might be a wise move.

Chapter 2

Hawker's Early Jet Designs

As explained in the previous chapter, both Gloster and de Havilland had been able to enter production of jet fighter aircraft before the end of the Second World War. At Hawker, Rolls-Royce had, in April 1944, given a presentation of their forthcoming RB.40 turbojet engine and yet it would be 1947 before Hawker would enter the jet aircraft ring. Why was it that the pre-eminent UK fighter design house was so late in coming to the jet party? What had the design office been filling their time with, while other companies stole a march on the Kingston company? To answer these questions, it would be useful to examine the Hawker design office output during the war years to see just what had been going on.

Hawker's ground-breaking Hurricane monoplane fighter had first flown in November 1935 and entered operational service at the end of 1937. Output of the fighter was, and continued to be, high and design improvements flowed from the Kingston design office to maintain the Hurricane's place as one of the RAF's pre-eminent fighters as war with Germany became a reality. Changes to the rear empennage were followed by replacement of the fabric-covered wing by use of a stressed metal wing and the early engine was replaced by the Rolls-Royce Merlin II with the Watts twin blade fixed-pitch propeller being replaced with three-blade variable-pitch units. Improvements in armament followed with the original eight browning guns being replaced by a twelve-gun battery in the Hurricane IIB and then four Hispano cannon in the IIC version. As Hurricanes poured out of Hawker's factory at Langley, (and at Gloster's Hucclecote factory and Canadian Car and Foundry in Montreal) the Experimental Drawing Office, Stress Office and various technical offices were relocated in mid-1940 to Claremont House near Esher to avoid the likelihood of bombing of the Kingston works. At this time a Project Office was set up under Robert Lickley with a staff of four. Here, work continued on the Hurricane's replacement. Seventeen marks of Hurricane would be built with construction continuing throughout the war until the last, a Mark IIC serialled PZ865 in July 1944, which was retained by Hawker and named 'The Last of the Many'.[1]

In discussing the move to Claremont in a lecture delivered in 1992, Ralph Hooper, a designer in Experimental DO at Kingston in the 1950s and latterly Executive Director and Chief Engineer (as well as the originator of the Harrier concept), noted that,

> at the beginning of the war the 'new types' part of Hawker's design organisation was moved into the stately home, which before the war had been a girls' school. The people engaged in current production support, modification and damage repair remained in the humbler surroundings of Canbury Park Road (Kingston-upon-Thames) and must have regarded themselves as the 'poor relations'.

In all, some 172 design staff moved over to Claremont, not returning to Kingston until the end of the war.[2]

Allied to the Hurricane was the Henley, designed to meet a requirement in the mid-1930s for a two-seat light bomber, construction proceeding in parallel with the Hurricane, with which it shared parts and design characteristics. However, although first flying in 1937, series production was reduced in favour of the Hurricane and construction of the 200 aircraft order hived off to Gloster (though design authority remained at Kingston). In the event, the Henley entered service as a target tug and rapidly left service again in 1942. A redesign of the Henley produced the Hotspur, a turret fighter in the Boulton-Paul Defiant mould. First

Hawker Aircraft Ltd Design staff at Claremont, Esher, 1944. Front row centre is Sydney Camm, Robert Lickley on his left and Roy Chaplin on his right.

The prototype Hurricane K5083 at Brooklands in November 1935, possibly prior to first flight. Of note are the tailplane struts and hinged undercarriage doors on the main wheels, both quickly deleted on production aircraft. Fitted at this stage is a twin blade Watts fixed-pitch propeller, later replaced with a three-blade variable-pitch unit.

The last Hurricane PZ865, a Mark IIC named 'The Last of the Many' aloft in 1944 with 'George' Bulman at the controls. The aircraft looks much more purposeful than that in the previous image.

flown in 1938, the type did not enter series production, the role being filled by the Defiant.

Designed to meet specification F.18/37, the Typhoon and Tornado would feature a twelve-gun armament and be powered by the Napier Sabre and the Rolls-Royce Vulture engine respectively. The Tornado first flew in December 1939 but problems with the Vulture engine resulted in the aircraft being trialled with a Bristol Centaurus radial engine, flying in October 1941. However, production of the Tornado was abandoned and effort transferred to the Napier Sabre-engine Typhoon which first flew in February 1940 and immediately became the subject of production contracts; an initial batch being manufactured at Langley before the remainder were sub-contracted to Gloster Aircraft. The original Typhoon IA was followed by the IB featuring strengthened rear fuselage and four Hispano cannon instead of the twelve-gun battery. The aircraft proved disappointing as a high-level interceptor due to its relatively thick wing but found renewed vigour as a close support aircraft where it excelled; particularly feared by the enemy were Typhoons carrying batteries of rocket projectiles with which they wreaked havoc on ground transport. The Typhoon would enter service in four different marks, some 3,330 aircraft being built but the type was being replaced at the war's end by another Hawker product.

Still seeking to design a potent interceptor with which to replace the Hurricane, the Hawker Project Office had, in discussions with the Director of Technical Development, schemed a Typhoon with a thin wing section and driven by a new Napier Sabre EC.107C (which would evolve into the Sabre IV). Known initially as the Typhoon II, the aircraft was tendered in November 1941 and first flew in February 1943 as the Tempest I. This mark was followed by the Tempest II, powered by the Bristol Centaurus radial engine (the result of continued development with the Centaurus powered Tornado) and later by the Tempest V with Sabre IIA and IIB engine and then the VI using a Napier Sabre V. The aircraft proved very effective in the fighter role, particularly at low altitude, as well as ground attack and was instrumental in successful attacks on the VI flying bomb. Post-war export orders for Tempest would be filled with suitably modified ex-RAF aircraft, numbers going to India and Pakistan.

The Fury and Sea Fury would be Hawker's last manufactured designs to be powered by reciprocating engine and propeller, the Sea Fury becoming a superlative fighter following in the footsteps of the Tempest. Its genesis was in 1942 when it was reasoned that a lightweight Tempest could be produced by eliminating the wing centre-section and bringing the wings together on the centreline of the aircraft. The resulting Tempest Light Fighter (Centaurus)

Typhoon IB R7881 at Langley c.1943. This aircraft later became the only NF.IB night-fighter prototype with AI Mk. IV radar fitted but was not proceeded with. Note the old farm buildings in the background and the barrage balloon.

Tempest Mk.VI NX201 at Langley 1946, fitted with Napier Sabre VA engine.

resulted in specification F.2/43 and a little later N.7/43 for a naval version and was first flown in September 1944 powered by a Bristol Centaurus XII driving a four-blade propeller. However, by January 1945, with the end of the war in sight, the RAF order was cancelled and the RN order reduced to 100 aircraft. The prototype Sea Fury first flew in February 1945, the aircraft being constructed at Kingston and Langley. The early machines designated F.X (F.10) were subsequently replaced by FB.XI (FB.11) in the fighter bomber role. Later redesign produced the two-seat T.20 training version of which sixty were built for the Royal Navy while export orders from Australia, Burma, Canada, Egypt, Iraq, the Netherlands and Pakistan, partly fulfilled by ex-RN machines and partly new-build (including licence production by Fokker) kept the aircraft in the inventories of various nations for some time after the war. Indeed, the aircraft would still be actively marketed in the late 1950s, to Cuba and as the TT.20, to West Germany in the early 1960s.

Such, then, was the prodigious design effort being undertaken at Hawker during the Second World War to fulfil numerous requirements for marks and sub-marks of their various fighter designs. One could easily forgive the failure to produce an entirely new form of aircraft powered by what was still a highly experimental powerplant in the circumstances. And yet …

Far from ignoring the potentialities of the new motive power available from the gas turbine engine, Camm and his design staff were already considering if, and how, such an engine might best be employed in one of their designs. That

Busy days at Langley, with many Tempest IIs powered by Bristol Centaurus V engines crowding the flight line.

Sea Fury FB.11 TF956, the first production aircraft, repurchased by Hawker Siddeley Aviation and refurbished, later being passed to RNAS Yeovilton where it was used as a display aircraft before its loss in 1989.

said, it should be borne in mind that Camm was conservative by temperament and the move away from traditional manufacturing methods to those exemplified by stressed skin aircraft powered by jets did not necessarily fill him with confidence. Roy Fedden (Chief Engineer at Bristol Aeroplane Company) once remarked that at the display of German aeronautical advances that Fedden had organised at RAE Farnborough in 1945, he came upon Camm 'looking with disdain at a model of the Messerschmitt P.1101 – the last word in swept wings and axial compressors'. Camm's response to Fedden's greeting was 'Did you ever see anything so ridiculous?'[3]

Sydney Camm, born in August 1893 in Windsor, Berkshire, had left school in 1908 to take up a carpentry apprenticeship. With his brothers, like many boys then and since, he developed an interest in aircraft and aeronautics in general, making model aeroplanes which they sold in the locality. In 1912, he was one of the founding members of the Windsor Model Aeroplane Club, an outlet that allowed him to develop his understanding of aircraft construction and aerodynamics. Around the beginning of the First World War, Camm had secured a position as a carpenter with the Martinsyde Aircraft Company (formed by H.P. Martin and George H. Handasyde) at Brooklands, Weybridge, before moving into the drawing office, but at war's end, the company – like many other aircraft concerns – went into liquidation and Camm moved in the early 1920s to premises acquired by George Handasyde at Mayford, Woking, before moving on to the fledgling Hawker Engineering Company in Kingston-upon-Thames in 1923 as a senior draughtsman. From 1925, Camm became in effect Chief Designer and, with Fred Sigrist, developed the tubular metal framework that would become a signature construction technique on Hawker aircraft for the next twelve years.[4]

The late 1920s and 1930s saw the company grow to become one of the largest in the

Sir Sydney Camm, Chief Designer for Hawker Aircraft Ltd and Hawker Siddeley Aviation from 1925 to his death in 1966.

Sir Sydney flanked by some of the Hawker Aircraft management team. Left to right: Roy Chaplin; Sir William Farren RAE; Sir Sydney Camm; Sir Tom Sopwith; Sir Roy Dobson, Hawker Siddeley Group Director.

country, producing designs that constantly found favour with the RAF. In 1934, Camm, having appreciated that the biplane was at the end of its development potential, began to scheme a monoplane fighter which would culminate in the Hurricane, which, with R.J. Mitchell's Spitfire, would become the backbone of the RAF in the forthcoming war.

The first opportunity to consider gas turbine engines as the motive power for a Hawker design arose while work was underway on the P.1005, proposed in December 1940 as a twin-engined high-speed bomber or long-range fighter powered by Napier Sabre or Bristol Centaurus radial engines (covered under P.1015 of 1942), the design being in response to OR.110. The design work was aligned with outline requirements (constantly changing) issued by MAP for a Mosquito replacement, later refined in various specifications (eg. 12/40, 3/41, F.7/41, 9/41, B.11/41) for a medium-range high-speed bomber or secondarily as a long range fighter, which was no doubt what had interested Camm initially since Hawker Aircraft was almost exclusively in the fighter business. The resulting design was an attractive streamlined mid-wing monoplane with twin fins capable of carrying a 4,000lb bomb load at over 400mph with a crew of three. As drawn, the aircraft had a wing span of 70ft and a length of 54ft, fuel capacity would be 1,100 gallons. For the fighter version, six 20mm cannon were envisaged, mounted in the belly under the cockpit.

The design appears to have had a troubled gestation; six months after work had started, the project was halted while the design was assessed. Work then began on a new version with a lengthened nose and a crew of four. Following mock-up construction of both types, a decision was made to continue with the first design but with the front fuselage of the second substituted. Work then again halted until December 1941 while work to increase the bomb load was schemed. Work then began again with refinement of the lines of the fuselage, which were incorporated in another rebuild of the mock-up. Although MAP appeared to be on the verge of placing an order for the aircraft, indecision abounded, not least because alternatives were available from de Havilland and Bristol. Although two prototypes were ordered in 1941, in March 1942 the decision as to whether to order was deferred for six months and by July, the project was essentially dead. However, another project, P.1011, was schemed in 1941 which was heavily based on the P.1005, but with the Napier Sabres replaced by gas turbine engines from Power Jets mounted in wing nacelles; no further information can be found. The last attempt to scheme a successful P.1005 derivative was the P.1034 using two Rolls-Royce RB.41 engines in 1944 but the design went no further, the Mosquito fulfilling all the requirements set out on the original Operational

P.1005 High Speed Bomber wind tunnel model.

Requirement. Eventually a 'jet Mosquito' would fly but not to a Hawker design. W.E.W. Petter's scheme for such an aircraft would emerge as the English Electric Canberra, one of the most successful post-war designs.[5]

Back at Kingston (or rather Claremont, where the project team had decamped), other project ideas incorporating gas turbines were schemed; P.1014 was a single-engined fighter of 1941, the powerplant to be a Power Jets unit; P.1031 of 1944, a fighter powered by Rolls-Royce RB.40 and the P.1035 of 1944, (which, as the P.1026, had been schemed around the F.2/43 Fury with a Griffon engine). The P.1035 then was drawn as a Fury but with a Rolls-Royce RB.41 gas turbine buried in the centre fuselage and exhausting at the tail. This would be further developed into the P.1040 which would become Hawker's first constructed essay in jet propelled flight.[6]

Further designs utilising gas turbine engines were the P.1038 of 1944, which was based on the P.1034 (itself a development of P.1005) but with a single Rolls-Royce RB.41 Nene engine; the P.1039 of 1945, an update of the P.1034 with two RB.41 Nenes buried in the fuselage, and finally, the P.1040, also of 1945 which will be examined in detail in the next chapter.

Yet, for all the designs for aircraft utilising jet turbine technology being schemed at Hawker, one cannot help feeling that this was mere tinkering. It must have been quite clear to the UK's aircraft design houses in the 1940s that aircraft powered by reciprocating engines and propellers were at the limit of their evolution. To go higher, faster, meant embracing wholeheartedly the revolution that jet engines now made manifest. Yet the industry's chief designers were hardly of one mind in this; at Bristol Aeroplane Company, Roche Swinchatt, the Development Engineer responsible for all piston and turbine engines in the late 1940s, was of the view that the gas turbine jet engine would never be any good, believing that the future belonged to Bristol's Centaurus radial engine, a position supported by the Managing Director, Norman Rowbotham and by Johnnie Attwood, the General Manager in charge of Production. At Hawker Aircraft, one might suspect that much the same opinion held sway, that there appeared to be a laissez-faire attitude that

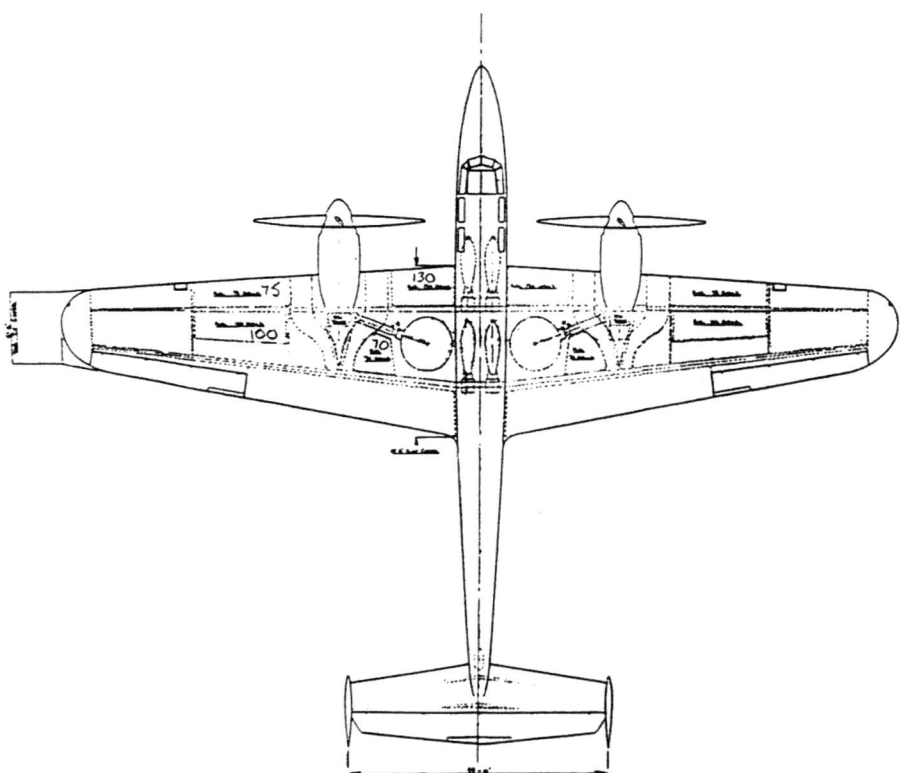

The High Speed Bomber schemed by Hawker, which was the basis of an investigation to replace the Napier Sabre engines with jet turbines. The design was envisaged as a 'sort of Mosquito replacement' and, with jet engines, might have supplanted the Canberra bomber, but was not proceeded with.

Hawker's Early Jet Designs   29

ignored the fact that the country's premier fighter design house was being left behind.[7]

However, in a letter to John Fozard – Senior Project Designer under Camm and later Chief Designer Harrier – in 1982, Robert Lickley, Chief Project Engineer at Hawker Aircraft in the 1940s, shone light on the background to the April 1944 Rolls-Royce visit.

> During 1943, Rolls-Royce kept visiting Kingston, generally Lappin, the then equivalent of Don Pepper and J.E. Ellor [Rolls-Royce Performance Engineer] who, like his successors, thought they knew more about aircraft design than Hawker. Their line was: now that the Mustang

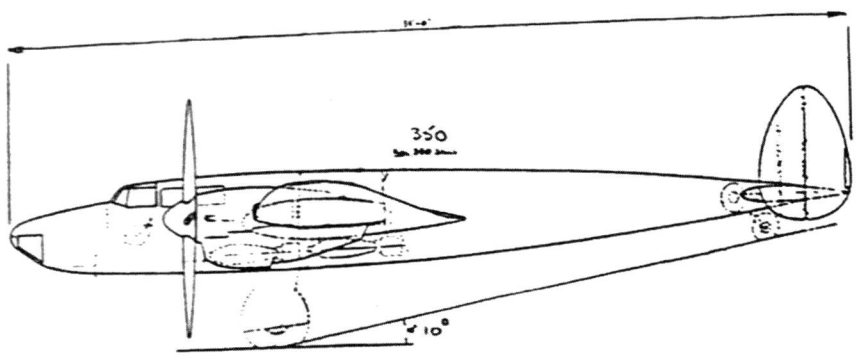

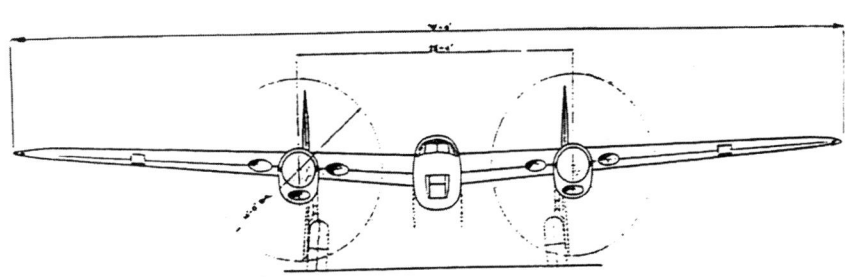

SPAN	70'
LENGTH	54'
TAILPLANE SPAN	22'
ROOT CHORD	13" 6'
FUEL	1,100 GAL

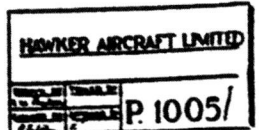

P.1005 High Speed Bomber at Canbury Park Road, Kingston-upon-Thames. One of several mock-up versions attempted before the project was abandoned.

[with RR Merlin engine installed] was so much better than Hurricane or Typhoon!, Hawker's only hope was to get into jets where the engine was simple, could be tailored to the airframe, could give whatever thrust you wanted and did not take any time to develop. In short Rolls-Royce were giving us this precious gift and couldn't understand why we didn't want it.

The truth, of course, was, until the B.41 came along you couldn't make a decent aeroplane, [with available jet engines] you got no range and the top speed was less than the Typhoon. The fight went on: in the Project Office we played with the 1037 [actually the P.1035] where the first bifurcated intake appeared and faint possibilities of a respectable aircraft emerged. Rolls-Royce immediately damned the intake, except a young intelligent fellow called Hooker who was at Barnoldswick and it led to the beginnings of the friendship between Sydney and him.

Finally we had the meeting at Kingston in April, Rolls-Royce fielded their whole team. Sydney [Camm] brought [Neville] Spriggs and [P.W.S. 'George'] Bulman [Hawker Pilot and Director] along to support the status quo. I was hauled up from Claremont to deal with Hooker! – and so we got down to it.

The upshot was Hawker would look into fitting an uprated B.41 … Rolls-Royce would accept the bifurcated intake and do all they could to

> help us develop it and so the P.1040 which led to the Sea Hawk was born. Rolls also agreed to stop pushing the Mustang and its radiator position as strongly as they had done, and so once again we started making the 'pilgrimage' to Derby.[8]

Following on from this meeting, on 10 May 1944 R.N. Dorey, Rolls-Royce engineer in charge of Nene development, wrote to Air Commodore Banks at the Ministry of Aircraft Production regarding the B.41 engine, noting that it was likely that Supermarine would use this in their new jet-propelled project and also that,

> It is likely that Mr Camm of Hawker's will also indicate that he is thinking on similar lines when we get his report. He is quite definite in his latest comments to us that he requires the smallest engine possible, as he visualises these engines must be fitted to nacelles on the wings.

Since Dorey had been present at the April meeting with Hawker, this suggests that design of a single-engined aircraft (such as P.1035/P.1040) had yet to be confirmed and that a version of the P.1005 was still being considered.[9]

However, it would be the single-engined P.1035/P.1040 that would go on to become the first Hawker jet aircraft.

As will become clear as this story unfolds, with the end of the Second World War in the summer of 1945, several events occurred in the political and military spheres of the UK that would immediately impact on the ability of the UK Government to pay for the materiel being produced by the aircraft companies, including Hawker Aircraft Ltd. In the first instance, the supply of military and other equipment from the USA under the terms of the Lend-Lease Agreement would cease with alarming abruptness in September 1945. Henceforth, the country would need to look to its own industries to equip the fighting services. Secondly, the arrival of a Labour Government in 1945, committed to massive social reform schemes and widespread nationalisation of industry at a time when the country was, to all intents and purposes, bankrupt, would mean that the UK Armed Forces would enter a period of extended contraction. The RAF saw squadron after squadron disbanded or merged and new equipment budgets tumble. Thus it was that, just as the UK stood on the threshold of a revolutionary new technology in the shape of the jet engine – and a world lead at that – it had neither the finances nor the political will to capitalise on the technology or the new aircraft that this offered.

The government and its Ministry of Supply promoted a 'make-do-and-mend' philosophy whereby those aircraft in use during the latter stages of the war would be kept in service until events showed that something else was required (and what that 'something' might be). This left the UK with just two jet aircraft in its inventory: the Gloster Meteor and the de Havilland Vampire, both first generation aircraft that, although capable of high speed and altitude, left much to be desired in terms of manoeuvrability and fuel consumption. It was left to the aircraft companies to seek to push the technology forward in the absence of any impetus emanating from Government.

This, then, was the background to Hawker's entry into production of jet engine aircraft. Though it would be a long journey, ultimately the effort would pay off as the Hawker Hunter entered RAF service in the next decade and would go on to fill the ranks of many other nations' air arms, remaining in use into the next century.

Chapter 3

P.1040 – Hawker's First Jet

So it was that early November 1944 saw two civil servants, Alfred R. Wardle (Director of Operational Requirements) and N.E. Rowe (Director of Technical Development) arrive at Hawker's country house design department at Claremont to 'discuss jet aircraft' and, with more powerful engines now becoming available, a single engine was discussed. This visit, following on the heels of briefings by Rolls-Royce and their first successful test run of the B.41 engine the previous month, appears to have kick-started Camm and his design team to get on with a realistic jet proposal.

Earlier work on P.1035 – essentially a jet engine dropped into a fuselage with Fury type wings – was brought out and dusted down. At a meeting later in the month with Sir William S. Farren – Director of RAE at Farnborough – various layouts were discussed and in December, the P.1035 scheme was upgraded to become P.1040. It was proposed that, to keep the jet pipe as short as possible (to reduce thrust losses), the exhaust would be bifurcated and ejected either side of the wing trailing edge. This novel arrangement appears to have been the brainchild of Vivian Stanbury, Project Engineer (succeeding Lickley as Chief in 1946), certainly it was patented under his name, and the scheme was sent off to Rolls-Royce for their comments as to its practicality. Quite how serious the P.1035 scheme had been is hard to tell, no general arrangement (GA) drawing for this has come to light, though there is an early GA for P.1040 that includes an air-brushed image showing elliptical wings a-la Fury and also images of a wind tunnel model with elliptical wings. The N7/46 tender document notes that the wings comprise 'a modified version of the high-speed section used on the Tempest'.[1]

As it stood at this stage, the proposal featured a centrifugal engine enclosed in the fuselage midships. Intakes in the wing root fed air into a plenum chamber encompassing the front of the engine face while exhaust was bifurcated and ejected either side of the wing trailing edge. Wings and tailplane were all conventional with no sweep. Armament consisted of four 20mm cannon in the nose under the cockpit located in the very front of the aircraft.

With the dawn of 1945, things now started moving with rather more haste. The Assistant Chief of the Air Staff/Technical (ACAS/T) visited and gave general approval to the proposal and a mock-up of the bifurcated jet pipe was ready for viewing at Rolls-Royce, Derby, by 26 January. The following month, the Comptroller of Naval Research, his deputy (CNR and DCNR) and Farren visited, also Sir Wilfred Freeman (former head of MAP, Vice Chief of the Air Staff), giving unqualified support for the proposal – in his words, 'Go right ahead' – a tender being submitted to the Directorate of Technical Development (DTD). On 27 February, Camm and Hawker Design and DO staff, Lickley,

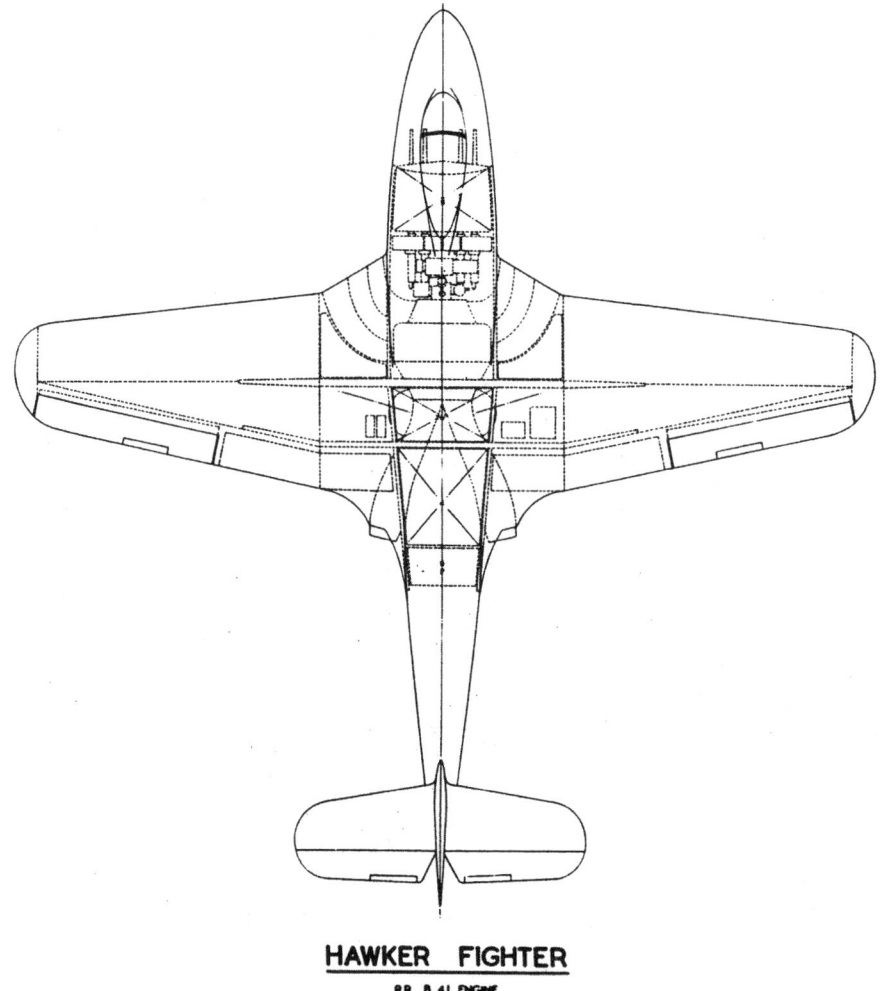

P.1040, general arrangement first iteration drawn by Vivian Stanbury in December 1944. All of the essentials of the later Sea Hawk are in place apart from the fin-mounted bullet fairing and naval equipment.

Stanbury and Lucas headed north to Rolls-Royce's great enterprise at Derby to assess the jet pipe mock-up and discuss the way forward. They also visited Rolls-Royce's jet engine plant at Barnoldswick where the new B.41 engine was being developed.[2]

Hawker would now have been expected to swing into action on the new project with all guns blazing, though the actuality was rather less formidable as the day diary makes clear: 'March 1945. Preliminary layout work was commenced in Experimental DO by one or two draughtsmen', out of the 305 design personnel available to Hawker at this period of the war. Hardly a ringing endorsement

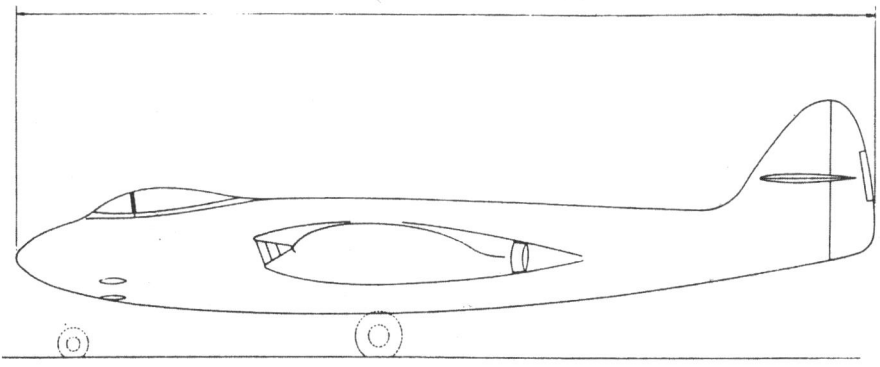

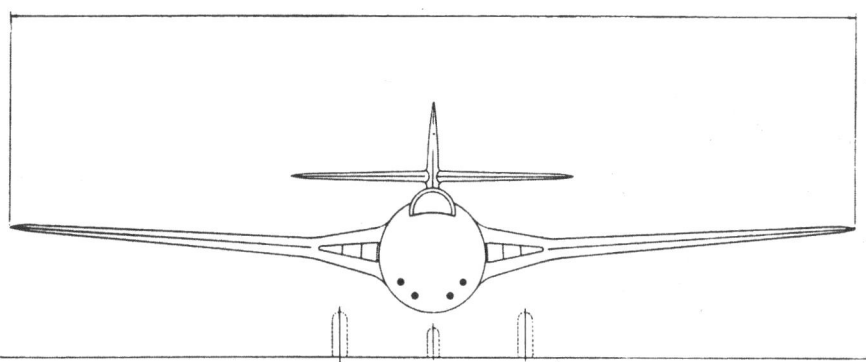

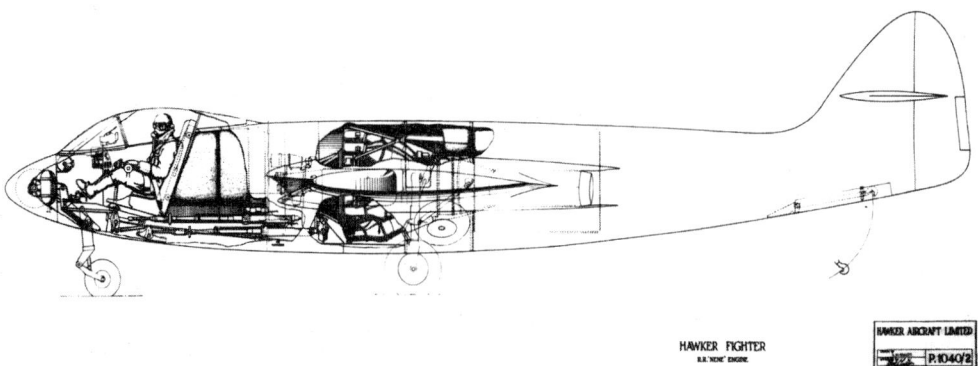

P.1040 cutaway side view showing early arrestor hook location, later moved further aft. Note how close to the front of the fuselage is the pilot's cockpit, which will allow an excellent view over the nose for carrier landings.

of the Directors' belief in the project though since all work was at company expense, perhaps understandable. The following month DTD revealed that they were less than happy with the air intake but it was agreed that if Captain Roger Liptrot at RAE was happy, then the project represented a considerable advance on existing types. With agreement that the intake arrangement should suffice, RAE agreed to carry out tunnel testing on models and on a full-scale intake arrangement. At this stage, Hawker had no wind tunnel of their own (Camm opining that he did not need wind tunnels because he could 'see' the airflow over a wing!) but would use those at Government establishments on an ad hoc basis.

The concern (shared by Rolls-Royce and DTD) regarding the intake design was due to the fact that, unlike the DH Vampire that also used wing root intakes to feed air to the engine, the Nene proposed for the P.1040 utilised a double-sided impeller, rather than the single sided unit used for the Halford H.1 engine. The intake air therefore had to be capable of use by both sides of the impeller and to achieve this, Hawker proposed that the front of the engine compartment should form a plenum chamber from whence the air could reach both sides of the compressor.

It appears that assistance on the finer points of intake design was obtained from Boulton Paul Aircraft, where Dr S.C. Redshaw (designer of the P.111) and John Dudley North (designer of the Defiant) advised on refinements to the air intake for the Sea Hawk and its predecessors to enable the most efficient intake to be applied to the Nene engine. This work would later be read across to the DH Vampire when plans were laid to replace the Goblin engine with the Nene, necessitating a revised intake shape akin to the Sea Hawk and plenum chamber in the aircraft.

By May 1945, interest had moved on to the construction of a mock-up of the proposal in the Experimental Department at Canbury Park Road (the mock-up engine had arrived in April). Drawings now began to be issued; wing drawings were disseminated to allow consideration of a single spar design with diffusion of load into heavy gauge skins. Drawings were also sent to Farnborough for the intake tests and for the model designs and to Rolls-Royce for the engine installation details. June saw the issue of wing drawings to the Production Department for construction of a test sample using the single spar design.

In September, the fuselage lines were issued to the Experimental Department, Dowty's was contacted with regard to design of suitable undercarriage and – good news – the intake arrangement was finally given clearance by RAE, with an estimated efficiency of 90 per cent. With six draughtsmen now at work on the design, in October a new tender was issued comprising three separate but related designs – P.1040, P.1046 and P.1047. P.1046 was submitted as a naval version of P.1040 with additional rocket engine/s to augment thrust, while P.1047 was based on P.1040 but with extreme sweepback on the wings and rocket engine augmentation. In time, the various elements of these proposals would be trialled but for now, just the P.1040 was the focus of attention.

In October 1945, attention turned to the gun installation, a mock-up being inspected and alterations proposed using a flat feed mechanism with ammunition housed behind the cockpit and in front of the engine bay. Also put in hand was the wing fatigue specimen to check torsional strength with the single spar arrangement. Finally on 13 October, a Production Order No. 599190 was raised for construction of one P.1040 to be allocated the serial VP401 and draughting staff was increased to ten.

At this point it became clear that all was not well with the design of the bifurcated jet pipe, Rolls-Royce apparently struggling to achieve a satisfactory design that would not impact on thrust. Unfortunately, none of this was known at Kingston, which continued with the original layout until belatedly informed of the requirement to alter the shape of the jet pipe. Early in December, representatives from Rolls-Royce came down to Kingston to refine the engine and jet pipe installation requirements. Having successfully resolved the jet pipe issues, the team was somewhat deflated to be told that, in fact, the RAF was not at this stage interested in the project, regarding it as insufficiently advanced over what was already in service. On 20 December however, following a visit by Admiral Slattery, who pronounced himself most interested in the project, Hawker was invited to submit a tender for a naval/RAF interceptor. By this stage the company had seventeen draughtsmen at work on the project.

Meanwhile, work had continued on refining the P.1047 project comprising a P.1040 type aircraft with extreme sweepback; the conclusions from the company's studies on this were now submitted to the Director General of Technical Development (DGTD) together with redesign around the forthcoming Rolls-Royce axial flow AJ.65 engine. At the end of January 1946, Hawker duly submitted their tender for an interceptor based on P.1040 for both the RAF and the Royal Navy. With twenty-six draughtsmen now beavering away on the project, clearly the company was becoming more confident of a successful outcome for the project and nagged Rolls-Royce to get on with making a start on manufacture of the jet pipe.

It was at this stage that considerations regarding pilot escape from the aircraft began to make themselves felt. The increasing speed of modern military aircraft meant that baling out of a stricken aircraft had become an increasingly risky activity. Work had progressed on assisted escape in the later stages of the war

P.1040 centre section under construction at Canbury Park Road. The integral stub wings would later be a feature of the Hunter.

P.1040 front and centre sections. The orifice for the bifurcated jet pipe is visible at left. Note the screening behind the fuselage to hide the work from prying eyes.

so that, by 1946, ejector seats were a reality, albeit an 'untested in anger' reality. In January, Camm had asked for a separate contract to allow for investigation of a pilot ejector seat for the project but the Ministry was of the opinion that this work was already sufficiently covered by work underway at RAE and CASR. However, the following month, RAE asked that Kingston submit a scheme regarding their thoughts on pilot ejection. Thus began a situation wherein Hawker was given little guidance for what might be required in assisted escape and plumped for an ejection seat designed by Marcel Lobelle manufactured by R. Malcolm Ltd, (M.L. Aviation Ltd from 1946). This seat would be used in all Hawker prototypes until the arrival of the P.1067 Hunter, at which time the Ministry and RAF had decided that Martin Baker would be the primary supplier of seats. The ML seat would figure large in the future for Hawker, but for now it was just one of many issues to be worked through.

On 21 February 1946 the P.1040 design passed its next hurdle with an order being placed for the construction of three prototypes (including the one already under construction to be serialled VP401) and a structural test specimen (serialled VP407) for a general-purpose naval fighter, the specification N7/46 being allocated against OR.218; contract cover being received in May. At this point, funding passed from company to government expense.

Now Camm, presumably having worried at the single spar arrangement for the wing, decided that a leading-edge spar should be introduced into the stub wing to give added strength to the wing base. Also revised (again) was the jet pipe design at Rolls-Royce; it did seem that this apparently straightforward piece of steelwork was receiving as much design input as the rest of the aircraft systems together. However, by April 1946, the naval requirements were to hand and preliminary work could begin on the second prototype design, while forty-five draughtsmen were allocated to the first aircraft. First flight of this aircraft was now intended for February 1947.

It was around this time that it became apparent that the P.1040 was becoming less and less representative of the N7/46 aircraft which would be much closer to the naval requirement. In particular, requirements for wing folding, assisted take-off (RATO), arrested landing and strengthened undercarriage would be omitted from the first prototype, and removal of non-essential equipment including armament would allow a less robust undercarriage to be fitted. As design work on the first prototype now lessened, that on the second aircraft, the first N7/46, increased to thirty-two draughtsmen, though in August, in an about-turn, the Ministry decided that the first aircraft would now feature an ejection seat, as well as catapult and arrestor equipment, thus increasing the weight which was now at risk of exceeding the undercarriage limits allowed. Also now raising its head was the request from Royal Navy representatives that the angle of incidence of the wing and the wing chord be increased to improve take-off performance; a request that did not go down well with Mr Camm

The P.1040 jet pipe assembly which would prove to be one of the most troublesome areas of construction.

P.1040 fuselage largely complete, awaits the tail assembly, nose cone and skinning of the stub wings. Note the wooden floor of the Canbury Park Road premises.

considering the work that would be required to increase the wing incidence at this stage. The concern of the Royal Navy was that the existing wing design would result in long take-offs and higher than desirable landing speeds, neither of which was welcome when operating from an aircraft carrier.

However, in November the front and centre fuselage sections of the first aircraft were removed from their jigs and mated, while discussion continued as to how wing incidence could be increased. Initial thoughts revolved around the suggestion that the nose leg be locked at maximum extension for take-off and supported on a trolley, thereby raising the nose by approximately 6in to obtain the 6.5 degree increase in incidence required. Also considered was the manufacture of a larger chord set of elevators and to design for power control of these units.

So ended another year of highs and lows for Hawker and their first sally into the world of jet propulsion; by the end of December, 81,076 man-hours had been devoted to the project. Come January 1947, the wings were offered up to the centre fuselage with minimal concerns. The ejection seat saga continued to rumble on with the suggestion that investigation be carried out on the structural test specimen to avoid delays on the actual aircraft. By now however, the ramifications of the Labour government's pursuit of the creation of a New Jerusalem – wherein would be available for all cradle-to-grave health insurance, care of a new National Health Service; pensions for all; jobs for all; education for all – were coming home to roost. With the end of the war, the UK was essentially bankrupt. The government's actions in promising to the electorate in 1945 the abolition of want, when it knew full well that the coffers were empty and the UK's export business, which might have supported such grandiose schemes had ceased to exist, culminated in the shutdown of great swathes of industry in February 1947 as energy supplies failed. Thus it was that the Hawker works closed its doors on the 10th of the month since there was no heat or light, and did not reopen till the 3 March.

March 1947 saw Hawker still awaiting the revised jet pipe and the first 'live' engine for installation. With the aircraft due to leave for Langley Aerodrome where a further 400 hours of work were required prior to acceptance for flight, delays now were unwelcome guests to say the least. The engine duly arrived on 15 April and, with the jet pipe, was installed in the aircraft on 18th and, on 29th, the aircraft was moved up to Langley for work to continue. In May, information regarding intake performance was received which showed that, while in flight the mass flow from the intakes was acceptable (due to ram effect), on the ground there would be a pressure depression in the engine bay of about 2lb per sq. in. To obviate this, it was recommended that the intake area be increased by 2 sq. ft. It was also found that additional stiffening of the jet pipe was required but,

P.1040, VP401 at Langley Aerodrome prior to engine runs. Canopy and rudder trim tab are not yet fitted. In the cockpit is pilot Bill Humble in discussion with Heathcote, the Rolls-Royce rep. The aircraft is fitted with squared exhaust fairings, later replaced with 'pen nib' type.

P.1040, VP401 undergoes engine running at the hands of the Rolls-Royce rep, Mr Heathcote at Langley. It would appear that ear protection was not considered necessary for the engineers. Behind are various marks of Sea Fury and Tempest fighters.

by 5 June, the engine and final jet pipe were installed in the aircraft. However, before any further work could proceed, Rolls-Royce coyly disclosed that the jet pipe had only been tested to a thrust of 4,500lb and therefore the first engine had been derated to this figure. A further redesign of the jet pipe would be required before the engine could be rated at 5,000lb. One can imagine the exasperation felt at Kingston regarding Rolls-Royce's handling of the jet pipe work.

Be that as it may, on 23 June 1947, VP401 had its first engine run at Langley, from which it was deduced that alterations to the jet pipe exhausts were required to direct the efflux away from the rear fuselage to avoid damage to the structure. Locally manufactured parts extending the pipe proved successful and engine runs and preliminary low speed taxying trials continued through July, and in August the aircraft was dispatched to A&AEE Boscombe Down for its first flight. Boscombe Down offered a long runway and sparsely populated areas, an important consideration for a new aircraft, while Langley had no concrete runway and was closely hemmed in by housing.

On 2 September 1947, VP401, the first Hawker jet, took off for a successful first flight at the hands of Bill Humble, Hawker's Chief Test Pilot, powered by the Rolls-Royce B.41 Nene.

On 5 September, the aircraft was flown up to Farnborough where testing would continue. Since Langley was not suitable for jet operations, Hawker had obtained permission from RAE to base themselves at Farnborough and had erected a small hangar and offices there for this purpose at a cost of £10,157. Early flight testing revealed that the aircraft was susceptible to an unpleasant buffeting in flight, and various remedies were tested in an effort to alleviate this, including changes to the trailing edge wing fillet adjacent to the jet pipe and blanking off the boundary layer exits. The aircraft was laid up in October for several days for updates to be applied including a fairing at the fin and tailplane intersection and further blanking of the boundary layer ducts. Good news arrived now to the effect that the aircraft was cleared to use the full 5,000lb thrust once the enhanced jet pipe was fitted and flying resumed in November. It was clear that the alterations to the aircraft had not improved the buffet problem.

Bill Humble recalled that, at this critical time, he had had a slight altercation with Sydney Camm.

P.1040, VP401 during an early taxi trial at Langley, Bill Humble at the controls. Only low speed taxying was undertaken at Langley due to the lack of suitable concrete runways.

P.1040, VP401 about to undertake its maiden flight at A&AEE Boscombe Down in the hands of Bill Humble. Note the attitude indicator mounted on the nose for the first few flights.

> It was when we were flying the 1040 down at Farnborough and he turned up. There was dense low cloud over Farnborough. The sun was sinking in the west and there was rain all over the place and the aeroplane was in trouble with this bloody vibration that we hadn't sorted out and the last thing I wanted to do was find myself in the aeroplane with failing light and rain and all the rest of it. And Sydney came up to me and he said 'Why aren't you flying?' and I said 'If you want it flown, fly the something thing yourself.' And he said 'Oh, if that's what you feel about it, perhaps you'd better not.'[3]

Humble, with limited jet experience, requested that Lieutenant Commander Eric 'Winkle' Brown RN fly the aircraft to assess the problem. On 11 November Brown flew the aircraft, commenting that in his opinion, the issue was related to engine rather than aircraft speed. Brown had been involved with the project from its earliest days as the Royal Navy pilot representative at RAE Farnborough (RDQF MoS), advising on cockpit layout, ejection seat arrangement etc.[4]

With the aircraft now amended to allow the full 5,000lb thrust to be used, flying continued under Trevor 'Wimpy' Wade as Chief Test Pilot, Humble having moved on to a sales role within the company. At this point, the indecision that had been rumbling on within the Air Ministry regarding which type of ejector seat to use in its aircraft appeared to have reached a resolution; Hawker's Resident Technical Officer (RTO) advising that henceforth, Martin Baker seats would be specified. Since the P.1040 had been constructed around the

P.1040, VP401 at Farnborough where flight testing was carried out until Dunsfold Aerodrome was available. The square heat shields on the exhaust are clear in this view.

P.1040, VP401 in its element, up from Farnborough with 'Wimpy' Wade. The clean lines of the design are evident in this view.

Malcolm seat and much alteration would be required to allow use of the Martin Baker product, Camm asked the RTO to refer the decision back to the Ministry. Meanwhile work continued on the buffet problem; the boundary layer ducts were un-blanked and a fillet on the intake lip removed. During the subsequent flight to provide a datum point to the buffet investigation, the hydraulic system failed and VP401 was landed without the benefit of a nose wheel, damaging the aircraft.

In January 1948, it was agreed that the aircraft could continue with the Malcolm seat, but should a production order be placed, the Martin Baker seat would be specified. On 10 March, the second set of flight tests resumed and in April, the fitting of leading-edge mass balances in the elevators appeared to have significantly lessened the vibration. In July, the issue of the pressure depression in the engine plenum chamber was finally addressed by the fitting of eight (later increased to twelve) suction doors in the engine cover and on 19 July, the existence of the aircraft was released to the press. In September, an assessment of the flying characteristics of the aircraft revealed that although

'Wimpy' Wade at the controls in this view of VP401, the P.1040. The heat shields have now reverted to the pen-nib shape that would be fitted on the Sea Hawk.

the top speed of 522 knots (Mach 0.81) was encouraging, the rate of climb was somewhat sluggish. As part of the work to alleviate this, a smaller chord elevator was successfully flown and, in November, spinning trials were successfully completed.

In March 1949, VP401, and VP413 (the second prototype and the first under the N7/46 specification) carried out assisted take off and arrested landing trials at Farnborough, VP401 principally in the hands of Eric Brown who flew stall handling sorties on 11 and 21 March and 1 April, and catapult launches on 4 April. Unfortunately on the same day, the aircraft was damaged when the 'rear fuselage was ripped open by hold back extension puller'. However, after suitable repair, VP401 was flown in August in the SBAC Challenge Cup Air Race at Elmdon by Wade at a speed of 510mph. In October, VP401, having completed its flight trials was returned to Richmond Road, Kingston for work to install a rocket motor for trials on behalf of Armstrong Siddeley and the Ministry of Supply, under project code P.1072.[5]

The P.1040, of which only one was produced, was of all-metal stressed skin construction with bolted transport joints at frames 12 and 29. A straight tapered

P.1040, VP401 shows off its aerodynamic profile and pen-nib heat shields. 'Wimpy' Wade in the cockpit.

wing was mounted midships onto stub wings formed integral with the centre fuselage and incorporating engine air intakes in the roots. The wings were not designed to carry any equipment and were not readily detachable on this aircraft. Hooper noted that,

> the P.1040's original design envisaged the use of front and rear spars but with no other span-wise stiffening of the skins. The intention was that the skin would remain unbuckled at 1g but that at high loadings it would operate in the 'post buckled' state. However, the sight of the buckled skin on test led to the hasty addition of two stringers ahead of and behind the main spar on the upper and lower skins. This arrangement survived the increase in span of 2.5ft and the introduction of wing fold on the production aircraft.

The undercarriage was a tricycle layout – Hawker's first – with nose leg retracting forward and main gear inwards, into the wing.[6]

The engine was a Rolls-Royce Nene 1, producing 4,500lb thrust initially, later increased to 5,000lb. The centrifugal engine was mounted in the centre section, the intakes feeding into a plenum chamber forward of the engine,

P.1040, VP401 at its Farnborough base undergoes checks between flights. Bob Marsh, Hawker Project Office, is checking the cockpit.

and the jet exhaust exiting via a bifurcated jet pipe aft of each wing root. The exhausts were kicked out slightly to direct the exhaust heat away from the rear fuselage where heat shields also protected the fuselage structure. These shields were originally finished with blunt 'spade' ends but were altered to a pen-nib profile to reduce buffet. The tailplane was unswept and all flying controls were manual; the cockpit was unpressurised.

Unlike its succeeding N7/46 aircraft, VP401 differed in that there was no provision for wing fold and armament was not carried (ballast was fitted in lieu); the fuel capacity was 390 gallons as against 410 gallons; the undercarriage was designed for a vertical velocity of 11.75ft/second rather than 14ft/second; radio fit was limited to a VHF radio TR 1520 rather than the TR 1501, TR 1502 and IFF TR; there was no provision for F.24 cameras nor for overload tanks; no airbrakes were fitted (but dive recovery flaps were) and numerous other smaller equipment items were not fitted. Provision was built in for assisted take-off hook and hold back attachment but these areas were faired. Provision for an arrestor hook was also included but the hook was not fitted and if required later, the rudder would be shortened and suitable hydraulic connections added.[7]

Leading Particulars

Wing span:	36ft 6in
Length:	37ft 7in
Wing area:	256 sq. ft
Thickness/chord ratio:	0.10 (10%)
Engine:	RR Nene RN.1 rated at 4,500lb, later RR Nene RN.2 at 5,000lb
Fuel capacity:	395 gall
Weight empty:	8,660lb
All up weight:	12,698lb
Performance:	Max speed at sea level 505 knots. At height level 0.815M, in dive 0.835M
Service ceiling:	43,500ft
Absolute ceiling:	47,500ft

Chapter 4

P.1072 – Rocket Propulsion

With the return of the sole P.1040 VP401 to Richmond Road, Kingston-upon-Thames in October 1949, work began on the conversion of this aircraft to admit the addition of an Armstrong Siddeley Snarler rocket motor rated at 2,000lb thrust.

The notion of aircraft powered by rocket had proved an attraction to aircraft manufacturers almost from the first days of flight. Early results from trials with solid rockets attached to the struts of biplanes ranged from less than successful to disastrous and it was not until the advent of liquid fuelled rockets developed principally in Germany, that this form of propulsion appeared achievable, though attitudes in the UK resulted in the idea essentially being dismissed at the Air Ministry as not feasible in the foreseeable future, much the same attitude as that shown pre-war for the use of jet turbines until the work of Whittle shattered such beliefs. However, as the Second World War entered its final phase in 1944 with the D-Day landings and Bomber Command beginning to encounter the rocket powered Me163 aircraft, the realisation of the rocket's practical application to flight began to be seriously considered. Part of the reason for the dismissive attitude of the Air Ministry was that Allied application of rocket power was envisaged as solid fuel powered which, once ignited, could not be controlled. The German use of liquid fuelled rockets, however, allowed the pilot to exert some control, the rocket being, at least theoretically, throttleable.

With the capture of German rocket research data in the closing stages of the war, UK scientists realised the great strides made in the subject and the potentialities of its application to aircraft propulsion. Armstrong Siddeley Motors, as an engine manufacturer, began research into the production of a workable liquid fuelled rocket in 1946. Following their Alpha rocket, designed for rocket assisted take-off (RATO) application, in 1948 the company designed the AS Beta developing 800lb thrust, derived from work at the Rocket Propulsion Establishment at Wescott in Buckinghamshire. This was used to power the Vickers Transonic model derived from the cancelled Miles M.52 project to M1.5. This motor used a water/methanol mixture with HTP (high test peroxide) as the oxidiser. The Beta was followed by the Delta rocket motor, this time using a kerosene/HTP fuel but the next motor – the AS Snarler – used liquid oxygen, a more amenable material. Work on this version had begun in 1947 and achieved the first firing in November of that year, development being extended and it was not until February 1950 that the motor was ready for testing, the motor being named Snarler in August 1951.

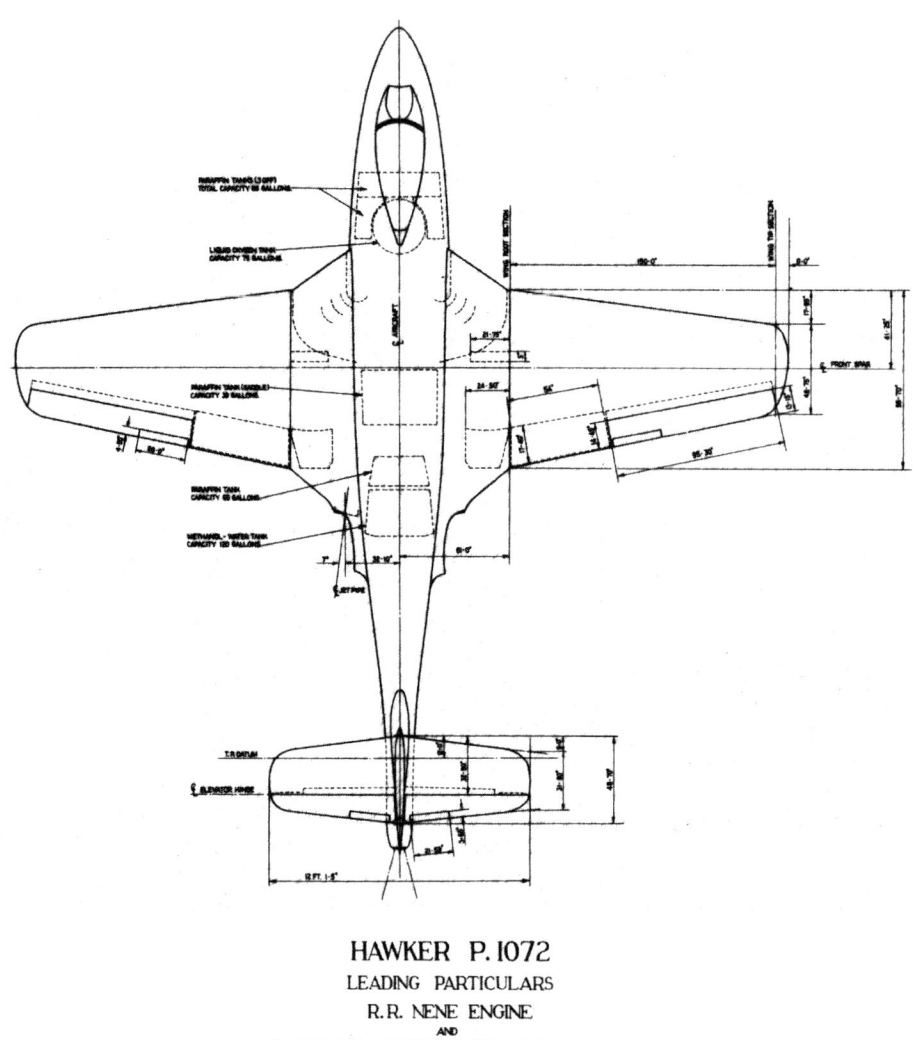

HAWKER P. 1072
LEADING PARTICULARS
R.R. NENE ENGINE
AND
ARMSTRONG-SIDDELEY 'SNARLER' ROCKET

P.1072 general arrangement showing the changes to the existing P.1040 aircraft due to the installation of the rocket motor system. A ventral keel carries pipework from the rocket fuel pumps driven by the jet engine back to the motor in the extreme tail.

P.1072 – Rocket Propulsion

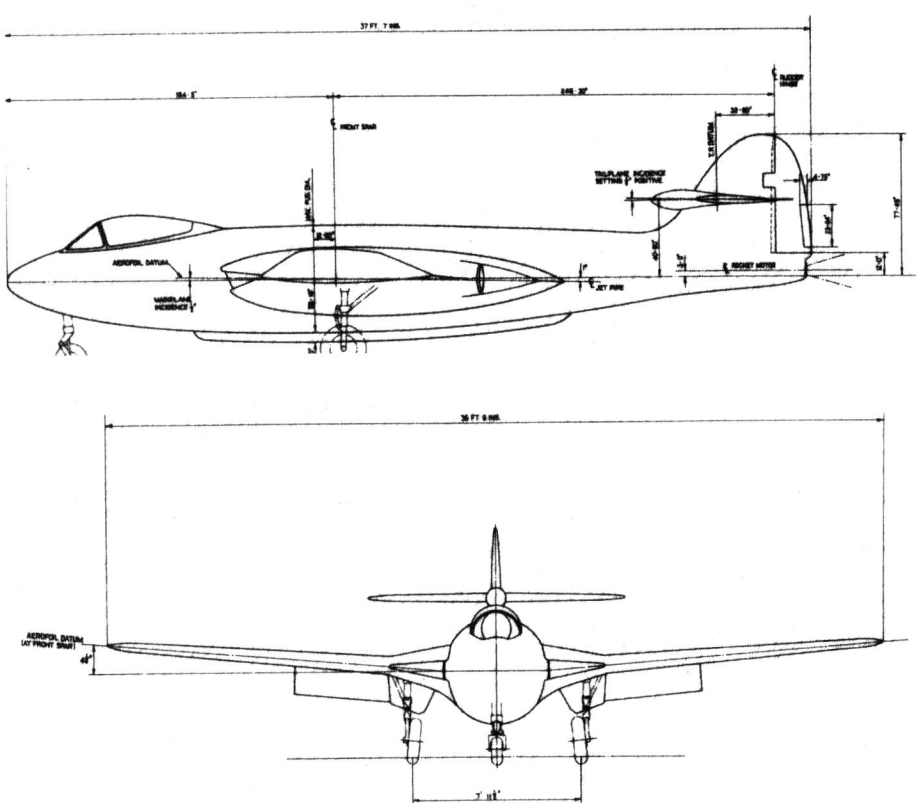

TOTAL FUEL CAPACITIES
PARAFFIN – 185 GALLONS.
METHANOL-WATER – 120 GALLONS.
LIQUID OXYGEN – 75 GALLONS.

SCALE 1/24

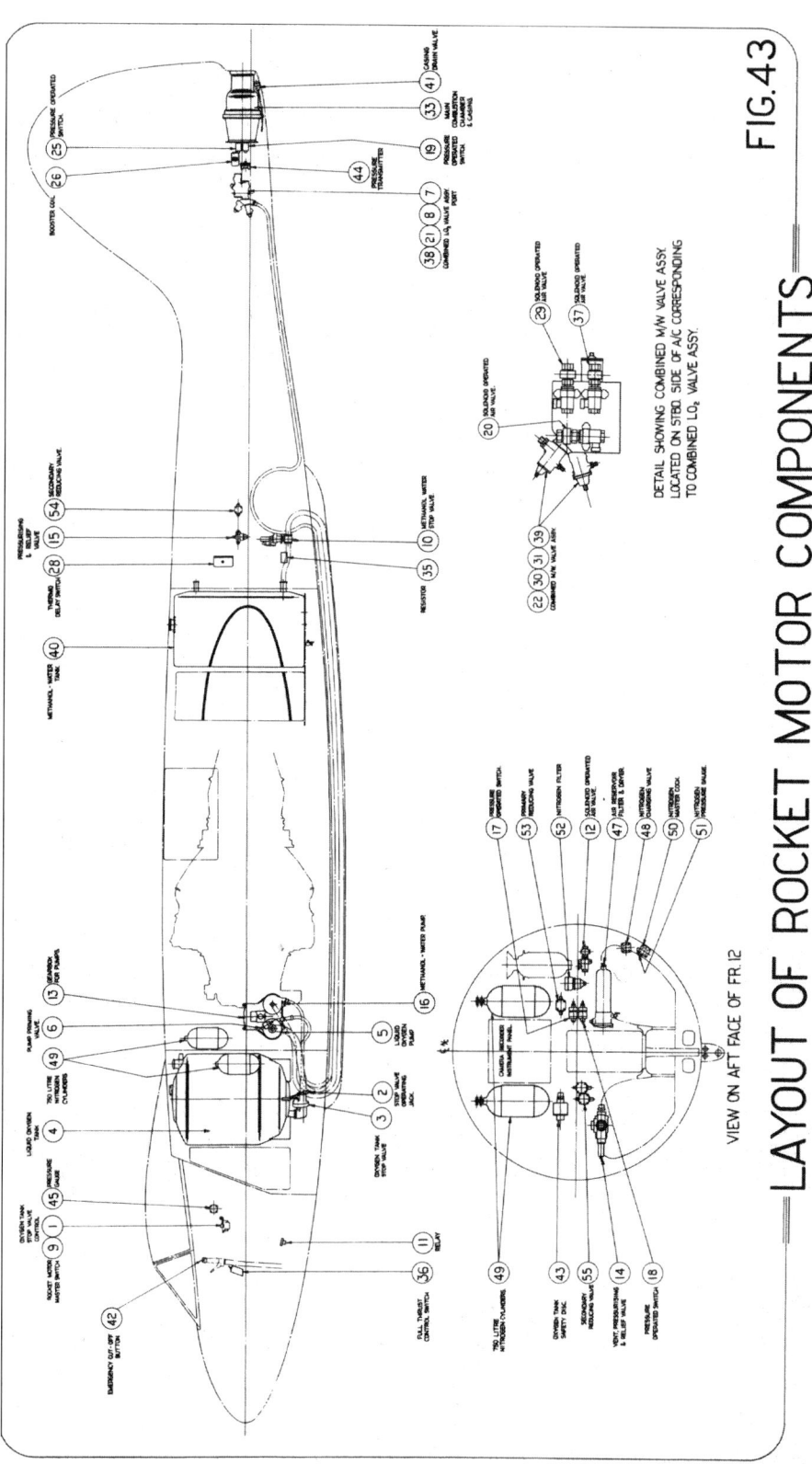

FIG.43 — LAYOUT OF ROCKET MOTOR COMPONENTS

P.1072 showing the layout of rocket motor components including the liquid oxygen tank in place of the front fuel tank and the water/methanol tank aft of the engine.

The advent of a resurgent USSR seemingly intent on an aggressive expansion of its influence into Europe and its possession of high-speed high-altitude bombers and nuclear weapons (from 1949) dictated a requirement within the UK for aircraft capable of interception of the bomber stream before it could get close enough to release its weapons. The answer to that requirement was seen by the Air Ministry as fighters able to reach altitude as rapidly as possible to engage the incoming forces and rocket power appeared to provide the answer, using rocket propulsion for a steep climb to altitude and then jet engine/s to manoeuvre during the attack and return to base. The attraction of such an arrangement was that, while a jet engine's thrust decreases with altitude, that of a rocket actually increases, making it highly suitable for high altitude interception.

Hawker Aircraft was in the fortunate position of having within their company combine – the Hawker Siddeley Group of companies – Armstrong Siddeley Motors and was therefore able to obtain information on progress with rocket motors. With this knowledge to hand, Sydney Camm had, in October 1945, submitted to the Air Ministry a combined tender comprising the P.1040, and P.1046 and P.1047, both the latter powered by rocket motors though only the P.1040 proceeded. (It should be noted that at this point there were no rocket motors available to fill the tender specification.) Two years later, with the idea of rocket propulsion still in vogue, it was suggested that one of the N7/46 prototypes (the Royal Navy version of the P.1040) be used for trials of a rocket motor.

A further attempt to design a workable rocket-augmented aircraft came with the P.1065/1 of February 1948 in response to Ministry specification F43/46 for a single seat interceptor fighter. This was designed around a Rolls-Royce Avon engine supplied via a chin intake, 35-degree swept surfaces with T-tail and long nose carrying four cannon. Accommodated at the rear of the fuselage was an unspecified rocket motor of some 3,000lb thrust but this was not proceeded with, the specification ultimately being replaced by F3/48 which would spawn the Hunter. By January 1948, the idea of producing a test aircraft was gaining ground with the intention now to use the P.1040 VP401 for trials once the preliminary testing to support N7/46 work was complete.

Between March and June 1948, interest and concrete proposals for the rocket trial had firmed up. Roy Chaplin and Vivian Stanbury were dispatched on 24 June to Armstrong Siddeley at Coventry to assess progress regarding manufacture of the rocket motor. At a Ministry meeting on the 29th to discuss the work, concerns were raised regarding the seeming impossibility of accommodating the pressurised tanks that would be required to hold the fuel for the rocket.

Notwithstanding this concern, the following month a contract was received covering the installation of a liquid fuelled rocket motor into either an N7/46 or E38/46 aircraft. The decision to use VP401, the sole P.1040 made much sense for, as the N7/46 prototypes progressed towards a definitive production version, VP401 became less and less representative of the Navy requirement.[1]

The concerns regarding the location of pressurised tanks for the rocket fuel were overcome by using pumps to pressurise the fuel, which could now be stored in unpressurised tanks. Space for these was created by removing one of the normal fuel tanks to create more space (though this left the aircraft with only 45 per cent of its normal fuel). While early liquid fuelled rocket trials in the UK had used hydrogen peroxide as an oxidiser (based on German research and military applications), the Armstrong Siddeley motor used liquid oxygen, the rocket fuel being a water/methanol mixture. Two additional tanks would therefore need to

Hawker Aircraft executives including Camm, Spriggs and Robertson with visitors including an Australian Air Marshal, presumably visiting with regard to the Australian interest in acquiring P.1052 or P.1081 for its Air Force. Behind is P.1072, VP401 undergoing modification; the front fuel tank is seen removed to allow accommodation of the liquid oxygen tank.

be accommodated in the fuselage of the aircraft as well as the rocket motor and its attendant fuel pumps. The final scheme (designed almost single-handedly by Reg Smythe in the DO), coded P.1072, was a minimum change arrangement which retained the Nene turbojet in the centre fuselage, the liquid oxygen tank containing 75 gallons was located immediately aft of the cockpit, while the water/methanol tank holding 120 gallons was housed just aft of the wing trailing edge giving fuel for 2.75 minutes' duration. This left room for just 185 gallons (175 actual) of fuel for the Nene engine. The rocket motor was installed on the centreline of the aircraft in the extreme tail, beneath the shortened rudder, and a ventral trunk carried fuel from the pumps located forward of the engine, to the motor with an additional gearbox fitted at the forward end of the engine to drive the fuel pumps. The aircraft skin on the under fuselage was replaced with

P.1072, VP401 during modification to accept the rocket motor. The front fuel tank has been removed to accommodate the liquid fuel tank, this being surrounded by smaller fuel cells, a volatile combination all mounted just behind the pilot.

10g light alloy to give increased protection to the liquid oxygen tank in the event of a forced landing. The aircraft had an adjustable incidence tailplane fitted, though for the early trials this would be fixed rather than adjustable.[2]

Interestingly, when the P.1040 arrived back at Richmond Road, it was found that the wing skins were buckled and there was some discussion concerning replacing them with a swept wing which would have the advantage of negating the requirement to fit ballast in the aircraft nose to achieve a suitable CG. In the event, the original wings were strengthened and retained (and presumably reskinned where required). With the aircraft ready to accept the rocket motor, all eyes turned to Armstrong Siddeley at Ansty near Coventry where the motor was to be tested before dispatch. Unfortunately, delays were incurred with non-delivery of the stainless steel piping for the fuel system and a requirement from the Ministry of Supply for modification to the test cell, concern being raised about safety at the site. Finally, in June 1950, the rocket motor was delivered and installed in VP401. The aircraft was then delivered to Farnborough and flight tested on 28 July before delivery to Armstrong Siddeley at Bitteswell the following day by Wimpy Wade for initial tests on the installation. It was returned to Kingston (via Langley) by Duke on 19 September for further work to be carried out to better accommodate the rocket installation. On 13 November,

P.1072, VP401 showing the rocket motor pipework emerging from the fuel pump bay to run aft in the ventral keel to the rocket motor.

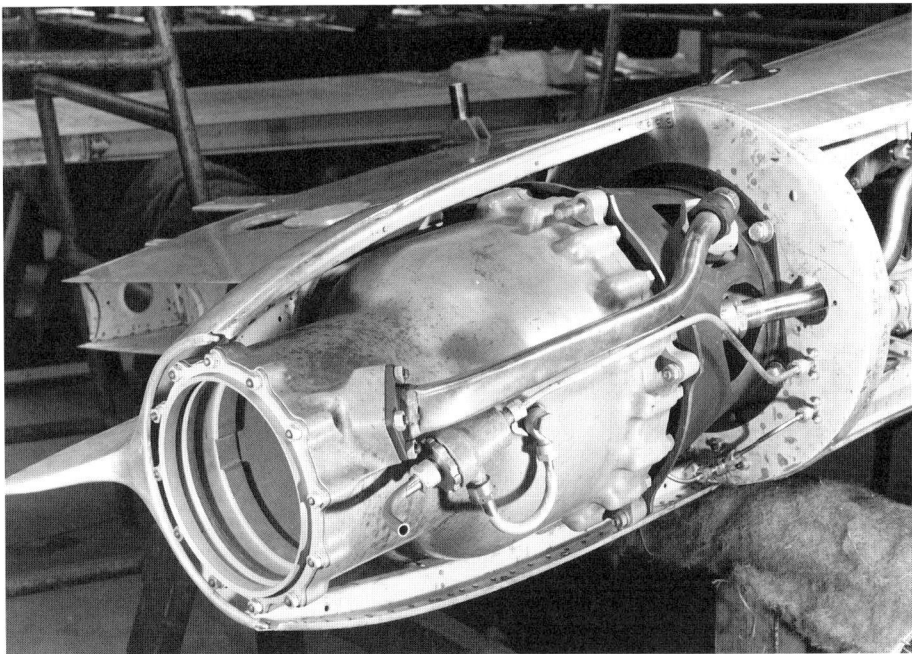

P.1072, VP401 with the Snarler rocket motor installed in the extreme tail, which is lying on its side in this view.

Duke flew the aircraft back to Bitteswell from Farnborough for ground running tests prior to flight.[3]

On 15 November 1950, the first flight under rocket power was successfully completed by Wade, all the fuel being used. During December 1950 and January 1951, a further six flights were undertaken though by whom is unclear. Duke records only two flights in his log during which he fired up the rocket, while Wade's log entries for the period are missing. However, in Duke's autobiography, 'Test Pilot', he notes that,

> Wimpy Wade and I made three flights each with the Snarler and found that it gave the P.1072 terrific climb performance, particularly at height. We took off normally on the jet engine, and then lit the rocket at a fairly low altitude, putting the aircraft into a climb. With the Nene jet engine working at full power, together with the thrust of the rocket, the aircraft went up extremely rapidly.[4]

During Duke's last flight on 18 January 1951, a faulty pressure gauge transmitter caused a small explosion resulting in substantial minor damage. The damage was repaired and a ground run and flight test carried out on

15 February. However, at the end of June 1951, the aircraft was still awaiting instruction regarding future use and in the event, appeared at the SBAC Farnborough display in September 1951 in the static park only. It was reported that the aircraft was made available to Armstrong Siddeley for further Snarler trials commencing 19 February 1951, but it is not known if these included flight trials. On 16 April 1952, the aircraft departed Bitteswell for storage at Farnborough where it appears to have featured in minimum drag flight trials from 8 August 1952 before being struck off charge on 10 August 1954 and presumably scrapped on site.[5]

Ralph Hooper described the P.1072 as,

> not the pilots' favourite aircraft. Firstly the gas turbine fuel was reduced to only 45 per cent of the P.1040's capacity. Also, the rocket was not throttleable and repeated stops and starts were not encouraged. Furthermore, the P.1040's cockpit was not pressurised and the flying controls were purely manual. On lighting the rocket, the aircraft would accelerate until it ran into Mach-induced buffet; if the pilot then sought to control the speed by climbing, he was soon at the limit for unpressurised flight![6]

The Snarler rocket motor and major components as installed in P.1072, VP401.

P.1072 – Rocket Propulsion

P.1072, VP401 with the rocket motor exposed during testing.

P.1072, VP401 with the rocket motor installation complete, possibly at Farnborough.

P.1072, VP401 prior to rocket test flights at Bitteswell Aerodrome.

P.1072, VP401 undergoing ground testing of the Snarler rocket motor.

P.1072, VP401 takes to the air at Bitteswell with rocket motor and main engine operating.

'Wimpy' Wade relaxing with the P.1072.

Although the project had provided useful data for the concept of rocket propelled aircraft, the thinking behind the provision of rockets to quickly obtain height to intercept incoming enemy bombers, gave way to the realisation that reheat offered a more flexible and less complex answer and rocket propulsion faded into the background. Reheat – the burning of fuel in the engine exhaust gases – allowed a more flexible use of thrust than the rocket and could use the existing aircraft fuel without need for more specialised fuels. Whittle had carried out research on reheat systems (or thrust augmentation as he called it) in conjunction with his development of the W2/700 engine for the Miles M.52 supersonic project. Afterburning was proposed for the Nene and Tay and later the Avon would feature a reheat system on various UK jet aircraft of the day.

However, although rocket power would not enter service in this form, the Ministry was at one time interested in continuing the trials, this time with the Armstrong Siddeley Screamer rocket motor which promised thrust of up to 8,000lb and was in development to power the Avro 720 project. Development had begun in 1946 and was first tested in 1954 at Armstrong Siddeley's test ground at Ansty. A requirement to flight test the engine resulted in Hawker proposing the P.1078, first schemed in August 1949; described as a P.1052 development, with the motor mounted at the rear of the fuselage and swept tail surfaces. Clearly a certain amount of work was carried out on this project; company accounts for 31 July 1950 show costs of some £36,546 being allocated to the project for labour (£10,638), materials (£2,311) and design work (£1,256). The project did not proceed and the Screamer motor project was cancelled in 1956 having never been air tested, though an engine was flown under a Meteor in 1951, but not ignited.[7]

Other rocket proposals included P.1053 of 1946, P.1071 of 1948 and P.1089 as late as August 1951. No further information is known of the P.1053 proposal other than its description as 'rocket fighter'. The P.1071 of October 1947 was altogether more ambitious and featured an early P.1067 layout with nose pitot air intake and 50-degree sweep on the wings; a delta tailplane set low on the fin and 2,000lb rocket motor housed above the Rolls-Royce Avon straight through jet pipe which included 20 per cent reheat ability. With such a layout, the aircraft should have been more than capable of level supersonic flight. Ultimately subsumed into P.1067 and P.1083 thinking but without the rocket, this project was also abandoned.[8]

Finally, on 21 February 1951, a revised specification F.124T was circulated to interested companies which called for a rocket powered interceptor, with or without an additional turbojet. Hawker's submission, P.1089, was a pure rocket interceptor, the design featured a delta wing with swept trailing edge, large fin and rocket installed in the tail. Thrust was proposed of 5,000lb and was probably derived from the Screamer project. Other designs for this specification included the Saunders Roe SR.53, the Avro 720 and the Boulton Paul P.122 but ultimately, the entire requirement was abandoned by the government and so the P.1089 was still-born.

Leading Particulars

Wing span:	36ft 6in
Length:	37ft 7in
Wing area:	256 sq. ft
Thickness/chord ratio:	0.10 (10%)
Engine:	RR Nene RN.2 at 5,000lb plus AS Snarler rocket motor at 2,000lb thrust
Fuel capacity:	175 gall turbojet fuel, 75 gall liquid oxygen, 120 gall water methanol rocket fuel
Weight empty:	11,000lb
All up weight:	14,050lb
Performance:	Max speed at sea level 505 knots. Max Speed in level flight: M0.82
Predicted rate of climb to 50,000ft:	3.5 minutes
Ceiling:	44,000ft

Rocket specification

Type:	rocket engine booster
Length combustion chamber:	23.4in
Nozzle diameter:	12.5in
Installation weight:	617lb
Propellant capacity:	120 gall fuel; 75 gall oxidiser
Fuel:	65% methanol, 35% water
Oxidiser:	liquid oxygen
Thrust:	2,000lbf at 20,000ft
Thrust duration:	2.75 minutes

Chapter 5

N7/46 – The Naval Project

Possible naval interest in the P.1040 design was first evident in October 1945, when a combined tender was submitted to the Air Ministry comprising P.1040, P.1047 – a swept-wing version with rocket thrust, and P.1046 – a naval version with rocket thrust. Whether this was as a result of previous discussion with naval contacts (Hawker's Sea Fury work would have resulted in plenty of these) or an unsolicited suggestion is unknown. Then, on 20 December, Hawker was invited to tender for the supply of an RAF/Naval interceptor aircraft, submitting this on 20 January 1946.

The tender was at pains to stress that the new aircraft bore multiple similarities with the Sea Fury, Hawker's current Royal Navy aircraft offering which had first flown the previous year and would enter service in 1947. Both structure and controls were 'similar to Sea Fury', 'as on Sea Fury', 'at least as good as Sea Fury', 'the cockpit is similar to Sea Fury' etc.[1]

One month later, the company was informed that contract cover would be made available for the construction of three prototypes and one set of parts for structural testing, for a general-purpose naval fighter based on the P.1040, specification N7/46 being applied to the project. In March, Camm had decided that strengthening of the wing would be desirable by introduction of a leading edge spar in the centre fuselage and stub wings to increase the wing base from a torsional perspective. Through April and May, various meetings were held to determine the particular requirements of the design with a view to naval use, including deck approach and landing problems (to be addressed with a revised leading edge radius), arrested landing and accelerated take off.

Finally, on 28 May 1946, contract 6/Acft/234/c.b.9(b) was received from the Ministry of Supply to cover the three prototypes (i.e. P.1040 and two N7/46). Weight was agreed to be in the region of 11,400 to 11,700lb and flight of the first aircraft (without folding wings) agreed as February 1947. The question of strengthened undercarriage for carrier landing occupied the design team during July; the naval requirement for an ability to land at a descent speed of 14ft per second (fps) for the two N7/46 aircraft and 11 fps for the first was agreed, while RAE Farnborough worked on checking various aspects of the design peculiar to shipborne use including safety barrier engagement using model tests and arrestor hook design. The Final Mock-Up Conference, held on 10-11 October was broadly successful though important queries were raised for resolution, including the layout of the gun installation, position of the gun sight (a retractable unit being requested), the arrangement of the reconnaissance cameras and wireless in the rear fuselage and the detachability of the bifurcated jet pipe. Also in October, Camm agreed that wings of increased chord would be fitted to the N7/46 aircraft to improve carrier handling but a request for increased wing incidence at this stage was a difficult issue to resolve. Later attempts to answer this, for the prototypes at least, centred on provision of a small trolley under the nose leg on deck to provide increased wing incidence and locking of the nose leg. In November, elevators of increased chord were drawn up with power control to be trialled on the prototypes once flying commenced.[2]

In August 1947, suggestions that to assist with control in the landing phase (a particular concern of the Royal Navy), the throttle should be interconnected with the airbrakes and flaps was under discussion at RAE. The concern here was to optimise slow speed approach while keeping engine speed up in case of a wave off, and requirement to go round again. In order to allow close control of airspeed in this phase, the aircraft was provided with a full array of devices including split landing flaps, dive recovery flaps and airbrakes on the upper and lower wing trailing edges. All were theoretically available during a carrier approach to offer slow speed but high engine revs. Also, on 19 August, tentative discussions began on a possible dual version of the aircraft and preliminary drawings were supplied to the Ministry on the 27th. This version, presumably seen as a trainer, did not proceed, a two-seat variant never being built.

By July 1948, work on the second prototype – the first N7/46 VP413 – with most of the navalisation work embodied, including hydraulically folding wings, catapult spools and armament, was nearing completion with hydraulic and fuel balancing tests underway. Taxi trials began on 31 August and continued over the next two days, presumably at the Farnborough outstation since the first flight occurred there days later on 3 September 1948 by 'Wimpy' Wade, the aircraft also being prepared for the static park for that year's SBAC Air Show.[3] Unfortunately the maiden flight was not as successful as the P.1040's; the landing flaps and airbrakes failed to function and emergency flap was used successfully; subsequent investigation on the ground could not reproduce the fault. Also evident on succeeding flights was a lateral out-of-trim situation which had not been present on VP401. Subsequent geometrical investigation of the wings, flaps and ailerons in October highlighted several inconsistencies in build standard which required remedial work.

As the year drew to a close, preliminary discussions began with the Admiralty on the production aircraft specification; one unwelcome piece of news arising from this was the fact that additional equipment being called for would increase all-up weight by some 400lb. However, notwithstanding the inevitable delays

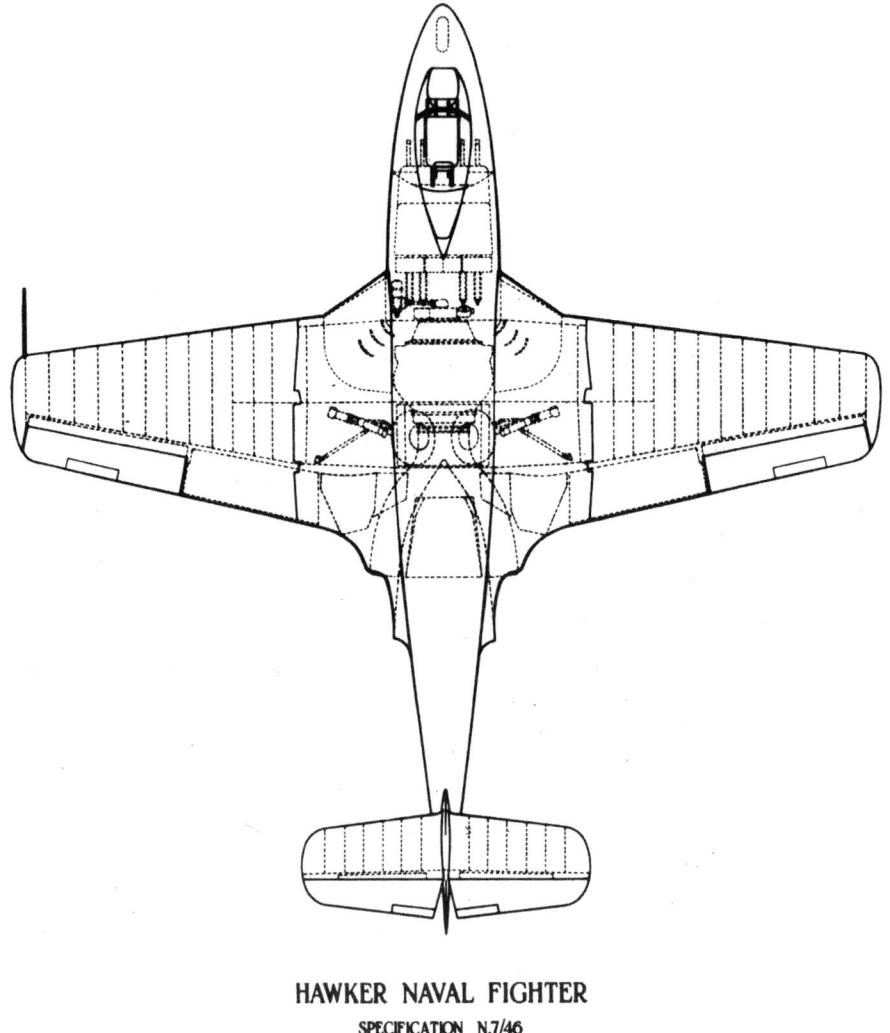

N7/46 general arrangement showing folding wings, four cannon armament, catapult pick-ups and initial arrestor hook design.

N7/46 – The Naval Project

that accommodation of the additional equipment would entail on the production aircraft, both VP401 and VP413 successfully completed trials at Farnborough of the assisted take-off and arrested landing arrangements, after which VP413 was allocated to A&AEE Boscombe Down for carrier deck assessment trials, the aircraft departing Farnborough in April 1949. Following these, the aircraft was flown onto HMS *Illustrious*, eight landings being carried out. Initial results from these trials indicated that the required high take-off speed might pose

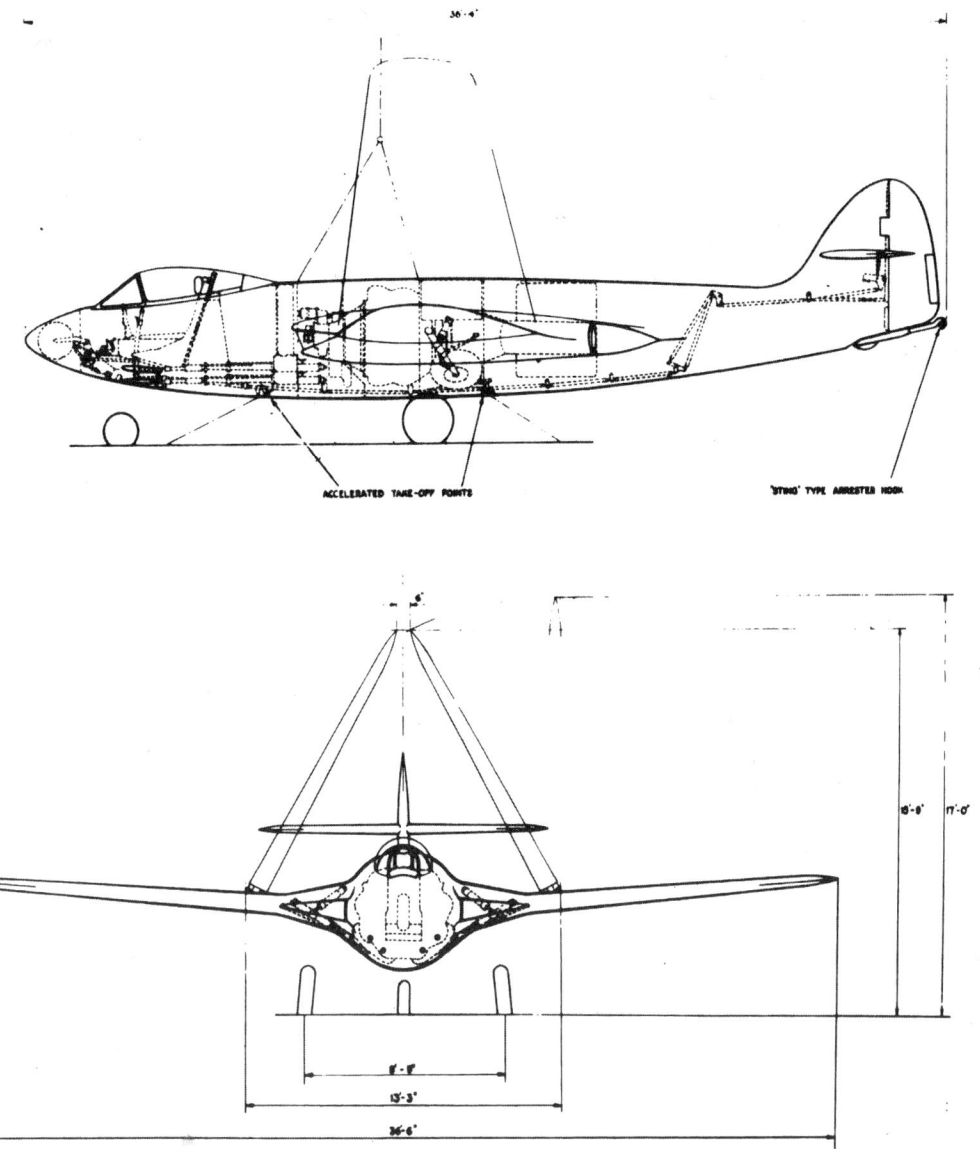

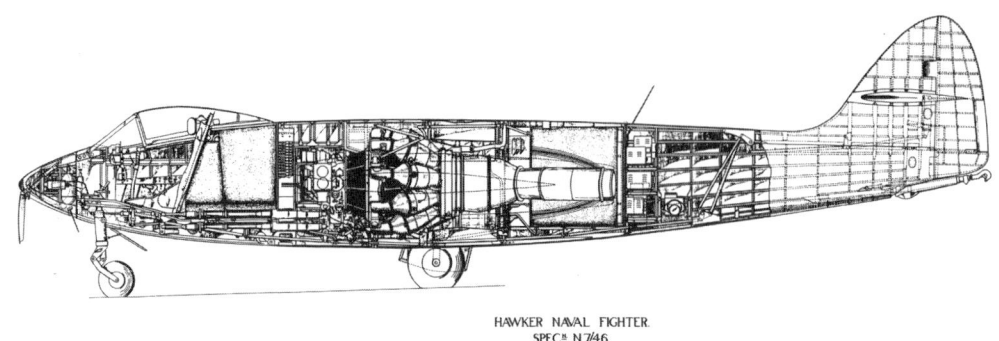

N7/46 cutaway view showing internal arrangement.

a problem with regard to available wind over deck and that the arrestor hook required further work.

Following the problem with non-actuation of the airbrakes and flaps on its maiden flight, arrangements were made in November 1948 for VP413 to be laid up in the near future for interim modifications to be made to the airbrake

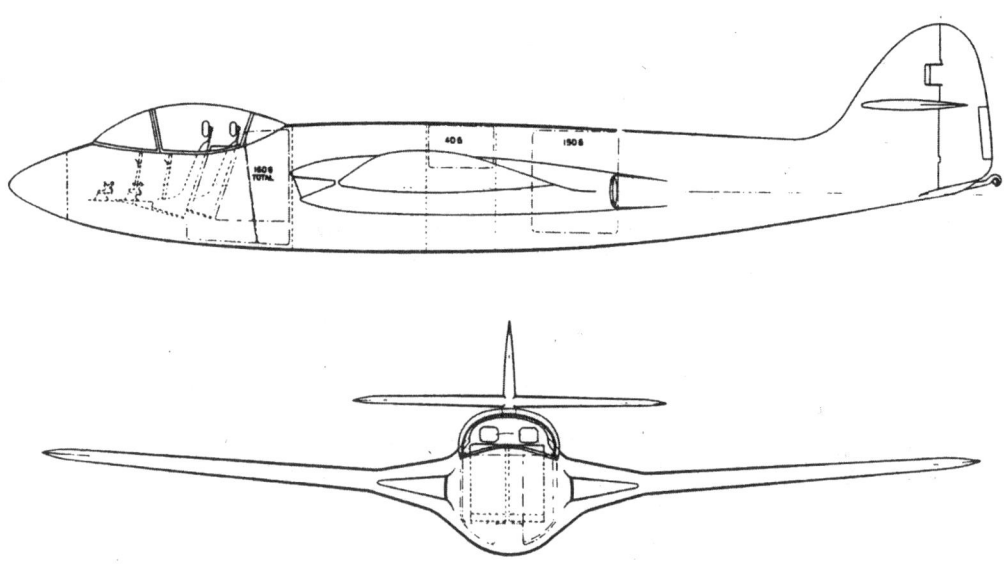

N7/46 designs for two-seat trainer version, both tandem and side-by-side seating. Note the elongated nose of the tandem seat version and the reduced fuel capacity required to maintain the CG. Neither scheme was built.

N7/46 – The Naval Project

system; this work being completed in February 1949 such that the upper portion of each airbrake (these comprised brakes both above and below the wing trailing edge) was locked in place, operation of the system now only moving the lower brake. In June of that year, plans were laid to fit a new airbrake arrangement along with work to increase torsion bar stiffness, the work being completed in July, allowing for the complete airbrake arrangement to be operable again. However, following its SBAC Display appearance and its delivery to Boscombe Down on 23 September for further assessment, the machine was returned the next day with a request that the airbrakes be deleted and the flaps returned to their original condition as on the original deck trials.

In July, works had been put in place to increase the wing span by 30in to 39ft and in September, the tailplane by 12in, to increase lift and improve control characteristics during take-off and landing. Also planned for future addition were increases to the fin and rudder area. In September 1949, VP413 appeared at the SBAC Farnborough Air Show in the flying display piloted by Neville Duke. Flying the N7/46 prototype VX413 on 9 September, his characteristic entry run at high speed, low level – and inverted – was a sensation for all the

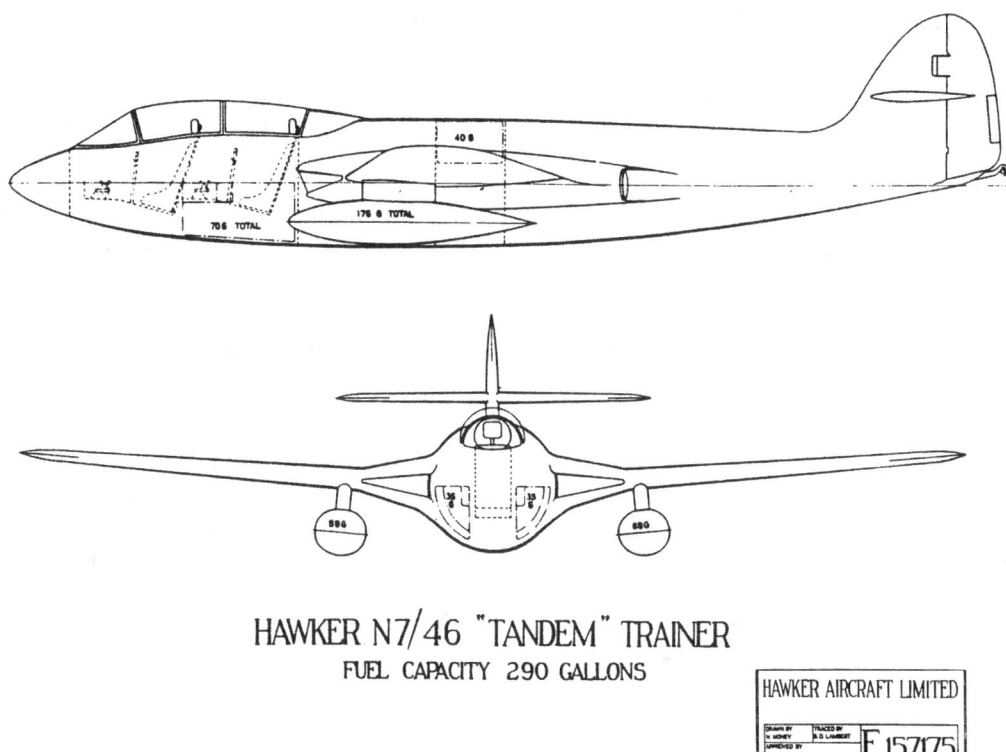

wrong reasons. Seeking to roll the aircraft upright at the end of the run down the display line, he let the nose drop, very close to the ground and in a desperate attempt to right the aircraft and climb away, suffered a high-speed stall and pulled 10G before successfully completing the display. On landing, the airframe was found to have wrinkled skins on the wings and fuselage and a distorted nose pick-up spar which laid up the aircraft for repairs. After the display, in Duke's words, 'On landing, I walked to the pilots' tent. I found it hushed – and the bar open, early.'[4]

In October, the second prototype N7/46 aircraft VP422 received its engine run. This aircraft differed from VP413 in having provision for RATOG and a faster undercarriage sequence time. The following month VP413 returned to HMS *Illustrious* for further deck trials, completing twenty-five landings successfully – though on the third, the arrestor hook hit the flight deck round down, but without damage. The aircraft then returned to Boscombe Down for further handling assessment. On 17 October, the first flight of the second N7/46, VP422 under 'Wimpy' Wade took place followed by complete handling trials. This aircraft was closest to the production specification and included a longer arrestor hook that protruded aft of the rudder, a shorter hook having been found to be less than satisfactory during carrier trials with VP413. Also built in were wing hard points for drop tank carriage and provision for rocket assisted take-off gear (RATOG).

Early January 1950 saw VP422 delivered to Boscombe Down and then to RNAS Lee-on-Solent to carry out aerodrome dummy deck landings (ADDLs) prior to further trials at sea. Unfortunately while there, the wings were inadvertently folded with the flaps down, causing damage. VP413 also came a

N7/46, VP413 at Farnborough, September 1948. No arrestor hook or tail bullet fairing has been fitted as yet.

N7/46, VP413 at Farnborough, September 1948 showing the wing fold arrangement. Behind are an eclectic variety of aircraft including a prototype Meteor and a DC-3 awaiting their fate.

cropper on its return to Farnborough on the 27th, when it overran the runway sustaining minor damage. Finally, in February, VP422 carried out deck landing trials, making twenty-eight landings successfully before embarking on trials with drop tanks, the shape of which had been causing the design team some sleepless nights. These trials were unsuccessful.

June 1950 saw the commencement of gun firing trials, VP422 being based at Boscombe Down for the duration before return to Hawker for modifications to the gun system in September. VP413 was also at Boscombe Down for handling trials through much of the early part of the year, returning in August for preparation for that year's SBAC Air Show, before being prepared for catapult trials, these being carried out in November at Farnborough in conjunction with 'ventral landing handling' tests.

The year 1951 proved to be a busy one for the two aircraft as they worked through the full flight test programme. VP422 continued with its gun firing trials, initially at Farnborough and then at RNAS Ford and RAF Tangmere in March. This was followed by another stint at Boscombe Down on hood jettison and seat ejection trials in the blower tunnel, both of which were satisfactory. In October, the aircraft suffered a fractured turbine blade in flight, requiring a replacement engine to be sourced. Meanwhile VP413 had, in February, returned to Richmond Road for modification work comprising the production version of airbrakes, ailerons and tailplane with the aircraft being prepared for return to flight in June. Subsequent flight trials in September revealed that further work was required on the airbrakes to render the system fit for production, the development work for this continuing into November.

The remaining items requiring clearance were worked through during 1952. VP422 continuing with gun firing trials at Boscombe from February to July, and in September these trials were signed off successfully. Also completed in September was the hood jettison trial. VP413 continued with airbrake trials which slowly yielded successful results. The continuing modification to the airbrake system and its associated landing and dive recovery flaps, would ultimately lead to a satisfactory airbrake solution for Sea Hawk, though it would also be a precursor to the ensuing attempts to achieve a satisfactory airbrake solution on the forthcoming Hunter, one that would threaten its entry into service.

It appears that one of the N7/46 aircraft was used to carry out trials of the flexible deck at Farnborough. This was a system that sought to allow aircraft

N7/46, VP413 at Farnborough, September 1948 showing the full panoply of speed reduction devices including airbrakes, landing flaps and dive recovery flaps.

N7/46, VP422, the second of the type up from Farnborough with 'Wimpy' Wade at the controls. This aircraft is fitted with the elongated arrestor hook which would be standard on the Sea Hawk.

to land without undercarriage on the flexible deck of an aircraft carrier, the idea being to reduce aircraft weight in favour of greater carriage of fuel or weapons. Lieutenant Commander Eric 'Winkle' Brown spent much of his time at Farnborough carrying out these trials using a DH Vampire beginning in 1947, before sea trials were carried out in HMS *Warrior* in 1948, again with few problems; indeed some 200 landings were completed without serious incident.[5]

Although the trials were broadly successful, the limitations imposed by the system (how to move the aircraft once it has landed; how would a diversion to a site without flexible deck arrangements be carried out) and the increasing thrust available from jet turbines resulted in the work ceasing in the 1950s. Geoffrey Cooper noted that VP413 was used on 12 November 1953 to test the system, making a take-off and landing on the Farnborough flexible deck with undercarriage retracted at all times.[6]

Be that as it may, the Hawker diary had noted that in June 1951, 'design work on mattress landing version started. Ceased in October.' In October and November 1950, as noted above, the aircraft was used at Farnborough for 'ventral landing handling' tests. Ray Sturtivant commented that,

> In June 1950, it was proposed to continue with development of the flexible deck using four Sea Hawks, it being envisaged that a prototype N7/46 would be available by March 1951, and that by the end of 1952, it would be possible to earmark at least three fully operational machines.[7]

As far as is known, however, only one Sea Hawk test was carried out at Farnborough, the machine being catapulted off, and landing on, the flexible deck without the undercarriage being lowered.[8]

On 14 November 1951, the first production Sea Hawk F.1 WF143 made its maiden flight at Farnborough at the hands of Neville Duke presaging the arrival over the next few years of substantial numbers of the aircraft. Meanwhile, the two N7/46 prototypes continued flight trials of various outstanding requirements, including a satisfactory working airbrake system (VP413) and fuel system clearance with drop tanks and gun firing (VP422) to be read across to the production machines.

Thereafter, information on further use of the two aircraft is difficult to come by. Bill Bedford had delivered VP422 to Boscombe Down on 4 March 1952 where it appears to have remained. On 20 January 1953, the aircraft, flown by Lieutenant A.I.R. Shaw RN, C Sqn A&AEE, on a familiarisation flight suffered problems with the problematic airbrake system which failed in flight and the undercarriage would not lower. Emergency hydraulics were then used which lowered only the nose and starboard main wheels and flaps. The aircraft swung on landing and struck the emergency services ambulance stationed on the perimeter track, the pilot was unhurt but damage was assessed as cat 3 (capable of repair). Thereafter it disappears from the record, presumably scrapped on site.[9]

Its stablemate VP413 continued with airbrake investigation under Bedford through early 1952 before being tested and cleared for delivery to Farnborough on 17 July 1953 by Frank Murphy. Apart from Cooper's note of its use in the flexible deck trials in November of that year, again the aircraft disappears from the record. Either struck off charge and scrapped, or allocated to a training establishment as an instructional airframe.

Leading Particulars

Wing span:	36ft 6in
Folded span:	13ft 3in
Length:	38ft 4.7in
Wing area:	268 sq. ft
Thickness chord ratio:	0.095 (9.5%)
Engine:	RR Nene RN.2 rated at 5,000lb
Fuel capacity:	430 gall
All up weight:	11,300lb

N7/46, VP413 during carrier suitability trials aboard HMS *Illustrious* during May 1949.

N7/46, VP413 aboard HMS *Illustrious* undergoes maintenance in a typically precarious location on the after deck.

N7/46, VP422 in its element, 'Wimpy' Wade at the controls.

DH Vampire about to take the arrestor wire on HMS *Warrior* as part of the trial to determine the effectiveness of the flexible deck concept.

Chapter 6

P.1052 – Swept Wings

On 8 October 1945, Hawker had submitted a tripartite tender to the Ministry of Supply which, as well as the P.1040 already considered, included a swept-wing version with rocket thrust augmentation under project code P.1047 which appeared to be armed with just two nose-mounted cannon. No more was heard regarding this scheme; however, on 2 May 1946, at a meeting held at Kingston with members of the Naval Aircraft Dept RAE, the issue of construction of a swept-wing version of N7/46 as an experimental aircraft was discussed, as were changes to the N7/46 wing itself, perhaps as a retrofit. Following this meeting, on 13 June, the company submitted a design for a swept-wing version of N7/46 under the project code P.1052. In August, the Deputy Director Aircraft Research and Development (DDARD) requested that Hawker proceed with construction of an aircraft to their P.1052 specification, though purely as a research aircraft.

The interest of RAE at Farnborough was evident in this suggestion since information on swept wings was sparse to say the least. The use of wing sweep to delay the onset of compressibility and therefore allow greater aircraft speed, had first been suggested by a German scientist – Adolph Busemann – at the Volta Conference in Rome in 1935, which British and American as well as German scientists had attended. However, while the German scientific community recognised and embraced the possibilities of the research, within the UK and US research community, the suggestion, for whatever reason, fell on deaf ears. Consequently, in the latter stages of the war, the Allies were faced, not only with aircraft powered by revolutionary jet engines, but which also displayed marked wing sweep. With the end of the war in 1945, the only research data that the UK establishments possessed was that 'lifted' from German research institutes and therefore the need for first-hand empirical data of their own was uppermost in the fertile minds at RAE.

Thus it was that the Ministry of Supply was requested to look favourably upon plans by UK manufacturers to construct swept-wing aircraft which could then be used to fill in the gaps (and there were many) regarding swept-wing flight. In

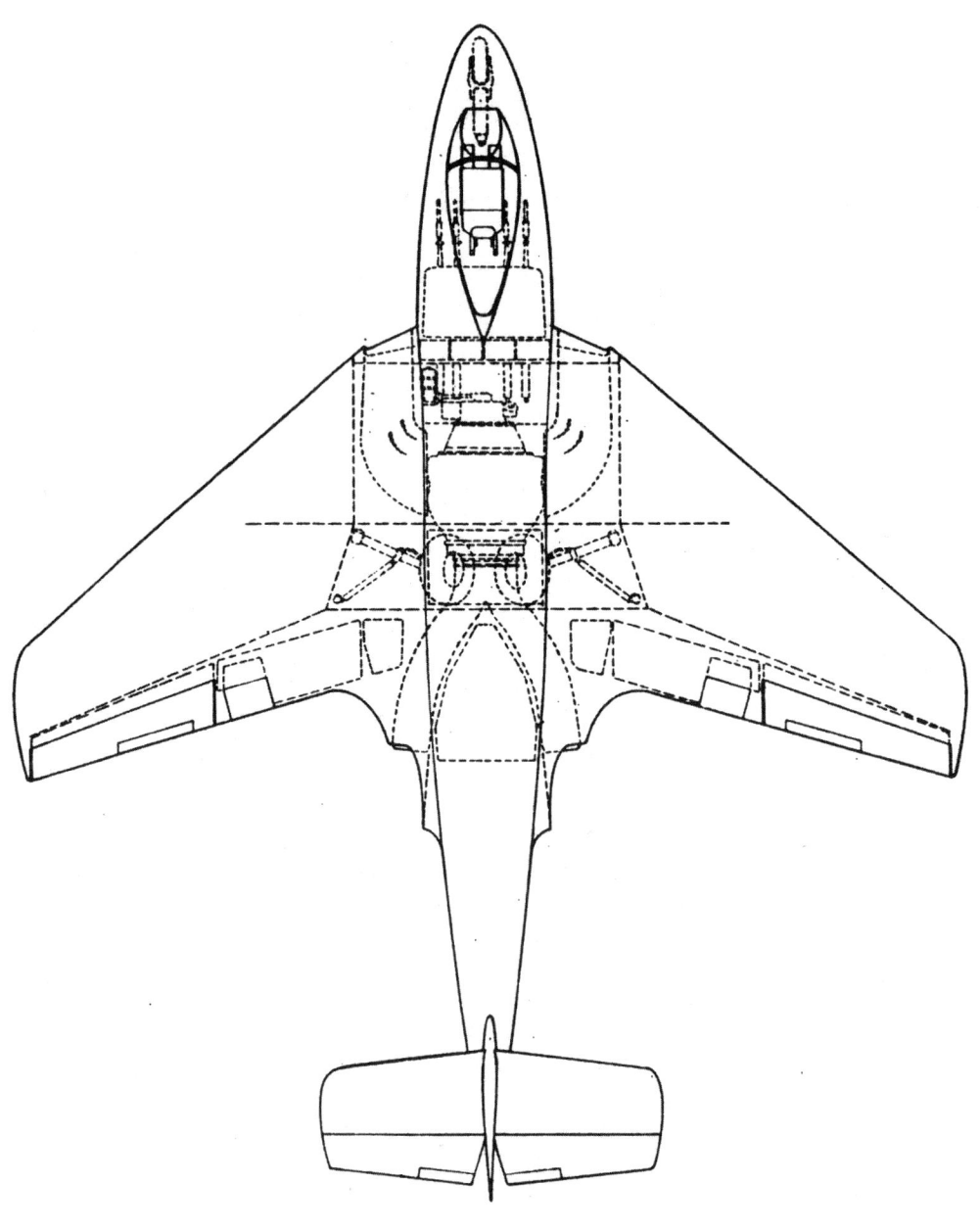

P.1052 general arrangement showing wing sweep at 35 degrees, straight tailplane and provision for 4 x 20mm cannon in nose.

this manner, then, both the Government research establishments and Hawker would benefit from the construction of an aircraft with wing sweep and the subsequent data that this would produce.

Contract detail was completed in September 1946, with DDARD requesting pricing for two aircraft, which was forwarded in November as preliminary design work for the P.1052 began on the 8th of the month. Work to investigate the stresses involved in extreme sweepback had commenced at Kingston in August and continued into November. On the 21st of the month a production order for one P.1052 under Hawker contract no. 599297 was raised.

At a meeting on 28 November with Ministry representatives, a Hawker draft specification for the design was considered which included external fixed slots to be fitted to wing tips for preliminary flights; a P.1040 type reduced area tailplane to be fitted, with ability to change the incidence on the ground (a swept back version to be considered later); provision for wing pressure plotting and stressing weight of new parts to be 10,000lbs. A tail parachute and ejection seat were definite requirements and power controlled elevators preferable to spring tabs. Six draughtsmen were now allocated to the project. Concern regarding the most

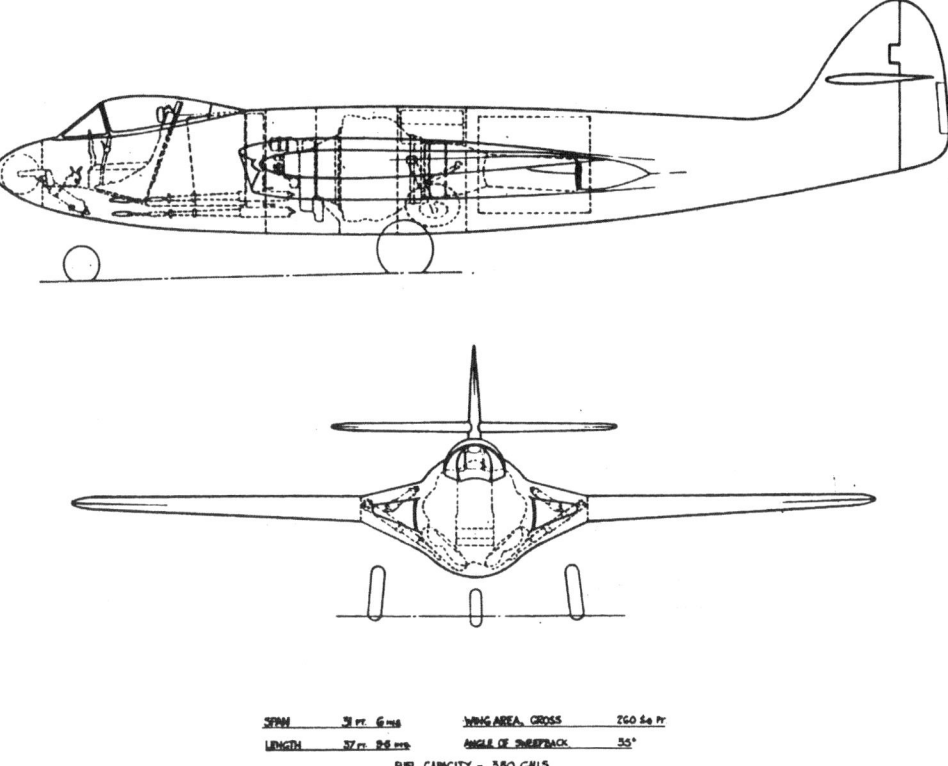

desirable wingspan saw this increased in December from 30ft 6in to 32ft 8in, which necessitated much recalculation of wing loads and stiffness. However, ten days later, a rethink saw the span reduced to 31ft 6in.

As 1947 dawned, Hawker received the revised specification E38/46, to which the company responded in March with their tender which was accepted, contract cover for two prototypes being received in May against contract 6/Aircraft/1156/CB.7 (b), with confirmation that first flight of the aircraft was expected at the end of the year. Before this, however, confusion at the Ministry of Supply in March resulted in the invitation to tender being received calling for the design and supply of an experimental swept back version of a Naval interceptor fighter. Hawker designers were non-plussed, pointing out that they had never agreed to supply aircraft to naval specifications, 'all we agreed to do was to produce two research aircraft with swept back wings. These would not in any way be fitted up to meet naval requirements.' Camm weighed in later with

P.1052 under construction in the Experimental Department at the Richmond Road premises.

a missive to Mr H.F. Vessey, AD/ARD/Research, the matter being resolved in April. During late 1947 and early 1948, work to determine the optimum position of the pressure plotting points for the wings was undertaken and of the instrumentation required to record this.[1]

The P.1052 would broadly follow the same layout as the P.1040, though the swept wings would necessitate minor changes to accommodate the altered CG. Also changed would be the engine air intakes which, on the P.1040, had been slightly swept in relation to the fuselage centre line; the swept wing would result in the air intake face being more perpendicular to the fuselage. Wing sweep settled at 35 per cent on the quarter chord and a thickness/chord ratio of 10 per cent (0.10). The intention to construct the wing to allow for pressure plotting at various points was significant since this would be the first time that the ability to collect data from a high speed swept wing would be possible and it was hoped that much useful data would be collected with which to advance knowledge within RAE and the wider scientific community in the UK.

In March 1948, some preliminary work was undertaken regarding a military version of P.1052 but this was retained in-house, not being shared with MoS. Work was now proceeding fairly smoothly on the first prototype at Richmond Road, though the wing skins appear to have been sub-contracted out to Westlands. However, by August the aircraft was sufficiently complete for the company to request it be displayed in the static park at that year's SBAC Display, though the Ministry declined on grounds of secrecy. As the new aircraft progressed through assembly, a new recruit to the Experimental Drawing Office was given the task of adding an additional row of blow-in doors to the plenum chamber cover, to provide an increase in the static thrust by a useful margin. P.1052 would have eight doors; Sea Hawk would have twelve. This new recruit – Ralph Hooper – would later find fame as the originator of the P.1127 VTOL aircraft. The addition of the extra doors was 'my only direct link with Hawker's first production jet aircraft. I always attribute any small success that the Sea Hawk subsequently achieved to this extra row of doors!'[2]

With the aircraft now undergoing stringent testing, a meeting on 16 October considered the possibility of putting the aircraft into quantity production, which must have cheered the Hawker Directors, though J.E. Serby at the Directorate of Military Aircraft Research and Development (DMARD) issued a note on 5 November 'not to proceed'. On 14 November 1948, the aircraft, now serialled VX272, was dispatched to Boscombe Down with taxi trials and first flight occurring on the 19th of the month at the hands of Squadron Leader Trevor

'Wimpy' Wade, returning to the Farnborough outstation on the 24th for further flight trials.

During January 1949 various modifications were introduced to VX272, including changes to the rudder to reduce the lightness of the control. Fitting of brake flaps was deferred until a suitable scheme could be designed and the tailplane incidence was adjusted to give one degree positive in an effort to address severe tail vibration. A short chord elevator was also fitted, flight trials showing a reduction in stick loads at high Mach number. Following a meeting with Vessey, it was agreed that an adjustable tailplane, electrically controlled, be designed

P.1052, VX272 at Farnborough, March 1949.

for the aircraft, this work being schemed in March. The following month, the aircraft was taken on charge by CS(A) and the second prototype VX279 completed its first flight on 13 April, again under Wade's control. In May it was decided that VX279 would go to Boscombe Down for preliminary handling trials 'in connection with the Australian enquiry'. The aircraft arrived in July for an assessment for the Australian Government during which twenty-two hours of flying were completed before engine problems necessitated a return to Hawker.

Assessment by A&AEE pilots revealed an aircraft which was pleasant to fly and free from any vices likely to endanger the aircraft. Two concerns were identified: first, the elevator controls were unacceptably heavy, and second, at high Mach number a tendency to Dutch Roll was experienced. In mock combat against the Meteor F.4, (VX279 in attacking mode throughout) elevator heaviness was confirmed and also the large elevator control inputs necessary to complete fighter type manoeuvres. The dive recovery flaps were found helpful in combat manoeuvring.

> Taken all round, the aircraft was fairly pleasant to fly in combat manoeuvres and the increase in critical Mach number and performance over current fighter types gave the pilot greater freedom of manoeuvre. However, the heavy and unresponsive nature of the elevator control was disappointing and more development of this control is required. Effective airbrakes are also necessary, particularly to prevent overshooting a target.[3]

Meanwhile VX272 was passed to RAE Farnborough for trials in June 1949, these being conducted by Lieutenant Commander Eric Brown and comprised:

2 June	Handling, stalls and dives from 35,000ft at M0.893.
2 June	Dive from 35,500ft. M0.935.
8 June	General handling.
9 June	Level flights at 20,000ft up to M0.88.
24 June	PE (position error) by aneroid method, up to 500 knots.
30 June	PE by aneroid method, up to 500 knots.
11 July	Stalls and PE with a 100ft trailing static (probe trailed at the rear of the aircraft).
12 July	Stalls and PE with a 100ft trailing static.[4]

Brown's verdict on the aircraft: 'Delightful … Here we had an aeroplane which could give a new lease of life to our compressibility work, which had got stuck at about Mach 0.9. We succeeded in pushing our top speed to Mach 0.94 but, to our disappointment, not beyond.' Brown went on to explain that this was not

P.1052, VX272 at Farnborough, March 1949.

P.1052, VX272 aloft in the hands of Neville Duke.

because the aircraft had any nasty characteristics, but because instead of nosing over in a compressibility dive, it would attempt to nose up out of it, making it an ideal candidate for the first swept wing deck landing trials.[5]

It was now (July 1949) that the Ministry decided that they would like to have a rocket motor fitted into one of the aircraft (a la P.1072) and it was decided that a separate rear end be manufactured which would incorporate both the variable tailplane arrangement and provision for a rocket motor, though the new back would at first be flown with the rocket orifice blanked off; the project code P.1078 being allocated for this. Come September and Hawker's new aircraft was flown at the SBAC Display, VX279 doing the honours. This positive publicity was somewhat mired on 29 September when the first prototype VX272 made a forced landing due to a sheared fuel pump drive, damaging the aircraft; repairs would ground it for the remainder of the year. However, the opportunity thus presented was grabbed and the new rear fuselage with electrically adjustable tailplane and rocket provision was fitted together with airbrakes on the wing. Comparing the rear fuselage of both VX272 and VX279 in later images, it may be that it was the latter that was given the fuselage with rocket capability rather than VX272, since this shows the base of the rudder cut back to a greater extent than VX272, but no definitive information has come to light thus far.

At this point, the P.1052 underwent complete structural tests with a view to increasing the minimum reserve factor to allow an increase in the aircraft's weight from 10,000lb to 12,500lb. It was deduced that this was possible by repair and reinforcement of the main spars in the centre fuselage and repair and reinforcement of the outer wings. This investigation would pay dividends when the later Sea Hawk was required to operate in the fighter bomber role.

Meanwhile the remaining aircraft VX279 was used to carry out a complete wing pressure plotting trial during October. At the end of the trial, the aircraft was laid up for a new rear fuselage to be fitted, incorporating a mechanically operated adjustable tailplane. However, resumed flight testing in the New Year of 1950 revealed severe vibration problems. Work to remedy this proved to be extended, February seeing various attempts to resolve the problem including additional hinged links, increased fin skin gauge, and fixed bullet fairing at the fin/tailplane junction. In March, the bullet fairing was hinged to allow adjustment of the tailplane incidence, testing showing improvement in the vibration though it was still apparent at high ASI, the aircraft being flown to M0.92. The opportunity was taken to fit the bullet fairing to VX272 also and this aircraft resumed flying on 24 March, principally engaged on trials to determine the optimum incidence for the tailplane, which settled at 1 degree, 20 minutes (1.33 degrees). The new

P.1052, VX272 in flight.

P.1052, VX279 prior to receiving its distinctive 'duck egg green' paint scheme.

P.1052 – Swept Wings 89

airbrakes were also tested in April with reasonably satisfactory results before the aircraft was handed over to RAE for assessment.

Also in April, VX279 was fitted with a swept tailplane to gather preliminary data prior to the aircraft being withdrawn from the flying programme for modification to P.1081 standard. On 11 May, the aircraft arrived at Richmond Road Experimental Department for conversion to an all swept aircraft with straight-through jet pipe to conform under project P.1081, not flying again till 19 June 1950. The further story of this aircraft is to be found in a later chapter.

With VX272 now the only P.1052, work continued with RAE into wing drop, but on 24 July 1950, the aircraft crash landed, thus bringing to a halt its research programme for some months. Indeed it was not until 4 September that VX272 took to the air again but with an ill wind blowing, a further emergency landing had to be made due to the failure of the port leg to lock down. Fortunately, damage

P.1052, VX279 in bare metal finish. Neville Duke in cockpit.

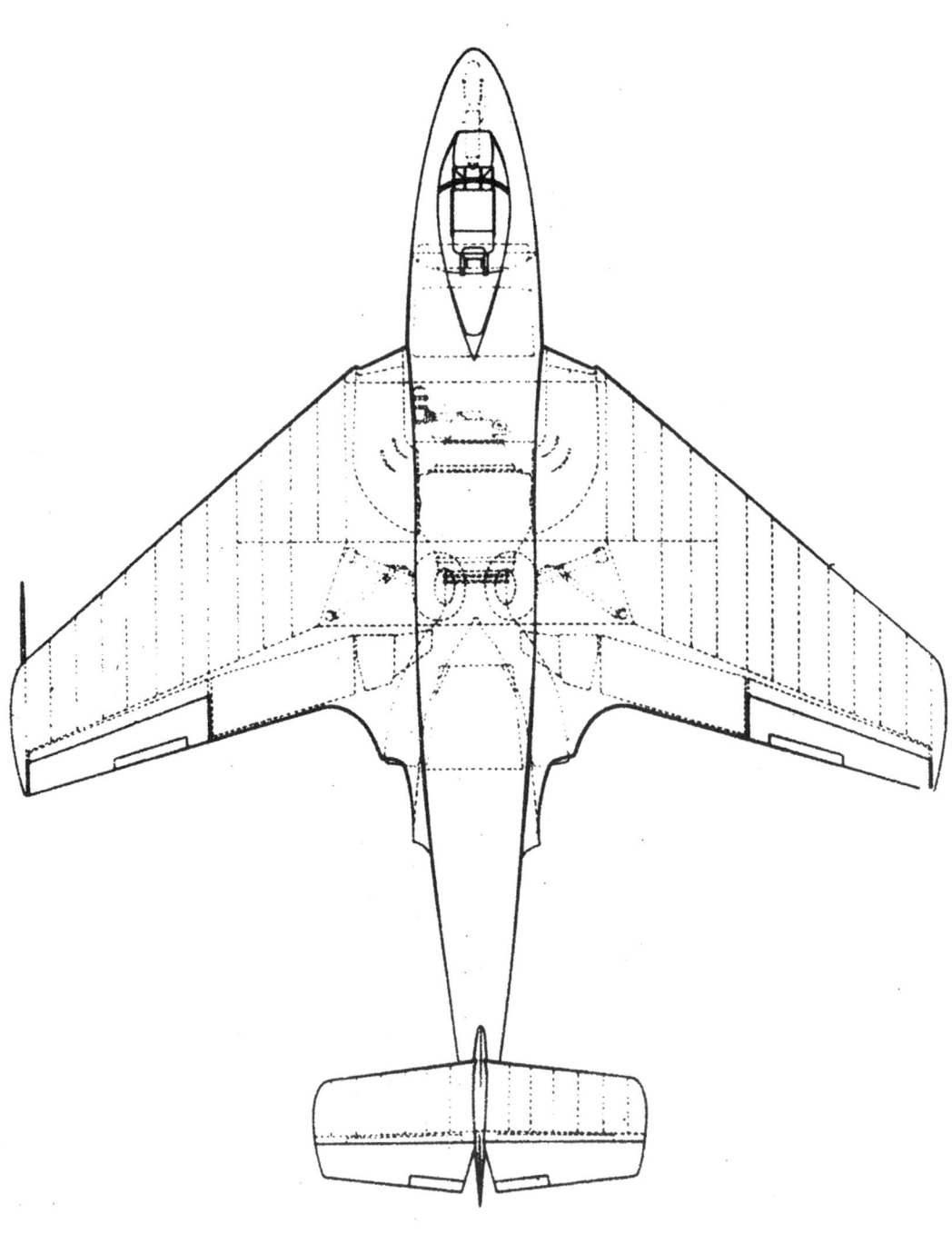

P.1052 layout showing revised cut back rudder.

was slight and was repaired within days. Work was now carried out to fit the Sea Hawk long-stroke undercarriage to the aircraft and delivered to RAE on 30 October for arrestor hook trials and later, carrier trials. However, the arrestor hook and the carrier trials were not carried out, the aircraft remaining with RAE until February 1952 when it was brought to Hawker's new Flight Test centre at Dunsfold Aerodrome for modification for high-speed research. At this point the bullet fairing at the fin tailplane junction was fitted and flying resumed, giving greatly improved high-Mach number performance before handing back to RAE. Thereafter, the aircraft returned to Dunsfold in April for modification back to deck landing condition. It had been intended that the rear fuselage from VX279, rendered redundant when this aircraft was converted to P.1081, should be fitted to VX272 for the carrier trials though whether this ever happened, in light of the delays caused by the various accidents the aircraft suffered, is unknown.

Following the carrier trials in May 1952 aboard HMS *Eagle*, a variable incidence swept tailplane was fitted for RAE research and handed over yet again. Finally, in September 1953, VX272 suffered a further forced landing, following which RAE announced that they had finished with the aircraft and did not

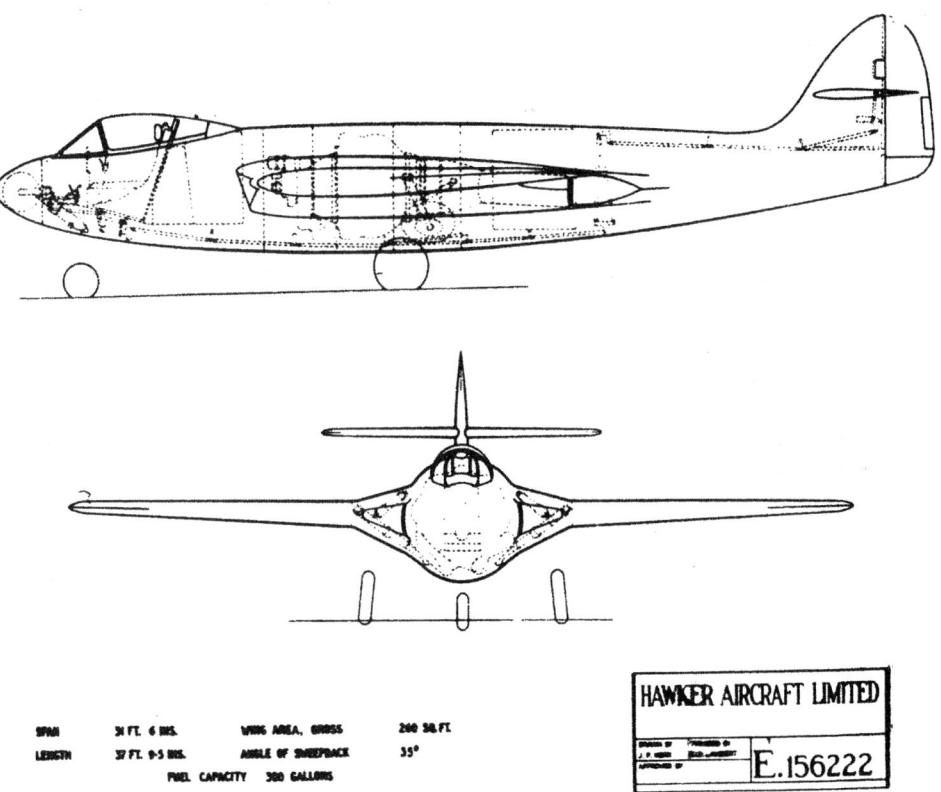

P.1052, VX279 with revised rear fuselage featuring shorter rudder and new paint scheme. 'Wimpy' Wade in the cockpit.

P.1052, VX279 in its element with 'Wimpy' Wade at the controls.

want it returned. Thereafter, following repair and a further flight test by Duke on 26 November 1953, the P.1052 was flown to Farnborough by Bedford. The aircraft then appears to have languished at various establishments, including RAF Cardington's gate, eventually arriving at RAF Halton as an instructional airframe coded 7174M in December 1956. Later the aircraft was placed in storage at RAF Colerne for the RAF Museum and now resides in the reserve collection at RNAS Yeovilton Museum.

Aircraft VX272 appeared to possess a charmed life, for despite being the subject of several accidents, it returned to flight after suitable repair work:

29 September 1949 – VX272, P.1052. Lieutenant J. Elliot RN, Naval Section, RAE Farnborough. Test flight. Engine failure in flight, force landed in a farmyard at Cove, nil casualties, cat 3.

17 April 1950 – VX272, P.1052. Flight Lieutenant J.G. Harrison, Aerodynamic Flight, RAE Farnborough. Trial to investigate wing drop at high Mach numbers. The engine failed due to fuel pump failure on a final approach to runway 25. Wheels up landing. Nil casualties, cat 3.

17 July 1950 – VX272, P.1052. Flight Lieutenant J.G. Harrison, Aerodynamic Flight, RAE Farnborough. Following repair after the forced landing on 17 April 1950, trials to investigate wing drop at high Mach numbers continued. The engine failed on the approach to runway 25, the aircraft crashed onto the RAE cycle sheds killing a contractor's painter, Mr J. Beale. 1 killed, cat 4.

4 September 1951 – VX272, P.1052. Neville Duke. During handling flight from Farnborough, forced landing at Langley due to hydraulic fault causing undercarriage malfunction. Flown out on 6 September to Farnborough.

31 August 1953 – VX272, P.1052. Squadron Leader W.J. Potocki DFC, Aerodynamic Flight, RAE Farnborough. High speed Mach number investigation. Hydraulic failure, the aircraft was diverted to Odiham after the port wheel failed to lower and landed on the starboard main and nose wheels. On 3 September, Potocki flew the aircraft out of Odiham to Dunsfold for repair. Nil Casualties, cat 3.

25 September 1953 – VX272, P.1052. Pilot unknown, RAE Farnborough. Repaired again after second accident on 17 July (or 24th, sources differ) and fitted with variable incidence swept tailplane. Trials recommenced but ceased on a final forced landing due to an engine failure in flight. Nil casualties, cat 5.[6]

94 Hawker's Early Jets

P.1052, VX272 at Dunsfold towards the end of its testing days, probably in May 1953 during a visit by the Duke of Edinburgh.

The swept wing P.1052 had, over a period of five years, given Hawker and RAE an excellent return on their outlay. RAE Farnborough had had available to them a swept wing, instrumented for pressure plotting research, which would form an important basis for future projects. Hawker had been able to trial various aspects of design that would come to fruition in the Hunter and gain experience in swept-wing design.

Leading Particulars

Wing span:	31ft 6in
Length:	39ft 7in
Wing sweep:	35 degrees at quarter chord
Wing area:	258 sq. ft
Thickness chord ratio:	0.10 (10%)
Engine:	RR Nene RN.2 rated at 5,000lb
Fuel capacity:	395 gall
Weight empty:	9,450lb
All up weight:	13,488lb
Performance Max speed:	at sea level 554 knots. At height level M0.87. In dive M0.9
Service ceiling:	45,000ft
Absolute ceiling:	49,500ft

Chapter 7

P.1081 – A Clean Sweep

As was discussed in the previous chapter, the P.1052 VX279 was withdrawn from flying in early May 1950 for modification work to convert it to P.1081 status. In January 1950, Hawker had issued a brochure relating to P.1081, a derivative of the P.1052 which would feature a straight-through jet pipe rather than the bifurcated design, but still be powered by the Nene turbojet with potential development in the future to take the Rolls-Royce Tay, an uprated centrifugal engine based on Nene and delivering around 6,000lb thrust. The straight-through jet pipe would be required because it was planned to trial reheat on the Tay aircraft, which could not be achieved with the bifurcated exhaust. The aircraft would retain the swept wing of the P.1052 but would also have swept tail surfaces with electrically powered adjustable incidence tailplane.

Discussion of a straight-through jet pipe had continued sporadically since July 1948, when Hawker had submitted preliminary data to the Ministry of Supply concerning the provision of a Nene 4 and straight-through jet pipe for N7/46 and the P.1052 aircraft in comparison to the P.1040. In January 1950, meetings with Rolls-Royce and Ministry of Supply in the person of Mr J.E. Serby discussed the engine requirements for the aircraft. Initially, it was agreed that the jet pipe would be suitable for the Nene and also the AJ65 Avon axial flow engine, while Rolls-Royce would work on developing a jet pipe suitable for the Tay engine. On 31 of the month, a meeting at the Ministry of Supply with Serby discussed the construction of a prototype P.1081 specifically for the Australian Government which was interested in obtaining jet aircraft for home defence. Hawker believed that they could deliver such an airframe within fifteen months of Instruction to Proceed, the aircraft to be fitted with the Rolls-Royce Tay engine.[1]

The issue of the tailplane design was revisited on 13 February since the proposed shape, when fitted to the P.1052 for flight testing, had been unsatisfactory, though a revised shape was agreed in the first week of March; it was also agreed to strengthen the wing of VX279. Problems with design and construction of a suitable jet pipe by Rolls-Royce were now delaying the project

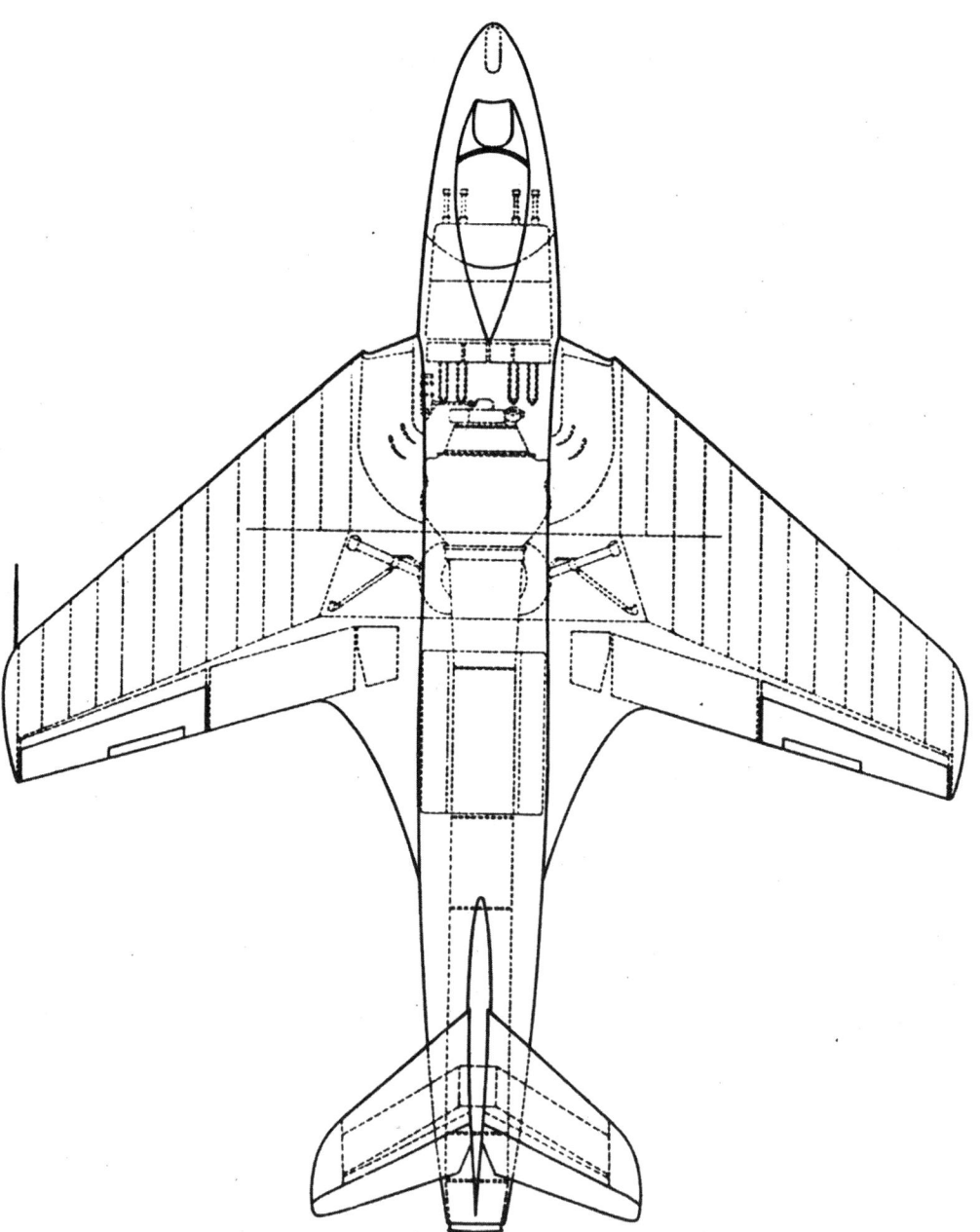

HAWKER INTERCEPTOR FIGHTER
ROLLS ROYCE 'NENE' ENGINE

P.1081 general arrangement showing revised rear fuselage incorporating straight through jet pipe, swept fin and tailplane and provision for 4 x 20mm cannon in nose.

and several visits to Kingston by Rolls-Royce personnel occurred during March. Part of the problem appeared to be the desire to allow for subsequent reheat in the new jet pipe. Eventually on 26 April, following further visits by Rolls-Royce design staff, a decision was taken to use a Supermarine Attacker type jet pipe on the first prototype, i.e. without reheat ability. With these decisions now cast, the aircraft was rapidly rebuilt at Kingston and made its first flight of thirty minutes on 19 June 1950, at Farnborough, flown by 'Wimpy' Wade.[2]

Such was confidence in the new design that VX279 was flown by Wade to the Brussels Aero Show on 23 June via London Airport (for Customs clearance) and returned on 26 June, exhibiting excellent speeds. The promise of the aircraft was, however, slightly dented (literally) when on 19 July 1950, Wade, on a flight from Blackbushe for filming, found himself unable to lower the undercarriage fully and also unable to retract the lowered port undercarriage due to failure of

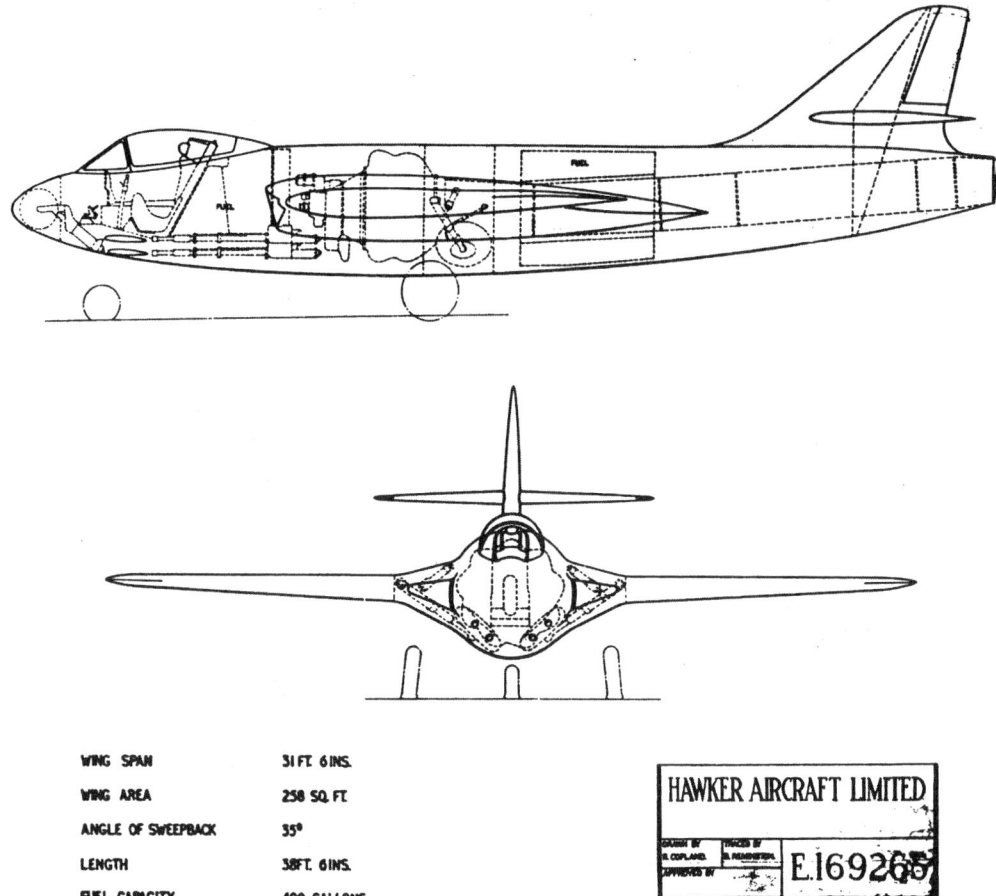

P.1081, VX279 undergoing modification in the Experimental Department at Richmond Road. Note in the background a nearly complete Sea Hawk, the fuselage of another and the aft fuselage from VX279, May 1950.

P.1081, VX279 at Farnborough, with new rear end still in bare metal. Note the much shortened rudder, July 1950.

the hydraulic pump, necessitating a diversion to Odiham and a landing on the port mainwheel and nosewheel. Minor damage was sustained to the starboard wing tip and fairing but following preliminary assessment, VX279 was flown back to Hawker's hangar at Farnborough the next day.

Through July and August, the full flight test programme was conducted and various changes to the jet pipe fairing, exhausting nozzle angle, and tailplane were trialled. At the same time, it was agreed that reheat would not be pursued on the prototype but would be incorporated in production aircraft, the company being quietly confident that a production order for Australia was within their grasp, either for a P.1081 derivative under project P.1062, or a P.1052 derivative under project P.1080 (against specification F.28/49). It appears that there was general uneasiness regarding the reheat proposal and following discussions with Wing Commander Richmond, a statement was produced for the Royal Australian Air Force (RAAF) recommending that reheat should not feature on the initial batch for Australia. In September, the aircraft performed flawlessly at the SBAC Farnborough Display under the control of 'Wimpy' Wade, after which it was laid up for yet more work on the tailplane, a larger unit being fitted, powered by an electrical actuator as well as increased chord rudder.

The interest of the Australian Government was driven by the requirement to deploy modern jet combat aircraft in Korea, a conflict to which Australia was committed to supplying support through the auspices of the United Nations (UN). Up till 1951, Australian fighter aircraft comprised F-51D Mustangs but it was soon clear, with the advent of the MiG-15 in the skies over Korea (powered by derivatives of the engines so helpfully supplied by the Labour Government), that urgent re-equipment was required in the form of jet aircraft. Australian High Commissioner in the UK, Sir Eric Harrison, reported that three types could be acquired from British sources: the DH Venom; the Hawker P.1081 and the Gloster Meteor. For maintenance reasons he gave priority to the Venom, second priority to the P.1081 and third priority to the Meteor T.Mk.7. De Havilland could deliver twenty aircraft, but only between January and June 1952. The P.1081 (by this time already disregarded) could not have been productionised in time to be of any use in the immediate conflict and therefore Meteors were supplied as a stop-gap until Australia could select the aircraft of its choice to modernise its forces in the long term.

Meanwhile, with the aircraft flying again in October 1950, high Mach number investigations were carried out, but unwelcome news hit the company on 14 November when Hawker was advised that the Australian interest had been dropped. The Australians had initially wanted P.1052, but Hawker had offered P.1081 as a licence built project. An Australian delegation visiting Kingston, however, reported that P.1081 required extra work to the tail to cure vibration and expressed concern regarding the company's ability to support a licence agreement in Australia when it was fully committed to projects at home. Clearly Hawker Aircraft had had expectations of an agreement with the Australian Government; company accounts for July 1950 show nominal entries for a licence agreement to run for five years, beginning in May 1950, valued at £35,000. However, by November a decision had been made that it would be the P.1067 that would feature in any agreement rather than the P.1081.[3]

Ralph Hooper noted that,

> The P.1081 flew well and could achieve Mach 0.89 in level flight. It was modified to provide an electrically actuated trimming tailplane and wing fences, both new features for Hawker at that time. But by the end of 1950, Australian interest had waned, the proposal for an Avon-powered version of the F-86 Sabre proving more attractive.

In the event, the Australian choice fell to a licence produced version of the F-86F Sabre fitted with a licence built Rolls-Royce Avon RA.7 engine, giving almost twice the thrust of the General Electric J.47 engine normally fitted. Built by the indigenous Commonwealth Aircraft Corporation of Australia, the type entered service in 1954, too late to see action during the Korean conflict.[4]

Following the loss of interest in the aircraft as a production item, flight testing continued through into early 1951 to refine the shape of the aircraft, especially at the rear, in order to achieve greater speed, a revised rear fairing of finer form giving an increase of approximately 7mph. Modifications were installed with the aim of addressing the buffet and vibration still plaguing the aircraft at higher Mach numbers, including a distributed mass balance rudder which markedly improved the situation. These modifications were successful in raising the top speed to Mach 0.94, most of the flying being carried out by Duke. The aircraft was also used to trial elements of the design of the F3/48 (i.e. Hunter) such as the combined use of landing flap and dive recovery flap, as an airbrake. Having completed these refinements, the intention was to hand off the aircraft to RAE for their own trials.

On 3 April, however a flight by Wade from Farnborough led to the complete destruction of the aircraft and the death of Wade through causes not understood.

The circumstances of Wade's death, and indeed the loss of the aircraft, were never fully resolved. At the subsequent enquiry into the accident, the following bald points were ascertained:

P.1081, VX279 at Farnborough, with new rear end still in bare metal. Note the much shortened rudder, July 1950.

P.1081, VX279 at Farnborough, Kingston Project Office staff in attendance, July 1950.

1) The aircraft VX279 had departed RAE Farnborough, pilot being Trevor Wade, to carry out a general air test which it was believed would comprise a climb to 35,000ft, a high Mach number run, operation of airbrakes, followed by a high speed level run.
2) Witness statements described 'a noise like a roll of thunder', that the aircraft was seen in an almost vertical dive followed by recovery close to the ground. The aircraft then began a slight climb followed by seat ejection, the aircraft completing a few uncontrolled manoeuvres before crashing near Lewes in Sussex.
3) The aircraft struck the ground in one piece apart from the cockpit hood frame and Perspex, these being found some distance from the aircraft.
4) The pilot had been ejected from the aircraft but had not released from the seat and was killed on impact with the ground.
5) The wreckage was inspected on site by members of the Accident Investigation Branch of MCA, Hawker Aircraft and the Accident Section of RAE Farnborough. The wreckage was then removed to Hawker's Experimental Dept; the hood and ejection seat going to RAE for detailed investigation.
6) The seat was manufactured by ML Aviation Company. The seat being fired by a single cartridge and initiated by operation of a blind in the seat head.[5]

Further investigation revealed the sequence of events as could best be reconstructed. It appeared that the hood detached from the aircraft at 9,000ft, either intentionally or by accident; the pilot's helmet and goggles at 8,500ft, pilot's oxygen mask at 6,000ft with seat ejection at 2,000ft; the aircraft experienced an almost vertical high speed dive before pulling out at low level. While pilot ejection had commenced and the seat had left the aircraft, the seat had rotated at a sufficiently high rate to render the pilot insensible and thus unable to free himself from the seat. During the ejection sequence, the face blind had ripped in half but had allowed ejection to be completed. Tests by ML Aviation to ascertain the speed at which seat rotation of this magnitude could be induced was calculated as M 0.987. The pilot was found after a search some 1,000yds from the crash site, in a small copse, still strapped into the seat.

While the investigation concentrated on the cause of Wade's death, there was no detail published of investigation into why the aircraft had crashed. Why was the aircraft in a steep dive when the test called for level high speed runs? At this remove, we shall never know. However, Wade had been part of a delegation to the USA to assess aircraft technology and had recently returned. As part of the trip he had flown the F-86 Sabre and may well have achieved speed in

P.1081, VX279 at Farnborough; Bob Marsh in glasses and Vivian Stanbury far right, from Kingston Project Office, July 1950.

P.1081, VX279 outside the Hawker hangar at Farnborough, July 1950.

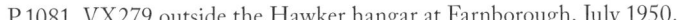

excess of Mach 1 (which the F-86 was capable of in a dive). It is feasible that he was attempting a similar manoeuvre in the P.1081 and witness statements lend support to a sonic boom. It is conjecture of course, but the fact remains that the aircraft was in a vertical dive (presumably out of control) when ejection was initiated at 9,000ft by pulling the seat face blind, thus releasing the hood before the seat followed at 2,000ft.

The ejection seat had been a constant problem for Hawker throughout the series of early jet aircraft. For whatever reason, Camm had decided to use a seat produced by ML Aviation (also known as R Malcolm) in the first jets, perhaps because it was lighter than alternative designs such as Martin Baker. In 1946, R. Malcolm became ML Engineering based at Slough and ML Aviation at White Waltham airfield. Camm's relationship with James Martin, of Martin Baker, appears to have been strained to say the least. Harold Tuffen, a Hawker designer, writing in 1971 about those early jet days recalled, 'I think Camm could not quite bring himself to use the Martin Baker seat. The two men at that time were not so well acquainted as later on and I remember some acrimonious discussions on blast tubes. Camm probably regarded Martin's aircraft efforts with some disdain.' Hawker, or rather Sydney Camm, decided that their new jet would incorporate the Malcolm seat. As described above, there was a certain amount of antipathy between Camm and James Martin; both were men with 'big' personalities who were renowned for not suffering fools gladly. The choice of Malcom's over Martin Baker, however, may simply have been that Marcel Lobelle and Camm had been trainees together at Martinsyde Aviation Ltd in the early 1920s and therefore knew each other and each other's strengths; the Malcolm seat was also lighter, a not unimportant consideration.[6]

The ejection seat as a piece of military hardware was new at this time and imposed requirements on new aircraft designs outside of the designer's previous knowledge. Stemming from a meeting at MAP in August 1944 to discuss improved means of escape from aircraft in the light of ever-increasing speeds attainable, both Marcel Lobelle, representing R Malcolm Ltd and James Martin for Martin Baker, expressed interest in developing a means of assisted escape based on ejection of the pilot and seat using an explosive charge. Both companies were to put forward schemes to achieve this; Malcolms working closely with RAE Farnborough on their design while Martin Baker preferred to work in isolation. The upshot of this was that both companies produced working systems and for a while, MAP was happy to allow both schemes to develop as an insurance should one fail later to make the grade.

P.1081, VX279 at London Airport, en route to Brussels, attracts much admiring attention. 'Wimpy' Wade by the starboard intake, June 1950.

P.1081, VX279 aloft in the hands of 'Wimpy' Wade. The aircraft has now been fitted with wing fences.

Come what may, in January 1946, Camm had been sufficiently concerned about the integration of the new technology to request consideration of a separate contract 'for development work necessary redesign of pilot ejection seat but DGTD [Director General of Technical Development] informed that, in view of extensive research being undertaken by RAE and CASR, this could not be considered.' Accordingly, Hawker submitted their proposed scheme to RAE the following month for consideration. A year later, it was agreed that tests on installation of the ejector seat would not be carried out on the actual aircraft but on a representative rig. In March 1947 it was reported that the Malcolm seat was already received, 'and modified to suit the aircraft', and would be used for the installation tests while another seat would be supplied for flight.[7]

Once the P.1040 was flying, it appears that the seat was not made live since, in September 1947, it was reported that 'the supply of cartridges for the ejection seat installation fitted to P.1040 would not be available for at least two months, and that it was essential that the utmost discretion be used in flying this machine.' By November, Hawker was advised that the Martin Baker seat would be the standard equipment for all future aircraft, leading the company to request dispensation for the ML seat in the prototypes in view of the modification work required to fit the Martin Baker seat. In January 1948, the Ministry stated

Poor image of P.1081, VX279 following its fatal crash near Lewes, April 1951.

that any production contract would have to use the Martin Baker seat and furthermore, development of the ML seat would be discontinued since it did not offer any appreciable advantage over the Martin Baker item. Thus was Hawker left with the need to continue using an ejection seat in prototype aircraft which would not receive any further development funding.[8]

In June 1948, the aircraft had been dispatched to Boscombe Down for initial trials but A&AEE had declared that they could not approve the ejection seat until it had been modified to their requirements; the modifications appear to have centred around increased leg protection for the pilot. In July, a meeting at RAE approved the fitting of leg guards and a meeting on the 16th was held to view suitable mock-ups, the modifications being approved in August. June 1950 saw belated trials with the ejector seat in the N7/46 prototype VP422 in the blower tunnel at Boscombe Down which appear to have been satisfactory though no details of applied air speed during the tests are known.

The accidental death of Wade in April 1951, then, appears to have occurred against a background of a modified ejector seat being used in anger for the first time with the aircraft at a speed above that at which the seat was likely to have been tested. The rapid rotation of the seat appeared sufficient to prevent the pilot from releasing himself from the seat and deploying his parachute in the short time available due to the low level at which ejection occurred. However, it had been noted earlier in the testing of the seat that there was a tendency for the seat to topple as it left the guide-rails and the Institute of Aviation Medicine, concerned that this could disorientate the pilot, had recommended that a stabilising parachute be fitted on future seats, which would deploy as the seat left the aircraft. It would appear unlikely that such a device was fitted at the time of the accident, though there had been failures of the stabilising parachutes due to the high speed of seat ejection. Unfortunately, the seat mark number is not stated in the official enquiry report and there is no mention of the stabilising parachutes.

It should also be noted that this was the first live ejection using a Malcolm seat, even the company had never conducted live trials, MAP believing that live tests were unnecessary and were not called for in either the Malcolm or Martin Baker contracts. Martin Baker, on the other hand, were adamant that live ejections would be part of their trials and successfully carried out numerous live ejections with their seat. In the event, this was only the third ejection from UK aircraft 'in anger'. The first two were via Martin Baker seats and were successful. The first Malcolm ejection was fatal for the pilot and a severe knock for ML Aviation.

As to why the aircraft entered what was clearly an uncontrollable dive, doubt has been cast on the fidelity of the tailplane electrical actuator, a malfunction of which could drive the tailplane incidence to one for which the pilot could not compensate. Such tailplane 'run-aways' have been an unfortunately recurring theme over the years. The theory appears to be supported by the story of an employee who drew an actuator from stores at Kingston for use on another project but found that it had malfunctioned in previous service and driven itself to the stops before 'fusing'. According to the records, its previous use had been on the P.1081, though whether it was on the aircraft at the time of the crash is unknown.[9] In any event, the P.1081 tailplane was designed to have an angle of incidence of plus or minus 2.5 degrees and one is left wondering whether such an angle could prove impossible to overcome with the pitch controls. It is more likely that the available elevator authority was just not capable of allowing control at the speed involved in the dive. Aircraft constructors were discovering that powered controls were an urgent requirement at high Mach numbers, Hawker incorporating these on the first Hunters.

Roy Chaplin (Camm's deputy) writing in 1987, was unequivocal in his opinion regarding Wade's death.

> I think he had the ambition to be the first pilot to go supersonic in a British aeroplane and was very conscious of fore and aft control at high Mach numbers. A major contribution to the improvement of this was the introduction of a swept tailplane and we had been engaged with him on various other tail end improvements until finally, on the fatal day, he must have felt that he should, without our knowledge or agreement, attempt a supersonic dive.
>
> Don Stranks, Harry Davis (RTO) and I were on the scene within an hour or so of its happening. I am quite clear in my mind as to what probably happened. Wade had no doubt gone supersonic – several witnesses had told us of 'a clap of thunder'. Presumably he found that he could not pull out of his dive and decided to eject.[10]

The response at ML Aviation was immediate. Des Armour recalled:

> My first day was eventful … in the late afternoon Bob Parsons and a section leader burst into the [drawing] office and with little or no explanation removed all the drawings from each man's board and plan chest. I remember the draughtsmen all looking on in amazement, while I was agog at such extraordinary practice …
>
> The reason for this sudden stop of work on the ML ejection seat soon leaked out; 'Wimpy Wade', the Hawker Chief Test Pilot, had been killed

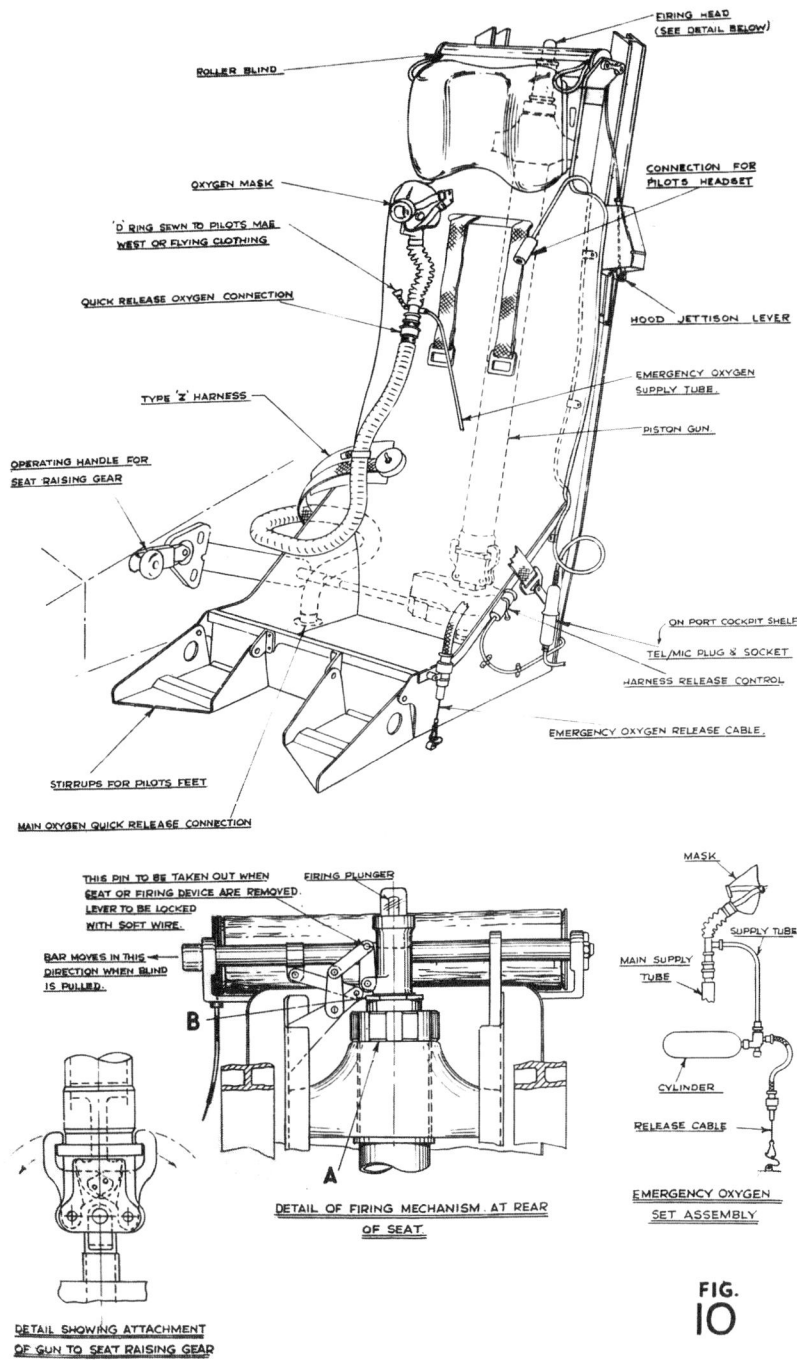

PILOT EJECTION

Detail of the ejector seat system as fitted to the P.1081.

The ejector seat from P.1081, VX279 following the fatal crash near Lewes.

earlier that day when his ML seat reportedly ejected through the unjettisoned canopy of the Hawker P.1052 [sic] he was flying. It was rumoured that the fatal malfunction was due to the failure of a Bowden cable operated system, and from that day on, no draughtsman dare incorporate a Bowden cable in any design without incurring the wrath of Chief designer, Marcel Lobelle.[11]

A final note on the accident is best left to the entry in the UK Flight Testing Accidents publication:

> 2nd April 1951 – VX279. Wimpey [sic] Wade. General air test flight flown from RAE Farnborough. The aircraft had last flown on 26 February 1951 after which modifications had been carried out including the interconnection of the dive recovery and landing flaps and the replacement of the tailplane actuator. During a high speed run some form of emergency occurred and the pilot elected to eject … After the pilot had ejected the aircraft flew a wide right-hand circuit performing various manoeuvres before finally striking the ground with the port wing and the aircraft nose at a steep angle at low speed and then cartwheeling, 850yds to the east of the ejected seat. The majority of the aircraft was destroyed by fire. It was considered possible that the aircraft had become transonic in the dive as several observers had heard what they thought was a sonic boom. The pilot had given no indication of his intentions before the flight, had not used the r/t after take-off and had not made use of the recording equipment fitted in the aircraft. 1 killed, cat 5.[12]

Leading Particulars

Wing span:	31ft 6in
Length:	37ft 4in
Wing sweep:	35 degrees at quarter chord
Wing area:	258 sq. ft
Thickness chord ratio:	0.10 (10%)
Engine:	RR Nene RN.2 rated at 5,000lb
Fuel capacity:	400 gall
Weight empty:	11,200lb
All up weight:	14,480lb
Performance Max speed at sea level:	554 knots. Max level speed M0.89. In dive M0.92
Service ceiling:	45,600ft

Chapter 8

Sea Hawk into Service

As seen in a previous chapter, Admiralty interest in the P.1040 project had been sufficient for an order for three prototypes of a navalised version under specification N7/46 to be raised, the first aircraft being a basic flying airframe and the latter two to be equipped for naval operation with items such as folding wings, arrestor hook, catapult spools etc. Once these aircraft were available for flight testing, continued modification to improve flight characteristics and Admiralty requirements were applied to the aircraft with the intention that the third aircraft should approximate as closely as possible to that required for production aircraft. Much of the Admiralty input in this respect came from Lieutenant Commander Eric Brown, while based at Farnborough.

In November 1948, a meeting was held with Commander Harrison RDQN to discuss the production specification though no order was in sight at that time, the final specification (25/48/P) being expected in December. It was at this meeting that the company was first informed that additional equipment for the aircraft was likely to increase all-up weight by some 400lb, a most unwelcome piece of news for Hawker. In February 1949, Camm wrote to Manning at MoS pointing out that the 'more serious modifications that we are putting through for the N7/46 production will undoubtedly cause some delay.'[1]

On 22 November 1949, a contract was issued to Hawker Aircraft Ltd for 151 aircraft to include a Martin Baker ejector seat and pressurised cockpit, production being undertaken at Kingston and Langley (though in the event Langley would not feature in Sea Hawk production) with flight testing to be undertaken at Dunsfold and, with the final design conference being completed on 27 August 1951, the first production aircraft, WF143 made its first flight at 14.45 on 14 November at Dunsfold Aerodrome in the hands of Neville Duke, fully seven years after design began. It should be noted that even at this point, fairly major design changes were in progress; an example being the fitment of the bullet fairing at the fin/tailplane intersection, which was omitted from WF143 during its initial flights.

The initial flight of WF143 lasted fifty minutes, the engine being a Nene RN.4 (Mk.101) of 5,000lb thrust. Ballast of 510lb was carried in lieu of ammunition and 394 gallons of fuel giving an all-up weight of 13,054lb at take off. Since this was a general handling sortie only, Duke restricted himself and the aircraft to an altitude of 21,000ft and speed of 360 knots (0.68 IMN). This first investigation of the flight characteristics appears to have been broadly positive, Duke noting that aileron control was heavy at higher speeds and that the gearing of the aileron and rudder trims was too fast. There was also concern regarding operation of the high-pressure fuel cock and the exhaust from the cartridge starter, both of which would require changes before release to service but all in all, a successful first flight.[2]

Flying of the first production aircraft WF143 continued at Dunsfold until January 1952 when it was laid up to allow fitment of the latest airbrake arrangement and instrumentation for the forthcoming contractor trials, flying again the next month in company with the second aircraft WF144 on 22 February. Production aircraft now began to leave the Dunsfold line at a regular pace, WF145 in March, WF147 in May (WF146 being a TI aircraft) and the sixth production aircraft in July; by year end, fourteen aircraft had flown. No time was wasted in clearing the aircraft for carrier qualification; in April, WF144 was despatched to RAE for assisted take-off and arrested landing trials while WF145 was delivered to Boscombe Down for assessment prior to carrier trials. In May, both aircraft flew to HMS *Eagle* and successfully completed on-board trials.

The A&AEE assessment of WF145, carried out between June and October 1952, assessed the production airbrakes fitted to the aircraft after negative reports of the prototype brakes. The production versions were found to be,

> … considerably more effective than the prototype installation previously tested but it is evident that the airbrakes still do not fully open at speeds above 275 – 300 knots IAS, and at high indicated airspeeds in particular the initial deceleration is relatively low. A further improvement is essential at such speeds at least.[3]

The first thirty-five aircraft were all built in the Experimental Department at Kingston and finished and flown at Dunsfold in three batches: WF143–WF161, WF167–WF177 and WM901–WM905. Concern and some anger was being expressed by the Royal Navy at this time because Hawker Aircraft Ltd was fully committed to work on the F3/48 (Hunter) jet for the RAF, this work

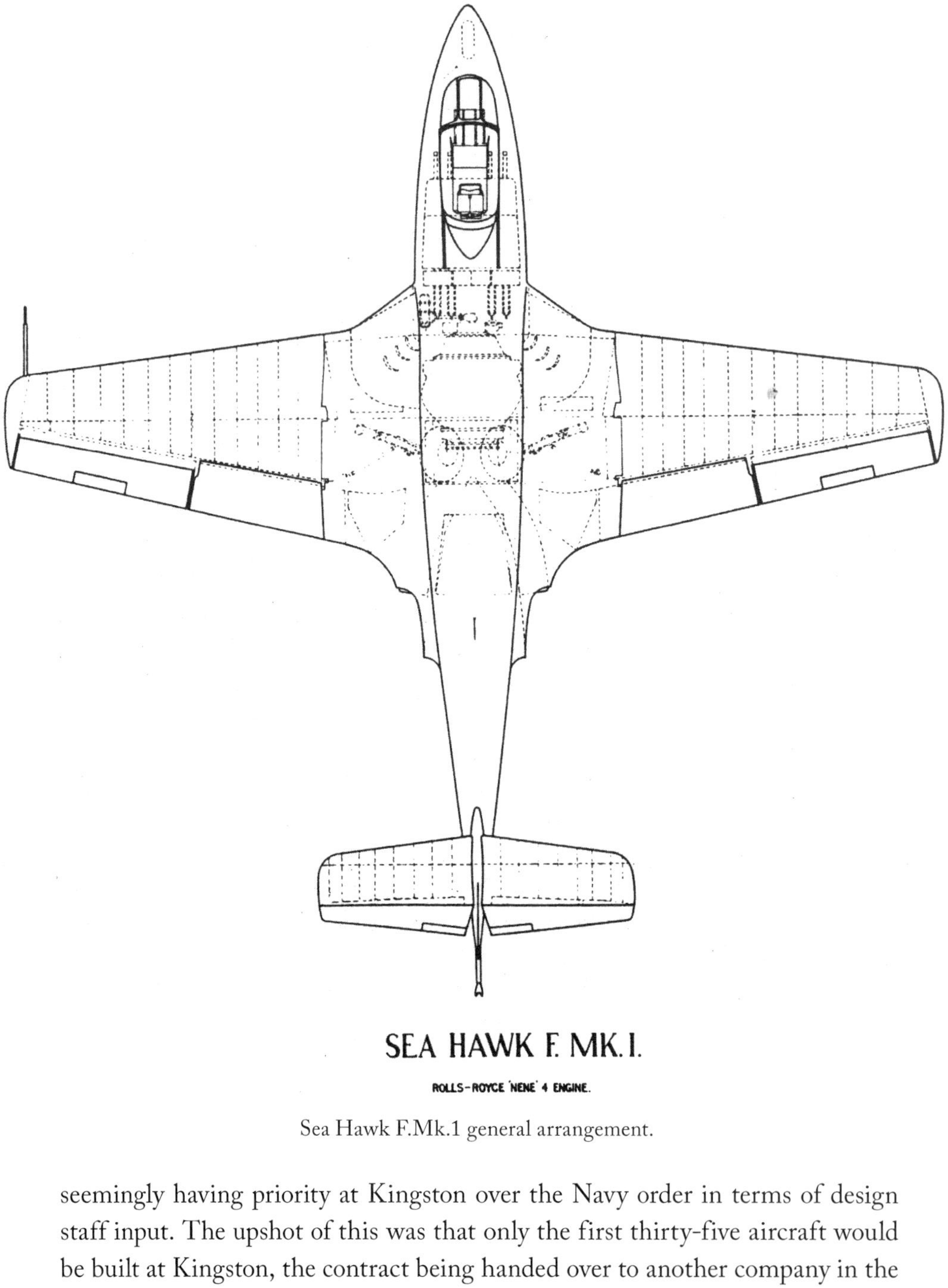

SEA HAWK F. MK.I.

ROLLS-ROYCE 'NENE' 4 ENGINE.

Sea Hawk F.Mk.1 general arrangement.

seemingly having priority at Kingston over the Navy order in terms of design staff input. The upshot of this was that only the first thirty-five aircraft would be built at Kingston, the contract being handed over to another company in the Hawker Siddeley Group – Armstrong Whitworth at Coventry. A further 399 would be produced for the Fleet Air Arm, making 434 altogether. Armstrong Whitworth, along with Gloster Aircraft, was used by the Hawker Siddeley

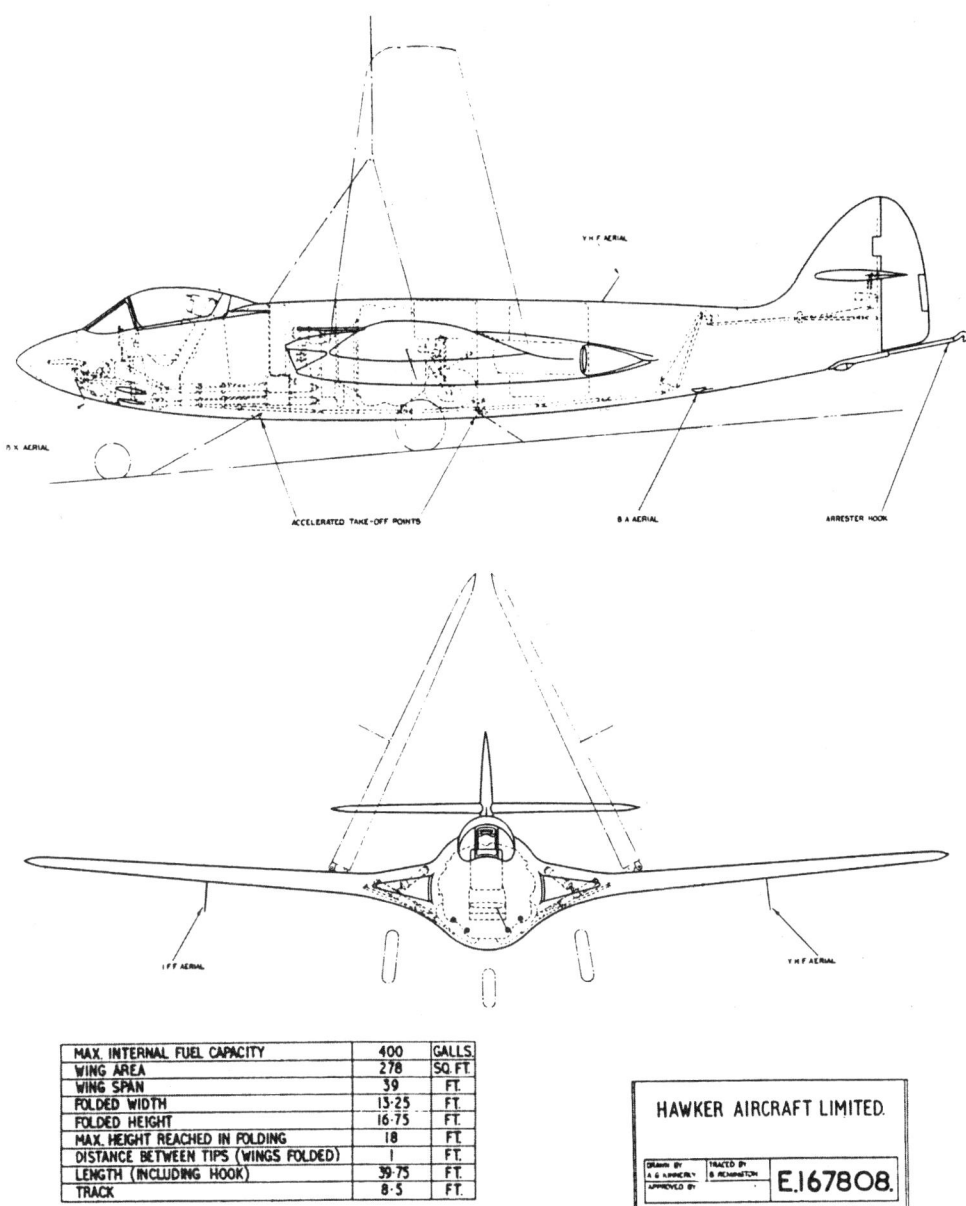

MAX. INTERNAL FUEL CAPACITY	400	GALLS.
WING AREA	278	SQ. FT.
WING SPAN	39	FT.
FOLDED WIDTH	13·25	FT.
FOLDED HEIGHT	16·75	FT.
MAX. HEIGHT REACHED IN FOLDING	18	FT.
DISTANCE BETWEEN TIPS (WINGS FOLDED)	1	FT.
LENGTH (INCLUDING HOOK)	39·75	FT.
TRACK	8·5	FT.

Group as an overload facility, to pick up excess capacity when not engaged on their own projects. This arrangement worked well, both for Hawker Aircraft Ltd and for the other companies in the group, providing work for factories when their own order books were slack.

The various trials of the first production aircraft revealed minor concerns with the design. WF143 was utilised for trials in June 1952 to remedy concerns

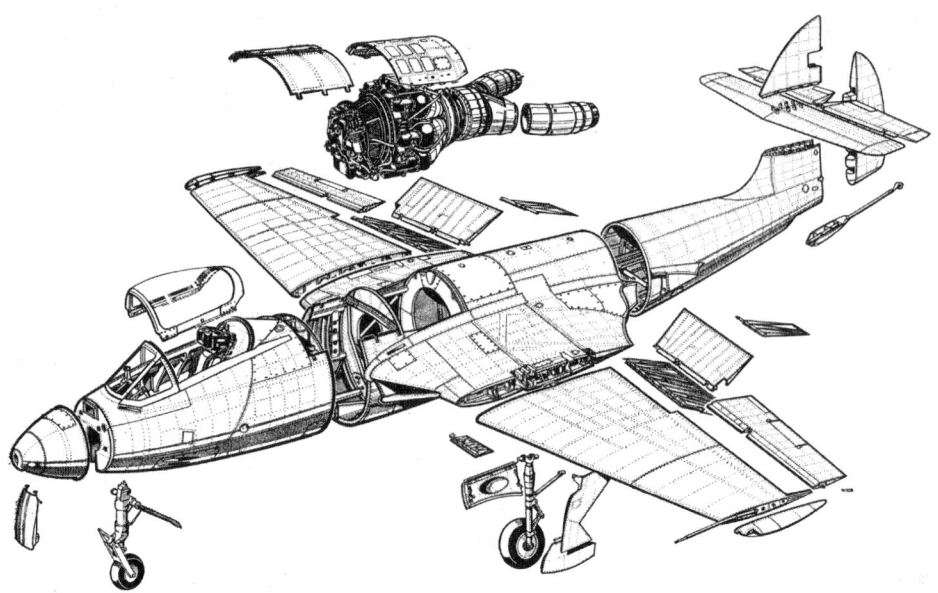

Sea Hawk F.Mk.1 breakdown of major components.

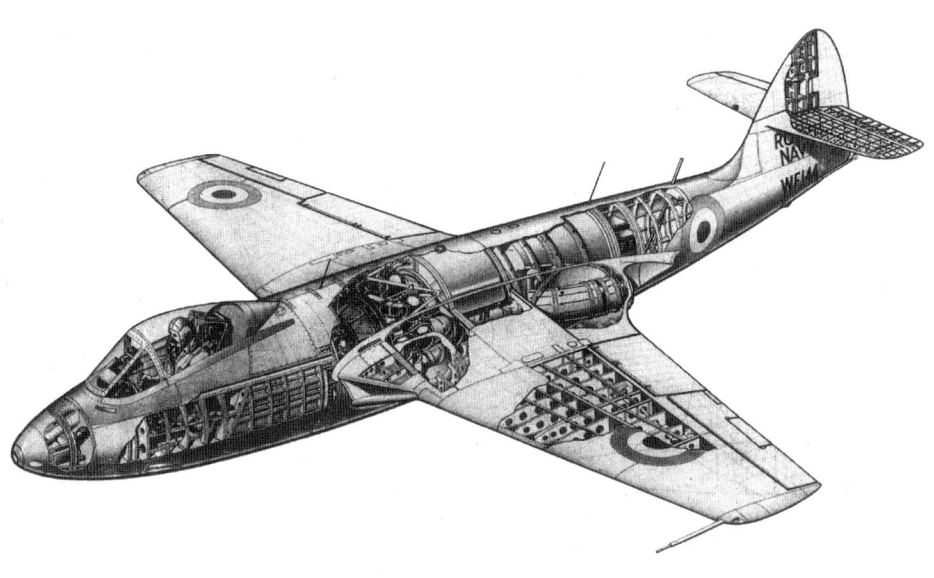

Sea Hawk F.Mk.1 cutaway view showing internal arrangement.

with lateral stability caused by aileron oscillation, investigation with various aileron spring tabs proving unsuccessful and leaving the company to consider power assisted ailerons as the best fix, these being designed in April for implementation on the production line at a suitable point. These were fitted to WF147 in November, effecting a complete cure, this aircraft becoming, in effect, the first Mk.2 Sea Hawk. Earlier trials with WF147 had revealed the inadequacy of the oil system to cope with inverted flight, this was believed to have been remedied by September though it appears that no one had told Bill Bedford as described below. Indeed Murphy had had to make a forced landing after inverted flight resulted in an engine running down and belching flame. After landing, the engine was found to be seized.

It was found that WF148 suffered from severe vertical vibration on its first flight for reasons unknown. However, application of 133 per cent over mass balance elevators showed a complete cure and it was proposed to apply 126 per cent to production elevators at a suitable production point. The aircraft was then despatched to Canada for winterisation trials at the Climatic Detachment of the Central Experimental and Proving Establishment (CEPE) Namou, Alberta, in September 1952, a trial that all UK aircraft had to pass since they were expected to be pan-climatic. Unfortunately, WF148's return to the air was delayed and was finally achieved on the last day of 1952 but appears to have spent most of the time in the hangar with unserviceabilities, its presence being held over for a further season; the aircraft finally leaving in June 1954. The pilot in charge, Wing Commander G.W. 'Johnnie' Johnson DFC, on leaving the RAF, would join Hawker Siddeley's sales team at Kingston and have a most interesting career, though he was never in the position of having to extoll the virtues of the Sea Hawk to potential customers.[4]

By March 1953, five aircraft had been dispatched from Dunsfold to squadron use by 806 Sqn at RNAS Brawdy, this being the first squadron to receive the aircraft, which later embarked on HMS *Eagle* for squadron-strength work up at sea. Subsequent aircraft equipped 800, 801, 802, 803, 804, 806, 807, 810, 811, 895, 897, 898 and 899 front line squadrons, as well as 736, 738, 764 and 767 Royal Navy Training Squadrons, together with 1832, 1835 and 1836 Squadrons of the Royal Navy Volunteer Reserve (RNVR). During the Suez Crisis, 800, 802, 804, 810, 897 and 899 Squadrons operated from the carriers HMS *Albion*, *Eagle* and *Bulwark*, providing close support to the Anglo-French landings in November 1956.

The Mk.1, of which ninety-five were produced, was followed by the Mk.2, essentially a Mk.1 with full powered aileron control and spring feel; forty were built and the order was completed by early 1954. For the Mk.3, the designation changed from fighter to fighter bomber, with 116 being produced. The FB.3 differed by having strengthened wings to allow for carriage of bombs in place of drop tanks, the first aircraft WF280, flying in March 1954. In August 1954, the next mark, the FGA.4 (fighter ground attack replacing fighter bomber in the Service lexicon) began delivery equipped to carry additional weapons on four underwing pylons, consisting of twenty rocket projectiles (RPs) or additional bombs under the wing. Some ninety-seven FGA.4 aircraft were built. All of these marks had utilised the basic Nene RN.4 (Mk.101) engine, but work to incorporate an uprated Nene Mk.103 engine producing 5,200lb thrust resulted in the Sea Hawk FGA.5, basically a Mk.3 with the uprated engine fitted. These aircraft were modified from earlier airframes, no new aircraft being produced. The next mark, the FGA.6, also with the more powerful engine, being based on the Mk.4 and eighty-six aircraft were completed to this specification. These aircraft completed the orders for the Royal Navy; henceforth, other orders would

Sea Hawk F.Mk.1 front fuselage jig with manufacture under way at the Richmond Road factory.

Sea Hawk F.Mk.1 under construction at the Richmond Road factory. The arrestor hook appears to have seen previous use.

materialise as the aircraft's docile handling and straightforward maintenance became well known among post-war navies.

All of the early test flying of production Sea Hawk F.1s was carried out at Dunsfold, under Neville Duke as Chief Test Pilot. Frank Murphy and Bill Bedford were involved in many of the flight tests and both suffered incidents when the aircraft did not behave themselves. Perhaps it was a tribute to the strength of the aircraft and the ability of the pilots that neither Murphy or Bedford was too seriously injured in these incidents.

Murphy, working as a Production Test pilot, was heavily involved in the day-to-day work of testing and on 19 December 1952, in WF159, found himself in some difficulty when the engine caught fire while over Sussex. A forced landing with wheels up followed at RNAS Ford, from which Murphy was able to walk away though the damage to the aircraft was assessed as cat 4. The aircraft had already completed its flight test schedule and was being flown to investigate a 'whistling noise'. The flight did not start off well, engine start-up was very slow and, on run up prior to take-off, the engine noise was considered to be 'rather harsh'. After approximately six minutes flying at low level to investigate the

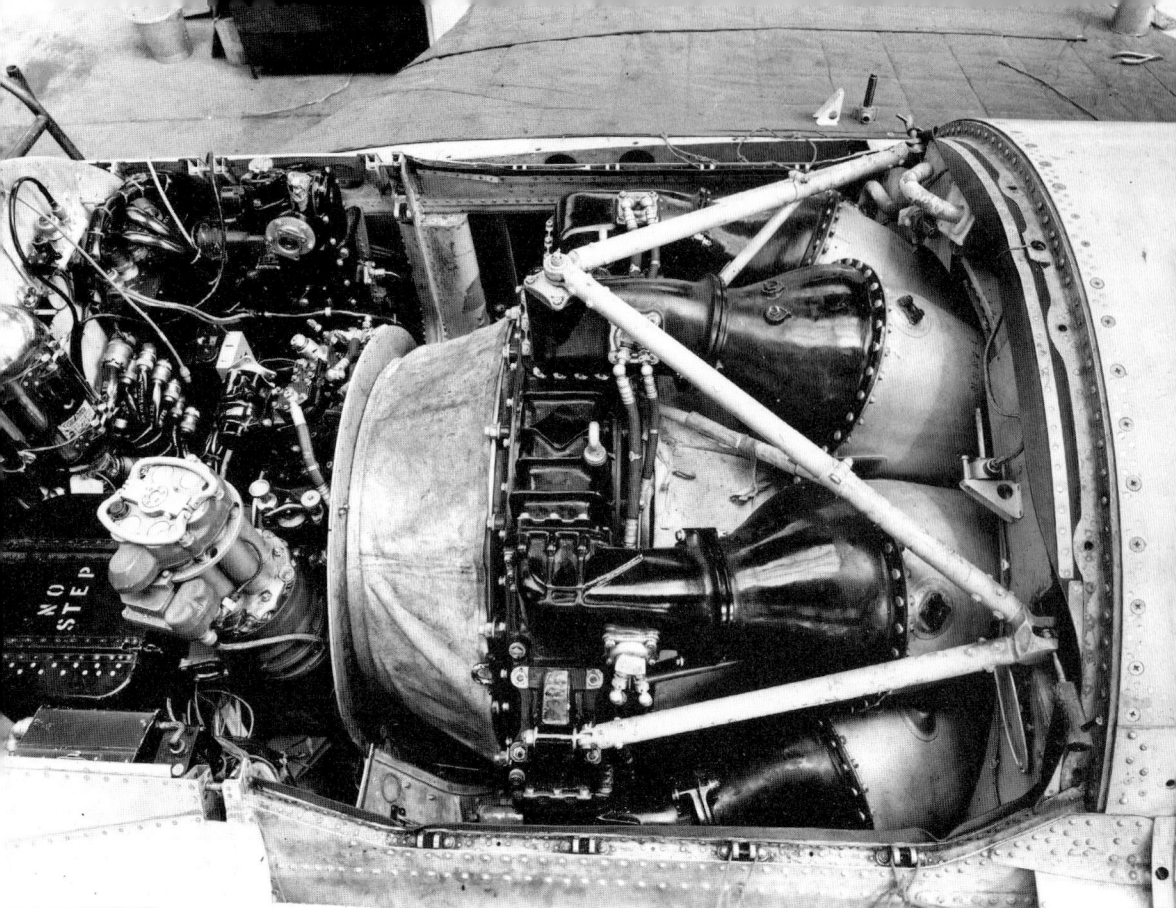

Sea Hawk F.Mk.1 showing forward engine bay and associated ancillaries and engine support struts.

whistle, attention was again drawn to the engine due to unusual noises, and the aircraft was meanwhile climbed to continue the investigation. At around 2,000ft a sudden drop in oil pressure and smell of hot metal and continued noises increased Murphy's uneasiness as it was clear that some failure was imminent. With engine rpm now decreasing, Murphy's forced landing at Ford was textbook and he was able to vacate the aircraft normally. The pilot of an Attacker, in the circuit nearby, reported flames issuing from the aircraft before touchdown and a cursory check of the engine revealed the turbine to be seized.[5]

Bedford had his incident rather closer to home when flying WF154 on 5 January 1953. Persistent problems with the oil system while flying inverted led to a trial with this aircraft entailing a timed inverted flight over the aerodrome to assess behaviour. At 10,000ft and 300 knots, the engine flamed out and could not be relit. Bedford announced his intention to force land on Dunsfold's runway 07. Selecting emergency undercarriage down (there being no hydraulics for normal operation) the port leg would not lock down. Selecting emergency flaps down was similarly unsuccessful, no response being apparent so, with time fast running out, the hood was jettisoned at 130–140 knots, coincidentally, the

Sea Hawk F.Mk.1 showing the complex wing fold joint.

flaps then operating successfully. At this stage, the runway had already passed beneath so a landing was made on the grass, followed by a run of about 600 yards across two drainage ditches before crossing the main Guildford–Horsham road at speed and coming to rest in the fields beyond, minus what undercarriage had by then lowered.[6] While Hawker's pilot lived to tell the tale, the crash appeared

Sea Hawk F.Mk.1 showing the landing flap and lower airbrake arrangement.

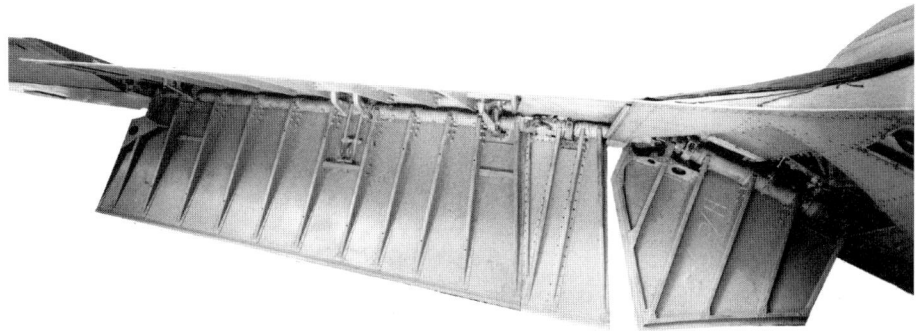

Sea Hawk F.Mk.1, WF143, the first production aircraft, at Dunsfold, November 1951.

to have exacerbated an earlier injury. A week after the accident, a medical check revealed problems internally which resulted in a three-month grounding and, in Bedford's words 'Returned to duty minus port kidney'. The aircraft was deemed to be damaged cat 4 and removed to Armstrong Whitworth at Coventry for repair and finally entered service at RNAS Brawdy in April 1954 before being involved in another crash, this time fatal, in June 1955.[7]

An unfortunate incident took the life of Squadron Leader D.W. Colquhoun of A Squadron A&AEE Boscombe Down on 27 June 1953, while flying Sea Hawk WF149. Briefed to undertake a gun firing sortie, the port wing inadvertently folded after take-off. The aircraft crashed into the rear of the officer's mess at Boscombe Down killing the pilot. The accident resulted in a redesign of the wing locking mechanism and an improvement in the visual locking indicators.[8]

As finally delivered to the Fleet Air Arm, 'Winkle' Brown thought the Sea Hawk, 'an altogether splendid machine, a beautiful piece of aesthetic and practical design which looked, and was, superbly airworthy. In full flight the Sea Hawk looked indeed like a graceful sea bird, when taking off and alighting more like a spray-dodging flying fish.'[9]

The aircraft also proved to be attractive to foreign governments. In 1956 the Netherlands placed an order for twenty-two Sea Hawk FGA.6 to be designated

Sea Hawk F.Mk.1, WF144, the second production aircraft up from Dunsfold with Neville Duke at the controls.

Sea Hawk F.Mk.1, WF159 aloft. Frank Murphy later carried out a forced landing at RNAS Ford in this aircraft due to an engine fire.

Mk.50, to be operated from their carrier the HNLMS *Karel Doorman* (the former HMS *Venerable*) and were delivered during 1957 and '58. These aircraft were later modified to carry the Philco Sidewinder infra-red homing missile. Following an upgrade to the carrier and a change within NATO of the Netherlands' role, in 1964 the Sea Hawks ceased to be seagoing and were decommissioned in the mid-1960s.

The next foreign customer was the West German Navy, which placed an order for sixty-four FGA.6 aircraft in 1956, thirty-two of this mark being sought as a day fighter designated Mk.100, and the rest as bad weather reconnaissance aircraft designated Mk.101 and fitted with a search radar carried in a pod under the wing. Ironically, West Germany possessed no aircraft carrier, its Sea Hawks being strictly land based. Deliveries began in 1958, with later aircraft being erected from kits within West Germany. These aircraft had a modified taller fin to improve directional stability and the Mk.100 would later also carry the Sidewinder AAM. Decommissioned in 1965, the Sea Hawks were replaced by the Lockheed F-104 Starfighter, a somewhat startling leap in aircraft and operational capability that resulted in a high attrition rate on German squadrons.

Finally, India contracted to purchase Sea Hawks in 1959, though these would initially be reconditioned ex-Royal Navy aircraft, nine FGA.6 being supplied, for operation from the carrier INS *Vikrant*. These were followed by fourteen new-build FGA.6 aircraft delivered during 1961. Over the next few years, further small batches of refurbished aircraft were supplied to supplement the Indian order, these being delivered in 1965 from Short Brothers and finally some twenty-eight ex-German Navy aircraft were supplied in the late 1960s. The aircraft saw action in the Indo-Pakistan Wars of 1965 and 1971 in the FGA role against Pakistani shipping, without loss. The Sea Hawk remained in service with the Indian Navy until the early 1980s, thirty-six years after its conception, when they were replaced by the BAe Sea Harrier. Some 539 aircraft of all marks were produced, not a bad start to Hawker's foray into the jet age.

The extended period between conception in 1944 and service entry in 1953, some nine years, and four years to move from contract to release to service of the Sea Hawk appears excessive from the perspective of history, when the Meteor and Vampire, both conceived and flown before the Sea Hawk, were produced within very tight timescales. One might point to delays caused by the novel jet pipe arrangement, to vacillation at the MoS and to peacetime timescales, but the fact remains that Sea Hawk entered service with minimal problems, served well in front-line service in the Royal Navy for eight years as the pace of aircraft development steadily grew. Still in second line service with several units many

Sea Hawk F.Mk.1s from 806 'Ace of Diamonds' Squadron based at RNAS Brawdy over the South Wales coast.

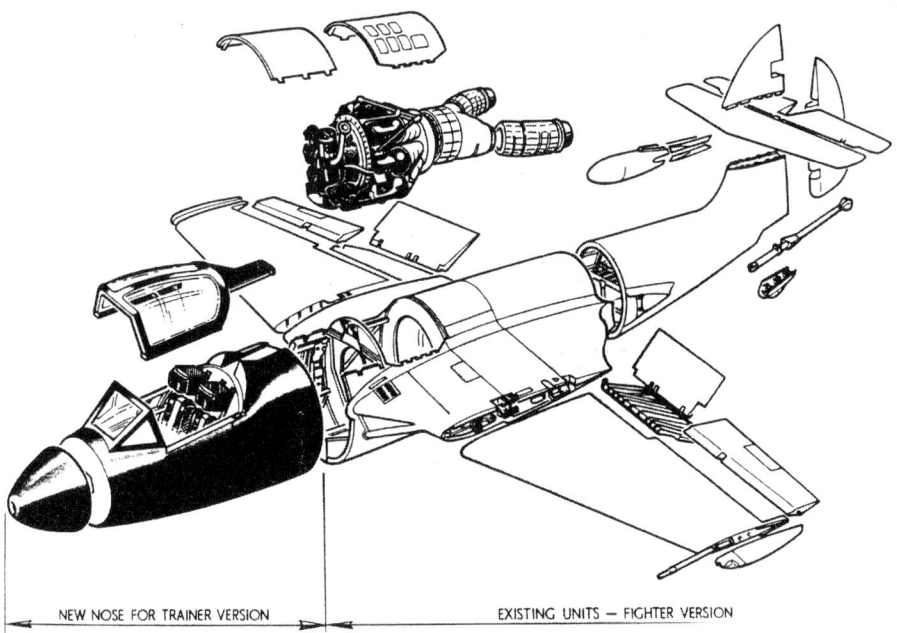

Sea Hawk F.Mk.1, proposed two-seat trainer version showing the minimal changes required from the single seat aircraft. The proposal was never taken up.

years later, Sea Hawk passed through six separate marks for the Royal Navy before replacement with more modern aircraft. 806 Squadron having been the first to bring the aircraft into service, was fittingly the last to relinquish their Sea Hawks, at Brawdy in November 1960, though in second line service, the Sea Hawk continued to serve the Royal Navy in the hands of Airwork Ltd, providing Fleet Requirement (FRU) services from 1958 before final retirement in 1969.

Leading Particulars (Mark 3)

Wing span:	39ft
Length:	39ft 10.5in
Wing area:	278 sq. ft
Thickness/chord ratio:	0.095 (9.5%)
Engine:	RR Nene RN.4 (Mk. 101) rated at 5,000lb. Later marks RR Nene Mk.103 of 5,200lb.
Fuel capacity:	395 gall clean, with drop tanks 575 gall
Weight:	empty 9,187lb
All up weight:	13,225lb
Performance:	Max speed at sea level 514 knots. At 36,000ft M0.823. In dive M0.85
Service ceiling:	43,000ft
Absolute ceiling:	47,000ft

Chapter 9

P.1067 – Dawn of the Hunter

In designing and constructing the P.1040/P.1052/P.1081 series of aircraft, Hawker was able to build up a detailed body of experience concerning jet engine technology, swept-wing theory and high Mach number flight. Much of the design work thus trialled would go into what was unarguably Hawker's most successful aircraft project of the post-war era. The aircraft that would arrive in 1951 as the P.1067 Hunter would feature mid-fuselage engine position, wing root intakes and fin mounted tailplane as in the P.1040; swept wings as in the P.1052 and swept tail with mid-set electrically activated adjustable tailplane as per the P.1081. What would be very different was the type of engine; for the first time, Hawker would build a fighter powered by an axial compressor turbojet, giving much more available power than the centrifugal engine for a lower cross-section.

In May 1947 the Chiefs of Staff at the Air Ministry, in deciding future defence policy, had concluded that 'the likelihood of war in the next five years was small, that the risk would increase gradually in the following five years, and would increase more steeply thereafter as the rehabilitation of Russia gathered momentum'. This assessment suggests an ignorance of the capabilities of the USSR, compounded the previous year by the Labour Government's decision to sanction the sale of Rolls-Royce turbojets to the Soviet bloc. Further policy decisions included the stipulation that the RAF should retain current types in service until more advanced aircraft became available, ruling out production of swept-wing fighters; and that supersonic flight would not be explored with full-scale aircraft since it was unlikely that speeds in excess of Mach 1 would be achievable with the current state of engine development. Thus was Government policy decided that would ultimately leave UK services seriously lagging when, before long, the time came to field aircraft with transonic capability. Unfortunately, the scales would not fall from Government eyes until the Berlin blockade in 1948, by which time, much damage, through neglect and ill-considered decisions, had already occurred.[1]

Initial design work on an axial jet powered aircraft at Hawker Aircraft had begun in September 1946 under the project code P.1054 which was for an interceptor fighter with swept wings powered by twin AJ.65 axial turbojets placed well forward on the fuselage sides and armed with a massive 4.5in recoilless gun that was located between the engines and fired through the extreme nose; a brochure and drawings being submitted to PDTD(A) on 27 September. Although the gun was an idea propagated in the Ministry of Supply; at a meeting the following month between Camm, Air Commodore Silyn-Roberts and J.E. Serby of DMARD, it was decided that work should proceed on the P.1052 instead (to gain initial experience with wing sweep) rather than continue with detailed work on P.1054; Scott-Hall at PDTD(A) expressing the opinion that experience gained now with P.1052 would allow Hawker to get P.1054 into the air much sooner. Somewhat bemused at this, Camm pointed out that the company had submitted their swept back version of the P.1040 back in October 1945 and that if the project had been allowed to go ahead then, much time would have been saved![2]

Be that as it may, on 24 January 1947, specification F.43/46 was issued, written around the P.1054 proposal and Hawker invited to tender. The specification called for an interceptor powered by either Rolls-Royce AJ.65 or Metrovick F.9 axial

Model of P.1057 proposal for twin-engined night fighter to specification F44/46. Not proceeded with.

jet engines to fulfil OR.228; Hawker submitting their tender on 26 February. In April, Serby visited to discuss the specification and asked if a conversion to straight wing together with tyre pressures of 110lb sq. in at overload weight would be possible; and any chance that they could fit a 20-inch radar dish in the nose? At this point Vivian Stanbury was dispatched to a meeting with Chief Engineer Armament Design (CEAD) at Fort Halstead (now Royal Armament Research and Development Establishment – RARDE) to gather information on the gun that the Ministry was keen to get into the air. It proved to be something of a monster – a barrel of 10ft and bore of 4.5in, weighing somewhere between 2,000 and 2,300lb. Immediate concern was felt at the large size of the weapon compared to the diminutive size of Hawker's aircraft, it was noted that the all-up weight would likely be in the region of 18,000lb and that 'the blast pressure, both at muzzle and the recoil jets is alleged to be most formidable.'[3]

In May 1947, the company had prepared a brochure for the straight wing version of F.43/46 as requested, but the entire project appears to have been overtaken by events and no more work completed against this project number after May 1947. However, in February 1947, Hawker had been invited to tender against a new specification F.44/46 for a twin-seat twin-engined night/all-weather interceptor and submitted their tender on 24 March under the project code P.1056 with a straight wing, and another with swept wing as per the earlier F.43/46 requirement. In the event, the straight wing project was also stopped in May, but the swept-wing design, now numbered P.1057 continued, with the company tender being accepted in June 1947 for three aircraft. This design featured a mid-wing swept at 35 degrees and delta tailplane set part way up the fin. The engines were blended into the fuselage/wing root, the semi-circular intakes being well forward adjacent to the cockpit with the engines exhausting aft of the wing. Four cannon were located beneath the cockpit though no mention is made of a search radar, which presumably could have been located in the nose.

Through July, Hawker geared up to produce the new aircraft, though at the same time, disquiet appeared to be growing at the Ministry regarding the weight of the aircraft against the power available, the company being advised that the number of guns or amount of ammunition might be reduced; and then in August, a request that armour protection for the crew be added.

On 25 August, the Advisory Design Conference scheduled for the following day was cancelled on the assumption that there might be a change of requirements in the offing and on 13 September, a letter was received from the Ministry stopping all work while further consideration was given to the requirement. By November, Serby had requested that the company consider an alternative

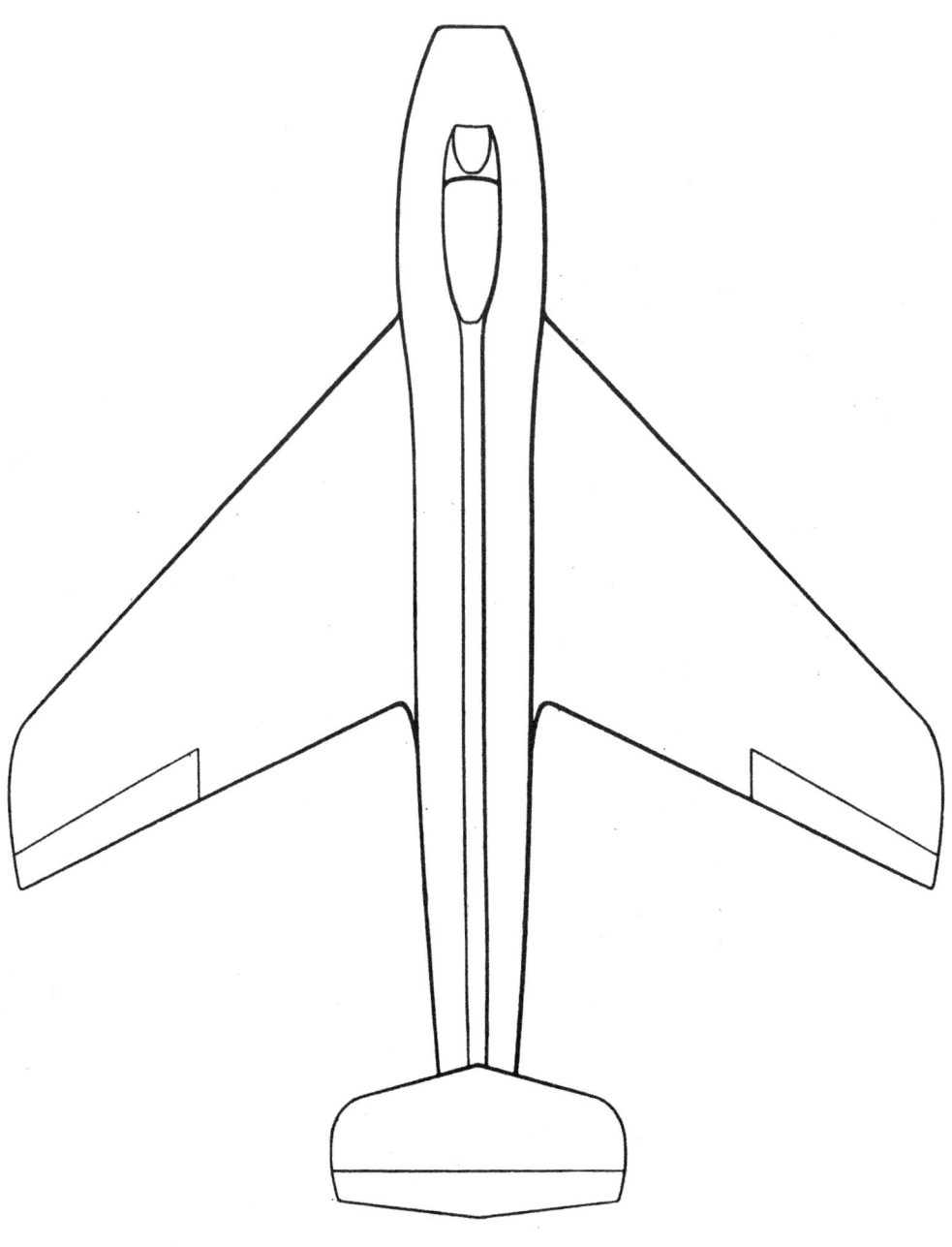

F3/48, initial thoughts on a single seat, single-engined day fighter featuring pitot intake, high-mounted non-swept tailplane and four-gun armament in the nose. Note the bulged forward fuselage to allow intake ducting to pass either side of the cockpit.

weapon fit – the 4.5-inch gun against either 4 x 30mm or 2 x 20mm guns, or even carriage of two Red Hawk missiles. Having received Hawker's thoughts on the alternative weapon fits, early in December 1947 all work was again stopped, a meeting with Serby being told that the emphasis of the requirement was now for a single-seat fighter with recoilless gun and radar ranging, and the company being asked to design around this requirement an aircraft of suitable size and wing loading capable of manoeuvring at 45,000ft.

Such then was the background to Hawker's attempts to fulfil the requirements of the Air Staff's OR.228 with tenders to specifications F.43/46 and F.44/46, but having tried various alternatives and having spent considerable time in trying to satisfy the OR with twin engines, the company decided to abandon this approach and instead design around a single AJ.65 Avon engine which was Camm's preferred solution anyway, indeed he had been attempting to 'sell' this proposal of the Ministry for some time. At this point in its development, the AJ.65 was producing some 5,500lb thrust as the RA.2, so Camm must have been confident that Rolls-Royce had the capability to develop this further if it

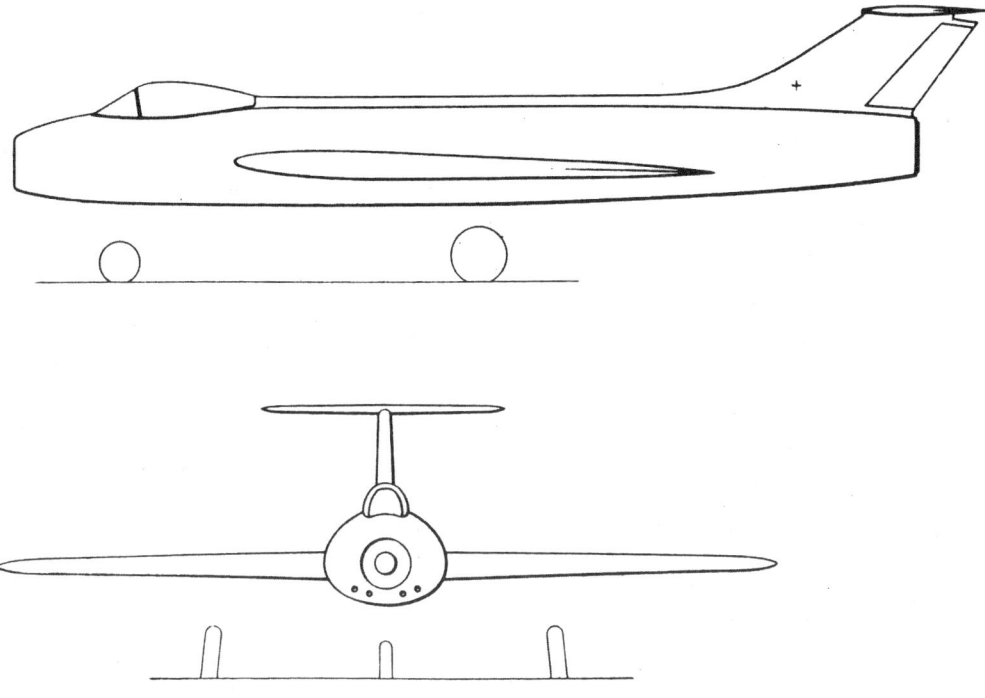

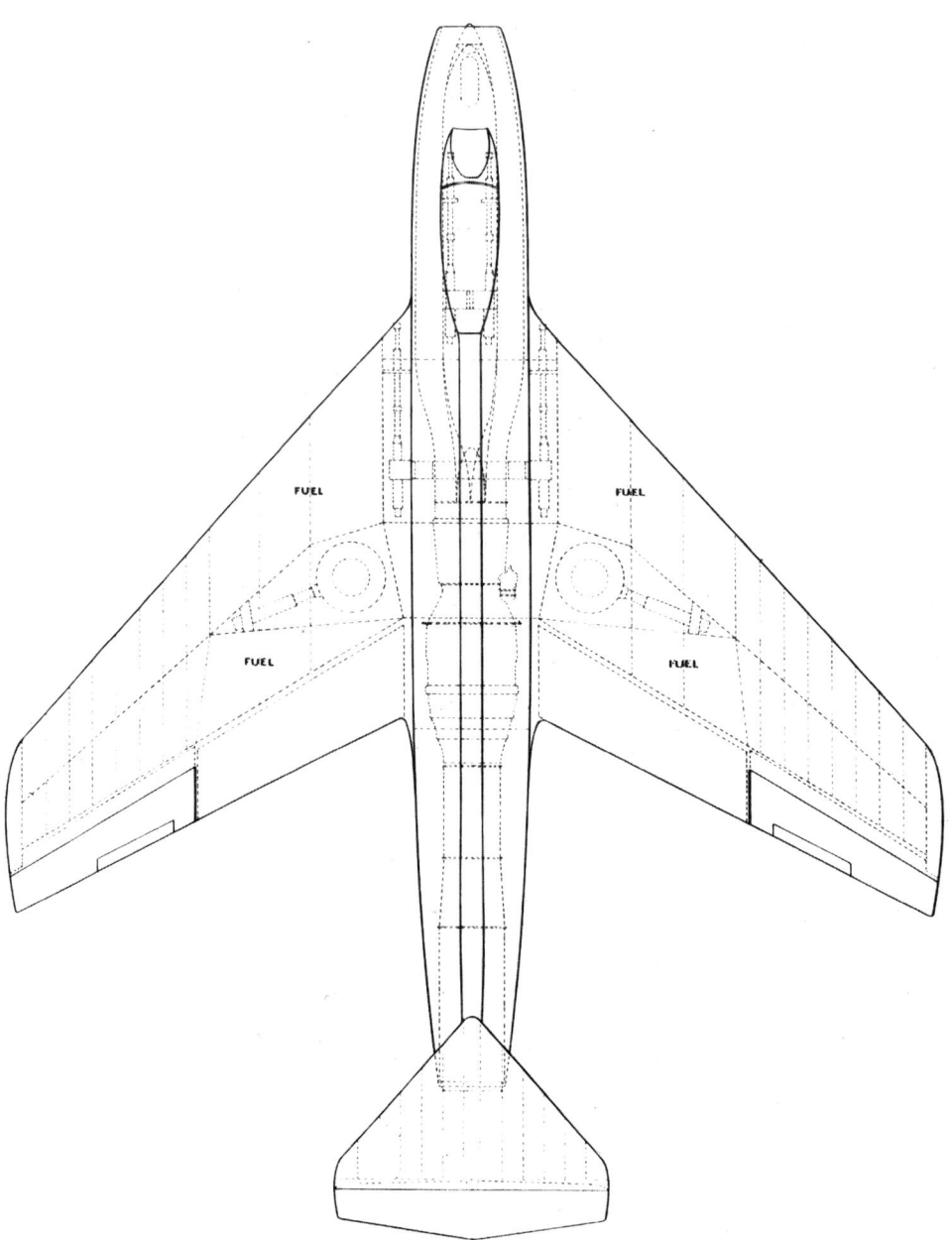

HAWKER SINGLE SEAT FIGHTER
SPECIFICATION F.3/48
ROLLS ROYCE 'AVON' ENGINE

F3/48, further development showing refined delta tailplane, 'wet' wings for internal fuel carriage and movement of two of the guns to the wing roots.

P.1067 – Dawn of the Hunter

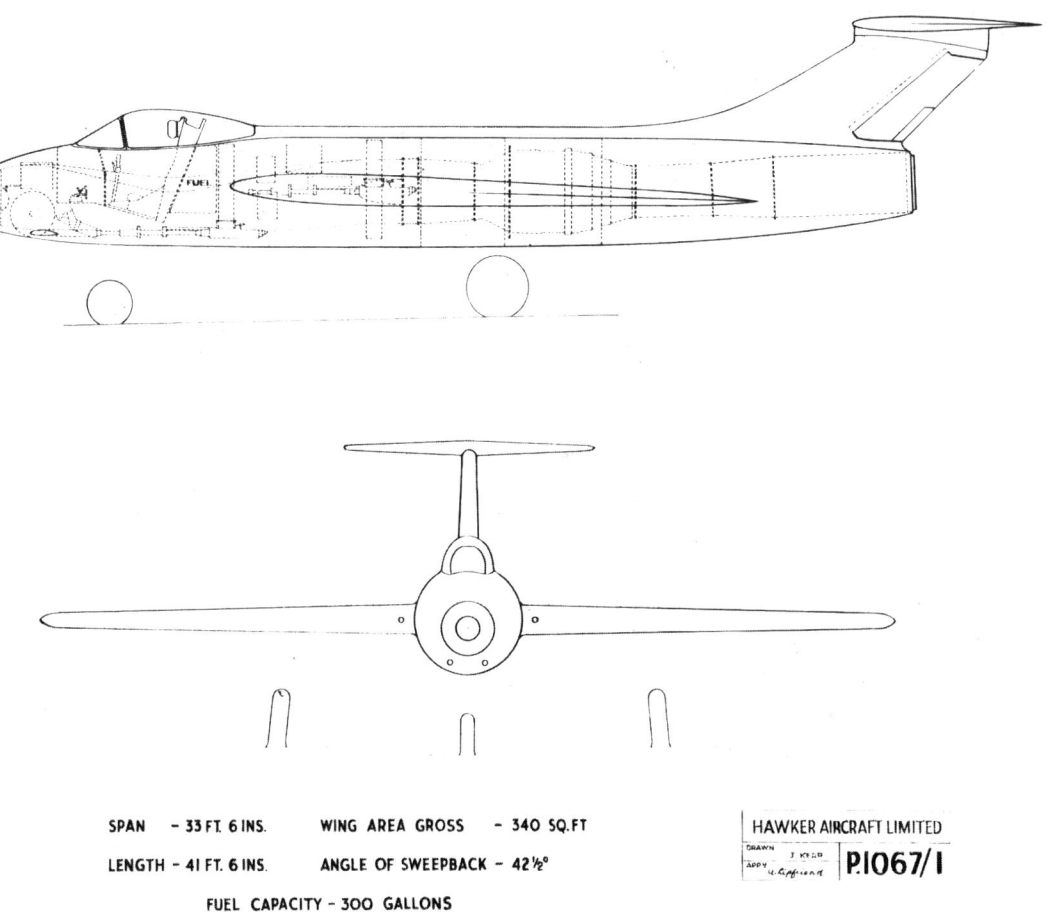

SPAN - 33 FT. 6 INS.   WING AREA GROSS - 340 SQ.FT
LENGTH - 41 FT. 6 INS.   ANGLE OF SWEEPBACK - 42½°
FUEL CAPACITY - 300 GALLONS

HAWKER AIRCRAFT LIMITED
P.1067/1

was to be a sole engine in his new design. This confidence was soon found to be well placed as the RA.3 engine produced a thrust of 6,500lb, these being used to power the early English Electric Canberra bombers. By the time that the P.1067 would be flying, Rolls-Royce was confident that the engine would be developing 7,500lb as the RA.7.[4]

Work began in January 1948 on an aircraft of some 12,000lb weight, armed with two 30mm guns, this initial approach being accepted by Serby who requested that the company continue on this design. Advice from RAE was 'to keep the project as slim and symmetrical as possible. The 8.5 per cent thickness/chord mid-wing and 50-inch diameter fuselage closely wrapped round the Avon engine was the result.' (Initial drawings show thickness/chord ratio as 9.5 per cent and sweep back at 42.5 degrees.) Hawker investigated at least twelve alternative layouts using four draughtsmen, involving wing loading, exhaust reheat and rocket assistance, together with single- and twin-engined configuration before

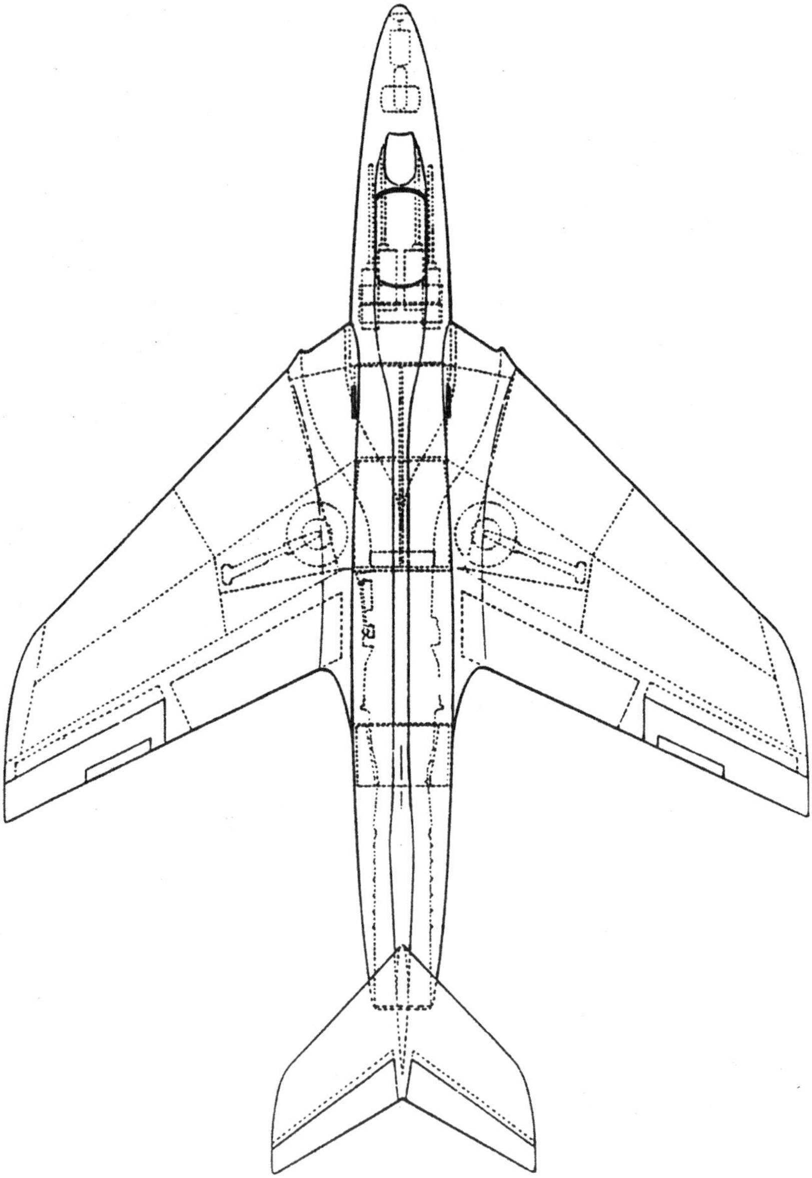

HAWKER SINGLE SEAT FIGHTER
SPECIFICATION F.3/48
ROLLS ROYCE 'AVON' ENGINE

F3/48, the pitot intake has been replaced by wing root intakes, allowing a solid forward fuselage to better accommodate the cockpit and radar ranging. All guns are now in the lower nose while the main fuel tanks have migrated from the wings to the fuselage. At the rear, the delta tailplane has been replaced by a swept form still located at the top of the fin.

a revision of OR.228 led to a new specification – F3/48 – which was issued to replace F.43/46.[5]

The new specification, written around Hawker's initial design and issued in February 1948, called for an aircraft capable of intercepting 'high speed, high altitude bombers in daylight as soon as possible after the bomber is detected on the radar warning system'. With this aim in mind, very fast starting was sought together with 'the greatest possible acceleration and highest possible climbing speed'. Once the fighter had been guided to within one mile of the target, 'interception would be completed visually'. Top speed at 45,000ft was to be not less than 547 knots (M0.953), and time to this altitude was to be not less than six minutes, with the ability to climb at 1,000ft per minute at 50,000ft. Endurance of at least one hour was stipulated from take off to landing, to include ten minutes combat at 45,000ft. Extension of endurance by means of drop tanks was to be investigated and importantly (in view of later problems), 'airbrakes are an essential requirement', though the only condition attached was that the brakes should

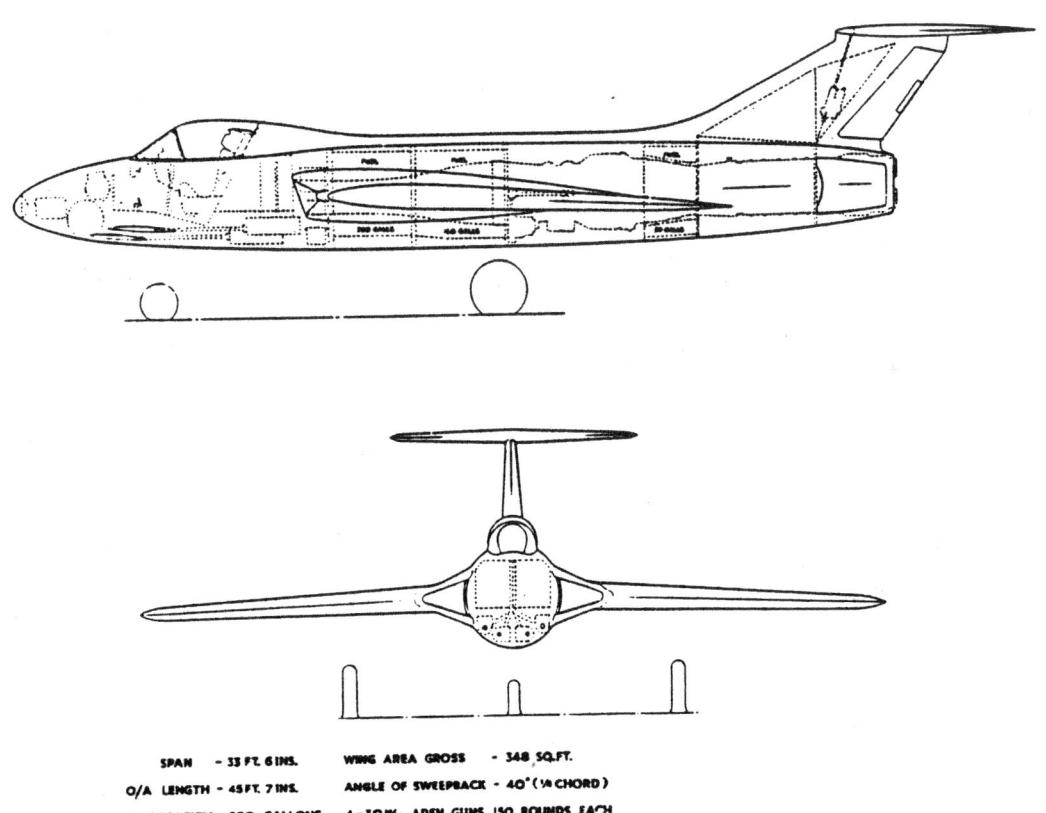

not cause vibration that might upset sighting of the guns. Armament would be either 4 x 20mm cannon with fifteen seconds of ammunition or alternatively 2 x 30mm cannon with ten seconds of ammunition. Still enamoured of large calibre weaponry for fighters, the specification offered the option of one 4.5in recoilless gun together with seven(!) rounds of ammunition. Aiming should be via a gyro

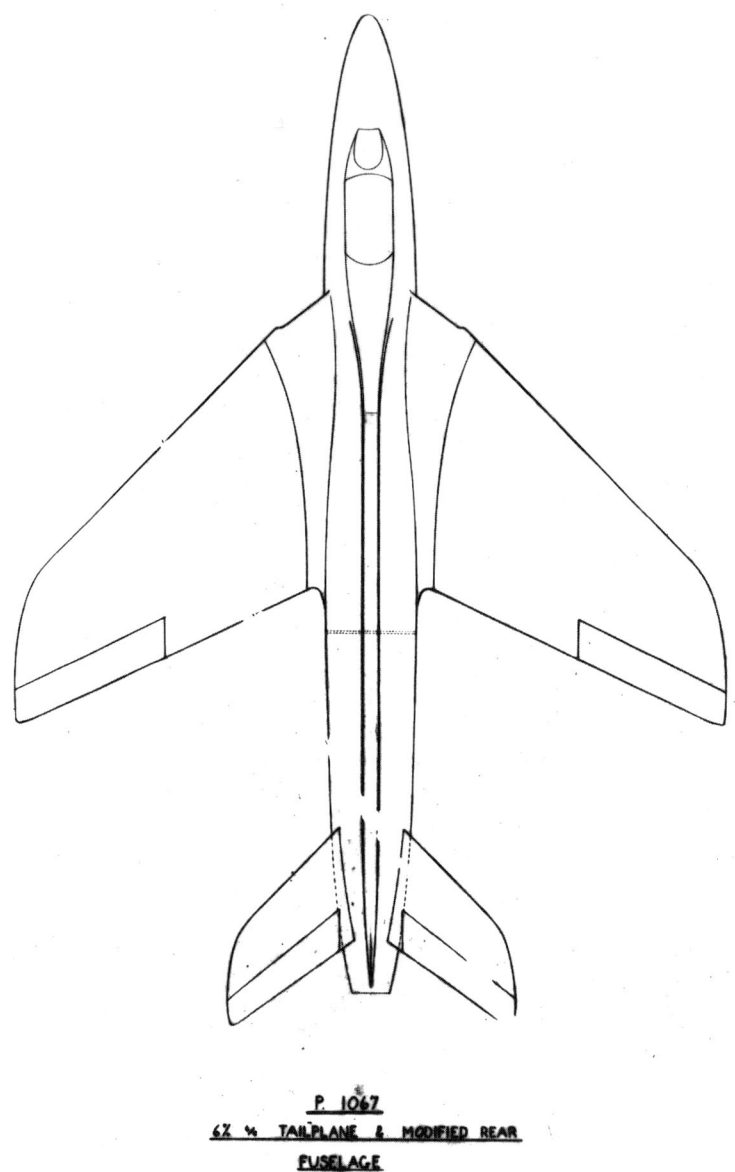

F3/48, showing the alternative low position for the tailplane and the remodelled rear fuselage.

gunsight slaved to ranging radar. A later amendment of October 1948 would call for provision for reheat, on the basis that it was unlikely that the performance required could be achieved without it.⁶

The Kingston Design Office set to, to scheme a number of alternative designs to meet this specification. Their tender response, which would be submitted in August 1948, offered an aircraft with highly swept back mid-wing (42.5 degrees at the quarter chord with thickness/chord ration of 10 per cent at the tip and 8.5 per cent at the root), small diameter fuselage with nose air intake ducted around the cockpit, and tail unit with delta tailplane planform and one-piece elevator set either on top of the fin or at its base. Performance was based on the then Avon engine delivering 6,500lb thrust together with 20 per cent reheat. At this rating, performance figures were expected to be 710mph at ground level, 595mph (517 knots) at 45,000ft, a rate of climb at this altitude would be in the region of 3,000ft per minute with an operational ceiling of approximately 53,000ft. Fuel capacity of some 300 gallons (carried in the wings together with a small fuselage tank) was expected to give an endurance figure of 1.25 hours. Armament was envisaged as 4 x 20mm cannon, two in the nose and two in the wing roots, though provision would be included to take 2 x 30mm Aden

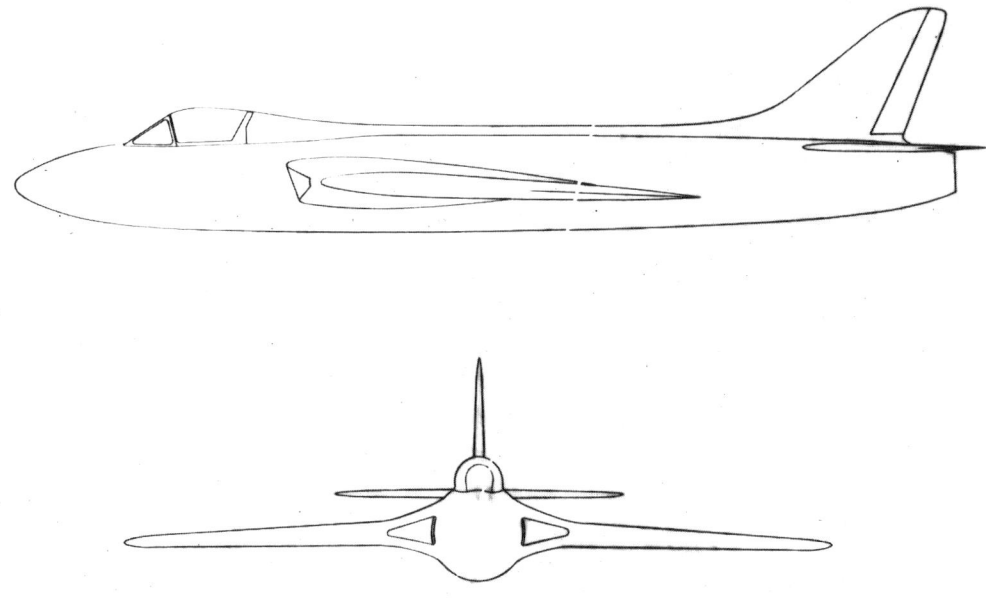

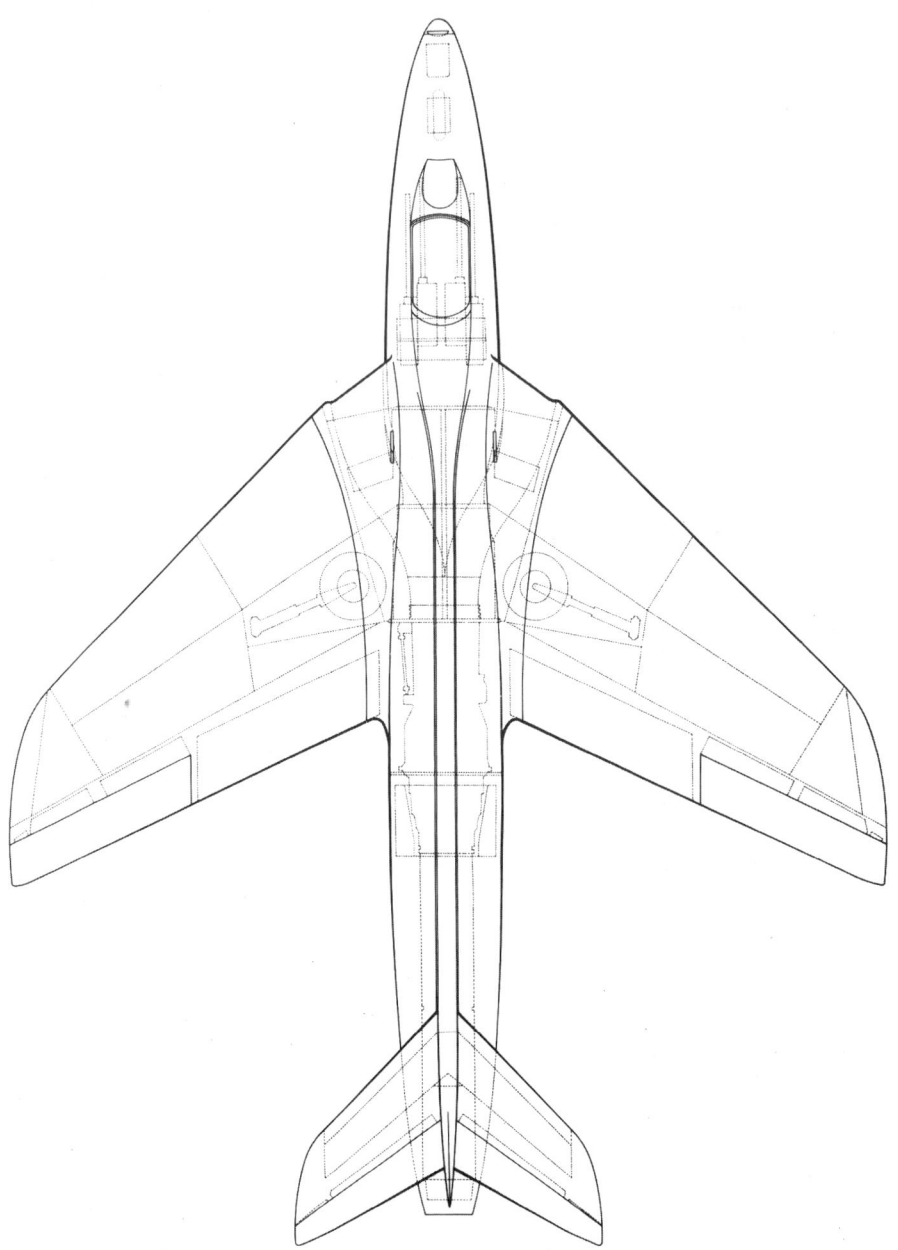

HAWKER SINGLE SEAT FIGHTER
SPECIFICATION F3/48
ROLLS ROYCE 'AVON' ENGINE

F3/48, general arrangement now looking like the definitive Hunter. Tailplane has taken up its final position low down on the fin.

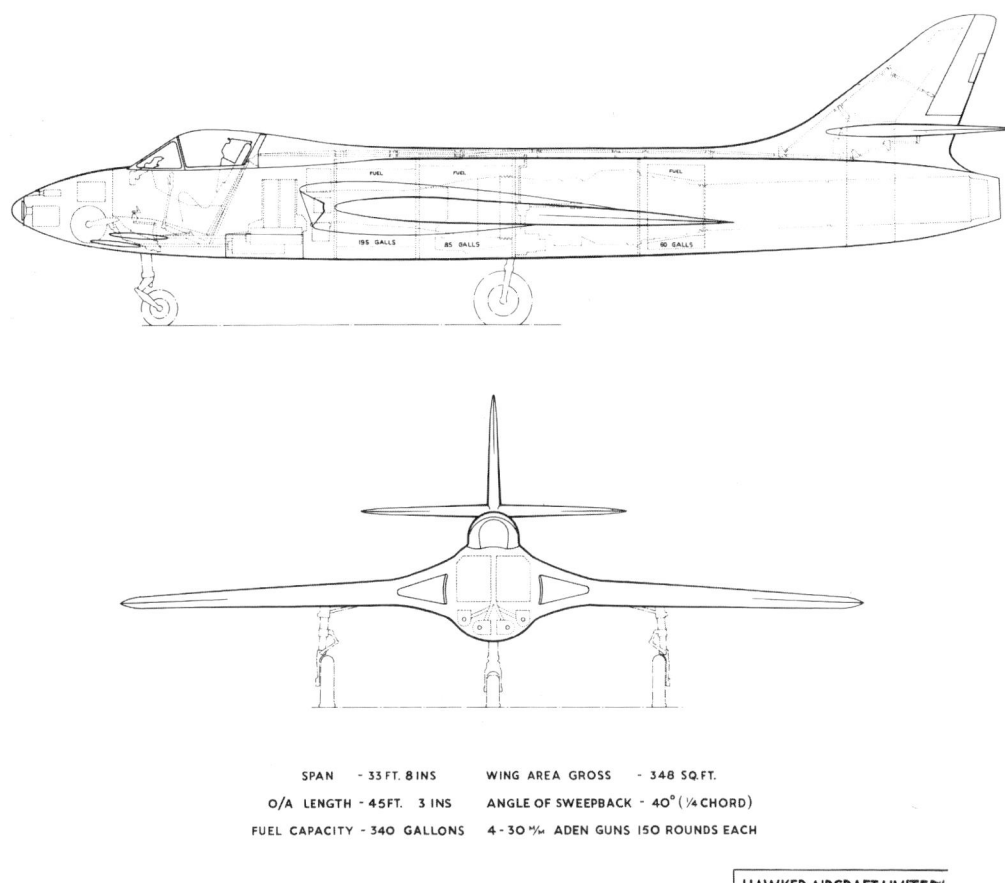

cannon when it became available. Radar ranging would be provided by a scanner mounted in a bullet in the nose air intake. Air braking was to be provided by the outer portion of the split landing flaps operating in conjunction with upper surface flaps as on the Sea Hawk. All up weight was expected to be in the region of 12,000-13,000lb.[7]

As well as the P.1067 series (first schemed by Stanbury), other ideas were schemed against projects P.1069, P.1070 and P.1071; all variations on a theme. Ultimately it would be a developed P.1067/7 which would best answer the requirement and which would proceed to production. By April 1948 a mock-up of the cockpit had been completed and preliminary investigation on increasing the armament to 4 x 30mm guns was submitted, though Hawker was not keen on this layout, presumably on weight and space concerns. At the end of May further requests for information from the Ministry regarding the fitment of a rocket motor and of armour plate resulted in this information being relayed back to DOR which promised answers on this and also the question of the armament fit.

In June 1948, word was received that the Armstrong Siddeley Sapphire engine might be considered as an alternative to the Rolls-Royce Avon. This engine, as the Sa.1, was already capable of producing around 7,000lb thrust and passed its acceptance test at 7,380lb by December 1949; as the Sa.2. Hawker was also informed, via the Hawker Resident Technical Officer (RTO), that an order for three prototypes was in the offing, with Roy Chaplin and Vivian Stanbury visiting Armstrong Siddeley on the 24th to assess the situation with their engine. By mid-summer, some progress on the armament situation was to be seen; it had been decided that there would definitely be four guns, but whether 20mm or 30mm was left for later – though it appeared that the Ministry was already assuming that the 4 x 30mm fit would be the normal load. The question of armament fit was finally confirmed on 19 June 1948 as 4 x 20mm cannon, to be replaced with 30mm cannon with 150 rounds of ammunition, when available. By the following month, interest had turned to the location of the tailplane; a low position offered certain structural advantages though a high position also had its adherents; in the event it was decided that one prototype of each position would be built.

At this point, the question of the ejector seat was raised, Camm being told that this must be a Martin Baker unit which, since this was a larger and heavier seat than the ML Aviation item previously used, would involve dropping the cockpit floor by 2in to avoid raising the cockpit canopy height. In January 1949, the requirement to fit in additional equipment, including the seat, led to a need to increase the fuselage diameter from 48in to 52.5in, and increase length by 12in to cater for the radar antenna. Wing sweep was also now reduced from 42.5 per cent to 40 per cent and thickness/chord ratio set at 8.5 per cent, and a decision made to construct two aircraft with the Avon engine and one with the Sapphire. The question of the ranging radar was now considered, with TRE advising that the antenna might be up to 12in in diameter, which could impact on the engine intake which at this point was a simple pitot design in the nose of the aircraft.[8]

By March 1949, with discussions still in progress with TRE, increasing concern regarding the nose intake and slim fuselage was being felt. Cockpit space (or rather lack of it), already constrained by the air intake ducting passing

Mock-up of the early pitot intake, the restricted space for the cockpit between the ducts is clear.

F3/48 mock-up of front fuselage with intake moved from nose to the wing roots.

F3/48 mock-up showing the early T-tail arrangement.

either side, was further constrained by the requirement to squeeze the Martin Baker seat in. Hooper recalled that,

> the intended wing (integral) fuel tanks were regarded with increasing scepticism so that more and more fuel was shoe-horned into the fuselage instead. The fuselage frames came to include an increasing proportion of stainless steel and work slowed as the mock-up work forced greater realism. By the middle of 1949 it began to look as if the whole project might have to be abandoned. Some of the credit for its redirection must go to Harold Tuffen who, with a background of Project Office experience himself, laid out the bifurcated wing root intake alternative which was to become familiar as the Hunter. The T-tail persisted for a while, but fell victim, I think, to Sir Sydney's conservatism (and who can say the decision was wrong?), the tailplane taking up a position on the fin similar to that of the Sea Hawk.

These changes were agreed in March with Serby and design commenced on this basis, though the loss of the wing fuel tank capacity would continue to dog the aircraft for some years.[9]

F3/48 mock-up with T-tail and mock-up Avon engine installed. Note the radar ranging unit in the nose.

Work continued on the gun installation through 1949; in September, given difficulties with removal of the guns from the mock-up, a suggestion for a completely removeable gun pack was aired, resulting in great interest from the MoS, the mock-up being altered accordingly. This would obviate the original concern posed by initial plans for gun arming. Hooper recalled, 'the guns were to be mounted individually and the ammunition boxes rearmed from the top of the fuselage. Some concern was felt about the weight of the 30mm ammunition belts which would have to be lifted up in this method of rearming.'[10]

Flying controls were also on the agenda in September; a decision to fit powered aileron controls was made, and the following month, investigation of powered elevator control begun and a decision made confirming the low position for the tailplane, to be operated by electric actuator. Airbrake provision would be met by means of strengthened landing flaps and dive recovery system, the two being interconnected (the dive recovery flaps were small – 3.16 sq. ft – spanwise flaps fitted under the wing forward of the undercarriage wells.

They did not make it through to the production aircraft, being found to be ineffective) though this would later prove to be completely inadequate once flight testing began.[11]

March 1950 saw work underway on the first prototype in the Richmond Road Experimental Department, and also a visit from DOR to discuss the development of F3/48 to include a wing sweep of 50 degrees under project code P.1083. By mid-summer, concerns were being aired regarding the available fuel capacity, with Hawker being pressed to increase this and also consider drop tank carriage of some 90 gallons per side and the possibility of provision of some 50 gallons of fuel per side in the wing leading edge adjacent to the root was discussed. Also in August, the Experimental Department went onto extended shifts to cover twenty-four hour working on the first prototype, the test airframe and the gun firing test fuselage. In December, a draft specification for the production aircraft was received by the company, leading to a design conference at the MoS on the 19th of the month.

In January 1951, the company received information confirming the strength and stiffness requirements for the production aircraft. The intention here was later made clear that the aircraft, although being designed as a pure interceptor, should be capable of operation in the ground attack role. Clearly the Air Staff

F3/48 close up of the mock-up rear showing T-tail, mock-up Avon engine and jet pipe fitted.

F3/48 mock-up with definitive tailplane location applied. Note the jet pipe model installed featuring contours suitable for reheat.

What appears to be a mock-up of a possible solution to buffet induced at the fin/tailplane junction as in the Sea Hawk, where a substantial 'bullet' fairing was used to cure the problem. The addition of a fairing aft of the fin/tailplane junction would be the preferred solution on the Hunter.

F3/48 mock-up with finalised nose contours and final tailplane location.

was looking ahead to future requirements, perhaps mindful that most interceptor aircraft latterly had a ground attack role added to their perceived roles. The fuel capacity of the aircraft, previously flagged as less than desired, was to be increased in the production aircraft by the installation of six fuel tanks against five in the prototypes and provision for drop tanks was to be built in from the start. Later, in August 1952, continuing concern regarding the limitations on the aircraft due to fuel capacity would lead to proposals for fuel storage in the production wing of around 85 gallons per side, a modification that would eventually appear on the Mark 4.

P.1067, WB188 at Boscombe Down prior to first flight. The external cabling was used for monitoring during engine running, July 1951.

By February 1951, the tailplane and elevator had been assembled onto the rear of the fuselage and the Avon engine offered up to the first fuselage for trial fit. Meanwhile work continued on the fuselage sections and flying controls. Also underway was a mock-up to accept the AS Sapphire engine to investigate the differences required for this engine in terms of aircraft structure, with Armstrong Siddeley representatives shuttling backwards and forwards between Coventry

P.1067, WB188 at Boscombe Down prior to first flight with anti-spin parachute housing above the jet pipe, July 1951.

and Kingston. Between February and May 1951, meetings were held between MoS and DOR and Hawker staff in an attempt to improve the rear view. This thorny problem had not been helped by the need to drop the cockpit floor by 2in in order to accommodate the Martin Baker seat. Added to this problem, the Mark 1E seat, which had replaced the earlier offering, had the parachute at the pilot's back, hampering the rear view, and the thickness of the dinghy pack, upon which the pilot would sit, further restricted the range of seating height.

At this late juncture, in an effort to off-set the increased weight and CG issues introduced by the provision of reheat, and to provide additional space for the radar, it was decided on 27 April to move the entire forward fuselage forward by 6in on the production aircraft.[12] By now, the first prototype WB188 was structurally complete and had begun resonance testing, control system functioning and impedance tests and finally, the big day arrived which saw WB188 loaded onto a transporter on 27 June for its journey to Boscombe Down for its maiden flight, with the first engine run being carried out there on 1 July.

On 8 July the first taxy run revealed problems with the brakes. Bob Marsh of the Project Office reported back to Camm and Roy Chaplin on the 16th that the first taxy runs at a weight of 14,900lb (full fuel could not be achieved due to a fault with the pressure refuelling valve) had taken place, the first run had been at approximately 60-80 knots and was without problems. Following the second run at around 100 knots, intermittent braking resulted in white puffs of smoke emanating from the wheels. Brought to rest at the end of the runway, flames were now apparent coming from the starboard mainwheel. Following replacement of brakes and pads, the next run at 15,200lb weight on the 13th saw the aircraft increase speed to 120kts and on braking, again white puffs of smoke were seen from the wheels.

> About two thirds down the runway, the aircraft was seen to zig-zag appreciably and it finally had to be turned off the runway at the far end to avoid overrunning onto the grass. Both brakes were observed to be flaming as the aircraft passed by near the end of its deceleration run.

Inspection revealed a complete fracture of the brake plates, disintegration of the pads and leaking piston seals. However, by the date of Marsh's less than glowing report, Dunlop representatives were well on the way to a solution.[13]

On 20 July 1951, the P.1067 WB188 lifted from Boscombe Down's runway for its first flight of fifty minutes in the hands of Neville Duke. For this flight, the power boosting of the aileron circuit was operative but elevator boost was not. All up weight on take-off was 15,465lb including 353 gallons of fuel, ballast in lieu of guns, plus a tail parachute in the fairing above the jet pipe. A comprehensive instrumentation fit was carried, comprising a wire recorder, V-G recorder, camera recorder in the nose, vertical and lateral vibrograph in the fin, and cockpit indication relayed from temperature sensors mounted at frames 40 and 45 to record structure temperatures adjacent to the engine bay. The flight was somewhat curtailed due to an undercarriage light staying on after retraction, but nevertheless the aircraft was taken to 19,000ft and 350 knots. Minor issues were noted including a lateral oscillation emanating from the aileron control system and there appeared to be no self-centring of the aileron circuit, an aileron displacement resulting in the control column continuing in the selected direction until full travel had occurred.[14]

Flying continued through August to accrue sufficient hours to qualify for display slots at the SBAC Show in September, which were duly carried out with no problems, and in October another nine hours of performance flying was successfully completed. Meanwhile, work continued with both Rolls-Royce and Armstrong Siddeley to agree suitable jet pipe schemes for the reheat system expected to be fitted in the F.3 version of the aircraft. In November, WB188 was laid up to allow fitment of an improved version of the Avon (an uprated RA.3 had been used for the initial flights, now replaced by an RA.7 engine of the same thrust), not flying again until January 1952; the following month, the height restriction of 40,000ft was removed to enable further expansion of the flight envelope. (15)

In September 1951, a delegation of armament experts arrived at Kingston to discuss problems being experienced with testing of the new Aden 30mm cannon on a Beaufighter aircraft. Damage was being caused to the tail surfaces by ejected ammunition cases and links, and Hawker was asked for advice on how these items might be stowed rather than ejected overboard. The main issue was the links, since these were light enough not to clear the aircraft quickly. The concern here was to avoid damage to the P.1067 from similar causes, and Hawker agreed to look at ways to retain the links on board. This led to a meeting at RAE in January 1952 with other industry members to discuss ways and means to deal with the spent ammunition problem.

Meanwhile, progress continued with WB188 at Dunsfold, the aircraft being flown by an American delegation, possibly with a view to approving it for MWDP funding for off-shore manufacture for continental nations within NATO. Once the Hunter had entered service, a US evaluation team including Major 'Chuck' Yeager (the first pilot to break the 'sound barrier') visited Dunsfold in April 1955 and, over four days, evaluated the aircraft prior to off-shore orders being

P.1067, WB188 aloft at last; Neville Duke at the controls, July 1951.

P.1067, WB188 aloft in the hands of Neville Duke, July 1951.

placed.[16] NATO interest was welcome though investigations in April had shown the aircraft structure to be potentially weakened under certain conditions. A failure on 28 November of the structural test specimen (probably in the Langley facility) at 57 per cent cp (centre of pressure) back case of Case B, led to additional strengthening being applied to take the failure point up to 112 per cent in the cp back case, which had added a mere 4lb to each aircraft, resulting in an extremely rugged and strong airframe. Also in May, design work continued on the P.1083 and the Avon RA.14 engine planned as the powerplant, while on the 5th of the month the second prototype WB195 took to the air at Dunsfold.

Directly the second prototype was available, work began on investigating the poor air braking available, or rather, the large trim change associated with deployment, identified by Duke on WB188. On the first flight, Duke had noted: 'Take-off flap was lowered at 230 knots and produced a nose-down change in trim which required a heavy pull force to hold and could not be trimmed out with the trimmer range available.' He also noted that, on the landing run, 'The

P.1067, WB195, the second prototype.

P.1067, WB202, the third prototype – powered by an Armstrong Siddeley Sapphire engine – at Dunsfold outside the Experimental Hangar.

increase in drag with full flap was very apparent and a large increase in rate of descent was noted, which required a considerable increase in power to check.' The original idea of using the strengthened landing flaps in conjunction with a dive recovery system now led to WB195 (and later WB188) being fitted with a small flap on the top surface of each wing above the existing landing flap. Initial trials suggested good results but it would soon become apparent that this was not a workable solution.[17]

The other major problem identified by WB188 was rear-end vibration, similar to that which had dogged the P.1040 aircraft. Fred Sutton – head of Flight Development – noted that the buffet was less severe when the anti-spin parachute fairing was fitted behind the fin. Thus a small trailing edge 'reverse bullet' fairing was fitted at the fin/tailplane junction which largely cured the problem. Once this matter had been cleared, transonic and supersonic flight trials began in earnest with WB188 being flown supersonically for the first time on 24 June 1952.

By July, thoughts of future developments were to the fore. On 1 July, MoS representatives paid a visit to Kingston to discuss their 'Blue Sky' project; this being the carriage of air-to-air guided missiles on UK interceptor aircraft in the shape of the Fairey designed Fireflash missile, a first-generation stern attack radar beam riding weapon. The missile would have limited success and be replaced by the passive infra-red homing missile produced by de Havilland under the name Firestreak. Work also continued with Rolls-Royce in refining the reheat system for the P.1083 extreme sweep interceptor, concerns being expressed about the level of ventilation of engine and jet pipe being insufficient.

As the latest and impressive fighter prototype in the UK skies, requests for appearances steadily accumulated; in June 1952, WB195 was flown at the Central Fighter Establishment at RAF West Raynham, while WB188 was flown by a team of test pilots from Boscombe Down. On 10 July, the aircraft was demonstrated at the Brussels Aero Show before coming home to join WB195, the star attraction at the September SBAC Air Show at Farnborough. The aircraft was then flown by NATO representatives Colonel Johnson and Major Davis (USAF) on 22 October. Hawker confidence in the basic P.1067 design thus far was emphasised by work beginning in the Richmond Road Experimental department on the first set of wings for the P.1083 developed version of the Hunter, though this would prove to be misplaced optimism. Also appearing for the first time on 25 November was the Avon RA.7R engine and reheat jet pipe for WB188, of which the developed RA.14R was planned to power the P.1083 aircraft.

With the now apparent failure of the revised airbrake arrangement on the aircraft, RAE was consulted and suggested airbrakes mounted at the rear sides of the fuselage, which it was agreed would be trialled when the rear end was remodelled on WB188 to take the new engine. Notwithstanding the thorny issue of airbrakes, the third prototype P.1067 WB202 arrived at Dunsfold and flew with the AS Sapphire engine installed on 30 November, which chimed nicely with the withdrawal of WB188 on 3 December and its return to Kingston for work to fit the new engine and reheat jet pipe and the revised airbrake arrangement. Meanwhile WB195 departed to Boscombe Down to begin trials, though it returned on the 20th with vibration problems, later diagnosed as elevator flutter.

While little of the flight test programme had been completed, a preliminary handling assessment report was compiled, containing good and bad news, and was issued on 2 March 1953. On the positive side, the pilots at Boscombe Down found the performance 'impressive by current standards, with creditably docile behaviour, even at high Mach numbers'. However, on the negative side, they listed a number of criticisms.

a) The rate of roll above about 0.75 INM below 15,000 to 20,000ft should be approximately trebled.
b) All control forces should be reduced considerably for adequate manoeuvrability. In particular, the heavy elevator forces at high IAS, coupled with large changes of trim and heavy forces at high Mach number, suggested that urgent consideration should be given to some form of 'flying tail.'
c) The airbrakes were unsatisfactory, and the aircraft could not be flown in safety to its limits.
d) The undamped and uncontrollable lateral oscillation at low and moderate speeds must be eliminated.

Not exactly a ringing endorsement, but in their reply Hawker stated that the issues were in hand, with the following steps being taken.

a) To increase the aileron and elevator boost ratios and thereby improve handling characteristics.
b) To test rear fuselage airbrakes.
c) To introduce other modifications recommended.[18]

January 1953 saw WB202 being earmarked for extended gun firing trials. Concerns raised by RAE regarding ammunition links being ingested by the engine had resulted in plans for initial trials to be flown with debris guards over the intakes. If subsequent observation revealed a tendency for ingestion, then either deflector plates would be fitted to the ejector chutes or some means of retaining the links aboard the aircraft in fairing containers would need to be designed. Ground firing trials then commenced on 16 February followed by air firing on 9 March.

Back at Richmond Road, the first production aircraft was coming together, a Mk104 engine being installed in February while the mock up P.1083 had its mock up RA.14 engine installed on the 17th. But while this work pushed ahead, concerns persisted regarding the outstanding issues on the prototypes – airbrake and reheat problems being the major concerns but the work to produce wing fuel tanks was also running into problems; partly due to structural limitations but also influenced by changes in the aircraft CG with 'wet' wings. In March, the problem of tailplane vibration, which the fin fairing was supposed to have cured, raised its head again and various remedies were trialled with limited success.

The problems associated with achieving a working reheat system in the P.1067 now took a different slant, with a visit to Kingston on 10 June by Air Commodores Silyn-Roberts and Kyle from Directorate of Operational Requirements (DOR) and Directorate of Military Aircraft Research and Development (DMARD) to obtain Hawker's views on application of the larger Avon engine (the Avon 200 series) to the aircraft. This was followed by another visit on the 22nd by Silyn-Roberts and Kyle, this time joined by Air Vice Marshal Tuttle (Comptroller of Supplies – Air), at which the news was broken that the DOR no longer had a need for P.1083, but favoured use of reheated engines in the standard Hunter rather than concentrating on larger engines. DMARD, on the other hand, appeared keen to preserve the P.1083 and on developing the Hunter with larger engines without reheat. This conflicting picture was clarified somewhat on 13 July with the official cancellation of the P.1083 project; thus closing the door to the chance of the UK fielding an interceptor capable of supersonic level flight until the advent of the EE Lightning in the 1960s. In August, it was announced that Hunter would proceed with the larger engine (10,000lb instead of 7,500lb thrust) in later marks of the aircraft.

P.1067, WB188 returned to Richmond Road to be modified with the reheated Avon RA7R and clam-shell airbrakes. In front is one of the N7/46 prototypes also being modified.

P.1067, WB188 modified for Avon reheat trials and an attempt on the World Air Speed Record. The nose contours have been sharpened and the aircraft given a bright red livery. Neville Duke in the cockpit at Dunsfold outside the Production Hangar.

Henceforth, with the first production aircraft WT555 making its maiden flight from Dunsfold on 16 May 1953, flown by Duke, attention would be focussed on the basic P.1067 Hunter airframe and efforts made to resolve the various problems already apparent with the aircraft. These are dealt with later, but for now Hawker Aircraft was intent on deriving some publicity from the vexed reheat installation, first trialled on 7 July in WB188 which worked successfully and was now to be used to undertake an attack on the world air speed record.

The proposal was seen as a means by which Hawker could publicise their brand-new fighter and also make use of the work already carried out on the reheated version of the aircraft. To this end, the aircraft was fitted with a sharply pointed nose and a clear-vision fairing of increased rake added to the cockpit windscreen. Vivian Stanbury noted the work required to bring the aircraft into racing trim. ' ... the airbrake jacks should be removed and the panels themselves rivetted shut.' Other subjects for attention included: 'curved windscreen, surface finish, unnecessary external excrescences, unnecessary air inlets and exits, leaks (tail unit), access doors, air intake doors, fit of cabin top, wheel doors, flaps and modified rear end.' Finally, 'We hope it will be very hot for the attempt so the cabin conditioning must be working properly.'[19]

On 30 August 1953, with WB188 resplendent in a coat of Cellon gloss red, Neville Duke began his work up for the speed record attempt, his fastest run over the course between Bognor and Worthing being 741mph. However, on 1 September the aircraft was damaged while airborne. At 540 knots and 1,000ft, 'a sudden loud bang was heard and the aircraft rolled violently to starboard and an acceleration of +6G was subsequently noted on the accelerometer. Control was regained and speed quickly reduced to 200 knots ASI in a climb when it was observed that the port undercarriage leg was fully down and appeared to be past the locked position.

'On further examination a hole was observed in the top skin of the port mainplane and the hydraulic pressure was falling.' Having attempted to get the leg to lock down using various manoeuvres, Duke brought the aircraft in for a landing at Dunsfold with only the starboard and nose undercarriage legs locked in position. 'Almost immediately on touchdown the port leg collapsed and the aircraft swung to port, coming to rest after a wide sweep of some 200 degrees.'[20] Work to repair damaged items was expedited by 'borrowing' from WB195, including a new leg and undercarriage door and wing tip and the aircraft was flying again by 7 September, ready for the actual record attempt. Three runs were made over the course just off-shore at Littlehampton, the best run giving 727.63mph, sufficient to gain the World Air Speed Record for the aircraft, Duke, Hawker Aircraft Ltd and the UK. Later in the month, WB188 was used again, this time for an attempt of the 100-kilometre closed course record, this being flown again by Duke who, on 19 September 1953, achieved 709.2mph, another record.

With the success of the Hunter gaining the world air speed record quickly overshadowed by the record being taken shortly thereafter by the Supermarine Swift, attention turned back to more prosaic issues. The airbrake situation was in danger of becoming a farce and was not helped by an adverse report from Boscombe Down following their assessment of WT555 concerning the landing flap type airbrakes and the poor results of the rear fuselage type of airbrake. At a subsequent meeting it was intimated that CS(A) release to service might be withheld until a satisfactory solution was available.

This galvanised the company into urgent action comprising full scale and wind tunnel tests at RAE with a view to making the present landing flap acceptable as an interim remedy while working to develop a new type of brake to more completely satisfy the requirement. Various alternative locations for airbrakes which would not result in unacceptable trim change were investigated, including trimming with a top flap (which Hooper mused had probably resulted in the longest ever take-off run at Dunsfold!) in May of 1952, dive recovery flaps and even opening the nose wheel door. The side airbrakes located under the tailplane were abandoned due to excessive pitch change, directional problems and buffet. Once the use of wing-mounted flaps had finally been discarded, alternative locations on the fuselage were assessed and positions just in front of and just behind the wing line were investigated as the positions least likely to induce pitch change. Subsequent trials resulted in the ventral location just aft of the wing trailing edge being tested and subsequently adopted, being retrospectively added to those production aircraft already flying, but it would always look like the 'add-on' that it was.

The prototypes, having performed sterling service during the work-up period to the first production Hunter, were soon removed from the MoS inventory. WB188 was allocated Maintenance Command serial 7154M and allocated to No.1 School of Technical Training at RAF Halton on 25 October 1954. Later it was moved to become a gate guard at RAF Melksham and later, in 1961, to RAF Abingdon. In 1964, the aircraft was moved to storage at RAF Colerne and in 1975, to RAF Museum reserve collection at RAF Cosford before being released on long loan to the Tangmere Military Aircraft Museum in 1992 where it resides today. WB195 also became an instructional airframe, serialled 7284M and allocated to RAF Henlow on 23 September 1955 before moving to No.1 School of Technical Training at RAF Halton in March 1959 and subsequently scrapped in December 1967. WB202 was struck off charge on 31 December 1957 and moved to Bedford for fire practice before scrapping in 1960.

Leading Particulars (WB188 initial flights)

Wing span:	33ft 8in
Length:	42ft 3in
Wing area:	340 sq. ft
Thickness chord ratio:	0.085 (8.5%)
Sweep angle:	39.9 degrees at quarter chord
Engine:	RR Avon RA.3 rated at 7,500lb (later replaced by RA.7 at same thrust).
Fuel capacity:	353 gall
All up weight:	15,465lb

Chapter 10

Early Hunter

That it took five years from initial design to getting the first production Hunter into the air (16 May 1953) may seem excessive, especially since much of the engineering had already been trialled on the earlier jet prototypes. Indeed, concern was expressed at the time within the Admiralty that Sea Hawk production was being slowed due to the design and production effort required on the P.1067. Part of the problem, however, was that during the war, government controlled work placements had been responsible for directing many of the design and engineering staff to Hawker (and other industries) as part of the war effort. With the conflict over, many lost no time in removing themselves from the shackles of central control and left the company to pursue their own employment elsewhere, leading to a drain of some of the brightest and best employees just when Hawker needed them most, to tackle the many new challenges thrown up by the new technology. The long gestation of the aircraft was partly responsible for its hasty entry into service before all of its foibles had been ironed out, but such was the perceived need, with the Cold War becoming intense, that operational evaluation was seen as paramount.

Some of the reasons for the delays in production of the Hunter may be perceived in a somewhat partisan history of Hunter procurement produced by Government civil servants in 1955.[1]

First, the decision within the Air Staff that the UK would not face external aerial threat from the USSR until around 1957 resulted in a lack of support for innovative design studies for future military aircraft. That this policy would prove to be misplaced is now obvious, but was a persuasive argument at the time when the UK faced years of penury following the end of the war; its Socialist Government struggled to accept that a threat from its former ally might manifest itself in the future. Not until the return of Churchill's Conservatives in October 1951 would the urgency of the situation begin to be realistically addressed.

Second, the pursuit of the F.43/46 and F.44/46 specifications for a day fighter and all-weather/night fighter able to replace the Meteor in the interceptor role had produced a number of design studies, not least from Hawker itself,

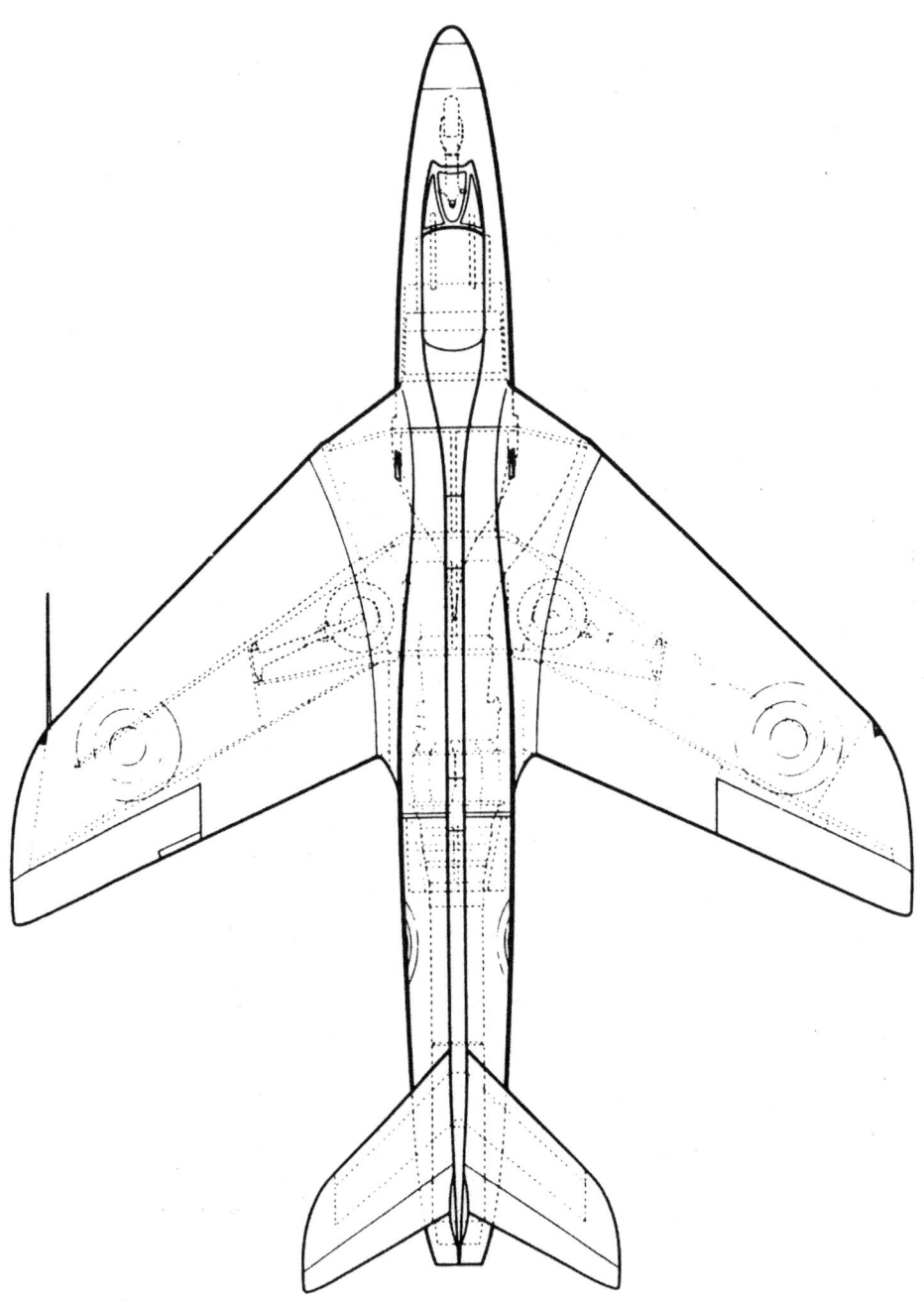

HAWKER HUNTER F Mk.1
ROLLS ROYCE AVON ENGINE

Hunter F.1 general arrangement, showing the aircraft as it entered service.

but none able to realistically fulfil the requirement as then envisaged. Work on this had occupied the design team during 1947 but led no further. With a new requirement against F.3/48, Hawker, rather than seeking to modify an existing design, started again with rather more success and produced a design that had the Ministry's backing. That said, numerous amendments and changes would be suggested during the gestation period, mainly springing from the Ministry of Supply and the Air Ministry.

The vexed issue of the airbrake on the Hunter had its roots in decisions made several years earlier. Ralph Hooper recalled that the Hunter specification 'called for "dive recovery" flaps'. But as work progressed, the 'emphasis gradually changing from "dive recovery" to "speed limiting"'.[2] The confusion surrounding the airbrake requirement was compounded by a visit to Kingston by a delegation of pilots from the Central Fighter Establishment (CFE) charged with assessing new aircraft operationally. Heretofore, Hawker had been working to produce an airbrake that would not impose a pitching moment on deployment (as opposed to dive recovery flaps which are often designed to impose a nose-up pitch) so that the brake could be deployed during an attacking run without upsetting the

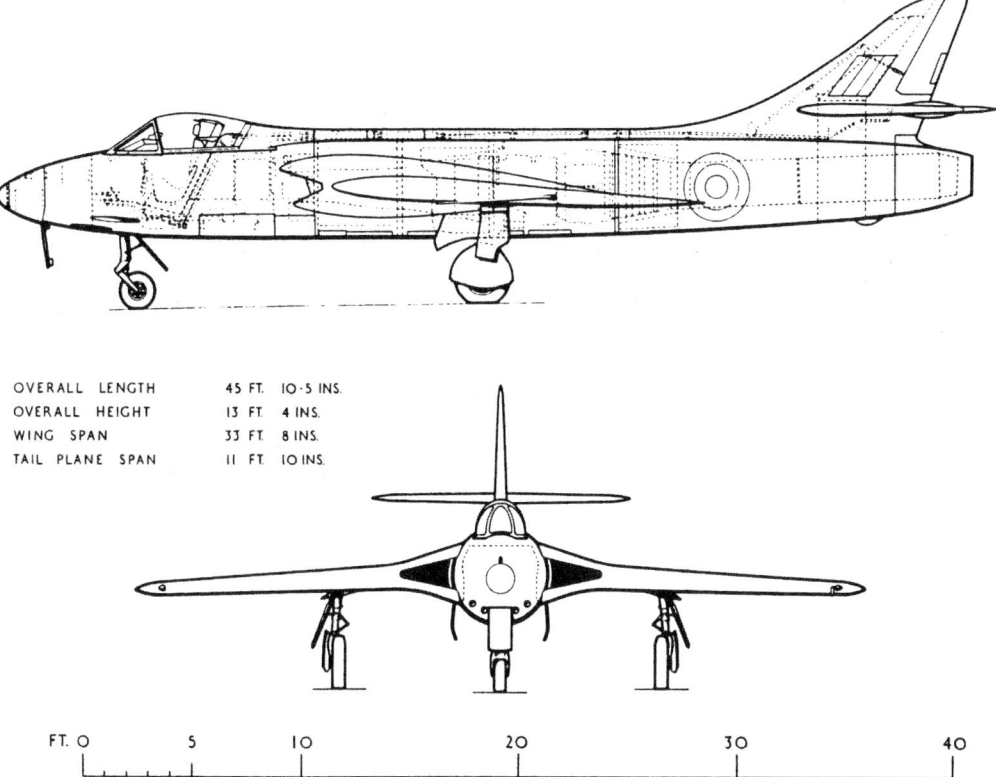

Hunter F.1 centre fuselage in its jig. To the rear can be seen an almost complete front fuselage. Probably at Langley.

Hunter completed front fuselage. The location for the gun pack and the apertures for the cannon barrels can be seen.

gun sighting. However, the opinion of the CFE pilots was that they required airbrakes purely as a means of not exceeding the critical Mach number! No wonder Hawker's design was 'confused'. The requirement to be able to fit either the 20mm or 30mm cannon (the 30mm Aden was not at that time available) and to be capable of fitting either the Rolls-Royce Avon or Armstrong Siddeley Sapphire into the same airframe also caused delay, as did differing and evolving requirements for UHF radio to be available.

The need for UHF radio and an additional navigation aid was not seen at Hawker as a requirement until approximately 1953 but in the meantime, an additional VHF set would need to be fitted into the radio bay which initial investigation suggested would not be possible without enlarging the bay. A frustrated Camm called a meeting at Kingston in August 1950 in an attempt to clarify just what the radio requirements were since 'no definite requirement for extra equipment had been received by him, but the numerous enquiries were causing confusion, and he must know what was required if they were to plan ahead'. Other helpful advice proffered by the Ministry was the requirement to fit armour protection for the pilot since this 'would have considerable morale effect in encounters with heavily armed bombers (TU.4) and make it easier for them to close in to make a kill'. The ability to dive at speeds of M1.2 was also latterly requested though the design had followed the original specification calling for stressing to M.1 only.[3]

In November 1950, Camm had estimated that production could start in 1952 and ramp up during 1953, but the various additional design changes (including that required to improve rearward view) had, by January 1951, resulted in initial production not likely until 1954, with one or two aircraft available in 1953 (an accurate assessment), with CA release in July 1953 (not an accurate assessment). Also of concern to Hawker was the difficulty of catering for the provision of reheat while keeping the CG correct. Although the decision was made by the Ministry to retain the reheat provision, it was decided that the company would also manufacture a rear fuselage without reheat. In the event, later in 1953, the reheat requirement was cancelled, superseded by the impending availability of more powerful engines in the not too distant future. With the rear of the aircraft causing design problems, in February 1951, the length of the 30mm cannon barrel was shortened by 14.5in, requiring more design changes to the nose section to accommodate new support structure.

By June 1953, such were the problems besetting the Hunter programme that the Air Staff now considered the Hunter less attractive than the Supermarine

Swift, which had previously been ordered in a limited capacity as an insurance should the Hunter fail to deliver. The following decisions were therefore made in June:

a) Cancel the Hunter Development (P.1083).
b) To restrict orders for the Hunter.
c) That as many Hunters which we have to accept should be Mk.2 (Sapphire and higher-powered Avon).
d) That as many of the remaining Hunters should be Mk.3 (Reheat).
e) Increased reliance should be placed on the Swift.[4]

These conclusions were communicated to the NATO MDAP Administration, which by then had placed an order for 450 Hunters as an off-shore purchase.

A major concern with the Hunter's Avon installation had come to light fairly early in the flight test programme, that of engine surging in certain flight configurations. That it was also apparent on the Swift suggested that this was an engine rather than an airframe problem, but at a meeting including Hawker and Rolls-Royce, no obvious answers were apparent. It was arranged that a Hunter be made available to Rolls-Royce and this was delivered on 11 January 1954. An early remedy involved derating the engine, thus impacting on the aircraft's operational effectiveness. Although it had not been realised at the time, the Avon engine was prone to surging at high level, particularly at high angles of attack (AOA) and when the aircraft was carrying out gun firing, during which the gun gases and disturbed airflow were ingested into the engine. Because the gun firing trials had been completed at Boscombe Down using the third prototype WB202 with the Sapphire engine, which had greater surge tolerance, the problem did not manifest itself in early testing. Ultimately, new versions of the Avon which were less prone to surging, together with the development of fuel dipping during gun firing would effect a cure and allow the Hunter to evolve into the formidable aircraft that it would later become.

Meanwhile the airbrake problem continued to cause concern, the existing arrangement of wing-mounted flaps doubling as airbrakes imparting a significant nose-down trim to the aircraft. By February 1954, by which time it was hoped to have had the aircraft in service, the use of wing brakes was finally abandoned and alternative means of slowing the aircraft initiated. At this point, locating an airbrake under the fuselage was investigated, positions just aft of the wing trailing edge and forward of the wing leading edge being identified as the most favourable positions and least likely to provoke trim changes. Trials began on the three prototypes as they became available with a brake mounted on Vernier

Hunter front and centre fuselage sections mated. This aircraft was the seventeenth production aircraft, first flown at Dunsfold January 1954. The aircraft would later feature a revised rear fuselage to trial Area Rule application.

Hunter front fuselage with primer applied. Note the cabling at the nose for the radar ranging unit.

rails aft of the wing trailing edge; this arrangement allowing limited positioning fore and aft. Trials showed this to give satisfactory braking with minimal trim change but trials continued with the prototypes and an early production aircraft WT566.

The political importance of obtaining a satisfactory solution to the airbrake problem, to allow the aircraft to obtain its CA release was emphasised by the dispatch of Air Vice Marshal Bird-Wilson, at that time Wing Commander and Officer Commanding the Air Fighting Development Squadron at the Central Fighter Establishment at West Raynham, to Dunsfold to see for himself what the problem was. Having flown the first production machine WT555, he summarised it thus: 'when the selection was made, the nose of the Hunter went hard down, while the pilot headed for the canopy. The trim was such that it was totally operationally unacceptable.'[5]

In the event, such was the pressure to get the aircraft into service that the forward location was only cursorily tested, and the rear position was hastily drawn up as an 'add-on' and incorporated onto the production line. While further design work was carried out to produce a more refined installation, the original 'bodged' design was retained and gave good service throughout the aircraft's life. The main drawback of the ventral location was that the airbrake's extended position of 67 degrees did not allow its use during landing, but this does not appear to have proved a concern over the life of the aircraft.

As production aircraft started to build up at Dunsfold awaiting CA release, the problem of the ammunition links striking the fuselage was still exercising Hawker and the men from the Ministry. Hawker's early attempts to retain the links internally had not been very successful due to space constraints, and attention now turned to some form of external slipper tank to retain the links. Finally, link collector tanks would be fitted under the gun pack to collect the discarded material, a system that again would stay with the aircraft throughout its operational life.

The last point of concern would be the tendency of the aircraft to tighten up in the turn (i.e. 'pitch-up'), a characteristic that it would share with the Swift, though not so marked. Until such times as the problem could be cured, a 4G limit was imposed on the aircraft. Initial trials using wing fences proved to be less than effective, but the addition of leading-edge extensions to the outer wings in October 1954 proved to be efficacious, the addition being read across to the Swift as well.

Eventually, on 1 July 1954, the Hunter F.1 was given a limited CA Release to Service with the following restrictions:

Hunter fuselage complete comprising front, centre and rear components. The next stage will be attachment of wings and tail surfaces.

A rather grubby front fuselage showing the modular gun pack and the hoist arrangements for installation.

An example of the engine installation technique. The aircraft rear fuselage is completely removed and the engine slid from its trestle into position in the centre fuselage. This later Avon has the annular combustion chamber rather than the individual 'cans' of the earlier engines. Note the flying control rods for rudder and tailplane on the spine.

Hunter wing sets under test for correct hydraulic function of flaps, undercarriage and ailerons.

a) Armament firing restricted until trials are completed.
b) 4g limitation at altitude to prevent tightening.

CA Release to Service for the Hunter F.2 followed on 31 August 1954 with the same restrictions.

In summary then, the problems that had beset the Hunter, to a large extent due to its hasty entry into service, were thus:

a) airbrakes, b) elevator flutter, c) tail end vibration, d) engine surge at high RPM, e) wheel brake judder, f) engine surge with gun firing, g) elevator ineffectiveness, h) pitch-up – tightening in turns, i) reheat installation, j) provision for extra fuel internally, k) ammunition link strikes on fuselage, l) heavy control forces, m) cabin misting.

Hunter in full scale production. Pictured are centre fuselages under construction. Completed units crowd the gangway between the jigs, some twenty-two units visible here. In the next bay are further fuselage sections and completed wings.

Hunter wings under construction, there are over fifty wings in this view.

Airbrake

That it took Hawker Aircraft two frustrating years to achieve a benign airbrake operation on the Hunter says much for the limitations of wind tunnel modelling at this time. Hawker had successfully produced an airbrake system on the Sea Hawk using the landing flaps in combination with upper wing flaps and this knowledge was read across to the P.1067 design, but appears to have been dropped before the first aircraft flew. However, it seems that the dive recovery flaps, fitted in front of the undercarriage wells, were flown on WB188 but were found to be ineffective and were thereafter deleted. The reasons for not fitting the top flap to the airbrake arrangement is unknown. Perhaps they were found to be unsuccessful in wind tunnel tests, but the greater inertia of the airframe and engine power available to the Hunter may have had a contributory effect. Later trials did indeed reinstate this top flap but the results were unsatisfactory, imparting severe trim change and vibration.

The main problem with the flaps as fitted to early Hunters was that although they were effective, they imparted a sharp nose-down pitch change when deployed. If the brakes were simply to be used to avoid exceeding the critical Mach number (as staff at CFE claimed), then this might have been just acceptable, but the Air Ministry insisted that they were required during a gunnery attack phase where large trim changes would upset the pilots aim and therefore braking had to be available without trim change.

Hunter front fuselages crowd the bay in this view, the front unit appears to be a Blackpool manufactured item. Behind these are numerous centre fuselages and semi-complete aircraft.

It seems that even before the P.1067 flew, Hawker designers were experiencing difficulty in finding an airbrake design that did not impart a trim change, DOR(A) being informed thus by Camm in January 1951. Hawker was invited to approach RAE with a view to identifying a suitable location, while flight trials from September 1951 confirmed the earlier theoretical studies that trim change would follow airbrake/flap deployment and were ineffective at high speed. By the end of 1952, attempts to alleviate the trim change had failed and further designs included a slotted finger flap arrangement, a rear fuselage brake or an interconnection between flaps and tailplane which would balance out trim changes. Whether such an interconnect (which was used successfully on the later T-45 Goshawk) would have been possible with the flying tail arrangement on the Hunter is open to question.

By January 1953, patience was wearing thin within the DOR which stated that airbrake improvement had high priority and a meeting at Kingston the following month with MoS and Air Ministry officers saw agreement reached that fuselage

Hunter erection at Dunsfold in bay 2 of the Production Hangar in late 1953. Aircraft would arrive with wings and tail removed, having been function tested at Langley, for re-erection and flight testing at Dunsfold. WT575 in the foreground first flew in January 1954.

airbrakes would be developed, while improvements to the flap/brakes would be pursued. Some progress was indeed made with the wing brakes and this was Hawker's preferred solution, Camm insisting that fuselage brakes would only be trialled if the flap/brake arrangement could not fulfil the requirement, due to the changes this would cause in CG (already giving cause for concern due to the reheat equipment requirements) and the involved changes that would be required on the production line. However, abandonment of reheat for the early production aircraft made fuselage brake fitment an easier proposition and interest in this as a long-term solution increased.

The fuselage brakes, designed to sit at the rear, under the tailplane on the aircraft mid-line, proved a disappointment when trialled between July and November 1953, causing considerable buffet and nose-down trim change on deployment; unsurprising given their location adjacent to the tailplane. Although WB188 was not fully representative of the production Hunter insofar as jet pipe was 18in shorter and this placed the brakes closer to the exhaust than would otherwise be the case, it appears that, apart from a redesign to move them forward by 12in, no further work was undertaken on this scheme, possibly because by then, the ventral fuselage brake was showing rather more promise. A full assessment of the aircraft in November 1953 by Boscombe Down reiterated their earlier concerns regarding the current airbrake situation, their report stating that:

a) The aircraft would be drastically restricted in the operational role.
b) it is doubtful if the aircraft can be considered safe for release.

The report added that use at high speed and low altitude was likely to be dangerous.[6]

With this damning assessment, ACAS(OR) and DOR stated unequivocally that safe and adequate airbrakes must be provided before the aircraft could be accepted by the RAF. Hawker was now given permission to use as many production aircraft on airbrake trials as were required and further, modification to the rear fuselage brakes was authorised in an attempt to improve the situation. A resume of the various trials regarding the search for satisfactory airbraking ability shows that work started in earnest in May 1952 with WB195, the second prototype, fitted with an airbrake flap on top of the wing (to deploy with the main flap). Through May until the end of 1952, work was also carried out on WB188 with various configurations, including a moveable top flap. Work continued into the spring and summer of 1953 with WB202 joining the airbrake trials including an extended trailing edge to the flaps and the fitting of one-third span flaps.

Hunter F.1, WT555; the first production Hunter, first flown at Dunsfold in May 1953. Note the clean lines and absence of the ventral airbrake.

Visit to Dunsfold by senior delegation of USAF staff to evaluate the Hunter against the F-86 Sabre. Left to right are General Albert Boyd, Colonel Fred Ascani, probably Bob Marsh, Neville Duke, Lieutenant Colonel Richard Johnson and Major Davis(?) apparently with the 81 Fighter Squadron, equipped with Sabres in 1953. Boyd was a highly respected test pilot within the USAF testing establishment, commanding many of the important test centres in his career. May or October 1952.

While WB188 then began work with the side-mounted airbrakes, production aircraft WT562 was added to the fleet trialling slotted flaps as well as holes in the wing surface. By February 1954, WT566 had been fitted with a ventral airbrake which showed promise; trials allowing the degree of extension to be increased from 60 to 67 and finally 75 degrees. Finally, with WT573 being added to the trials fleet, this successfully flew with the production version of the airbrake, extending to 67 degrees. While this was being signed off in June 1954, allowing CA Release the following month, WT566 carried out several flights in June with the ventral airbrake mounted forward of the wing leading edge though the rear position would be read across to the production Hunter F.1 and F.2 aircraft.

Elevator Flutter and Ineffectiveness

This problem, which Hawker had already encountered on the earlier jet aircraft designs and which was causing concern around the second half of 1952, was ultimately cured by use of fully powered controls for the flying surfaces, including the elevators and an increase in the elevator boost ratio. Allied to the flutter were high stick forces at high IAS and poor longitudinal control which an early assessment by Boscombe Down highlighted, with the recommendation that some sort of flying tail be fitted. This was carried out as a TI on a Mark 1 aircraft in April 1954 using an interlink between elevator and tailplane powered by an electric actuator as per the P.1081 and fitted as a full 'flying tail' to the Mark 4 onwards.

Tail End Vibration

Vibration emanating from the rear of the aircraft was another problem that had been apparent on the early jets, from the P.1040 onwards and which, on the Sea Hawk, was cured by introduction of an 'acorn' fairing at the junction of the fin and tailplane leading edges. On the P.1067, this was partly caused by elevator flutter but mainly by buffet. Fred Sutton noticed that the vibration was less severe when the streamlined fairing housing the anti-spin parachute was fitted at the back of the fin, giving a clue as to where the airflow was breaking down. Eventually a conical fairing was trialled fitted at the rear of the fin at the tailplane junction, leading largely to a cure and was introduced on all production aircraft.

Hunter F.1, WT594 first flown July 1954.

Hunter F.4, WT701, the first Mark 4 first flown October 1954, at Dunsfold.

Engine Surge at High RPM and During Gun Firing

The problem was largely one associated with the earlier mark of Avon engine which appeared to be particularly prone to compressor surging, especially at high RPM and high altitude; this same engine was in use in the Swift fighter which was similarly affected. In January 1954, a Hunter was made available to Rolls-Royce for flight investigation of the problem and in March of that year, a short-term solution involved derating the engine, though this would involve operational limitations for the aircraft. A long-term solution was being sought and was expected to be available within about three months. An associated concern was surging occurring during firing of the aircraft cannon armament, again a problem apparent on other aircraft. Indeed, it was first noted by US forces, and in May 1954, DOR asked MoS to arrange trials of the Hunter to identify whether this was an issue, this being confirmed in June when the guns were fired at altitude. Steps made to remedy the problem included work to produce a more surge resistant Avon engine by Rolls-Royce, and the development of a fuel dip system which reduced fuel to the engine when explosive gases and disrupted airflow were ingested by the engine during gun firing. The problems associated with the early Avons caused much bad feeling at Hawker towards Rolls-Royce.

Wheel Brake Judder

Problems with wheel braking had dogged the aircraft even before its first flight; Duke suffering from burnt out brakes on the first taxying trials at Boscombe Down. By 1953, it was apparent that the two-plate brakes currently in use were causing excessive juddering, potentially leading to failure of the undercarriage. To avoid the judder, the only remedy was a gentle use of braking which was resulting in landing runs of around 2,500yds, clearly not helpful on shorter runways. The introduction of single plate brakes in later 1953 led to a complete cure.

Pitch-up – Tightening in Turns

Tightening in turns or pitch-up was yet another concern shared with its transonic stablemate the Swift, (and indeed with the Sabre) though not to such an extent and a limitation of 4G was placed on the aircraft while investigation work sought a cure. Work by RAE on understanding the phenomenon had given Hawker some advanced notice of the problem and the understanding that increasing the wing chord at the tip offered the likelihood of controlling the problem but with increased detriment to the low speed stall.[7]

Hunter F.4, WT707 following Frank Murphy's unconventional landing at RNAS Ford in January 1955. Unsurprisingly, the aircraft was struck off charge.

Initially, wing fences were trialled but without much success; this was followed by trials during 1955 and 1956 of drooped leading edge extensions on the outer wings on a Mark 1 Hunter WT568 and later, on a Mark 6 XF380 at Boscombe Down. A&AEE reported that the modification 'has resulted in a definite improvement in the pitch-up characteristics of the type. Pitch-up has been alleviated and buffet and manoeuvre boundaries have been raised to an extent readily appreciable in mock combat.' The modification was then introduced on the Mark 6 and retrospectively on some Mark 4s. The leading edge extension effectively increased the chord of the wing at its extremity, thus delaying stalling of the wing at the tip, induced by spanwise airflow.[8]

Reheat Installation

The requirement for reheat was presumed rather than explicit, and originated with DOR believing that reheat would be necessary for the early Avon RA.7 engine since it lacked the power to deliver the speed requirement explicit in OR.228. However, issue of specification F3/48 did include the requirement for reheat and on that basis, Hawker worked to incorporate it into P.1067. Work to design this was protracted since the fuselage had been designed to be as slim as possible and the reheat jet pipe increased weight at the rear, throwing out the CG, already causing embarrassment, due to the parallel requirement to fit fuel into the swept wings; reheated engines being notorious for their prodigious thirst. By December 1950 RAE had carried out an assessment of the likely performance of the P.1067 and considered that, with reheat, the aircraft would just meet the OR.228 requirement but without it, performance would be down on level speed and fail the climb performance criterion by 60 per cent. With the reheated WB188 flying in July 1953, trials' work began, culminating in the successful air speed record runs along the south coast, but because of the modification work implicit in fitting reheat into the production aircraft and the still to be resolved difficulties with CG and fuel capacity, the decision was made to abandon reheat and instead fit the uprated RA.21 Avon which could deliver greater thrust than the earlier reheated Avon.

Ammunition Link Strikes on Fuselage

First identified as a problem while trialling the Aden cannon on a Bristol Beaufighter in the summer of 1951, Hawker first looked at retention of the links internally as part of the detachable gun pack, though space limitations made this unworkable. The eventual solution was external retention of links in collector boxes or fairings mounted below the gun pack – the so-called 'Sabrinas'. Successful ejection of the ammunition cases themselves was achieved by lengthening the shell ejector tubes to encourage their exit without impacting the fuselage.

These, then, were just some of the problems incurred while attempting to get the Hunter into service as quickly as possible. By March 1955, work was continuing to bring about a truly successful transonic interceptor, including that relating to the airbrake – where further deceleration was sought; engine surging – ultimately cured by better surge tolerance in the Avon engine; elevator ineffectiveness – the full-powered elevator largely curing this; pitch-up – largely cured by leading edge extensions and flying tail and ammunition link strikes – collector boxes being fitted.

Entry of the Hunter F.1 into squadron service had begun with allocation to the Central Fighter Establishment at West Raynham and to 43 (Fighter) Squadron at Leuchars in Fife in August 1954. The Hunter F.2 powered by the AS Sapphire engine was issued initially to 263 and 257 Fighter Squadrons, based at Wattisham, Suffolk beginning in September 1954. Thereafter six squadrons took delivery of the aircraft, which was welcomed for its advance on its predecessors. Realistically, the Hunter was not, at this stage, suitable for operational use, but it did allow the RAF to become familiar with the aircraft systems and the opportunities that its performance promised. That said, four Hunters were deployed by the Central Fighter Establishment during Exercise 'Dividend' in July 1954, the results were claimed to be 'very successful', in 'enabling the fighter once again to take its proper place in relation to the performance of the bomber'.

The main concern expressed by pilots was the critically short flight duration caused by the available fuel capacity and it was this aspect that the F.4 addressed on its entry into squadron use in April 1955 with 98 and 118 (Fighter) Squadrons. The internal fuel capacity was increased from 337 to 414 gallons and ability to carry a 100 gallon drop tank under each wing increased this to 614 gallons or, with two further drop tanks on the outer pylons, to 814 gallons. While the Mark 4 offered greater duration, the continuing restrictions on gun firing grated with the service and it was not until the arrival of the F.6, with this restriction removed and leading edge extensions to counter pitch-up, that the RAF finally got the aircraft promised back in 1954.

The path to squadron acceptance for the Hunter had hardly been a 'walk in the park', particularly for Hawker's pilots. With the aircraft now in service, Duke's team continued to refine the Hunter, sometimes with less than perfect control of the beast. On 27 January 1955, Bedford had taken Hunter F.1 WT628 to Idris in Libya to carry out hot weather performance trials with an Avon RA.115 engine installed. No sooner had he and the team arrived than an urgent telegram was received on 2 February. 'Murphy in hospital, Duke in plaster,

Hunter F.6, WW593, the second Mark 6 prior to fitment of wing leading edge extensions, first flown August 1955.

return immediately.' The sparse phrasing revealed the reality of test flying, that death or serious injury could await the unwary at every turn.

On 25 January, Murphy in Hunter F.4 WT707 suffered engine failure. He recorded the event thus:

> Crash landed RNAS Ford – wheels up. Flame out 44,000ft above 8/8 stratus at 1,500ft. Relight circuit U/S then radio U/S while still above cloud. Unable to lower emergency flaps so aircraft of necessity belly landed at high speed – initial impact 240mph – 19 bounces then aircraft slewed port went through caravan site – 3 fatalities, 2 injured – hit sunken road sideways still about 80mph – Aircraft broke up and self in cockpit tumbled further 100 yards. Sustained cracked vertebrae severely torn back muscles superficial cuts and abrasions and deceleration bruising. Royal West Sussex Hospital and RAF MRU Headley Court. Discharged 11/5/55.[9]

Quite why Duke was 'in plaster' is a mystery, but he returned to flying on 15 February only to suffer his own unscheduled visit to RNAS Ford in August. Flying Hunter F.1 WT562, he suffered an engine failure and carried out a forced landing at Ford. The aircraft engine was replaced and on its next flight on 6 August, the engine again failed, this time at 1,000ft after take-off. A forced landing was attempted at RAF Thorney Island but the aircraft, landing fast, bounced to destruction while crossing the airfield boundary and came to an abrupt halt in a ground depression. The aircraft was destroyed and Duke severely injured with a fractured back. Duke described the aftermath of his unconventional landing:

> When I came to, the aircraft was in pieces around me. I was still strapped safely to the seat but my body smarted and ached with cuts and bruises … Slowly, I heaved myself out of the cockpit and staggered to a hillock to contemplate the scene. My back was broken but I was still alive. Never again would I fly as a test pilot. When I looked at the Hunter, I realised how lucky I had been. The nose was broken off, the rear fuselage had snapped at the bulkhead right behind the ejector seat.[10]

Duke was, in fact, flying again within a month. However, the injury had weakened his back so that when, on 9 May 1956 while flying the P.1099 prototype XF833 modified with a P.1121 type cockpit layout, he made a heavy landing at Dunsfold and suffered further injury to his back, described in his log as: 'slipped disc – fractured back'. As a fast jet test pilot, this really was the end, though Duke would continue to fly right up to his death in 2007.

Ultimately some forty-eight RAF squadrons and seven RNAS squadrons would be equipped with the Hunter, becoming by far the most numerous aircraft in UK military service throughout the later '50s and into the 1960s. By 1971, 1,972 Hunters of all marks had been built, including license production in Belgium and The Netherlands. Refurbished aircraft would total another 526, many going to overseas customers. Indeed it seemed at times, in the middle decades of the twentieth century, that almost every country in Europe, the Middle and Far East, was operating one mark or another of Hawker's superlative Hunter.

The first production Hunters did not remain in service for long, being quickly superseded by the F.4 Mark. WT555, the first Avon engine Hunter F.1 was retired from active use in November 1953, having flown for just six months. Allocated to Boscombe Down in June 1957 the aircraft was stored at No.5 MU Kemble before becoming a Ground Instructional Airframe serialled 7499M and allocated to No.7 Radio School, RAF Locking in November 1957. In 1967, it was transferred to No.2 School of Technical Training at RAF Cosford before entering the reserve collection of the RAF Museum, also on site. In 1989, the aircraft was auctioned and sold to Vanguard Holdings which displayed it on the roof of their premises in Ealing, London until 1998. After a period in storage, it was returned to the roof in 2002 where it is believed to remain. WN888, the first Hunter F.2 suffered a mishap resulting in cat 3 damage in July 1956 with 257 Squadron and was subsequently moved to No.5 MU at Kemble in December of that year before issue as a Ground Instructional Aircraft serialled 7486M and issued to No.1 School of Technical Training at RAF Halton in November 1957. Subsequently scrapped at Halton.

Leading Particulars – Hunter F.1

Wing span:	33ft 8in
Length:	45ft 10.5in
Wing sweep:	40 degrees on the quarter chord
Wing area:	340 sq. ft
Thickness chord ratio:	0.085 (8.5%)
Engine:	RR Avon RA.7, 7,500lb thrust
Fuel capacity:	334 gall
Weight empty:	12,648lb
All up weight:	16,145lb clean
Performance:	0.93M at 36,000ft
Service ceiling:	48,800ft

Chapter 11

Other Companies' Projects

It comes as no surprise that Hawker and Supermarine – the pre-eminent UK fighter design houses during the Second World War – should have entered the field of gas turbine powered aircraft at around the same time. They were, after all, great rivals; Hawker with the Hurricane, Typhoon and Tempest, and Supermarine with successive iterations of the Spitfire, had provided the RAF with the bulk of fighter aircraft throughout the war. Hawker had been in the fighter business since its inception in 1920, building on the success of Sopwith Aviation during the First World War, while Supermarine had come late into the fighter business with R.J. Mitchell's superlative Spitfire. Yet, of the two, it would be Supermarine, now under the designer Joe Smith, which would be the first to get a jet fighter into service use with the Attacker F.1 for the Royal Navy in January 1951, Hawker's Sea Hawk F.1 replacing the Attacker in 1953. As each company sought to design a successful second-generation jet fighter, building on their earlier work, the rivalry between the two design houses would reach its peak in the early 1950s, with Hawker emerging the undoubted winner with the Hunter.

Supermarine

The last iteration of the Spitfire – successively improved throughout the war – was the Spiteful, for the RAF (first flown in June 1944) and a navalised version named Seafang (first flown in 1946). Although both variants were ordered in quantity, with the end of the war most orders were cancelled and only a few of each type built. The Spiteful/Seafang featured a completely new wing incorporating laminar flow characteristics and, in an attempt to retain some of the effort that had been expended on the design, the wing was used as the basis for a new aircraft, powered by a Rolls-Royce RB.41 Nene engine. This – the Type 392 – featured a bulky fuselage with low set wings and air intakes mounted adjacent to the cockpit feeding the Nene engine of 5,000lb thrust, exhausting through a long jet pipe to the rear. Conventional tapered tail surfaces matching the plan of the wings were incorporated together with the Spiteful's tail down undercarriage. Early concerns from the CFE requested that the wing-mounted armament (four 20mm Hispano cannon) be repositioned in the nose of the aircraft and that a tricycle undercarriage be fitted, neither of which happened.

Constructed to Air Ministry specification E10/44, the aircraft first flew on 27 July 1946 in the hands of Jeffrey Quill, the prototype TS409 performed well, though directional snaking was evident at higher speeds, this being resolved by small changes to the rudder trailing edge. Although the aircraft was viewed as broadly viceless, following trials by Boscombe Down criticism was levelled regarding the low Mach number limit (M0.82), the low G threshold (2-2.5G) before onset of buffet, high elevator forces at low and high speed and the poor layout of the cockpit controls. Not surprisingly, the RAF felt it had nothing to gain by ordering the aircraft into production and it was the Navy that kept the project alive, issuing specification E1/45 for a navalised fighter prototype. With naval equipment fitted, the second prototype TS413 undertook carrier trials on HMS *Illustrious*, which were considered broadly successful, though the view over the nose on the approach was considered less than adequate.

By 1948, Navy interest in the aircraft was lukewarm at best, its performance could now be compared with Hawker's first jet, the P.1040, first flown in September 1947, which offered comparable performance with the Type 392. Nonetheless, with much work required to bring the P.1040 into line with the Navy requirements specified in N7/46, the Type 392 came to be seen as a useful interim type before the Sea Hawk became available and on that basis, an improved design to specification NR/A.17 (written in October 1947 and issued November 1948) was produced and an order for sixty-three aircraft placed in October 1948 for the Supermarine Attacker F.1. Entering service with the FAA in August 1951, it would remain in service for just three years before being supplanted by the Hawker Sea Hawk F.1, but would provide the Royal Navy with useful jet handling experience before the arrival of Hawker's replacement.

Interestingly, a comparison of the performance of the Attacker and the Sea Hawk shows that the Supermarine and Hawker aircraft were evenly matched:

Supermarine Attacker F.1: Max speed sea level 565mph; fuel internal 293 gallons; duration 2 hrs 30 mins clean; service ceiling 48,500ft; rate of climb 5,765ft/min; limiting Mach no. 0.825.

Hawker Sea Hawk F3: Max speed sea level 591mph; fuel 395 gallons clean; duration 2hrs 15min clean; service ceiling 43,000ft; rate of climb 5,700ft/min; limiting Mach no. 0.85.

Supermarine Attacker taking the arrestor wire on unknown aircraft carrier. Note the tail-down attitude required to engage the wire. (*Courtesy of Chris Goss*)

However, performance isn't everything and pilots preferred the Sea Hawk for its docile handling, stability in combat, good manoeuvring capability and excellent view from the cockpit, particularly on landing. Maintenance access was also considered easy and the aircraft broadly trouble free.

With the Attacker entering Royal Navy service, attention now turned to the third prototype and its potential use for swept-wing research. As with the Hawker P.1052, Supermarine had been approached by MoS and RAE with a view to getting aircraft with swept wings into the air to allow UK scientists to attempt to catch up with the US and USSR in the field of high Mach swept-wing performance. While Hawker was allocated research specification E.38/46 for what would become the P.1052, Supermarine was allocated E.41/46 against their swept-wing design, the Type 510. Based on the Attacker design, the Type 510 featured wings swept at 44 degrees, coupled with swept tail surfaces, the Rolls-Royce Nene engine and tail down undercarriage configuration being retained. The first prototype VV106 made its maiden flight from Boscombe Down on 29 December 1948 and poor handling soon became apparent, believed to be caused by the manual controls, fully powered controls being considered the likely cure. However, the aircraft showed a far superior speed to the Attacker, being displayed at the 1949 SBAC Display at speeds in excess of 600mph. Deck landing trials the following year on HMS *Illustrious* saw VV106 become the first swept-wing aircraft to land on a British carrier in November 1950. The second prototype, VV119, first flew in March 1950 but was soon returned to the factory to be heavily modified, emerging as the Type 535 with new longer nose, tricycle undercarriage and provision for reheat with a slightly more powerful Rolls-Royce Nene RN.3 of 5,100lb thrust. In this configuration it more closely approximated to Hawker's P.1081.

With the Air Ministry now finally awake to the reality that the country was being left behind in the aeronautical field by American and Soviet research and industry, a call for a production version of the Type 535 was made against specification F105P, two prototypes and 100 further aircraft (later increased to 150) being requested in November 1950, powered by Rolls-Royce's new axial flow engine the Avon RA.7, with provision for reheat. The specification was something of an attempt at a quick fix in terms of getting aircraft into the air to bolster the RAF but throughout its life, the Swift, as the aircraft became known, would suffer from the rush to get it into service, a problem initially shared with Hawker's Hunter which was being designed against the same OR.228 (issue 3). This called for Mach 0.95 at 45,000ft and a time to height of six minutes. Unfortunately, unlike the Hunter, which would be almost a 'clean-sheet' design, the Swift would enter service with 'baggage' from its earlier versions including lack of fuel, poor short-field performance and a wing identified by RAE as unlikely to satisfy high-level requirements without a major redesign.

Supermarine's Swift prototypes – allocated code Type 541 – WJ960 and WJ965, first took to the air in August 1951, (a month after the Hunter prototype) with WJ960 being flown from Boscombe Down by Mike Lithgow. Although grounded for some months due to engine problems, Supermarine staff were happy that the aircraft displayed significant improvements over the earlier types. The second prototype WJ965 more closely matched the production design, this flying for the first time at Boscombe Down in July 1952. The second aircraft carried additional fuel but to off-set the increased weight, the outer wing skins had been reduced in thickness, leading to concerns regarding flutter, and further investigation revealed that this was indeed happening, the spring tabs on the ailerons being replaced with geared tabs to dampen the problem. Later, powered ailerons and increased stiffening of the outer wings was carried out to resolve the problem.

Supermarine Swift FR.5 WK281 of 79 Squadron, pictured at RAF Abingdon in 1968. (*Courtesy of RuthAS*)

The first pre-production Swift WK194 was complete by November 1952 when it was flown by Chris Clarke at Boscombe Down. His report revealed problems with stability prior to the stall, wing drop at the stall, tightening in turns and severe aileron buzz at higher speeds. By July 1953, several Swifts were available for further evaluation, though early problems with the Avon RA.7 caused delays to the programme. With the Air Staff insisting that the aircraft be in service with 56 Squadron by the end of 1953, Supermarine redoubled efforts to achieve the deadline, but loss of WJ965 (which was being used to gather instrumentation data) in a spin, meant that further delay attended the possibility of achieving CA Release in the time available, this was eventually obtained on 12 February 1954 but with restrictions. The aircraft was limited to 500 knots at sea level and 0.9 IMN at 25,000ft. Spinning was not permitted.

So it was that the Swift F.1 entered restricted service with AFDS and 56 Squadron, only five months before the Hunter was released to service. In several areas, continuing problems with the Swift were mirrored by the early Hunter; both suffered from pitch-up, engine surging and concerns regarding damage caused by ammunition link strikes, lack of elevator authority and trim changes on airbrake selection. Both the Swift F.1 and Hunter F.1 should really be considered as pre-production aircraft, given the restrictions under which they were released to service and the continuing battle to cure the various problems manifesting themselves. For the Hunter, these problems were broadly resolved by the Mark 4 and certainly by the Mark 6, while for the Swift, these were not really put to bed until the Mark 6. Attempts to fit the full armament suite of four 30mm Aden cannon into the lower nose (the F.1 carried only two cannon) now revealed insufficient space for the ammunition. Accordingly, the wing roots were extended to house the ammunition and in doing so, severely increased the pitch-up tendency, only resolved by increasing the nose ballast, impacting on performance further. The conclusion of Boscombe Down was that the F.2 was actually worse that the F.1!

While it is not intended to pursue the Swift through its operational use, its place as an 'insurance policy' against Hunter failure had not been particularly successful. Although it would remain in limited use for photographic reconnaissance as the FR.5, most of the orders for Swift were cancelled; twenty-two x F.1; sixteen x F.2; twenty-five x F.3 (none entering service); eight x F.4; ninety-one x FR.5, one x PR.6 (not flown) and five x F.7 – totalling 198 – were built.

Pursued in parallel with the Swift development at Supermarine was work on a twin-engined fighter for the Royal Navy. Stemming from the Type 508, with straight wings and all-moving V tail, the prototype first flew in August 1951, upgraded to Type 529 on the second prototype. Further upgrading, including the provision of swept wings, produced the Type 525 and from this, the Type 544 featuring swept wings and blown flaps. The prototype for this, to specification N.113, would have its first flight in 1956, entering service as the Supermarine Scimitar F.1 in 1957, of which 100 were ordered but only seventy-six built. Like its Swift relative, the Scimitar would suffer from retention of the earlier wing design, meaning that control at altitude and high angle of attack would be marginal at best. This was not helped by early aircraft entering service suffering from pitch-up since leading edge extensions were not fitted, despite being applied to the Hunter several years prior.[1]

Its service history was somewhat marred by a high accident record, but it did remain in service until replaced by the Blackburn Buccaneer in 1969.

Gloster

During the same period of the late 1940s – early 1950s, other companies were also busy on jet propelled fighter projects. Gloster, which had stolen a march on other companies by being the first to achieve flight in the UK of a jet propelled aircraft – the E28/39 – in 1941, had quickly followed this with the F9/40 Meteor jet aircraft, entering service in 1944.

Ultimately, the Meteor would be produced in a number of marks, each improving on the last; the F.8 was a very different aircraft to the first production jets of 1944, the aircraft achieving wide export sales to some sixteen countries. Also modified to take up the night fighter role, the NF.11, NF.12 and NF.14 marks remained in service until the late 1950s, their role being taken over by the Javelin. In RAF service, the Meteor was issued to sixty-three squadrons as well as serving with the Royal Navy, twelve squadrons operating the aircraft. In all, some 3,881 Meteors of all marks were produced, not bad for Gloster's first operational jet fighter.

However, since the production of engines at this crucial period of the war was slowed due to continued failures at Rover, tasked with production of the Power Jets W2B, MAP requested that Gloster also consider the design of a single-engined fighter. In an effort to minimise the use of the precious engines

A Gloster Meteor III, EE393 coded US-J of 56 Squadron, pictured at Lubeck on 28 May 1948. The pilot is Denis Hailey. (*Historic Military Press*)

Gloster GA.2 "Ace" TX145, the second prototype and the first to fly.

MAP issued specification E5/42, calling for a single-engined jet fighter, but little work was done before the take-over of Rover's jet engine interests by Rolls-Royce led to an increase in available engines and the cancellation of the E5/42 specification. However, interest in the proposal at Gloster resulted in continued design work on such an aircraft with power likely to be supplied by a Halford H.1 engine, followed later by the Rolls-Royce Nene and, in 1944, a revision of E5/42 led to E1/44, around which Gloster's work now concentrated.

The result was a mid-wing stressed-skin single-engined aircraft with straight tapered wings and low-set tailplane, with the Nene turbojet rated at 5,000lb exhausting at the tail, the name 'Ace' and company designation GA.1 being bestowed on the aircraft. With the constant revisions to the design, the first two prototypes ceased to be representative of the latest thinking and work ceased on these. The third prototype, serialled SM809, became the prototype GA.2 on which work began in late 1944 and it was this aircraft which, in July 1947, began the road journey to Boscombe Down for its first flight. Regrettably it never arrived, the transporter crashed en-route, damaging the aircraft beyond repair. Despite this major setback, Gloster began work on a replacement – TX145 –

which flew at Boscombe Down in March 1948. Results were encouraging; top speed was 620mph and service ceiling 44,000ft with good climb ability, though handling was problematical until the tailplane was reset higher on the fin and thereafter, results proved excellent. Indeed, so good were the results with the new tail design that it was subsequently incorporated into the later marks of Meteor.

In 1946, MAP (absorbed into Ministry of Supply from April 1946) had issued two pre-production orders for twenty production aircraft each under designation GA.4, suggesting that Gloster was about to embark on another winner; yet within a week, the second order for twenty aircraft was cancelled by MAP and although work would continue on the GA.2, from this point there was really no likelihood of the aircraft entering series production. The second aircraft – TX148 – flew in 1949, joining the test programme already underway with TX145. Although the results were excellent, with the new tail now being fitted on the Meteor, transforming its performance, the GA.2 was little better than its predecessor and the first pre-production order was also cancelled. With little use for the two flying aircraft, TX145 and TX148 were transferred to RAE ownership and used at Farnborough for various trials. The third prototype – TX150 – never flew, being used by Gloster for structural testing until transferred to Cranfield College of Aeronautics. After a total production run of four airframes (six if the uncompleted airframes for E5/42 are included), Gloster's attention turned to production of the UK's first dedicated night fighter, the Javelin. The Javelin was the eventual winner of the search by the Operational Requirements branch of the Air Ministry to obtain an all-weather fighter to complement the day-fighter role eventually awarded to Hawker's Hunter.

The Javelin was the UK's first delta winged aircraft to enter service, the design requirements for two crew operation and twin engines resulting in a big aircraft. With fairly massive T-tail surfaces, it was a hard aircraft to miss and did give the UK a useable all-weather fighter in advance of the interim types it replaced, such as the Meteor and Venom in the night fighter role. Initially designed to specification F.44/46 (later revised to F.4/48) as the Gloster GA.5 in competition with the de Havilland DH.110, the first prototype took to the air in November 1951, entering service in February 1956 as the Gloster Javelin FAW.1. Some forty FAW.1 were built, the aircraft being continually upgraded through successive marks until replaced in 1968 after a production run of 436.

De Havilland

While Gloster had been busy investigating ways to build on their early success with the Meteor, de Havilland had similarly been occupied with their Vampire aircraft. Like the Meteor, the Vampire was produced in multiple marks and was distributed to numerous RAF squadrons as well as selling widely abroad, some 3,268 aircraft being produced. Over thirty overseas forces operated the jet during its active life, and it remained in service for many years after relegation to second line use.

Seeking to build on this success, de Havilland upgraded the Vampire design; the result would be the DH.112 Venom. Heavily based on its predecessor, it would feature a thinner wing section reducing the Vampire's thickness/chord ratio from 14 per cent to 10 per cent, and with a swept leading edge but straight trailing edge; the DH.103 Ghost engine, in place of the Goblin, delivering 4,800lb thrust and the ability to carry fuel tanks on the wing tips. While the design was still essentially first generation, it was seen from the outset as a means of providing an improved fighter bomber to take over the role which the Vampire currently fulfilled, and to fill an interim role until the arrival of their second-generation fighter, the DH.110 Vixen.

Designed around specification F15/49, this called for an improved aircraft capable of replacing the Vampire in the fighter bomber role. First flying in September 1949, VV612 was joined by the second prototype VV613 in May

De Havilland Vampire T.11 XD506. (*Courtesy of Chris Goss*)

Other Companies' Projects   193

the following year. Following broadly successful evaluation at Boscombe Down, the first production aircraft was delivered for restricted service with CFE, the first of 375 of the Venom FB.1. Performance of the Venom gave a top speed of 640mph and a service ceiling of just under 40,000ft against the Vampire's speed of 548mph and a ceiling of 42,800ft. De Havilland also modified the design to create the Venom NF.2 night fighter, intended as a replacement for the Vampire NF.10. The Venom NF.2 had a crew cockpit of increased size to accommodate a second crewman equipped with AI intercept radar and entered service during May 1953. Early mark Venoms were replaced by the FB.4, some 250 being constructed while the NF.2 (ninety-one produced) was upgraded to the NF.3 with ejector seats and improved radar, 123 being built.

As an interim aircraft, the Venom successfully filled the gap between the first-generation Vampire and the RAF's Hunter day fighter and the Javelin night fighter, remaining in service with the RAF till 1962. Export success followed that of the Vampire, a number of countries taking up the option of acquiring a cheap, easily maintained jet fighter bomber. Indeed the Swiss Air Force took a licence for domestic production, building some 136 of the fighter bomber variant and did not finally retire their aircraft from first line duty until 1983. In all, some 1,431 Venoms were produced, greatly assisting the company and the nation's finances at a critical period.

With their Venom design thus making a useful contribution to the RAF, de Havilland had, in 1946, begun design of a powerful, twin-engined aircraft capable of supersonic flight. The DH.110 would earn enduring notoriety due to its aerial disintegration during its showcasing at the 1952 SBAC Farnborough Display, leading to the deaths not only of its crew, but of numerous members of the viewing public. But despite this tragedy, the DH.110 would enter production for the Royal Navy as a successful all-weather fighter named the Sea Vixen FAW.1 which would provide all weather fighter protection to the fleet until 1972. Like the Javelin, with which it had been in competition during the early days of the F.44/46 specification, the Sea Vixen was a big aircraft. As with its company predecessors, it featured a twin boom tail layout, with power being derived from twin Rolls-Royce Avon 200 series engines giving transonic performance. Armament comprised air-to-air guided missiles, a first for the Royal Navy, though the aircraft could also be used in the ground attack role. The Sea Vixen remained in service until replaced by the McDonnell Douglas Phantom II, some 145 being built, and was viewed in service as a successful aircraft, though somewhat long in the tooth at its retirement.

Heretofore, the trend of the second-generation fighter aircraft, not only in the UK but globally, had been one of ever-increasing weight and complexity. In the UK, this trend would be exemplified by the English Electric P.1B Lightning, a third-generation supersonic fighter armed with air-to-air missiles. The second-generation aircraft in the UK were all following the same upward trajectory, as the Air Ministry's desire to fit ever more equipment into airframes with greater endurance was inevitably met with larger airframes. However, several aircraft designers, not least in the UK, realised that the trend was capable of reversal to produce a simple, lightweight, low-cost fighter that might prove attractive to air arms unable to afford the increasing cost and complexity of industry's output. The main proponent of this thinking in the UK was none other than W.E.W. Petter, ironically the chief designer at English Electric under whom the P.1 Lightning supersonic fighter prototype would be evolved.

Folland

Leaving English Electric in later 1949, Petter soon found employment with the small Folland Aircraft Ltd at Hamble near Southampton under Henry Folland, soon to retire. Petter joined as deputy Managing Director in 1950 but on Folland's retirement shortly after, took on the role of Managing Director. Work soon began on the design of a lightweight fighter, the Fo.139 Midge, to be powered initially by the Armstrong Siddeley (later Bristol) Viper engine producing 1,640lb thrust, construction work starting in 1953, the completed prototype arriving at Boscombe Down in August 1954. Its first flight at the hands of Squadron Leader 'Ted' Tennant was successful, the aircraft being soon flown to Chilbolton, where Folland had established their Flight Development department. The Folland Midge had a wing span of 20.33ft and a length of 29.25ft. Powered by the AS. Viper Mk.V, producing 1,640lb thrust, the aircraft was transonic in a shallow dive, a maximum permissible Mach number of 0.95 IMN being allowed. Weighing just 3,455lb, the Midge augured well for its developed offspring, the Fo.141 Gnat fighter.

Work on the Gnat proceeded quickly under Petter's rather autocratic regime, the first aircraft being rolled out in June 1955. The Gnat was larger than the Midge but not by a great deal: wing span was 24ft and length 31ft 9in. Power was now provided by a Bristol Orpheus 101 giving 4,520lb thrust for a total empty weight of 5,560lb. Limiting Mach number was now raised to M1.3 with a maximum level speed of M0.95. Armament would be two 30mm cannon

Folland Gnat F.1 XK741 at Dunsfold c.1961.

mounted in the air intake lips. First flight was on 18 July 1955 in the hands of 'Ted' Tennant. Although the RAF did not have a place for the Gnat in its inventory, the Air Staff were sufficiently interested to place an order for six Folland Gnat F.1 pre-production aircraft for assessment. Sadly for Petter, and Folland Aircraft Ltd, no RAF order was forthcoming though small orders were placed by several countries, including India, which would also licence-build the Gnat.

By the mid-50s, a replacement for the obsolete Vampire trainer aircraft in RAF service was well overdue. While the weapon training requirement would be covered by T.7 Hunters, the need was for an aircraft able to allow ab-initio training on jets for the new pilots entering the RAF. Folland looked to their Gnat as the basis for an airframe capable of fulfilling the trainer requirement and schemed an enlarged aircraft with tandem seating, the resulting aircraft being just 9in longer than the fighter variant, but with a wing of greater span. The resulting design met with favour at the Air Ministry and an order for a batch of fourteen Fo.144 Gnat trainers (eight development and six pre-production aircraft) was received in March 1958, the first aircraft flying in August 1959. But a production order was not forthcoming; rumour and speculation at Folland equating this with presumed pressure from Government to persuade the company of the sense in being absorbed into the Hawker Siddeley Group as part of the

Government's current craze for rationalisation in the aircraft industry. While this was partly correct, in fact, the company's financial position was not strong and Petter, realising that changes would have to be made, entered negotiations with the Hawker Siddeley Group which resulted in the company becoming a member of that Group while Petter retired to Switzerland.

Eventually, with the takeover of Folland Aircraft agreed, an order for thirty Gnat T.1 aircraft powered by a single Orpheus engine rated at 4,400lb thrust was received in February 1960 with further orders for twenty aircraft in July 1961 and forty-one aircraft in 1962. While this was good news for Hamble, where the aircraft would be constructed, it meant the closure of Folland's flight development centre at Chilbolton, the work being transferred to the Hawker Aircraft Ltd site at Dunsfold where the majority of the flight testing and future development work would take place. A total of 105 trainers was built, remaining in service with the RAF until replaced by HSA Hawk in the mid-1970s.

Of all of the aircraft projects described above, it was really only the Swift with which the Hunter was in direct competition and which at one stage threatened to oust Hunter as the Air Ministry's preferred aircraft. However, various Hawker proposals were schemed against F.44/46 – P.1056 and P.1057 – though just how serious Camm was in trying to secure these projects is unclear. The specification was ultimately withdrawn and replaced by F.4/48, the Gloster Javelin fulfilling the requirement for the RAF and the de Havilland Sea Vixen for the Royal Navy. Supermarine did though obtain a consolation prize in the shape of the Scimitar which gave the Royal Navy a rather more potent fighter than Hawker's diminutive Sea Hawk which it replaced in service.

Chapter 12

Future Hawker Projects

P.1083

In August 1950, the Directorate of Operational Requirements within the Air Ministry (DOR/C) had carried out an assessment of the likely performance of the P.1067 (or F.3, short form of F3/48, as it was termed within DOR), particularly when flown against the new Soviet fighters. In a note to the Ministry of Supply, DOR stated that 'although the F.3 was superior to the MiG-15, the margin was not outstanding. The MiG-15 was already in service and presumably was capable of some improvement. The Air Staff were therefore interested in any plans the Ministry of Supply might have for developing the F.3.'[1]

As it happened, the Air Ministry was knocking at an open door; even as the design that would become the Hunter was in its earliest stages, ideas for its development were being discussed in Kingston's Project Office. In September 1948, the Hawker investigation into a transonic design bearing the project code P.1069 was forwarded to PDSR. This retained features of P.1067 as it then stood, with nose air intake and tailplane mounted low on the fin, but with 50 degree sweep on the wings and alternative engines – Avon or Sapphire – both with 20 per cent reheat. This was followed the next month by P.1071; a similar P.1067 design with reheated Avon but with the addition of a 2,000lb thrust rocket in the tail. A preliminary visit by DOR to Hawker in May 1950 had resulted in initial discussions on such a project which would feature a wing sweep of 50 degrees to facilitate supersonic speeds in level flight, with a note being written up the following month on the project, now coded P.1083.

Following discussions with RAE on 31 May 1951 a technical brochure was submitted by the company to DMARD showing a development of the F3/48 design with 50 degree swept wing and AS Sapphire engine. In November 1951, serious work in the design and stress offices at Hawker Aircraft on the P.1083 began while the following month on the 10th, at a conference at the Air Ministry, it was agreed that the proposed further development of the F.3/48 should go ahead.

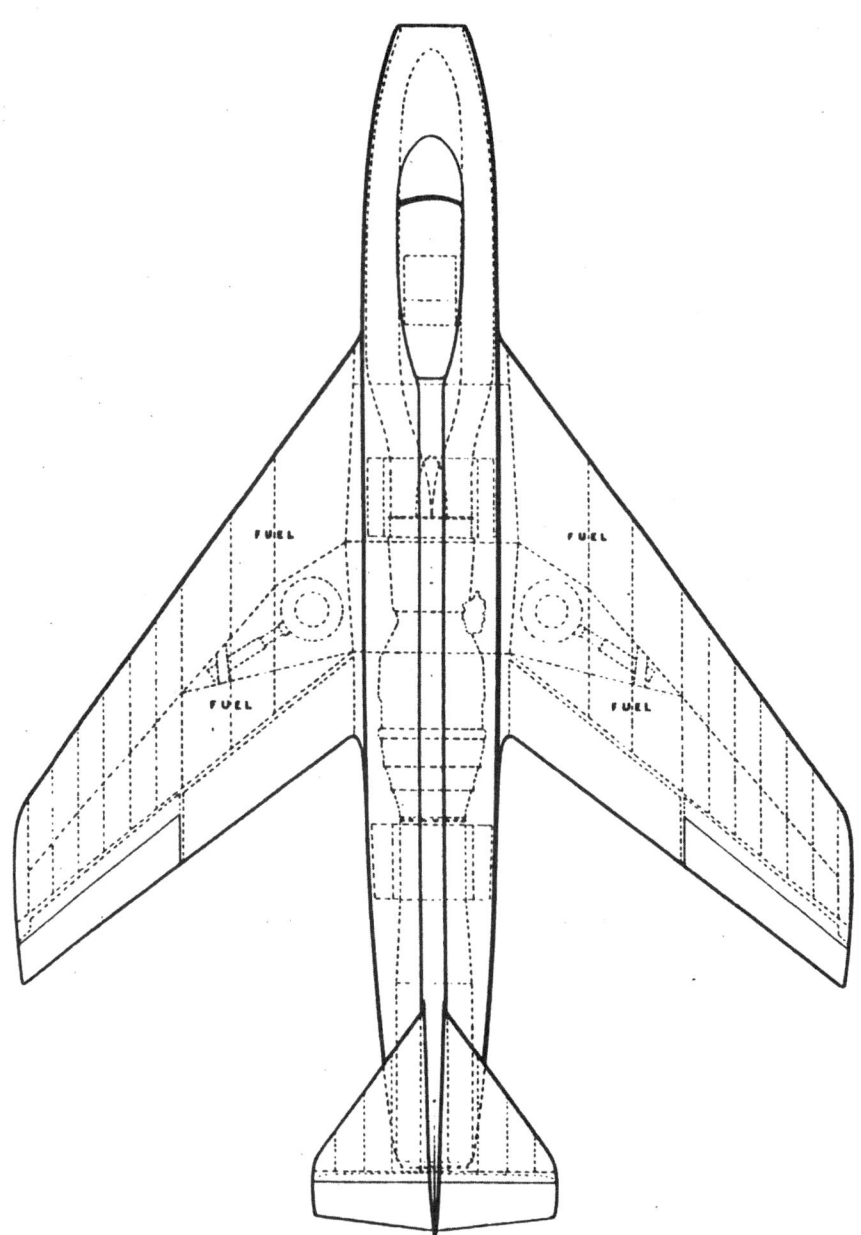

HAWKER TRANSONIC AEROPLANE
ROLLS ROYCE 'AVON' ENGINE
ALTERNATIVE POWER UNITS :-
ROLLS ROYCE 'AVON' WITH 20 % RE-HEAT
ARMSTRONG SIDDELEY 'SAPPHIRE' WITH 20 % RE-HEAT

P.1069 general arrangement showing pitot type intake to a reheated engine, 50 degree wing sweepback and low mounted delta tailplane.

Future Hawker Projects 199

The Air Staff felt that the need to develop this aircraft was important. The Hunter would be superior to the MiG-15, but not necessarily to a developed MiG-15, or a new Russian fighter. In addition, although the Hunter was adequate against the current bomber threat it would need maximum possible performance against a jet bomber threat which might soon arise.

The Air Ministry was right to be worried. The following year, the first flight of the Tupolev Tu-95 (NATO code Bear) occurred. This swept-wing bomber was powered by turboprop engines, giving a useful performance of 520mph, a range of over 8,000 miles at an altitude of 45,000ft. In 1953, the Soviet Union flew its first pure jet bomber, the Myasishchev M-4 (NATO coded name Bison), a swept-wing jet with a range of some 3,000 miles, a top speed of 588mph at an altitude of 36,000ft.[2]

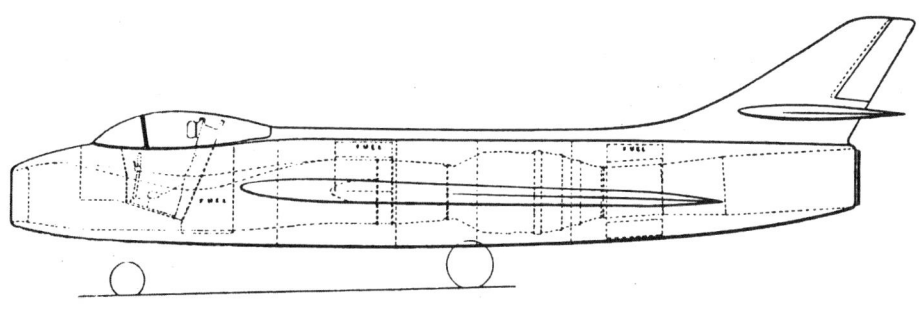

SPAN 25 FT. 9 INS.   WING AREA GROSS 235 SQ.FT.
LENGTH 36 FT. 6 INS.   ANGLE OF SWEEPBACK 50°
FUEL CAPACITY 300 GALLS

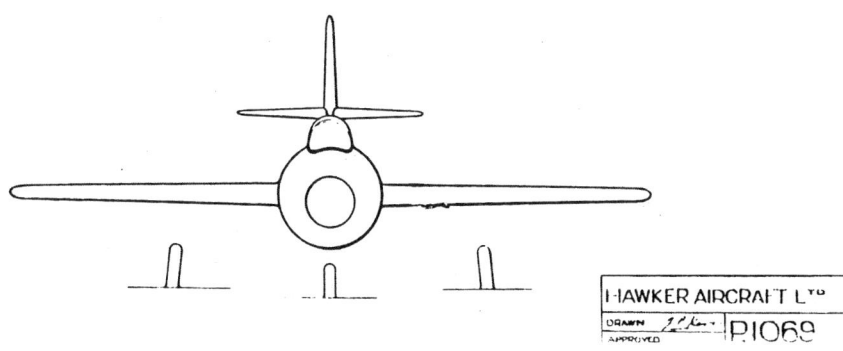

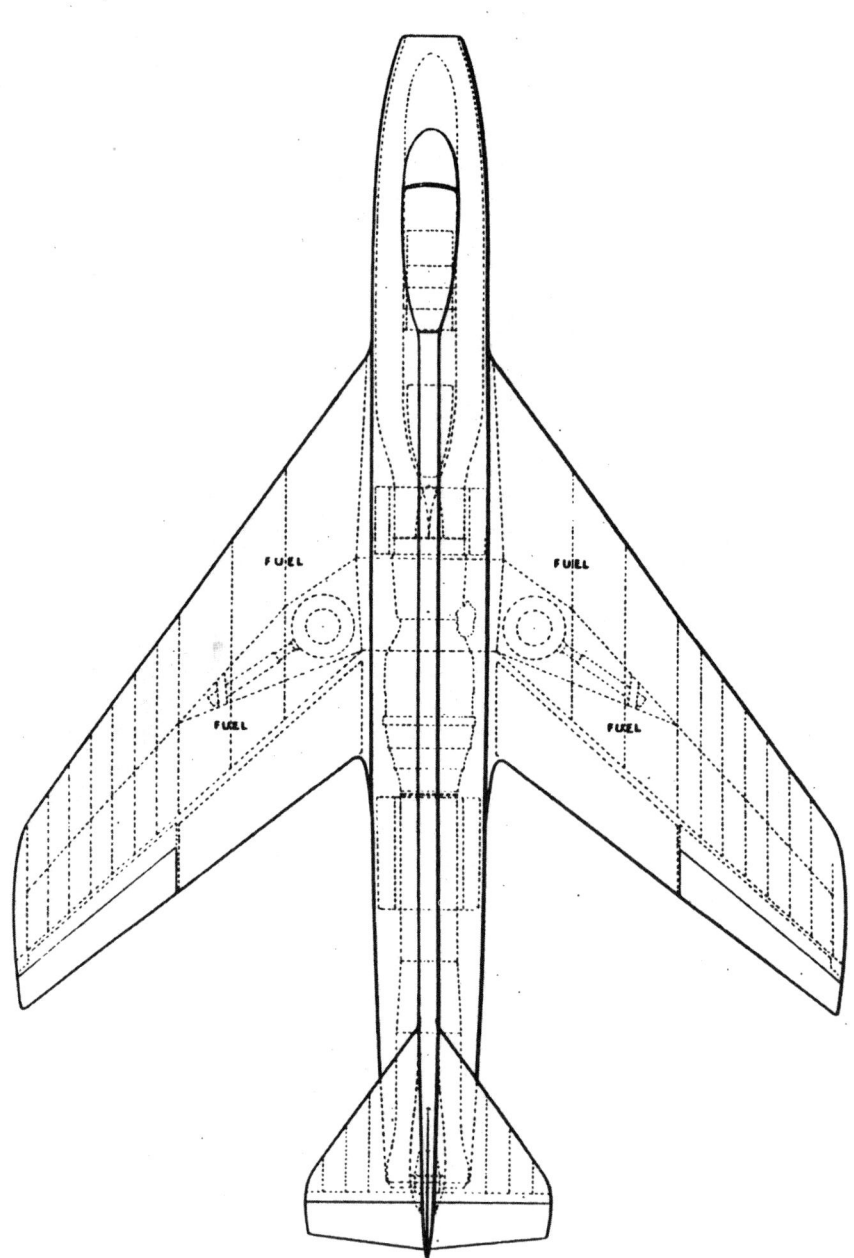

HAWKER TRANSONIC AEROPLANE
ROLLS ROYCE 'AVON' ENGINE WITH 20% RE-HEAT AND
2000 LB ROCKET UNIT
WITH ARMAMENT

P.1071 general arrangement as per the P.1069 but with the addition of armament and AS Snarler type rocket motor in the tail.

Future Hawker Projects 201

With agreement that the Hunter should be developed without delay, on 26 February 1952 the Hawker RTO wrote to the company with arrangements for manufacture of the 50 degree development of F3/48, leading on 18 April to the receipt of a draft specification for P.1083.

Notwithstanding the brochure suggestion of the development aircraft being fitted with an Armstrong Siddeley engine, on 15 May Messrs Herd and Kerry visited Kingston to discuss installation of the more powerful Rolls-Royce RA.14 with reheat capability into P.1083. While this was entirely feasible, Hawker

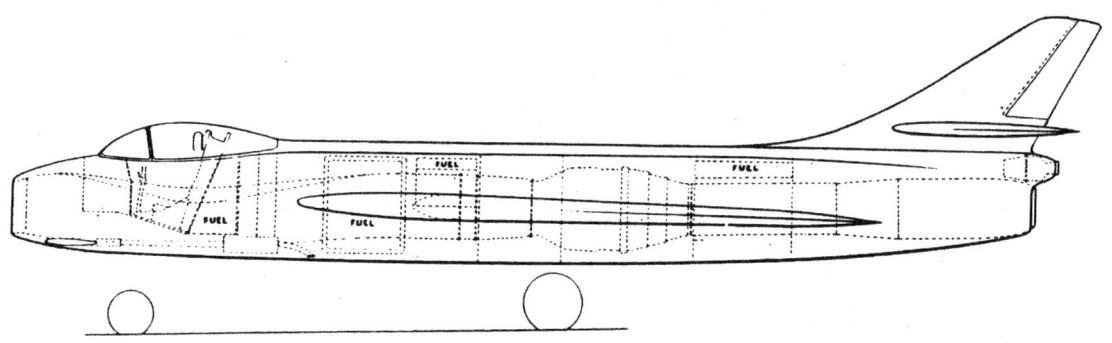

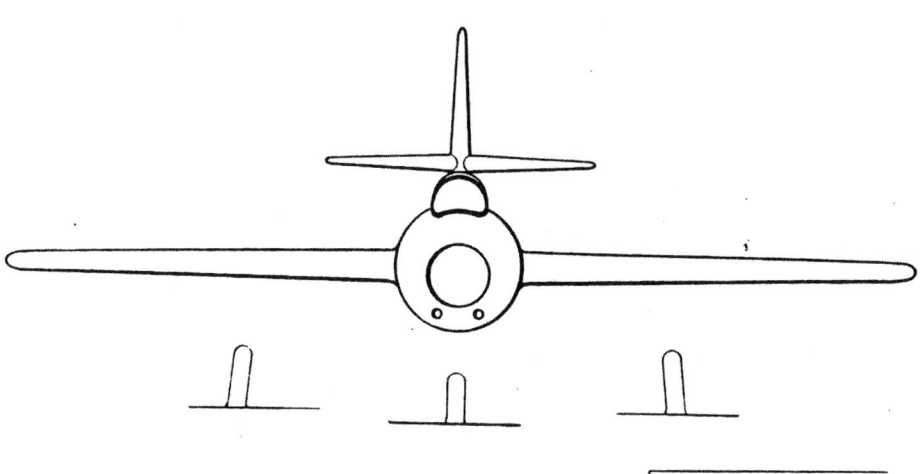

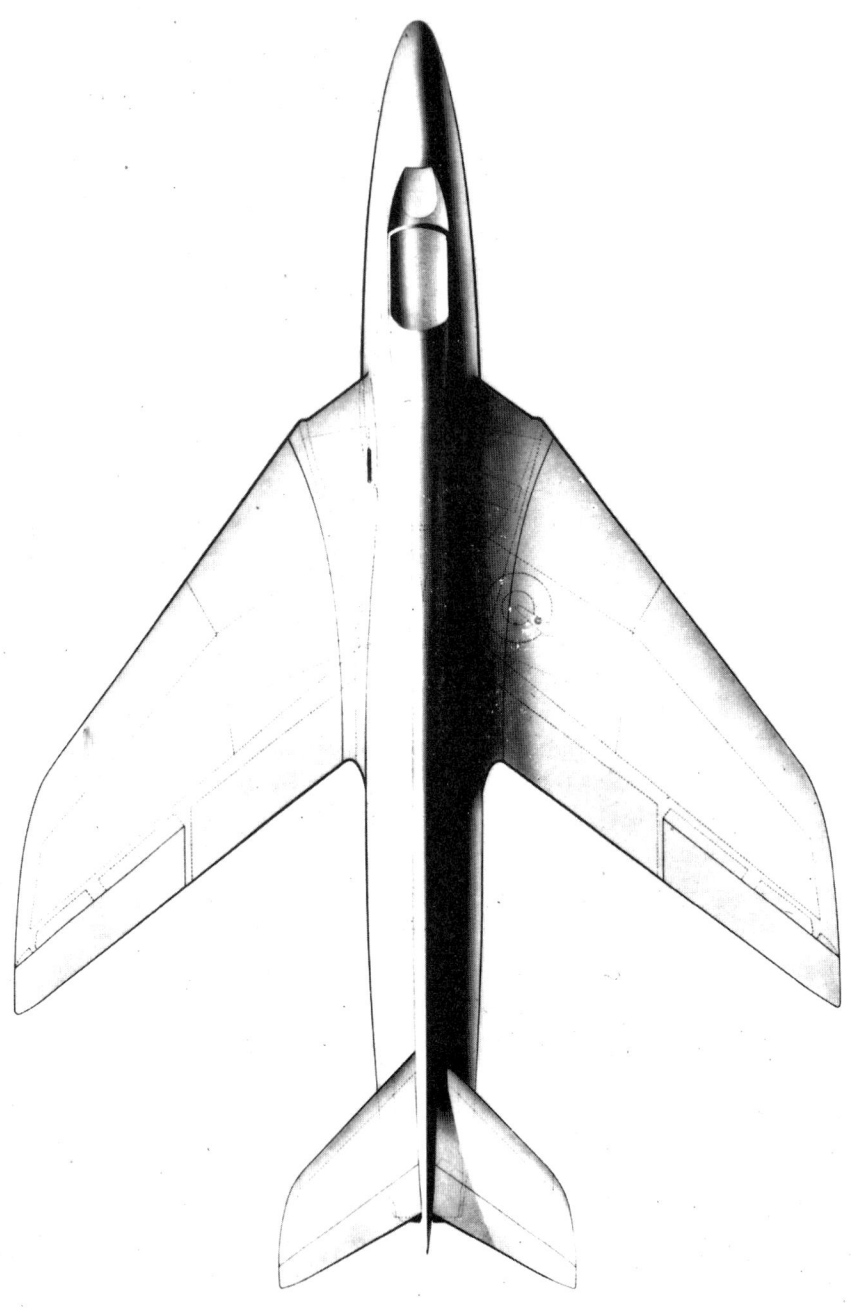

HAWKER F.3/48 FIGHTER
WITH 50° SWEEPBACK
ROLLS ROYCE 'AVON' ENGINE

P.1083 general arrangement showing reversion to Hunter style but with 50 degree sweep to the wings. Note that only two cannon are featured and fuel capacity has increased to 400 gallons.

Design was concerned that such an installation would require rather more fuel than presently available and with the existing airframe, space for this addition could not easily be found. At a further meeting with Air Ministry and DOR Staff in June 1952, held to discuss the development programme, the MoS representatives disagreed with Hawker's estimate of July 1953 for first flight of P.1083 and opined that due to the conflict between Hunter and Sea Hawk production, the company would be in 'production difficulties for at least twelve months. They thought the developed Hunter could be delivered off production during the summer of 1955' – less than the good news that DOR was looking for.

With specification F.119D being issued in August 1952 to cover the project prototype, in October metal was cut for the first time for P.1083 when construction of the wings was begun in the Experimental Department at Kingston-upon-

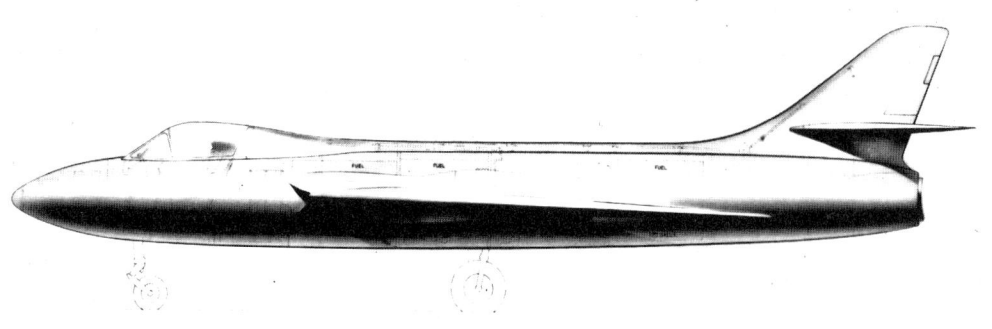

SPAN - 31 FT. 0.INS   WING AREA GROSS - 340 SQ.FT.
O/A LENGTH - 45FT. 3 INS   ANGLE OF SWEEPBACK - 50° (¼ CHORD)
FUEL CAPACITY - 400 GALLONS   2 - 30 ⁒ ADEN GUNS 200 ROUNDS EACH

SCALE ¹⁄₂₄

HAWKER AIRCRAFT LIMITED
P. 1083

Thames, the aircraft being allocated serial WN470 and ordered under contract 6/Aircraft/6296/CB.7b. A mock-up was also constructed and on 15 February 1953, a mock-up of the Rolls-Royce Avon RA.14R engine was installed, but as noted earlier, Hawker was now struggling to find space for the additional fuel required for the reheat version of the Avon engine.

At about this time, it was clear that all was not well with the basic Hunter and the various shortcomings requiring rectification prior to entry into service. It became apparent to the Air Staff that This unsatisfactory state of affairs on the existing Hunter was an indication of the difficulties which confronted the Hunter Development, quite apart from the aerodynamic changes involved in fitting a larger engine (also reheated) and the complication attendant on the fitting of guided missiles (Blue Jay). It therefore seemed clear that the Hunter Development must be virtually a new aircraft and was unlikely to be available to the Service within two years after the first Hunter, as originally planned. Because of the delays inherent in getting the developed machine into service and the additional costs that Hawker was now highlighting (£130,000), the conclusion within DOR was that, to allow Hawker to concentrate on clearing the Hunter F.1 for service, 'the Hunter Development should be cancelled in favour of the Swift Development which was scheduled for introduction into the Service in 1956'.

This proposal was submitted and discussed at a meeting under the chairmanship of DCAS on 29 May 1953, a decision being made that 'the Hunter Development (Hawker P.1083) should be cancelled, and reliance placed on the development of the Swift (which must be tailored to take Blue Jay)'. Ironically, while it looked like Swift had stolen a march over Hunter, the Swift Development was itself cancelled in late 1954. It was therefore in complete ignorance that Hawker Aircraft hosted a visit on 10 June 1953 by Air Commodore Silyn-Roberts (Directorate of Operational Requirements – DOR) and Air Commodore Wallace Kyle (Dept of Military Aircraft Research and Development – DMARD) at Dunsfold to discuss with Hawker the application of larger engines to the P.1067 Hunter. Quite what was said is unknown, but shortly after this meeting, on the 22nd of the month, Silyn-Roberts and Kyle were back, this time with Air Vice Marshal Tuttle (Comptroller of Supplies, Air – CS/A) to break the news that P.1083 was no longer required, progress with larger engines being such that required thrust would be available without reheat and, on 13 July, the company was officially notified of the cancellation of the P.1983 requirement, Tuttle stating in August that the company should now proceed with a large engine non-reheat version of the Hunter.

Such a design was duly begun under the project code P.1099, featuring the Hunter with the uprated RA.14 Avon engine, though a revised brochure was sent out in September 1953 to Woodward-Nutt, perhaps illustrating the P.1083 with the dry Avon engine, without reheat. With the P.1083 aircraft 80 per cent complete, all work stopped but the front and centre fuselage sections were retained and formed the basis of what would become the Hunter F.6 with the 200 series Avon engine rated at 10,500lb thrust, the prototype P.1099 being serialled XF833. Thus, the UK's chance of possessing a supersonic fighter in its inventory would have to wait till the 1960s and the advent of the English Electric Lightning.

The P.1067 Hunter would spawn a number of different marks and design derivatives over the period 1948–53 in an effort to increase the performance of the Hunter still further. P.1076, of 1949, was an investigation of the potentialities of the P.1067 design for further development, but work stopped at an early stage. P.1090, first schemed in August 1951, was based on the P.1083 Hunter design but with the Avon replaced by the de Havilland Gyron with reheat, the air intakes being enlarged to cater for the greater power of this engine which would have produced a formidable supersonic interceptor. Another investigation schemed was to apply a delta wing to the Hunter under project P.1091 of October 1951 in conjunction with Avro, schemed by John Fozard, to produce a tailless delta powered by AS Sapphire 4 with reheat of some 8,000lb dry, the leading edge angle of sweep being 60 degrees. Although this would give only transonic performance, the wing should have allowed a significant increase in fuel capacity though only 420 gallons was specified.

In June 1952, project P.1095 investigated the application of larger engines to the P.1083 Hunter airframe, the AS Sapphire 4 and the RR Avon RA.14 with 2,000k degree reheat but did not proceed beyond initial scheming, the fitting of a larger dry engine under P.1099 superseding it. While the Project Office was busy attempting to develop the Hunter theme, it was also more than happy to look to other design possibilities in a period of the 1950s when boundaries were being pushed and broken daily by aircraft companies.

P.1077

The P.1077 design, of July 1949, was described as a 'General Purpose' fighter with two Avon engines. This bald description obscured the remarkably futuristic design encompassed by the project number. A tailless, streamlined twin-seat fuselage of 55ft housed two Avon engines stacked above each other mounted

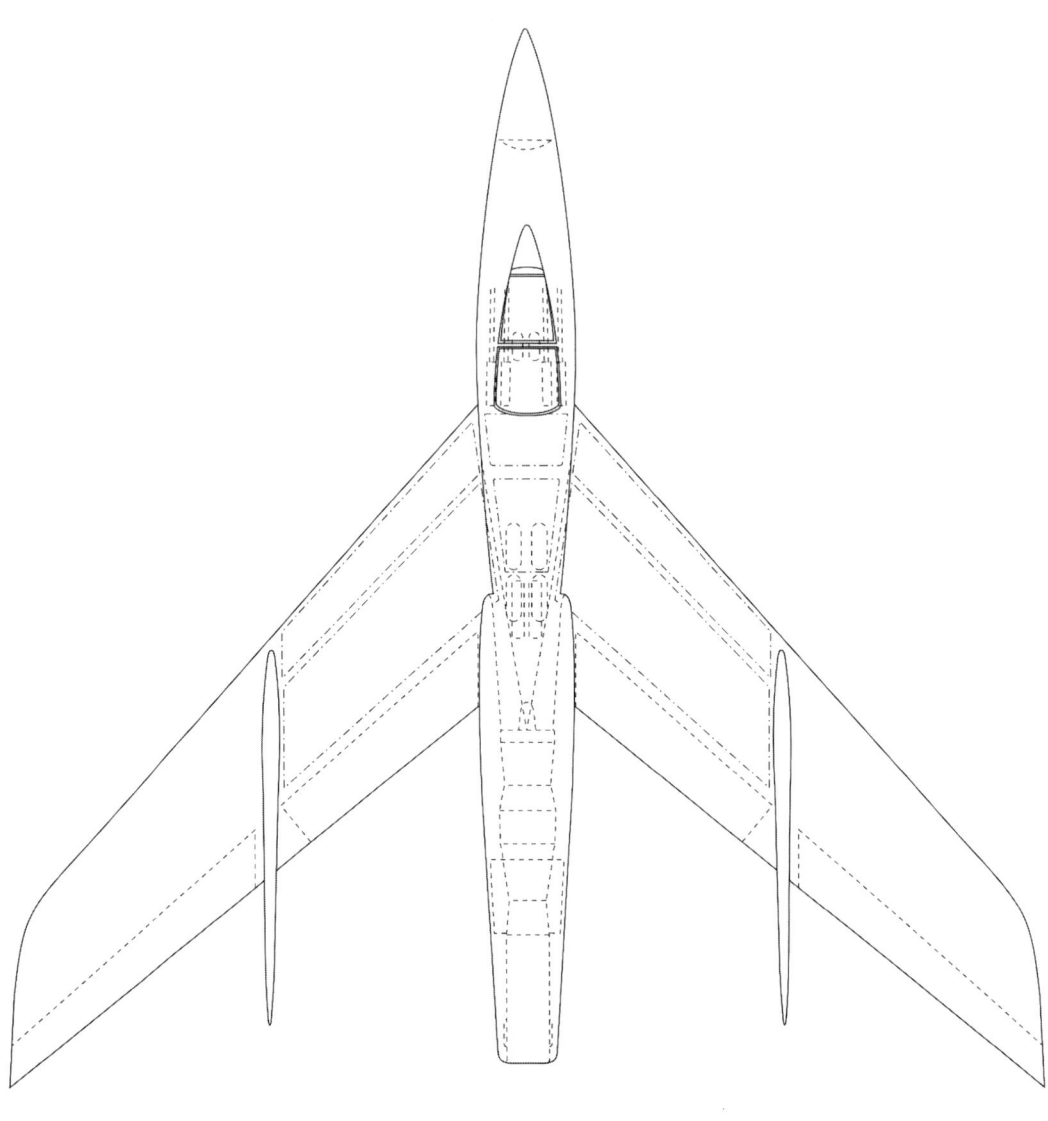

HAWKER P.1077 CP FIGHTER

P.1077 general arrangement. This very advanced concept featured a tailless streamlined twin-seat fuselage of 55ft housing two Avon engines stacked above each other mounted to the rear, and nose mounted radar dish. Wings spanning 58ft, swept at 45 degrees, supported large tail fins at mid-span separating the flaps and ailerons and extending both above and below the wing. A bicycle undercarriage allowed for a thin unencumbered wing without air intakes, these being mounted above and below the wing at mid-span.

to the rear, and a nose-mounted radar dish. Wings spanning 58ft, swept at 45 degrees, supported large tail fins at mid-span, separating the flaps and ailerons and extending both above and below the wing. A bicycle undercarriage allowed for a thin, unencumbered wing without air intakes, these being mounted above and below the wing at mid-chord. The aircraft would have had a fuel capacity of 1,000 gallons stored in wings and rear fuselage and a battery of four cannon mounted low, adjacent to the cockpit. The design appears to have some similarity to the Junkers EF128, a late war design that never reached construction. Hawker Project Office did have access to German designs which must have been a fertile source of new ideas.[3]

P.1088

The P.1088 of August 1951 was an altogether different approach to design for the Hawker Project Office. Designed as a single-seat light fighter, the result was diminutive, with a wing span of just 24ft and a length of 28ft. Slight sweep of 14 degrees on the leading edge resulted in a wing area of just 120 sq. ft. Air intakes mounted either side of the nose fed directly into twin Avon engines of 3,000lb thrust mounted at the front of the aircraft and exhausted on the fuselage sides under the high mounted wing. Strangely, the cockpit was mounted at the rear of the fuselage just in front of the sharply swept fin, topped with straight tail surfaces, and one has to wonder about the pilot's field of view when taking off and landing. A most unusual design that needless to say, did not proceed.[4]

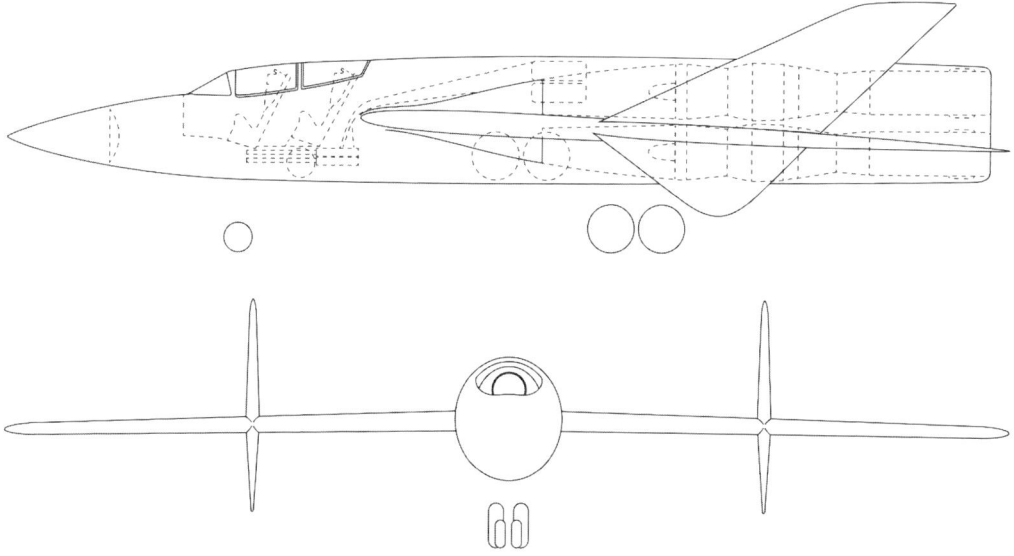

P.1089

This design dated August 1951 dispensed with turbojets and relied upon rocket power. Designed in response to F.124.T first issued in 1949 calling for a ramp-launched rocket fighter, the specification was amended to allow conventional undercarriage and mixed powerplant installations. Hawker's response to the proposal was a sleek single seat low wing semi-delta design powered by a single rocket motor producing 5,000lb thrust. A large, highly swept fin was the only tail surface while the undercarriage was conventional and retracted into the wing. No detail of the proposed armament is known, early drawings do not include this. Though other companies tendered for the project, Hawker do not appear to have done so; Bristol's 178, Avro's 720 and Saunders-Roe's SR.53 all offered similar approaches to the requirement, with Saunders Roe offering a mixed powerplant fighter with a design speed above Mach 2 which was actually built and test flown, though ultimately, the entire rocket interceptor concept would fall with the advent of the Sandys White Paper of 1957.[5]

While Hawker would continue to pursue various Hunter derivatives through the early 1950s, including the P.1100 supersonic Hunter powered by Avon RA.24 and 2 x 2,000lb rocket motors, and P.1102, a thin-winged Hunter; thoughts in the mind of Sydney Camm and the Projects Office were now turning to a completely new design to replace the Hunter which would progress through P.1103, P.1121 to P.1129, submitted to the contest that spawned TSR.2 – and we all know how that ended.

P.1092/P.1093

A design by John Fozard, P.1092 of November 1951 was an advanced design for a twin-seat supersonic delta all-weather fighter. Designed around a blended delta wing featuring leading edge sweep of 65 degrees and a span of 33ft, the aircraft would be powered by a Rolls-Royce Avon engine with 800 gallons of fuel and armed with the standard four Aden cannon armament in the wing leading edge adjacent to the air intakes. P.1093 of February 1952 was yet another scheme investigating the supersonic all weather delta interceptor, this time as a single seat fighter featuring nose air intake, with radar in centre body-fairing and powered by the Avon RA.14 or de Havilland Gyron, with 1,000 gallon fuel capacity. The wing was swept at 64 degrees on the leading edge and spanned 41ft, and housed the armament, now increased to six high-velocity cannon mounted in the wing root.[6]

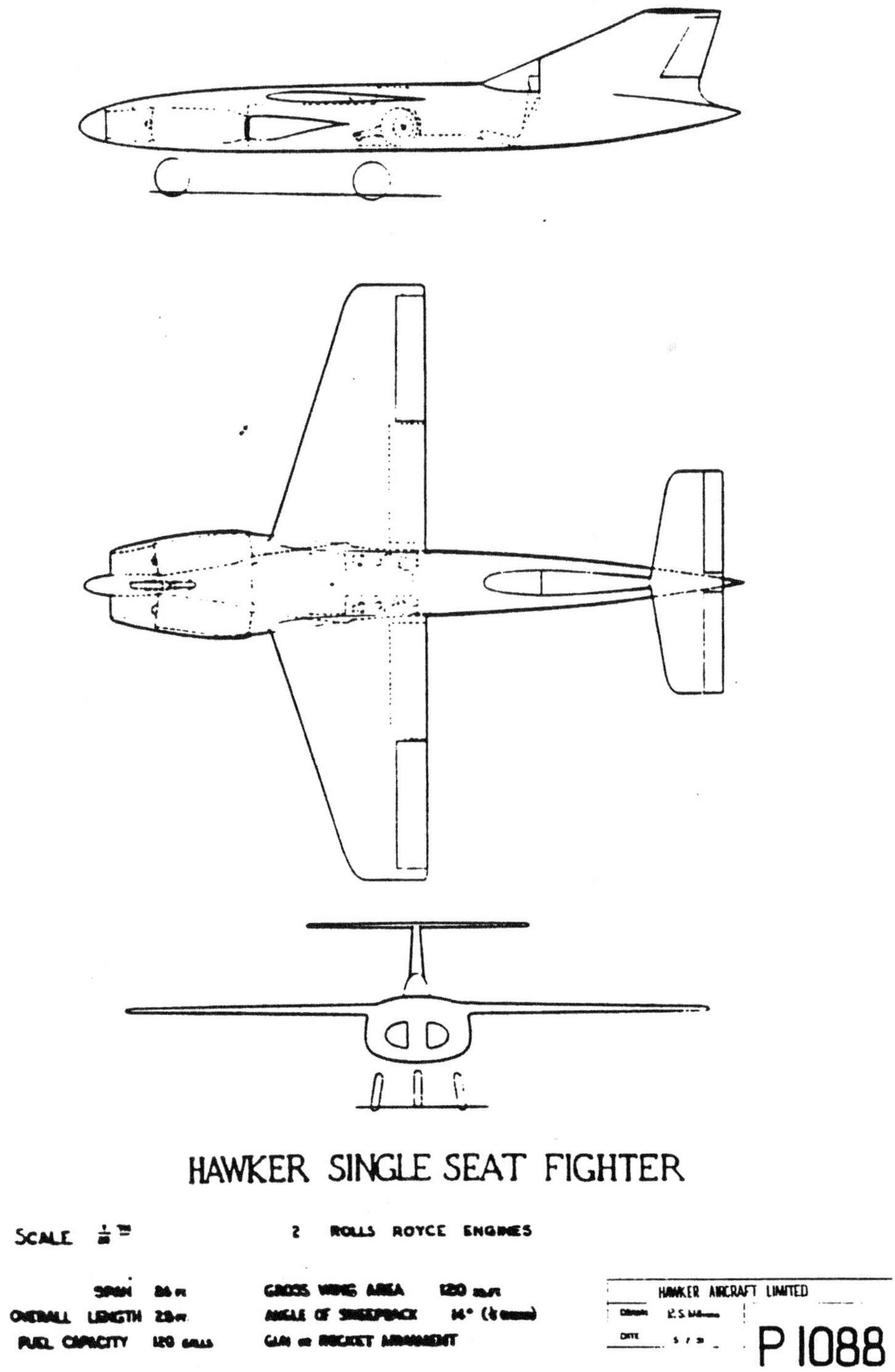

Future Hawker Projects   209

HAWKER SINGLE SEAT FIGHTER

SCALE ⅛" = 1'   2 ROLLS ROYCE ENGINES

SPAN   36 ft   GROSS WING AREA   120 sq ft
OVERALL LENGTH   29 ft   ANGLE OF SWEEPBACK   14° (¼ chord)
FUEL CAPACITY   120 galls   GUN or ROCKET ARMAMENT

HAWKER AIRCRAFT LIMITED

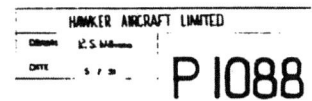

P.1088 general arrangement featuring straight tapered wing, two engines mounted in the nose, highly swept T-tail and strangely, the cockpit mounted to the rear just forward of the tail.

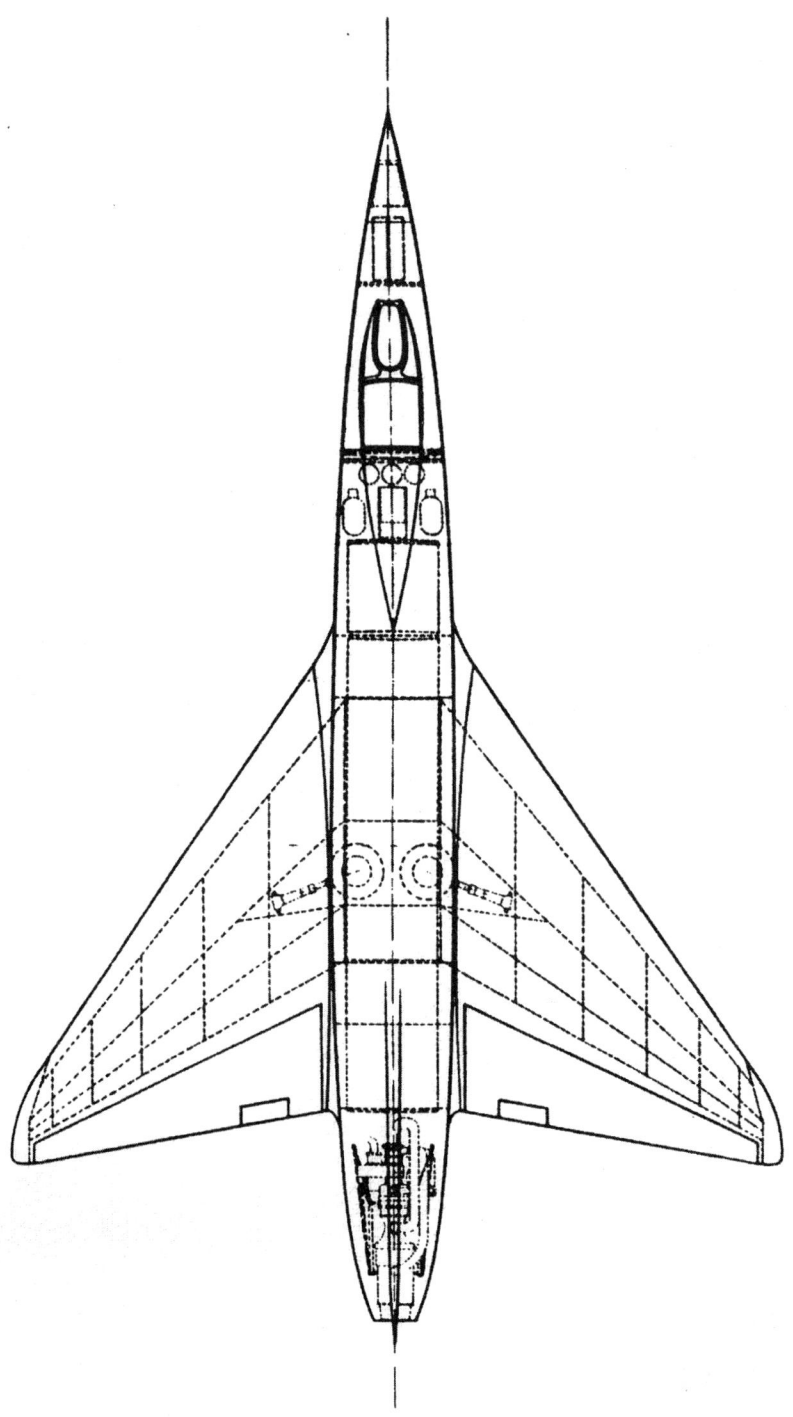

P.1089, a delta-wing rocket fighter with large tail designed to specification F.124.T.

P.1096/P.1097

P.1096 of May 1953 was schemed in response to ER.134T, which called for a research aircraft capable of sustained Mach 2 performance. Another Fozard design, this one featured a single-seat semi-delta high-wing layout swept at 56.5 degrees, and with additional tail surfaces mounted low on the fuselage. Power was to be supplied by a single RB.106 engine fed by intakes in the wing roots and fuselage-mounted airbrakes ahead and above the tailplane. The narrow track undercarriage retracted into the fuselage, while the nose leg retracted aft behind the cockpit. The P.1097 design offered a differing approach to layout. The semi-delta wing was replaced by a mid-set blended wing swept at 52 degrees, span increased from 33 to 35ft. Tail surfaces were moved from the low position to one atop the fin. Fuel capacity was increased from 650 to 800 gallons. The RB.106

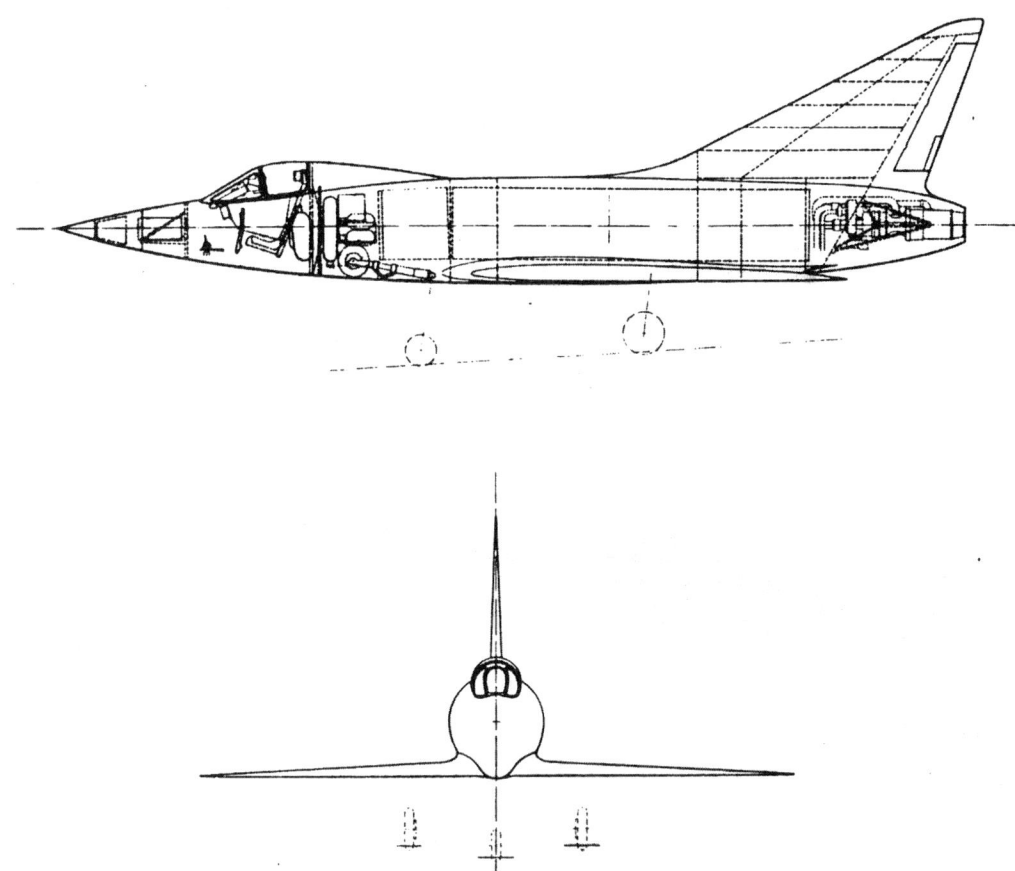

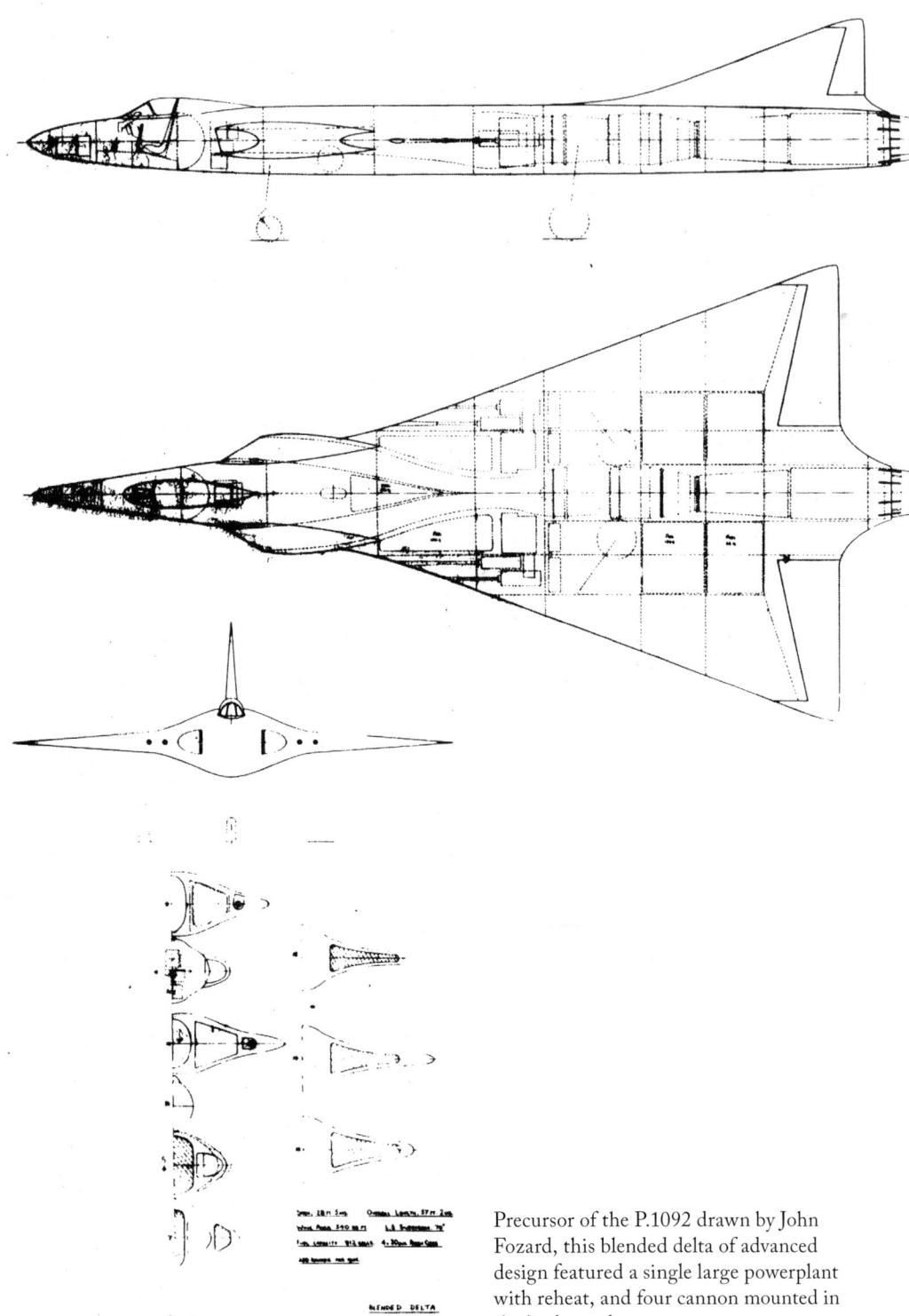

Precursor of the P.1092 drawn by John Fozard, this blended delta of advanced design featured a single large powerplant with reheat, and four cannon mounted in the leading edge.

Future Hawker Projects 213

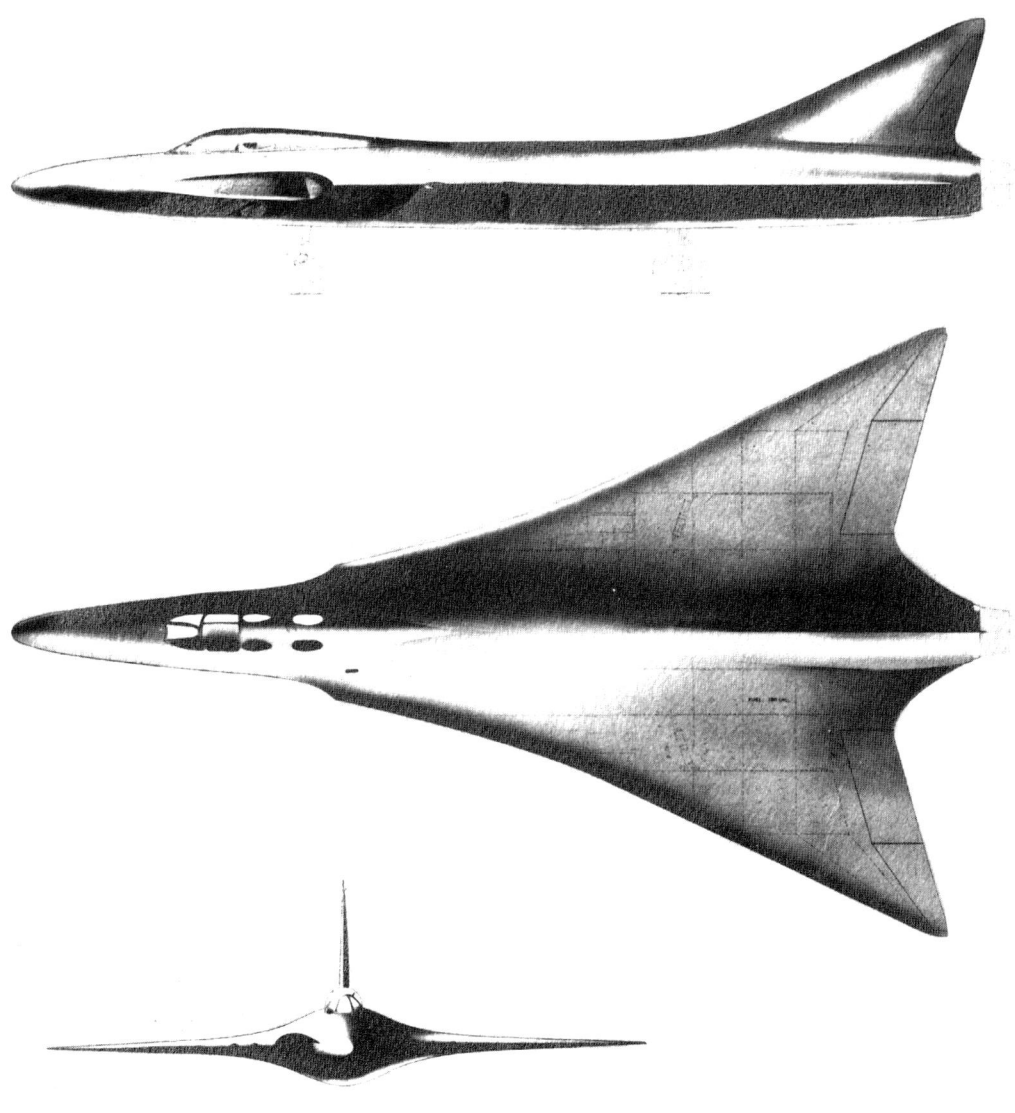

P.1092 general arrangement of this all-weather supersonic fighter was another Fozard creation of advanced design with wings swept at 65 degrees, single large Avon engine and four-gun battery in the leading edge.

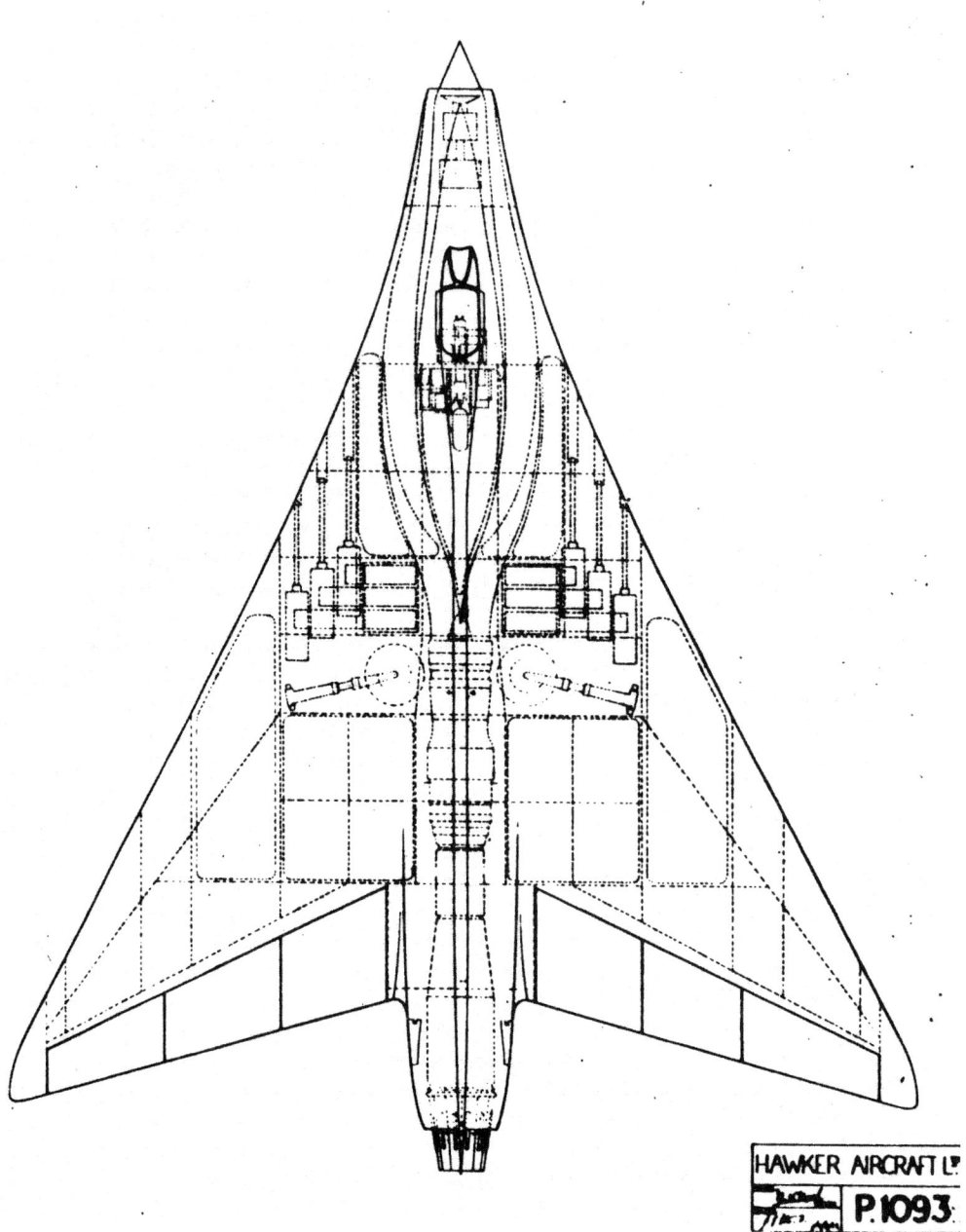

HAWKER SINGLE SEAT SUPERSONIC FIGHTER.

ROLLS ROYCE R.14 or De HAVILLAND GYRON ENGINE.

P.1093, a development of the P.1092, now with pitot intake in the nose and armament increased to six high velocity guns in the leading edge.

Future Hawker Projects   215

engine, comparable in size to the Avon but more powerful, offered thrust of up to 21,750lb but fell victim to the 1957 Defence White paper which cut all funding, the project being scrapped.[7]

P.1103/P.1121

No sooner had the prototype Hunter flown than Camm had directed the Project Office to begin a search for its successor. As early as 1951, as noted above, project P.1092/3 had been schemed for a delta-winged supersonic all-weather fighter in twin- and single-seat configurations, followed by P.1096, a

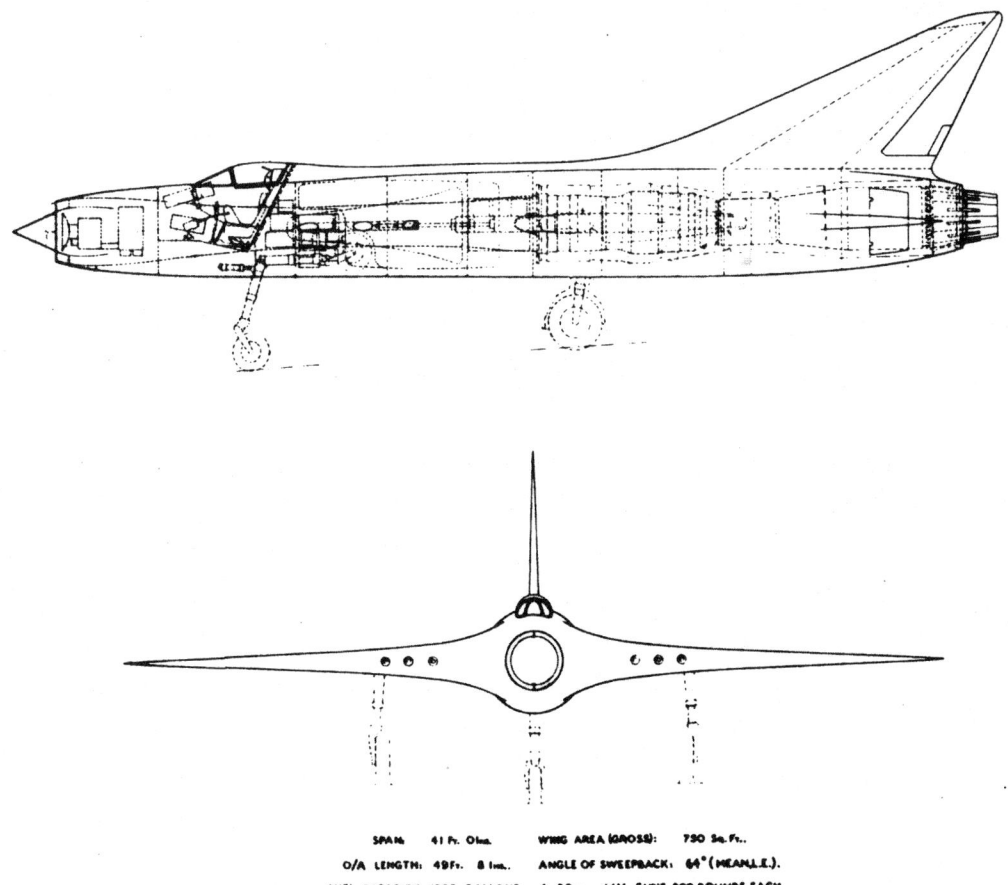

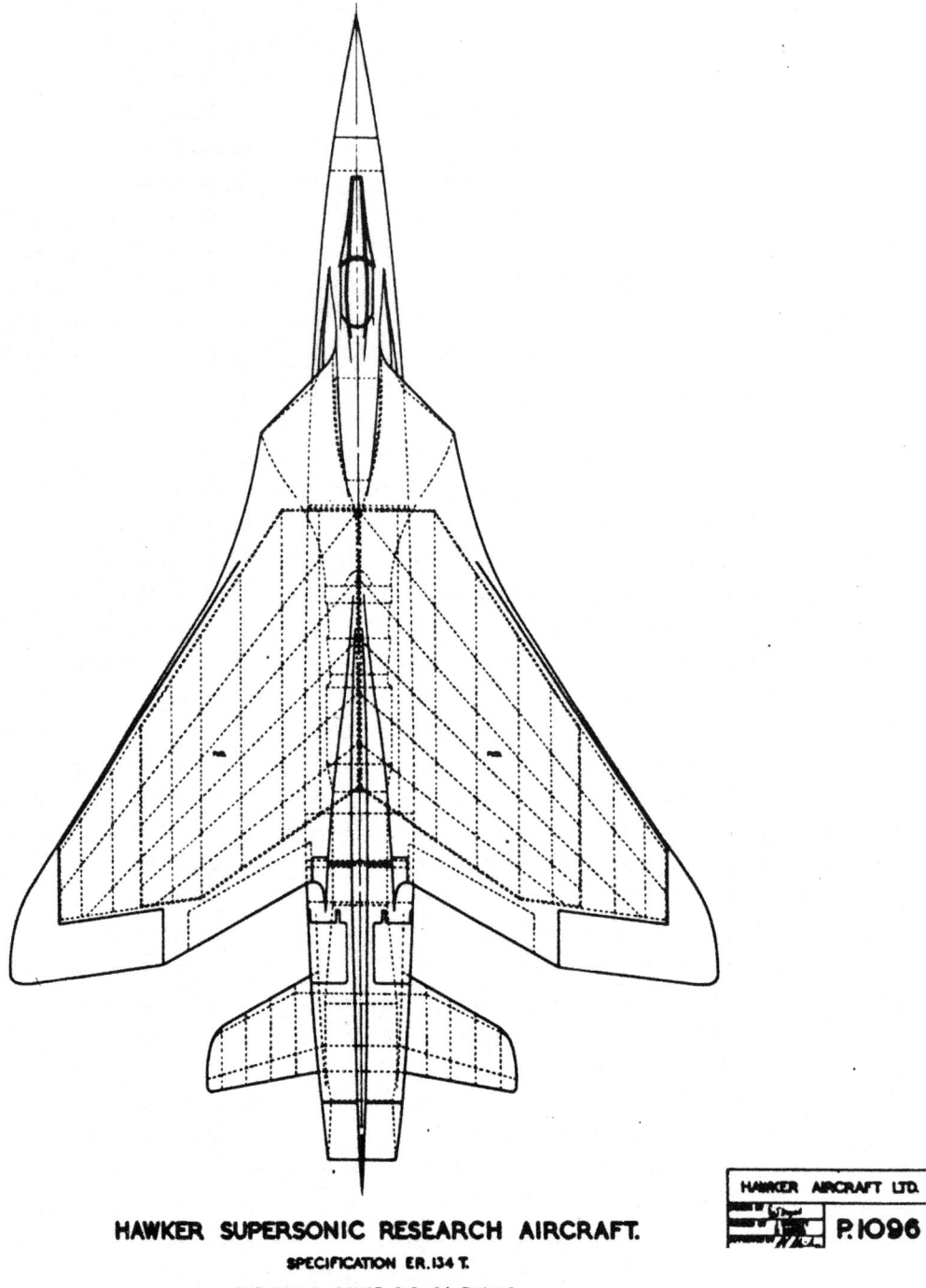

HAWKER SUPERSONIC RESEARCH AIRCRAFT.
SPECIFICATION ER.134 T.
ONE ROLLS-ROYCE R.B. 106 ENGINE.

HAWKER AIRCRAFT LTD. P.1096

P.1096, designed to specification ER.134T which called for a research aircraft capable of sustained Mach 2 performance.

highly swept supersonic research vehicle. The following year, P.1100 sought to achieve supersonic capability with a reconfigured Hunter powered by an Avon RA.24. In early 1954, following initial information on draft specification OR.329 becoming available to design offices, Hawker produced two designs that they felt would meet this specification – P.1103 and P.1104. These early studies were in the 'developed Hunter' fold, with twin crew requirement seen as necessary for the role and powered by a DH Gyron engine with reheat. By early 1955, with an official specification F.155T issued, concern about the ever-rising weight and size of the aircraft had seen P.1103 redrawn as a smaller single-seat design with ventral intake, Gyron Junior engine and rockets in the wing roots for additional thrust.[8]

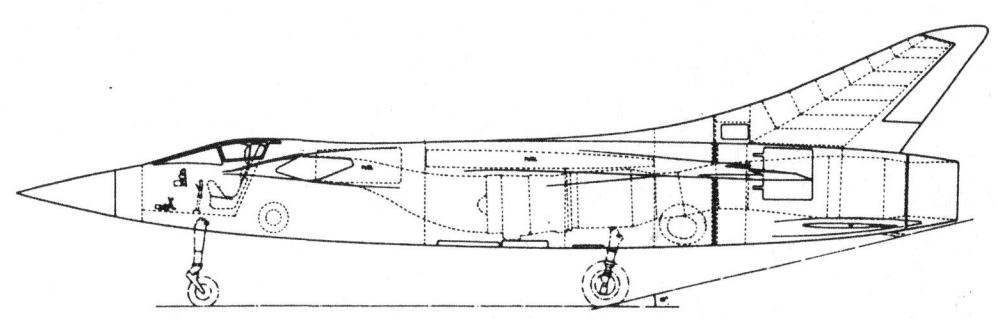

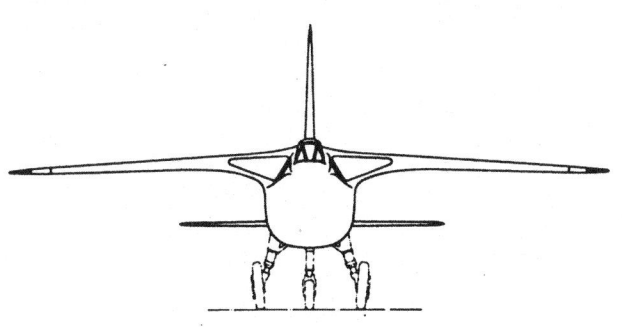

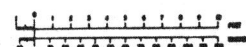

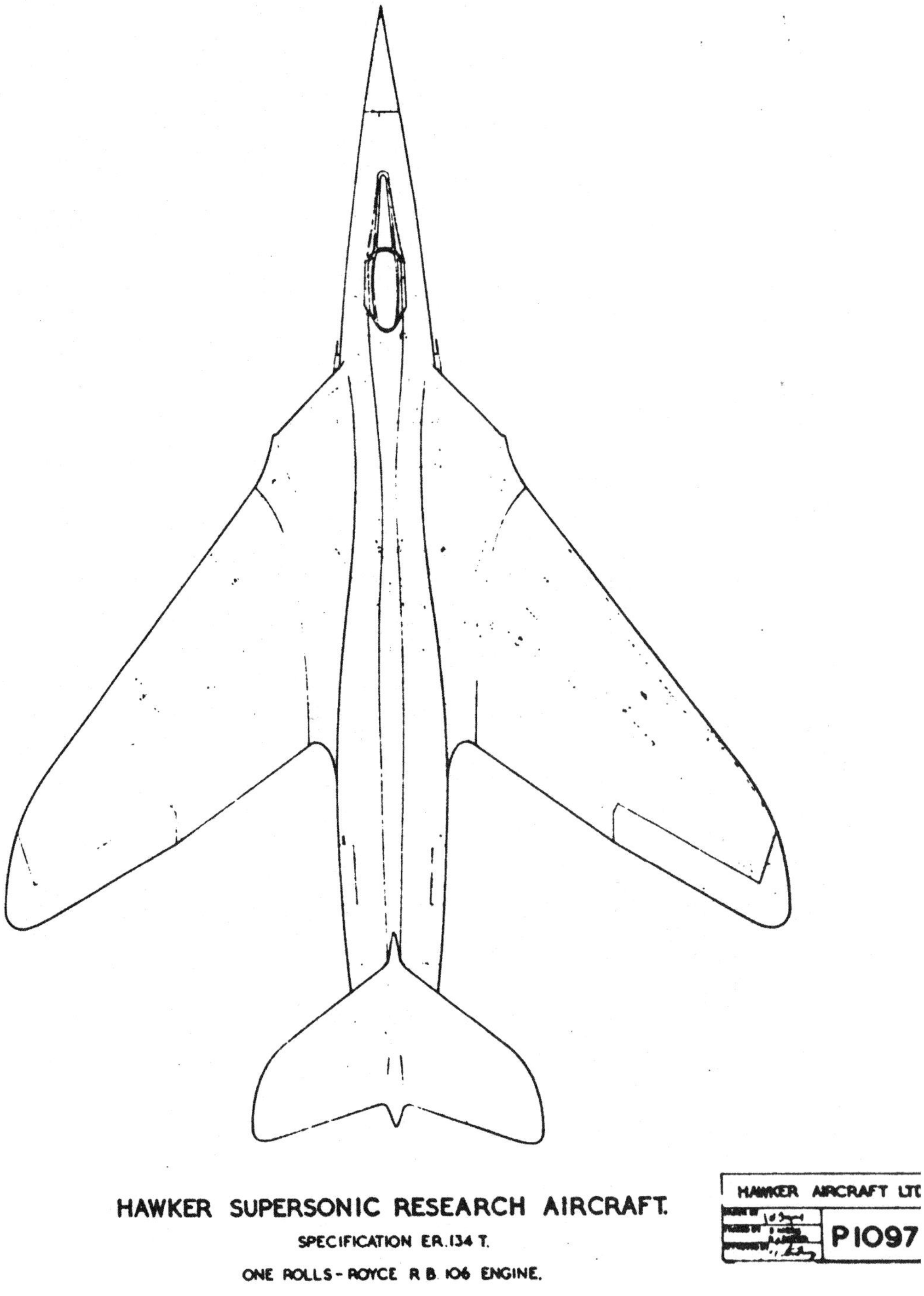
HAWKER SUPERSONIC RESEARCH AIRCRAFT.
SPECIFICATION ER.134 T.
ONE ROLLS-ROYCE R.B. 106 ENGINE.
HAWKER AIRCRAFT
P1097

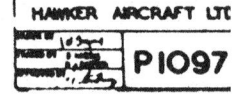

P.1097, developed from the P.1096 and now shown with highly swept T-tail, reduced wing sweep and increased fuel capacity.

By the summer, in the face of continually changing load-carrying requirements, Hawker's single-seat offering was already looking outmoded, and indeed Camm questioned industry's ability to fulfil the requirement. However, a revised issue of F.155T suggested that they were on the right track with changes aimed at reducing weight in the tendered designs and by September, Hawker had finalised its submission. The design submitted on 5 October 1955 featured a mid-wing aircraft with large ventral intake and Hunter-type tail, plus a 32-inch radar dish in a nose radome. Speed was expected to be Mach 2+ from a 25,000lb-thrust DH Gyron engine. With the requirement continuing to change within the Air Ministry, by December of that year Hawker's submission was out of the race, though the company was not officially informed until April 1956. While no submission had been accepted in its entirety, Fairey and Armstrong-Whitworth were selected for further development work, a sure sign that the Air Ministry was still unsure what it wanted.

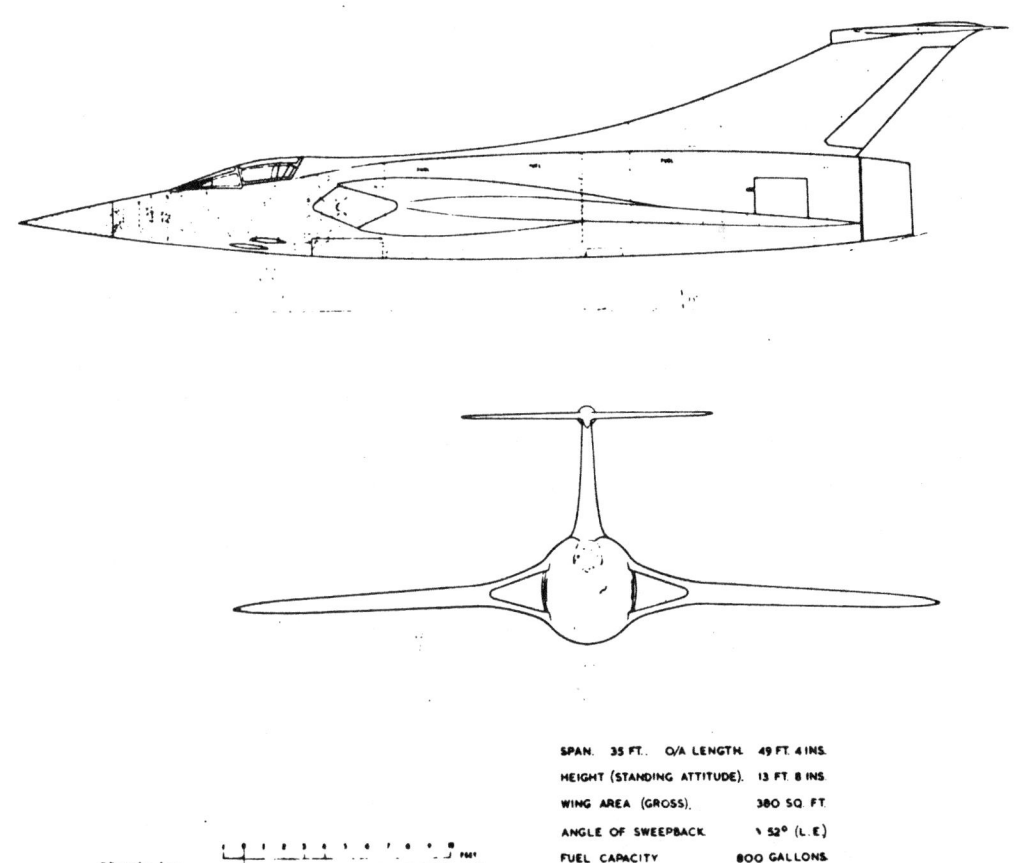

Far from being put out at this turn of events, Camm – believing he had support for his actions within the Air Ministry – set about reinventing the P.1103 design to fulfil a strike role for use in more limited war situations. By 16 May 1956 brochures were with the Air Ministry for a revised aircraft design under P.1116, which featured a similar aircraft but with smaller wing and nose, more akin to a direct Hunter replacement, and two fixed Aden cannon. Following lukewarm responses from the Ministry to this latest submission, design effort reverted to the P.1103 as a single-seat aircraft minus its wingtip missiles for use in the strike role, a brochure being submitted to the Ministry to this effect under the project code P.1121. Although some departments within the Ministry were averse to any further development of the design, others gave sufficient encouragement for Hawker to continue the work on a company funded basis and by July 1956, work was in hand for the construction of a full-sized mock-up in the Experimental shop at Kingston.[9]

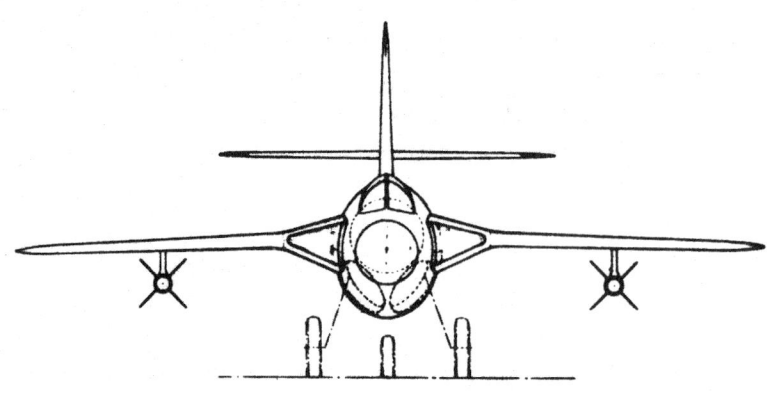

P.1103 general arrangement, the first thoughts on a Hunter replacement. Armament suggested as radar guided missiles and no cannon fitted. At the wing trailing edge root are suggestions of rocket boosters.

Future Hawker Projects 221

The amount of time and effort which Hawker was pouring into the design of P.1121 was a reflection of the fact that, in essence, the aircraft represented the company's future; there was no other sizeable project emanating from the Air Ministry, or within the Hawker Project Office, that offered the numbers of aircraft for manufacture that the success of the Hunter had suggested was possible and desirable. The decision of the Hawker board to countenance continued work on a privately funded basis reinforced the company belief that a sizeable contract might be within their grasp.

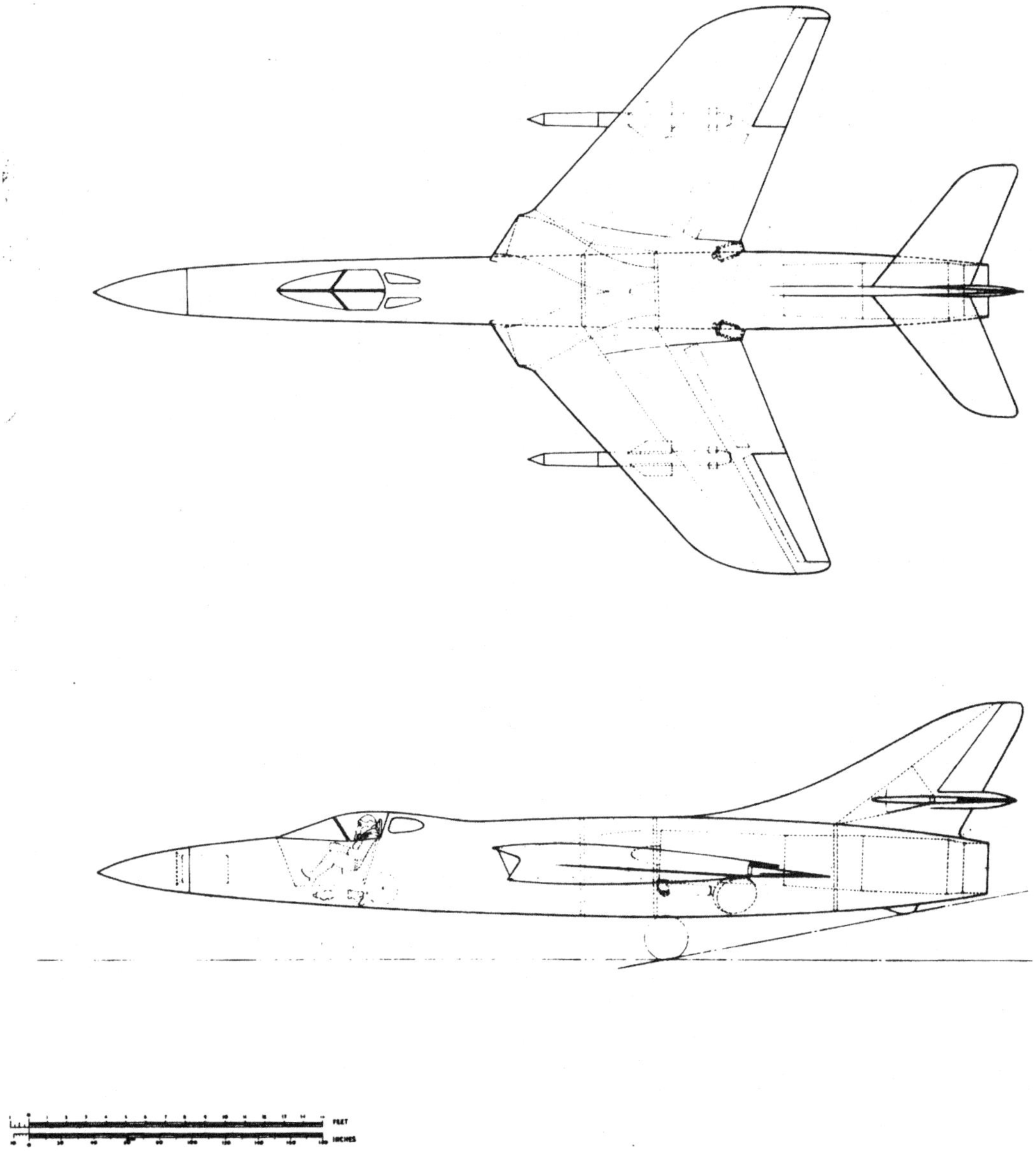

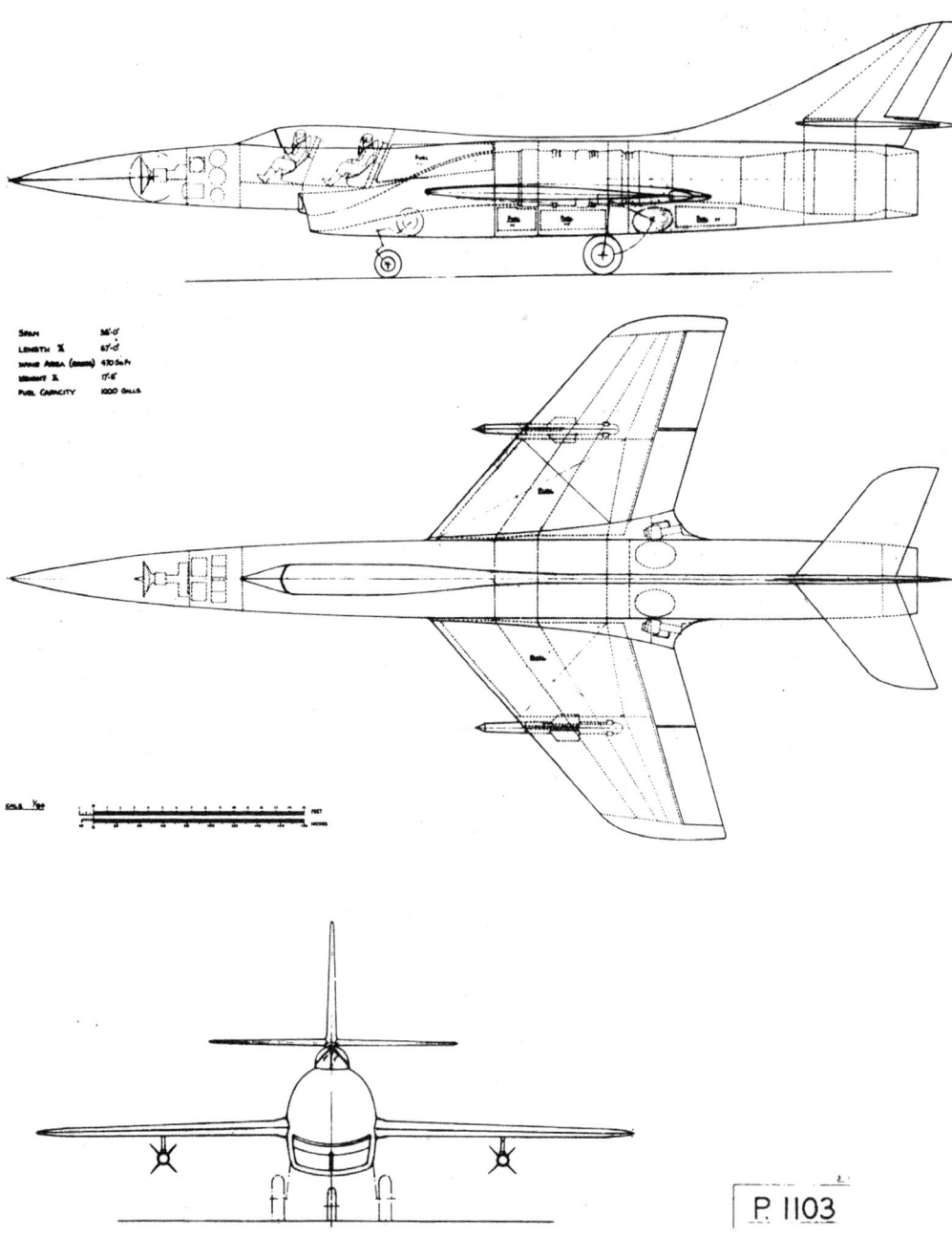

P.1103 development showing an altogether larger aircraft accommodating two crew, a chin mounted 'letter-box' air intake, larger span and increased length and the trailing edge rocket boosters. Armament consists of radar guided missiles.

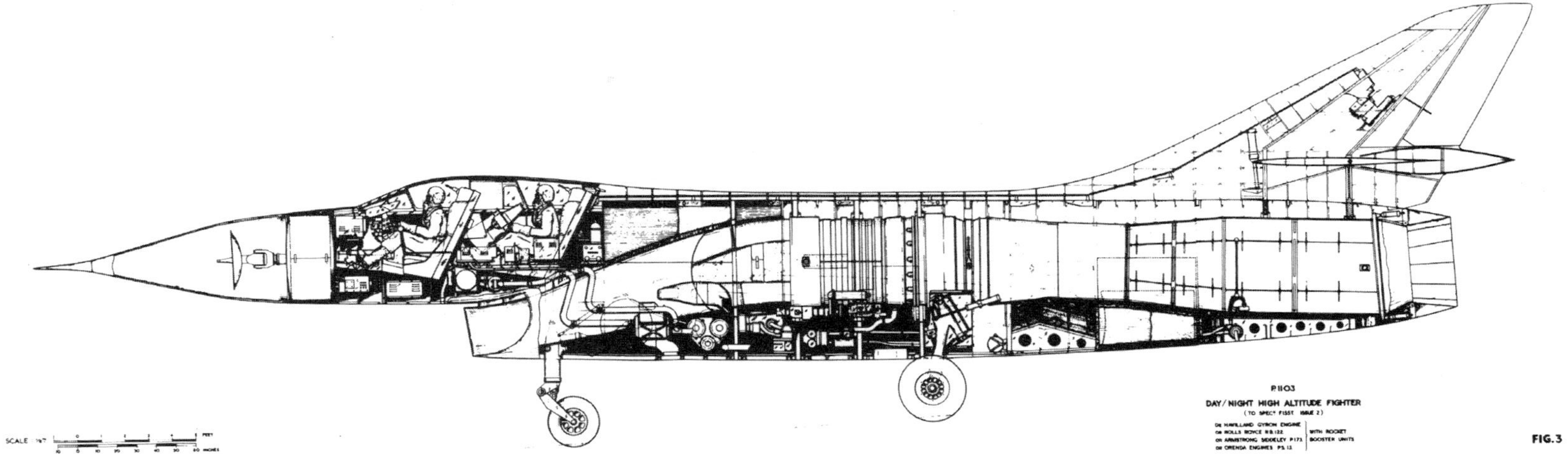

P.1103 cutaway view now showing a scarfed chin intake and large reheated engine in the DH Gyron range.

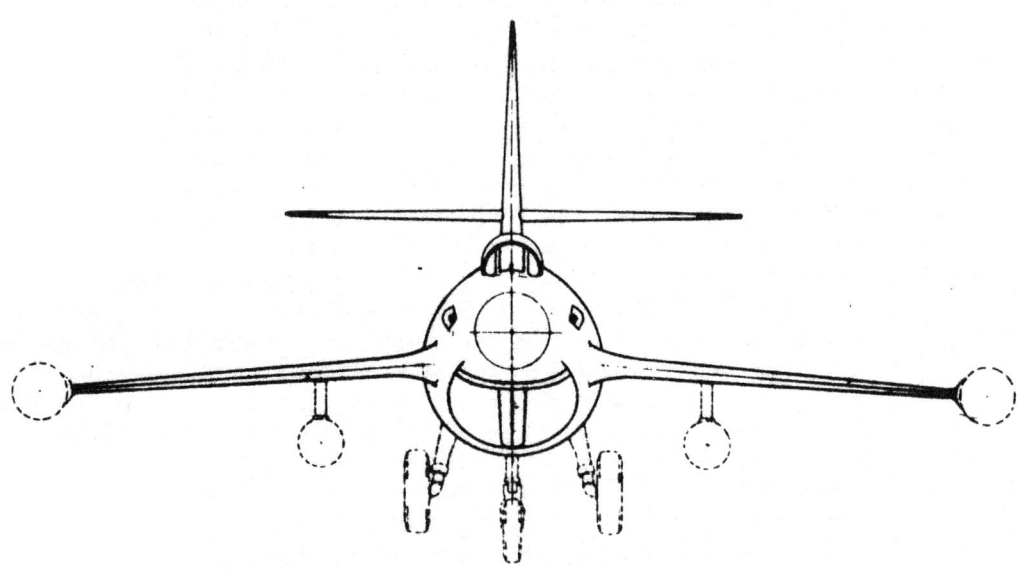

P.1116

MACH 2 INTERCEPTOR AND
LONG RANGE STRIKE FIGHTER

De HAVILLAND GYRON TURBOJET

P.1116, successor to P.1103 shows a reversion to single crew and the addition of conventional armament in a the form of two cannon. Capability of mounting wing-tip fuel tanks and underwing mountings for bombs reveals the move away from pure interceptor towards a strike role.

Future Hawker Projects 225

Meanwhile the OR.329 competition for the new interceptor that Hawker had failed to win was withering on the vine due to lack of funding – but was not dead yet. More than ever, it looked as if Hawker's decision to pursue their present course was the right one and, with memories of the private venture background to the Hawker Hurricane still fresh in some minds, the company's stance on the privately funded P.1121 was noted in the press of the day. In January 1957, two Air Ministry officials visited Kingston to view the now completed P.1121 mock-up, their response was underwhelming and worryingly, during the subsequent discussion, they informed Hawker that they did not see a requirement for an interceptor after 1960, the import of this was surely not missed by the Hawker team but the detail of what it all meant would become all too apparent in the following months.

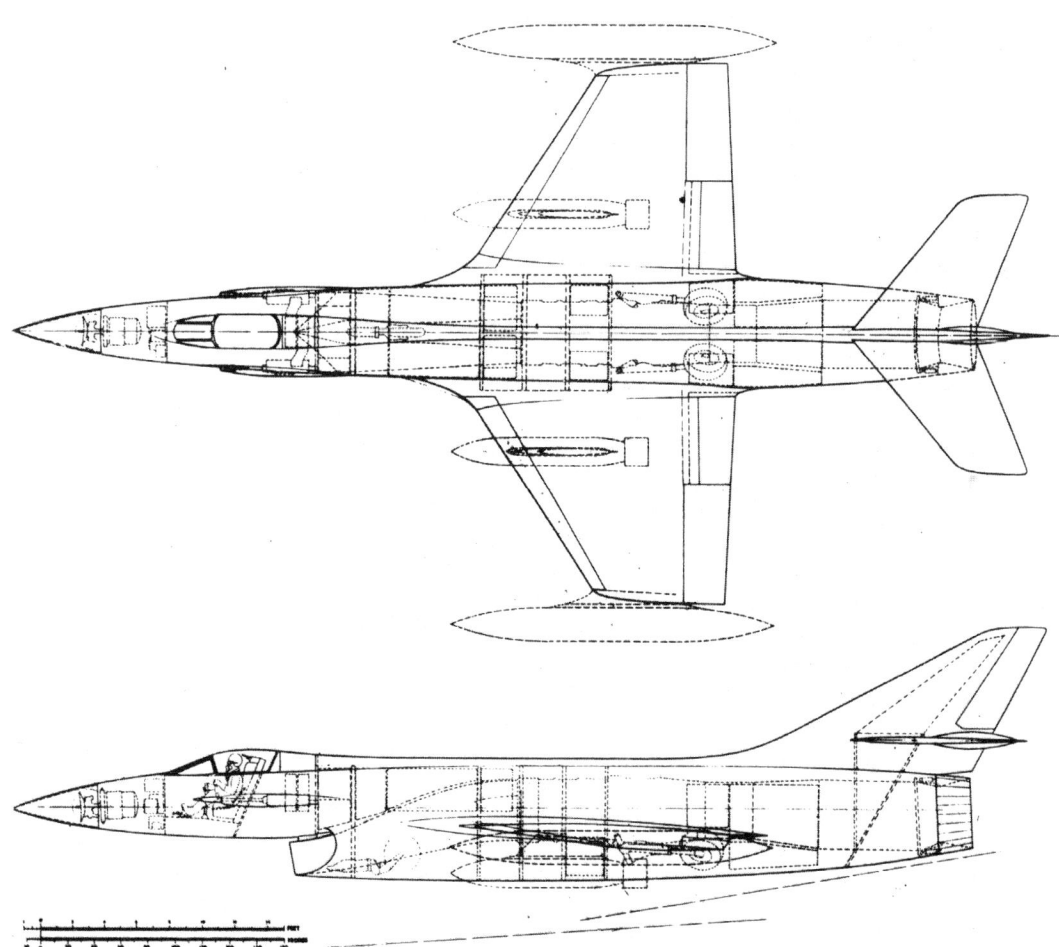

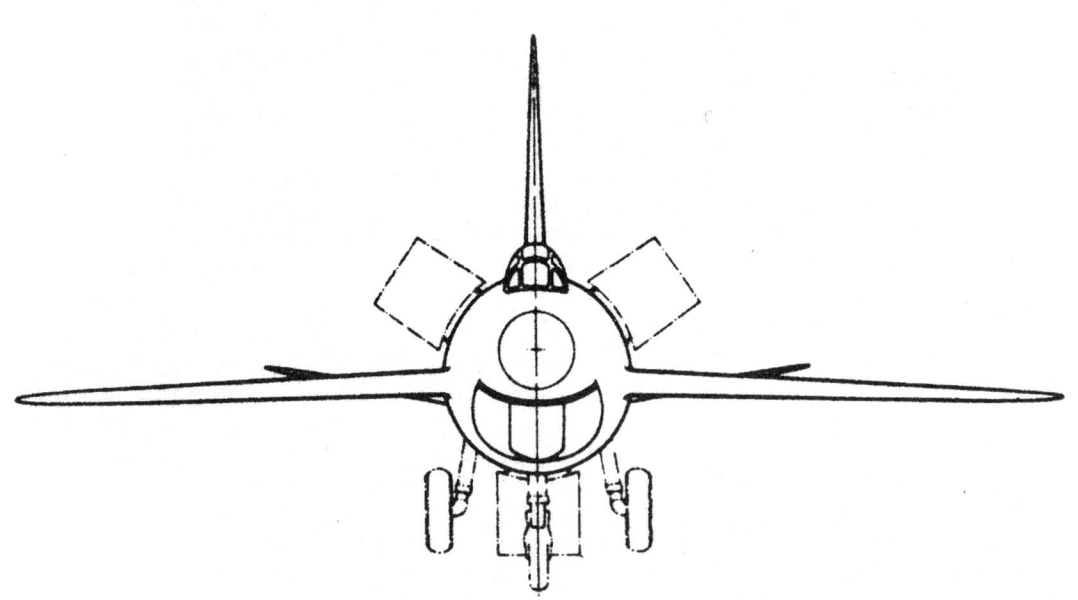

P.1121

HIGH PERFORMANCE FIGHTER

de HAVILLAND GYRON TURBOJET

P.1121 in its initial form with single crew and weapon system optimised for close air support in the form of rocket batteries mounted aft of the cockpit and provision for underwing bombs. The tailplane has taken up a low position on the fuselage and features dihedral; engine would be the DH Gyron.

Future Hawker Projects 227

On 4 April 1957, the notorious White Paper on the future of the United Kingdom's defence was announced by the Defence Minister, Duncan Sandys, which foresaw protection of UK airspace by guided missiles and the end of manned interceptors. While the cost-cutting policies that drove the paper would have severe implications for British aircraft manufacturers, especially fighter design houses of which Hawker was the prime example in terms of its implications for P.1121 the impact was less since the project was privately funded and P.1121 was now being offered as a strike rather than interceptor aircraft. It did, however, spell the immediate end to the OR.329 requirement and to government funding of the DH Gyron engine that was being considered as the powerplant for Hawker's aircraft. Although de Havilland agreed to continue development of the Gyron on a private venture basis, more bad news followed when initial engine runs with the P.1121 intake fitted proved disappointing, the engine repeatedly stalling.

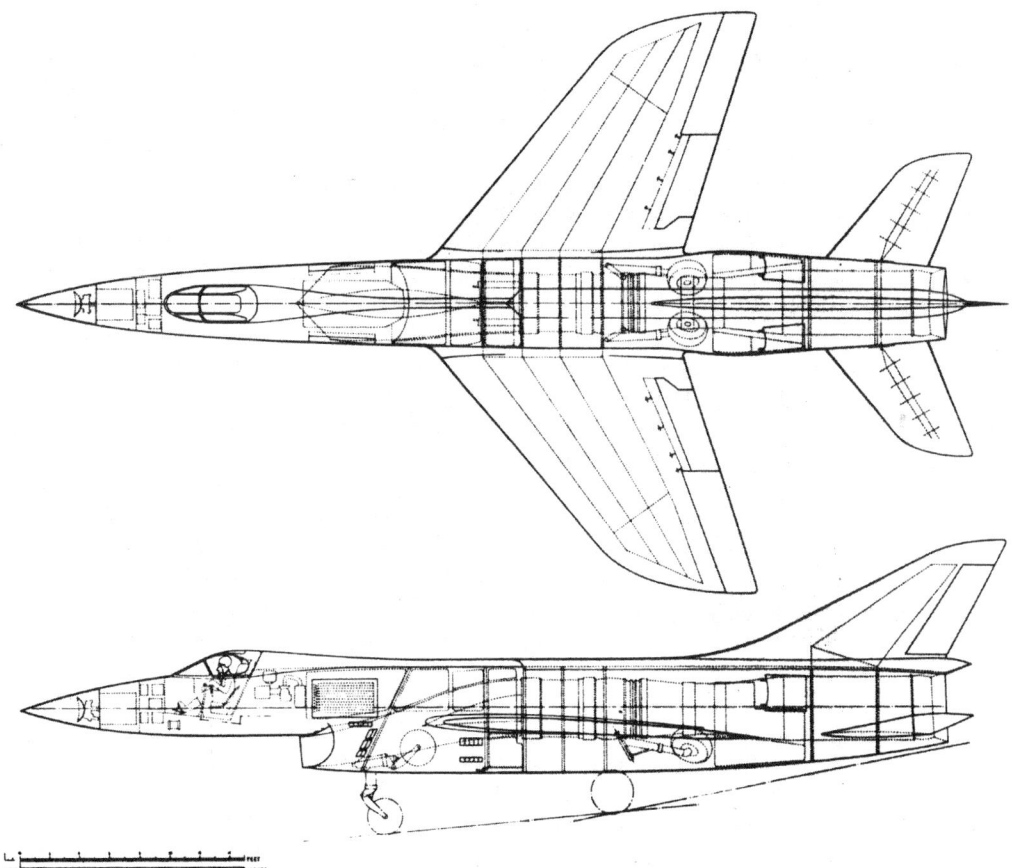

STRUCTURE

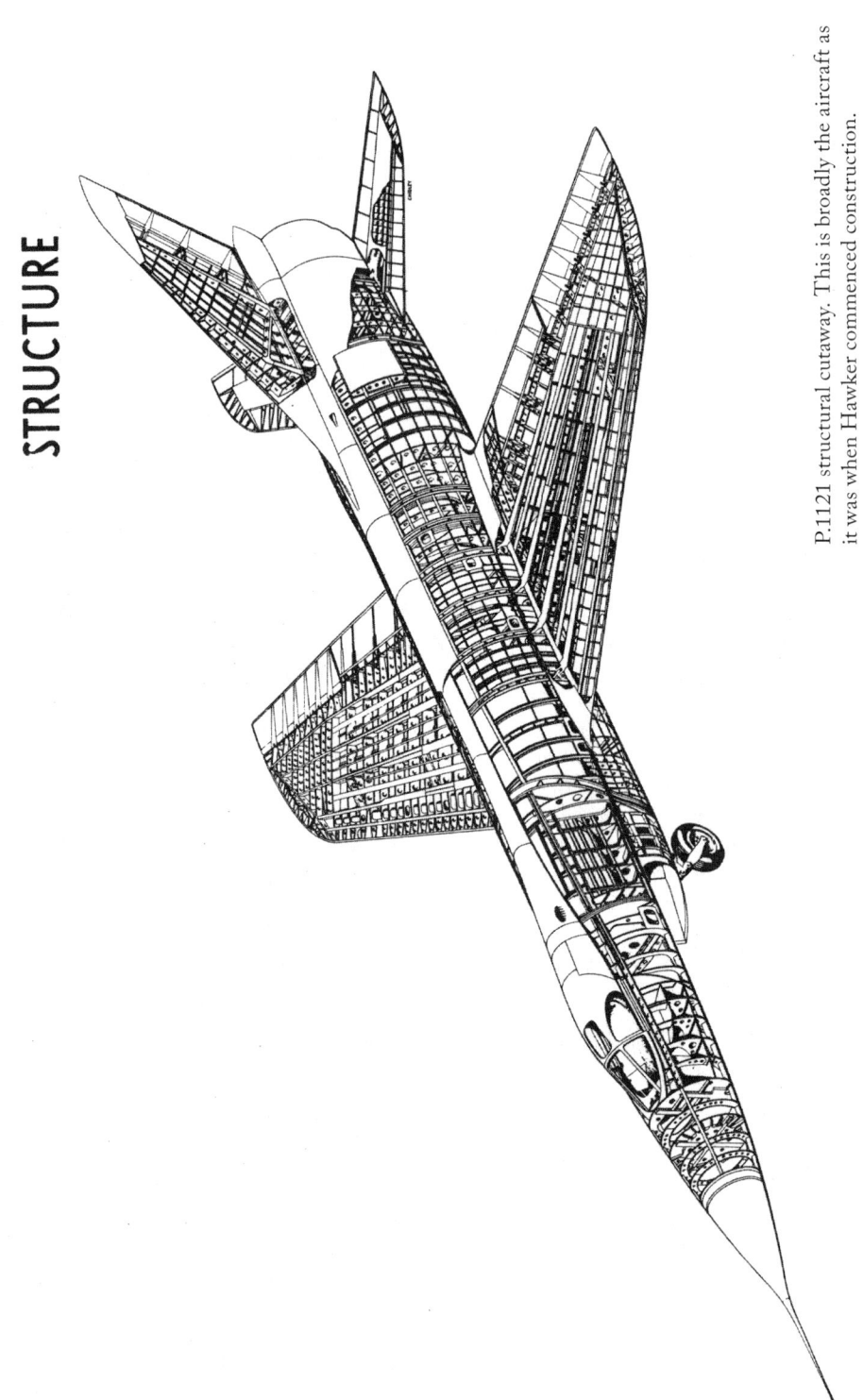

P.1121 structural cutaway. This is broadly the aircraft as it was when Hawker commenced construction.

Following the news that one of the few aircraft requirements that would continue post-Sandys would be a Canberra replacement under GOR.339 (which eventually gave rise to TSR.2), P.1121 would be reinvented as a twin-seat, twin-engine, low-level strike aircraft which would become Hawker's submission as the P.1129. In the meantime, in October 1957 the Hawker Board agreed to reduce work on the first prototype by 80 per cent, given the problems with the Gyron engine and lack of any interest from potential customers. While attempts to interest customers in the P.1121 continued, the Hawker Siddeley Group Board agreed to a joint submission to GOR.339 by Hawker and Avro which was submitted in November 1958 and, with no customer in sight, all work on the P.1121 ended the following month. In January 1959, Hawker learned that

P.1121 mock-up in the Experimental Department at Richmond Road, c.1956.

GOR.339 had been won by English Electric and Vickers, which would go on to construct the ill-fated TSR.2 amid a fog of political interference.

Hawker had put a great deal of work and money into the various projects leading up to P.1129, it was really the only realistic project that Kingston had at that time. Its loss left a large hole in Hawker's design department and on the shop floor, where work had to be brought in from other parts of the Hawker Siddeley Group to retain some semblance of a worthwhile workforce.

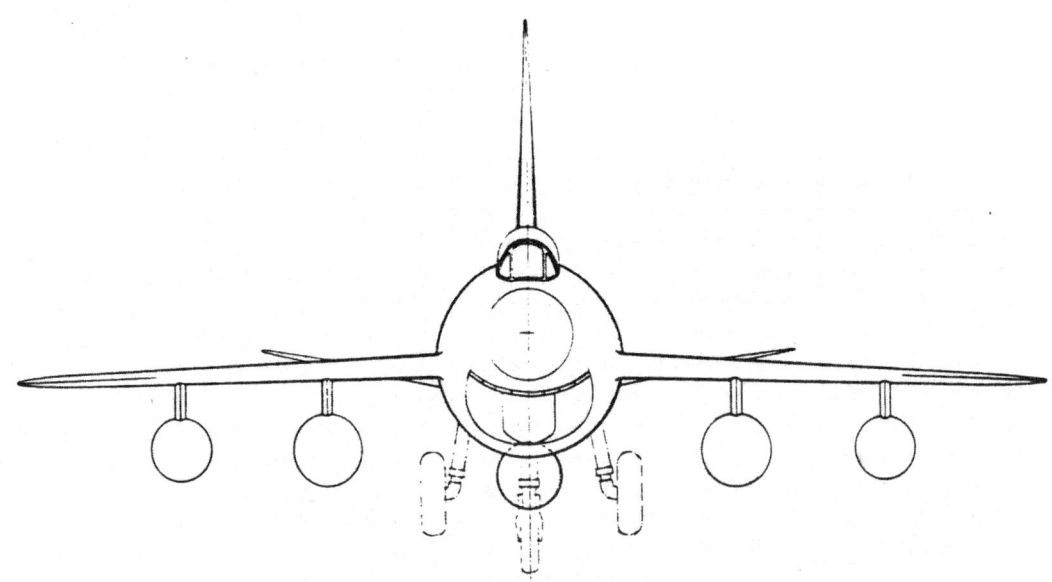

P.1121 as an alternative design with two crew and an alternative engine in the Bristol 21R.

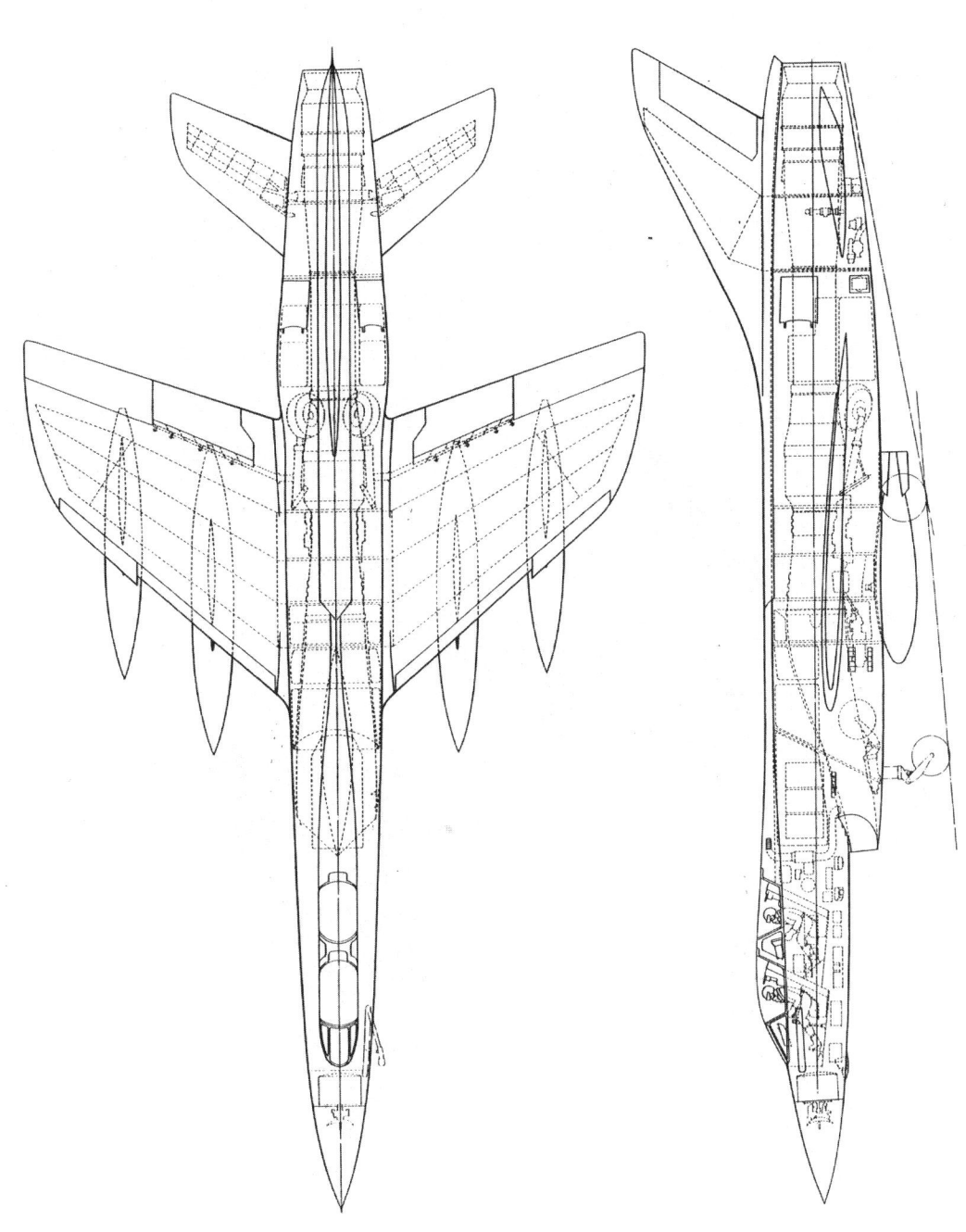

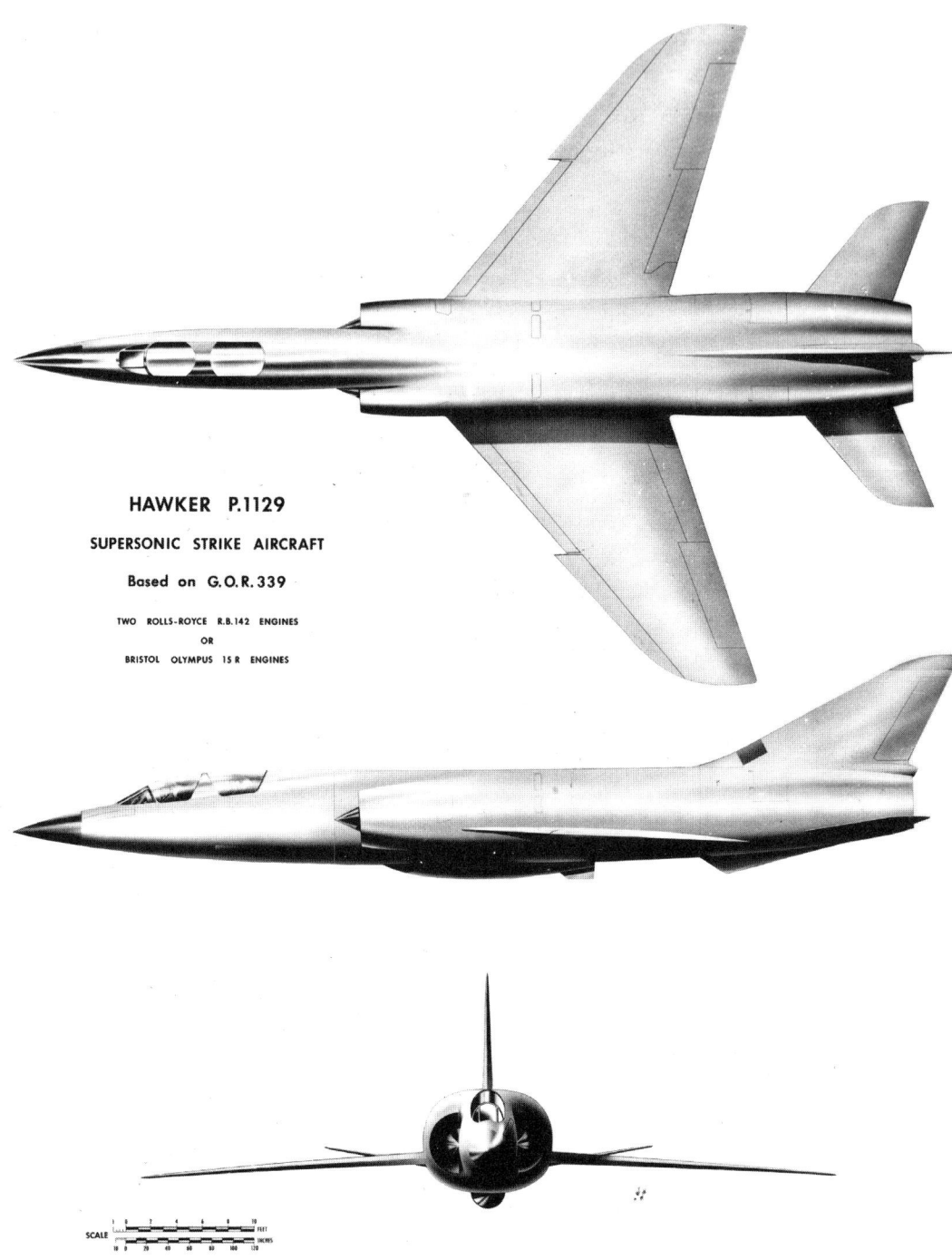

P.1129 general arrangement; the joint submission to GOR 339 combining the Avro and Hawker designs to the tender that would spawn the TSR.2.

These are just some of the projects schemed in the Hawker Project Office between 1945 and the 1960s. Ultimately, Hawker, and later Hawker Siddeley at Kingston upon Thames, would go on to produce the V/STOL family of aircraft based on the Harrier as well as the Hawk trainer, surely the most profitable trainer project in history. Later merging into the British Aerospace monolith resulted in a loss of design authority for the Kingston team and ultimately the closure of both the Kingston and Dunsfold facilities. Nonetheless, their products became the stuff of legend and produced some of the best engineers of the day.

Notes

Chapter 1
1. Jet: Frank Whittle and the Invention of the Jet Engin, John Golley, Datum Publishing 2010. P.257
2. Pyestock: Its Contribution to R&D. Ian McKenzie. FAST 2015. P.8
3. Jet: Frank Whittle and the Invention of the Jet Engin, John Golley, Datum Publishing 2010. P.2
4. Not Much of an Engineer Sir Stanley Hooker, Airlife 2014. P.81
5. Turbojet: History and Development 1930-1960, Volume 1 Antony L. Kay Crowood 2007. P.50-51
6. Ibid. P46-49
7. Not Much of an Engineer Sir Stanley Hooker, Airlife 2014. P.84-99
8. Ibid. P101-105
9. Jet: Frank Whittle and the Invention of the Jet Engine John Golley, Datum Publishing 2010. P.245-251

Chapter 2
1. Hunter Roy Braybrook, Osprey. p.18
2. Brooklands Museum HAL/HIS/003
3. By Jupiter: The Life of Sir Roy Fedden Bill Gunston, Royal Aeronautical Society 1978. (Hawker's use of stressed skin construction was used on the front fuselage of the Typhoon and the complete fuselage of the Tempest).
4. The Life and Work of Sir Sydney: First Sydney Camm Lecture, Robert Lickley, Royal Aeronautical Society 1971. P.1-3
5. Brooklands Museum HAL/PRJ/044
6. Brooklands Museum HAL/PRJ/037
7. Not Much of an Engineer Sir Stanley Hooker Airlife 2014. P.126
8. Brooklands Museum HAL/HIS/005 image 4263
9. Brooklands Museum HAL/HIS/005 image 4262

Chapter 3
1. Brooklands Museum HAL/SHK/001
2. Brooklands Museum HAL/HIS/082
3. Brooklands Museum HAL/CMM/006-009
4. Eric Brown Logs: Camm diary has this flight as 3 Nov but Brown's log has it as 11th as 'handling', via Peter Amos.
5. Ibid

6. Brooklands Museum HAL/HIS/003
  7. Brooklands Museum HAL/SHK/006

Chapter 4
  1. Brooklands Museum HAL/HIS/082
  2. Brooklands Museum HAL/SHK/006
  3. Brooklands Museum Sqn Ldr Trevor Wade Flight logs. Tangmere Aviation Museum Neville Duke Flight Logs. 2007.084.001.004.
  4. Test Pilot Neville Duke Allan Wingate 1953. P.172-3.
  5. 'Rocket Science' Tony Buttler, The Aeroplane, October 2019. P.103-106
  6. Brooklands Museum HAL/HIS/003
  7. Brooklands Museum HAL/HIS/113
  8. Brooklands Museum. Hawker Project GA Drawings P.1000 – P.1149

Chapter 5
  1. Brooklands Museum HAL/SHK/001
  2. Brooklands Museum HAL/HIS/082
  3. Brooklands Museum. Sqn Ldr Trevor Wade Flight Logs.
  4. Test Pilot Neville Duke Wingate 1953. P.193
  5. Brooklands Museum HAL/MIS/106
  6. Farnborough and the Fleet Air Arm Geoffrey Cooper, Ian Allan 2008. P.198-205.
  7. British Research and Development Aircraft Ray Sturtivant, Haynes 1990. P.163
  8. Farnborough – the Story of RAE Reginald Turnill and Arthur Reed, Robert Hale 1980. P.124.
  9. Brooklands Museum. HAL/MIS/092

Chapter 6
  1. Brooklands Museum HAL/HIS/082
  2. Brooklands Museum HAL/HIS/003
  3. Brooklands Museum DSCN8219 HAL/SHK/023
  4. Eric Brown Pilot Logs
  5. Wings on my Sleeve Eric Brown, Weidenfeld & Nicolson. 2006. P.181
  6. Brooklands Museum HAL/MIS/092

Chapter 7
  1. Brooklands Museum HAL/HIS/082
  2. Brooklands Museum. Sqn Ldr Trevor Wade, Flight Logs
  3. Brooklands Museum HAL/HUN/063
  4. Brooklands Museum HAL/HIS/003
  5. The National Archives AVIA 6/16904
  6. Brooklands Museum HAL/SHK/001
  7. Brooklands Museum HAL/HIS/082

8. Ibid
9. Via Peter Amos
10. Brooklands Museum HAL/CMM/002
11. ML Aviation Ltd – A secret world Graham Carter, Keyham Books 2006. P.60
12. Brooklands Museum HAL/MIS/092

Chapter 8
1. Brooklands Museum HAL/HIS/082
2. via Peter Amos
3. Brooklands Museum HAL/SHK/022
4. Finals – Three Greens Wg Com G.W. Johnnie Johnson, Cirrus Associates. 2000. P.73-78
5. Brooklands Museum HAL/SHK/026
6. Via Peter Amos
7. Bill Bedford Flight Logs
8. Brooklands Museum. HAL/MIS/092
9. Wings on my Sleeve Eric Brown, Weidenfeld & Nicolson 2006. P.162

Chapter 9
1. Brooklands Museum HAL/HUN/062
2. Brooklands Museum HAL/HIS/082
3. Ibid
4. Ibid
5. Brooklands Museum HAL/HIS/002
6. Brooklands Museum HAL/HUN/017 and 061
7. Brooklands Museum HAL/HUN/017
8. Brooklands Museum HAL/HUN/063
9. Brooklands Museum HAL/HIS/002
10. Brooklands Museum HAL/HUN/018
11. Brooklands Museum HAL/HUN/049
12. Brooklands Museum HAL/HUN/063
13. Via Peter Amos
14. Via Peter Amos
15. Brooklands Museum HAL/HUN/049
16. Bill Bedford Pilot Logs
17. Via Peter Amos
18. Brooklands Museum HAL/HUN/062. The National Archives AIR2/13058
19. Brooklands Museum HAL/HUN/116
20. Brooklands Museum HAL/HUN/116

Chapter 10
1. Brooklands Museum HAL/HUN/062
2. Brooklands Museum HAL/HUN/115
3. Brooklands Museum HAL/HUN/062

4. Ibid
  5. Brooklands Museum HAL/HUN/116
  6. Brooklands Museum HAL/HUN/062
  7. Brooklands Museum HAL/HUN/018
  8. Brooklands Museum HAL/HUN/115
  9. Frank Murphy Pilots Logs
  10. Brooklands Museum HAL/HUN/018 (The Tangmere log book summer 2014.

Chapter 11
  1. Scimitar F.1 Preview Flight Tests. ETPS 30 November 1968. D. Thigpen (General Dynamics) and Ft Lt H. Frick

Chapter 12
  1. Brooklands Museum HAL/HUN/062
  2. Ibid
  3. Brooklands Museum Hawker Project GAs
  4. Ibid
  5. Ibid
  6. Ibid
  7. Ibid
  8. Brooklands Museum HAL/PRJ/058
  9. Hawker's Secret Cold War Airfield Christopher Budgen, Pen and Sword 2020. P.56

Appendix I

Hawker Pilots Involved in Early Jet Testing

William 'Bill' Humble was born in 1911. Having begun his career in the mining industry, Bill Humble graduated to flying, obtaining his pilot's licence in 1929 with the RAFVR and flying with 504 Squadron in Westland Wallaces and Hawker Hinds. On outbreak of war Humble was posted to 11 FTS at Shawbury, but due to his earlier work in mining engineering, he was seconded back into the coal mining industry, which at that time was desperately short of manpower. Having eventually extricated himself from this situation, Humble was posted to Hawker's airfield at Langley in 1941 as test pilot on Hurricanes and Typhoons, and later the Tempest and Fury series. On the retirement of Philip Lucas in 1945, Humble took over the role of Chief Test Pilot, responsible for all flight testing at Langley, mainly Tempest and Sea Fury. On 2 September 1947, Humble joined the club of pilots with jet experience, piloting the P.1040 prototype VP401 from Boscombe Down for its first flight. Having carried out almost all of the early flying of this aircraft, in 1948 Humble relinquished the Chief's role to 'Wimpy' Wade and moved away from flying to take up a role in Hawker's sales team, becoming responsible for Middle East sales campaigns and being awarded the MBE in 1949. Bill Humble died in 1992.

Trevor 'Wimpy' Wade was born in 1920. Wade joined the RAFVR in 1938 and was posted to 92 Squadron, Northolt in 1940, mainly flying Spitfires. Wade and Neville Duke served together while 92 squadron was based at Biggin Hill, in B flight in 1941. In 1943, Wade was posted to Wittering to take charge of the Air Fighting Development Unit, testing captured Axis aircraft. Following on from this work, in 1945 he was part of a team sent to the USA to assess captured Japanese aircraft. With the rank of Squadron Leader and having received both the DFC and AFC, Wade left RAF service in 1946 to work for The Aeroplane magazine, but joined Hawker Aircraft at Langley 1947 at the invitation of Bill Humble; when Humble retired in 1948, Wade took over as Chief Test Pilot. Wade had started his test piloting career with Hawkers on production Sea Furys, but with Humble's retirement, took over the work on Hawker's first jets and Sea

Hawk prototypes, carrying out much of the flying of the P.1040 and sharing the N7/46 and P.1052 work with Duke. With the advent of P.1081, again Wade took on the lion's share of the work before being joined by Duke. On a flight in the P.1081 VX279 out of Farnborough on 3 April 1951, the aircraft failed to pull out of a dive and although apparently initiating a late ejection, Wade died in the subsequent crash.

Francis (Frank) 'Spud' Murphy was born in 1917. Having overcame infant paralysis that left him partially disabled in a hand and foot, in 1941 Murphy joined the Royal New Zealand Air Force before travelling to England and flying Hurricanes and Typhoons with the RAF, the latter with 486 NZ Squadron. Murphy was later seconded to Hawker at Langley on test pilot duties flying Hurricanes, Typhoons and Tempests. On leaving the RAF as a Squadron Leader and a recipient of the DFC, Murphy joined Hawkers in July 1945 on test pilot duties, taking the position of Chief Production Test Pilot at Langley in 1948. With the advent of the jet aircraft, Murphy obtained one flight in the P.1040 before becoming more actively involved with the Sea Hawk prototypes and then with the production Sea Hawks. Due to their experimental nature, Murphy was not involved in the swept wing P.1952 (though he did fly VX272 twice in 1953) or P.1981 aircraft. On 19 December 1952, Murphy was involved in a forced landing at RNAS Ford in a Sea Hawk F.Mk.1 WF159, from which he escaped relatively unscathed. With the arrival of production Hunters, Murphy was soon heavily engaged in clearing these for release to service, including the maiden flight of the first production Hunter WT555 in May 1953. On 25 January, while testing Hunter F.1 WT707, engine problems saw Murphy once again heading into RNAS Ford for a forced landing at high speed and with no flap or undercarriage. Landing at some 230mph, Murphy and the Hunter bounced repeatedly before leaving the airfield and careering through an adjacent caravan park resulting in three fatalities. Soon after this brush with mortality, Murphy moved from test flying to a role within the company as a sales manager, retiring in 1976 with the award of an OBE. He died in May 1997.

Neville Frederick Duke was born in 1922. Duke joined the RAF aged 18 in 1940 and was posted to 92 squadron at Biggin Hill in 1941, flying Spitfires in the same B flight as 'Wimpy' Wade. Soon posted to the Middle East flying Kittyhawks based in Libya, he was shot down twice in five days by Messerschmitt Bf 109 aircraft but lived to tell the tale. By November 1942, 92 Squadron had arrived in Libya and Duke managed to rejoin his old unit. By 1944, Duke was based in Italy and managed to survive being shot down again, this time by AAA.

As a Squadron Leader, he ended his tours as the top scoring pilot in the Mediterranean theatre with twenty-seven victories and in October 1944 was seconded to Hawker Aircraft at Langley as a production test pilot, on Tempest and later, Furys. With his year at Hawker quickly up, Duke's next posting was to no.4 course at ETPS in 1946; following this, he was selected as one of three pilots in June of that year to form the RAF High Speed flight, together with Group Captain E.M. Donaldson and Squadron Leader Bill Waterton to carry out an attempt on the world air speed record using suitably modified Gloster Meteors. This group was successful in raising the record to 616mph on 7 September 1946, after which Duke moved to Boscombe Down.

Upon leaving the RAF in 1948 with the rank of Squadron Leader and in receipt of the DSO, DFC and AFC in recognition of his service during the war, Neville Duke joined Hawker Aircraft in June, returning to Langley as a production test pilot on Tempest and Sea Fury. Fairly soon, Duke was brought into the experimental test flying under 'Wimpy' Wade, being involved in display flying of the N7/47 Sea Hawk prototype at the SBAC shows at Farnborough in 1949 and '50, and the P.1052 aircraft VX272 at the 1951 show. Also at the 1951 Farnborough show was the prototype P.1067 Hunter WB188 and it fell to Duke to debut the aircraft to the world's public, causing something of a sensation with its sleek lines and formidable speed.

Two years later and after much work to bring the Hunter to a standard acceptable to the RAF, Duke was back in the cockpit of WB188 for another attempt on the World Air Speed Record. Now referred to as a Mark 3, the aircraft featured a reheated engine and modifications to wring the maximum speed from it. On 7 September 1953, Duke took the speed record at 727.6mph, a triumph for both him and the company. Continuing his work on subsequent marks of Hunter, Duke was injured in a forced landing at RAF Thorney Island in August 1955, damaging his back and requiring time off to recover. A heavy landing the following year at Dunsfold resulted in further damage and Duke realised that the time had come to retire from such high risk activity. Subsequently resigning from Hawker, Duke carried out freelance work for many years, being awarded an OBE, before his death in April 2007.

Alfred William 'Bill' Bedford was born in 1920. Having served an apprenticeship with Blackburn Starling Ltd, Bedford joined the RAF in 1940 with a posting in September 1941 to 605 Squadron flying Hurricanes, with his next posting taking him to India and the Far East with 135 Squadron, still on Hurricanes and later, P-47 Thunderbolts. By 1945, Bedford was with 65 Squadron flying Mustangs and with the award of the AFC, the following year obtained a posting to Central Flying School (CFS) as an instructor where he remained until 1949. This was followed by Course no.8 at ETPS from which he graduated in 1949, being posted to Royal Aircraft Establishment (RAE) at Farnborough, becoming something of an expert on spin recovery of swept-wing aircraft. During his time at Farnborough, Bedford continued to indulge his passion for gliding, achieving several notable records in this pursuit, including the first UK holder of the International Gold 'C' with two diamonds.

In 1951, Bedford retired from the RAF with the rank of Flight Lieutenant and in September was recruited to the Hawker test pilot team, in process of moving from Farnborough to Dunsfold, working as Duke's deputy on the experimental aircraft as well as production flight testing, at this time mainly on Sea Hawk and early production Hunter. As Sea Hawk flying tailed off, much work was carried out to bring the Hunter into service, Bedford's abilities in demonstrating spinning in swept-wing aircraft now proving most useful in clearing the Hunter for this manoeuvre and in displaying the multiple spin at Farnborough Air Shows in the twin seat Hunter G-APUX trailing smoke to the delight of the crowds. With Neville Duke's retirement from testing at Hawker, Bedford took over the role of Chief Test Pilot in October 1956.

With the advent of the P.1127 and developed Kestrel V/STOL aircraft, Bedford returned to public prominence and acclaim as his work on bringing the wonder of V/STOL into the realms of operational use was demonstrated to amazed crowds at Farnborough displays. His flying skills enabled him to survive an ejection at very low level from one of the prototype P.1127s when a cold nozzle was lost and, in 1963, to emerge unscathed when a fault with the nozzle control of XP831 resulted in the aircraft dropping to the ground from a hover in front of the world's press at the Paris Air Show.

In 1967, having taken the little P.1127 from its maiden hover to operational aircraft for entry into the RAF inventory (and been awarded the OBE), Bedford retired from test flying, passing the reigns of CTP to Hugh Merewether. At this point, Bedford followed the well-trodden route of former test pilots and joined the Hawker sales team, promoting company products until retirement in 1986. Bill died in October 1996.

Appendix II

Flights Undertaken during Testing of Early Hawker Jets

The flights listed below are the most complete record so far available for the various jet aircraft prototypes produced by Hawker Aircraft. It is compiled from the flight logs of the company pilots involved and includes other flights, where known. It does not include flights by pilots attached to Government establishments such as RAE Farnborough or A&AEE Boscombe Down except where these have come to light, such as Lieutenant Commander Eric Brown's involvement.

Flights are listed for P.1040, P.1072, P.1052, P.1081, P1067 and early Hunter F.1; early Sea Hawks are listed for completeness. The flight details are those listed by the pilots in their logs, which can sometimes be abstruse to the point of mystery; 'Wimpy' Wade's being particularly dense. For example, when investigating the lateral instability, Wade would indicate this by simply a 'wiggly' line in his log! The entries under 'Flight details' are verbatim from each pilot's log. Author additions are in square brackets. Missing/undecipherable text is denoted by question marks.

P.1040 Flights		VP401		
Date	Pilot	Location	Flight Detail	Time (mins)
02/09/1947	Bill Humble	Boscombe Down	1st flight	
03/09/1947	Bill Humble	Boscombe Down	Flight	
04/09/1947	Bill Humble	Boscombe Down	Flight	
05/09/1947	Bill Humble	Boscombe Down to Farnborough	Ferry flight	
15/09/1947	Bill Humble	Farnborough	Flight	
15/09/1947	Bill Humble	Farnborough	Flight	
16/09/1947	Bill Humble	Farnborough	Flight	
17/09/1947	Bill Humble	Farnborough	Flight	
19/09/1947	Bill Humble	Farnborough	Flight	
08/10/1947	Bill Humble	Farnborough	Test flight	
08/10/1947	Bill Humble	Farnborough	Test flight	
10/10/1947	Bill Humble	Farnborough	Test flight	
20/10/1947	Bill Humble	Farnborough	Test flight	
21/10/1947	Bill Humble	Farnborough	Test flight	
27/10/1947	Bill Humble	Farnborough	Test flight	
31/10/1947	Bill Humble	Farnborough	Test flight	
03/11/1947	Bill Humble	Farnborough	Test flight	
11/11/1947	Eric Brown	Farnborough	Handling. Second pilot to fly this prototype	
26/11/1947	Bill Humble	Farnborough	Test flight	
11/12/1947	Bill Humble	Farnborough	Test flight	
17/12/1947	Bill Humble	Farnborough	Test flight	
22/12/1947	Bill Humble	Farnborough	Test flight	
10/03/1948	Wimpy Wade	Delivery to Farnborough	Vibration noted	15
11/03/1948	Wimpy Wade		Fixed tab. Vibration - here we go again	15
12/03/1948	Wimpy Wade		More vibration but less with new elevator	15
12/03/1948	Wimpy Wade		More vibration but less with new elevator	40
15/03/1948	Wimpy Wade		Vibration	20

Date	Pilot	Location	Flight Detail	Time (mins)
16/03/1948	Wimpy Wade		Fuel load variations with new elevator	25
16/03/1948	Wimpy Wade		Fuel load variations with new elevator	35
17/03/1948	Wimpy Wade		Fuel load variations	15
18/03/1948	Wimpy Wade		Ballast variations	25
18/03/1948	Wimpy Wade		Ballast variations	25
19/03/1948	Wimpy Wade		Back to old elevator	20
20/03/1948	Wimpy Wade		Increased weight on old elevator. Same vibration	25
24/03/1948	Wimpy Wade		Vibrograph recordings	35
25/03/1948	Wimpy Wade		Vibrograph recordings	35
30/03/1948	Wimpy Wade		Vibrograph recordings	30
14/04/1948	Wimpy Wade		Demo for Swiss. Two burst tyres.	15
16/04/1948	Wimpy Wade		Vibration checks - wot? No vibration?	25
19/04/1948	Wimpy Wade		Vibration checks	30
20/04/1948	Wimpy Wade		Vibration checks	45
20/04/1948	Wimpy Wade		Vibration checks	25
22/04/1948	Wimpy Wade		Photos and levels	55
26/04/1948	Wimpy Wade		High and low levels	45
29/04/1948	Wimpy Wade		Performance. Stability. Stick force recordings and general handling	45
29/04/1948	Wimpy Wade		Performance. Stability. Stick force recordings and general handling	45
29/04/1948	Wimpy Wade		Performance. Stability. Stick force recordings and general handling	45
03/05/1948	Wimpy Wade		Stick force per G	60
10/05/1948	Wimpy Wade	Farnborough	Farnborough to Boscombe	15
10/05/1948	Wimpy Wade	Boscombe Down	Position Error runs (BD record 606mph)	55
10/05/1948	Wimpy Wade	Boscombe Down	Return to Farnborough	15
12/05/1948	Wimpy Wade		Admiral McIntosh	25
21/05/1948	Wimpy Wade		Stick force per G	60

Appendix II

Date	Pilot	Location	Flight Detail	Time (mins)
25/05/1948	Wimpy Wade	Farnborough	To West Raynham	25
25/05/1948	Wimpy Wade	West Raynham	Demonstration	15
25/05/1948	Wimpy Wade	West Raynham	Return to Farnborough	25
27/05/1948	Wimpy Wade		New tailplane setting test	60
27/05/1948	Wimpy Wade		Photography (Chas Brown)	1,10
01/06/1948	Wimpy Wade		Hood pressure and fuel vent? Test flight after mods	50
02/06/1948	Wimpy Wade	Farnborough	To Lee on Solent	15
02/06/1948	Wimpy Wade	Lee on Solent	Demonstration	15
02/06/1948	Wimpy Wade	Lee on Solent	Return to Farnborough	15
10/06/1948	Wimpy Wade		Pressure measurements and high Mach no dives 31,000 ft	25
10/06/1948	Wimpy Wade		More Machery	50
14/06/1948	Wimpy Wade	Farnborough	To A&AEE for prelim handling	20
21/06/1948	Neville Duke	Boscombe Down	Local flight	45
26/06/1948	Wimpy Wade	Boscombe Down	Return to Farnborough. A&AEE on strike	25
06/07/1948	Wimpy Wade		Stick forces	45
06/07/1948	Wimpy Wade		Stick forces	50
20/08/1948	Wimpy Wade		Air test after tail mod (land at Langley)	30
24/08/1948	Wimpy Wade		Press show (a line being shot)	20
24/08/1948	Wimpy Wade		Return to Farnborough. Vibration	15
25/08/1948	Neville Duke	Farnborough	Handling and mach no investigation	
25/08/1948	Neville Duke		Handling and mach no investigation at 30,000 ft	
26/08/1948	Wimpy Wade		Back to normal (high up)	55
27/08/1948	Neville Duke		Combat climb to 35,000 ft. Levels and 35,000. Landed Langley	
30/08/1948	Wimpy Wade		To Farnborough and roll data	35
01/09/1948	Wimpy Wade		Flight test	10
07/09/1948	Wimpy Wade		SBAC flying.	10
08/09/1948	Wimpy Wade		SBAC flying.	10
09/09/1948	Wimpy Wade		Air test for elevator trimmer	30

Date	Pilot	Location	Flight Detail	Time (mins)
09/09/1948	Wimpy Wade		SBAC flying.	10
11/09/1948	Wimpy Wade		SBAC flying. Display	10
12/09/1948	Wimpy Wade		SBAC flying. Demonstration	10
13/09/1948	Wimpy Wade		Test flight	40
14/09/1948	Neville Duke	Farnborough	Mach no. investigation to M 0.845	
13/10/1948	Wimpy Wade		Climbs	55
14/10/1948	Neville Duke	Farnborough	Elevator assessment	
24/11/1948	Wimpy Wade		Spinning tests	20
25/11/1948	Wimpy Wade		Spinning tests	40
25/11/1948	Wimpy Wade		Spinning tests	35
26/11/1948	Neville Duke	Farnborough	Spinning trials 20,000 ft	
10/12/1948	Wimpy Wade		Air test	15
13/12/1948	Wimpy Wade	Farnborough	To Moreton Valence	20
14/12/1948	Wimpy Wade	Moreton Valence	Return Farnborough	20
17/12/1948	Wimpy Wade		520 mph for 420 odd miles	60
17/12/1948	Frank Murphy		Test	
10/03/1949	Wimpy Wade		Air test, spin and demonstration to Argentines.	30
10/03/1949	Wimpy Wade		Landing at Langley and return Farnborough	30
11/03/1949	Eric Brown		Stalls	
21/03/1949	Eric Brown		Stalls	
01/04/1949	Eric Brown		Stalls	
04/04/1949	Eric Brown		Cat launches. Rear fuselage ripped open by hold back extension puller	
09/06/1949	Wimpy Wade		Up and about. External elevator balance	40
10/06/1949	Wimpy Wade		Up and about. External elevator balance	35
15/06/1949	Wimpy Wade		External elevator balance	50
21/06/1949	Neville Duke	Farnborough	Handling without mass balance weights	
20/07/1949	Wimpy Wade		Air race practice	35
20/07/1949	Neville Duke	Farnborough	Practice race circuits	
28/07/1949	Wimpy Wade		Air race practice	55
28/07/1949	Neville Duke	Farnborough	Race practice Elmdon course	

Date	Pilot	Location	Flight Detail	Time (mins)
29/07/1949	Neville Duke	Farnborough	Farnborough to Elmdon (plus course × 2)	
30/07/1949	Neville Duke	Elmdon	Kemsley trophy race - 1st	
31/07/1949	Wimpy Wade		Dress rehearsal at Elmdon	40
01/08/1949	Wimpy Wade		National Air Races. 1st SBAC Challenge Cup Race	20
02/08/1949	Neville Duke	Elmdon	Elmdon to Farnborough	
16/08/1949	Wimpy Wade		External elevator balance	55
16/08/1949	Wimpy Wade		External elevator balance	1,05
17/08/1949	Neville Duke	Farnborough	Elevator assessment, external mass balance	

| P.1072 Flights || VP401 ||
Date	Pilot	Flight Detail	Time (mins)
28/07/1950	Wimpy Wade	Air test	20
28/07/1950	Wimpy Wade	Air test	25
29/07/1950	Wimpy Wade	Deliver to Bitteswell	20
19/09/1950	Neville Duke	Bitteswell to Langley	?
13/11/1950	Neville Duke	Farnborough to Bitteswell	20
20/11/1950	Wimpy Wade	Snarler test flight	11
11/12/1950	Wimpy Wade	Snarler test flight	10
12/12/1950	Wimpy Wade	Snarler test flight	13
15/01/1951	Neville Duke	Firing Snarler rocket motor	25
18/01/1951	Neville Duke	Firing tests rocket motor. Exploded	25
15/02/1951	Neville Duke	Flight test	25

N7/46 Flights		VP413 and VP422		
Date	Pilot	Flight Detail	Time (mins)	Aircraft
03/09/1948	Wimpy Wade	First flight	15	VP413
15/09/1948	Neville Duke	First flight. General handling, stalls		VP413
16/09/1948	Wimpy Wade	Performance and handling	40	VP413
24/09/1948	Wimpy Wade	A bit of everything	60	VP413
24/09/1948	Wimpy Wade	A bit of everything	50	VP413
08/10/1948	Wimpy Wade	Air brake investigation	55	VP413
08/10/1948	Wimpy Wade	Air brake investigation	1,05	VP413
14/10/1948	Neville Duke	Stalls. Air brake assessment		VP413
28/10/1948	Neville Duke	Handling. Stalls		VP413
29/10/1948	Neville Duke	Handling		VP413
03/11/1948	Wimpy Wade	Figures	55	VP413
03/11/1948	Wimpy Wade	Figures	60	VP413
04/11/1948	Wimpy Wade	Combat climb. Mach no stick force per G.		VP413
05/11/1948	Wimpy Wade	Figures	55	VP413
25/11/1948	Neville Duke	Partial climbs 10,000 ft		VP413
25/11/1948	Neville Duke	Partial climbs 25,000 ft		VP413
07/12/1948	Wimpy Wade	Climbs	45	VP413
05/02/1949	Wimpy Wade	Air brake test	60	VP413
05/02/1949	Wimpy Wade	Air brake test	50	VP413
Feb-49	Wimpy Wade	Deck landing course at RNAS Milltown. 60 ADDLS, 5 deck landings in Seafire XV & XVII.		
08/02/1949	Neville Duke	Air brake assessment. Trimmed speeds		VP413
08/02/1949	Neville Duke	Stalls and deck landing assessment		VP413
10/02/1949	Neville Duke	Farnborough to Boscombe Down		VP413
10/02/1949	Neville Duke	ADDLS		VP413
10/02/1949	Neville Duke	Boscombe Down to Farnborough		VP413
11/02/1949	Neville Duke	Measured take-offs		VP413
22/02/1949	Neville Duke	Stability 10,000ft and deck landings		VP413
08/03/1949	Neville Duke	Deck landing assessment, modified flaps		VP413
08/03/1949	Wimpy Wade	Deck landing assessments	30	VP413
13/04/1949	Neville Duke	Demonstration		VP413
27/04/1949	Neville Duke	Demonstration		VP413

Date	Pilot	Flight Detail	Time (mins)	Aircraft
05/05/1949	Wimpy Wade	Boscombe to Farnborough		VP413
10/05/1949	Wimpy Wade	Return to Boscombe	20	VP413
23-30/5/1949	Wimpy Wade	Three days with HMS *Illustrious* N7/46 carrier trials		VP413
08/07/1949	Wimpy Wade	Test flight	60	VP413
14/07/1949	Neville Duke	Static stability 25,000 ft		VP413
20/07/1949	Neville Duke	Stability tests. Abortive - hood		VP413
20/07/1949	Neville Duke	Stability tests. Acln [acceleration?] on Re?????		VP413
21/07/1949	Neville Duke	Static stability 25,000ft		VP413
21/07/1949	Neville Duke	Stick force per G		VP413
21/07/1949	Neville Duke	Demonstration		VP413
09/08/1949	Neville Duke	Static stability 25,000ft		VP413
09/08/1949	Neville Duke	Acceleration in out of trim		VP413
10/08/1949	Neville Duke	Acceleration in out of trim dives		VP413
12/08/1949	Neville Duke	Static stability 5,000ft		VP413
12/08/1949	Neville Duke	Stick force per G, 5,000ft		VP413
17/08/1949	Wimpy Wade	Aircraft stability	55	VP413
17/08/1949	Neville Duke	Static stability 25,000ft		VP413
18/08/1949	Neville Duke	Acceleration in out of trim 1,000ft		VP413
24/08/1949	Wimpy Wade	Stability and stick force	55	VP413
26/08/1949	Neville Duke	Stick force per G, 5,000ft		VP413
05/09/1949	Neville Duke	Flight test and aerobatics		VP413
06/09/1949	Neville Duke	SBAC demonstration		VP413
07/09/1949	Neville Duke	SBAC demonstration		VP413
08/09/1949	Neville Duke	SBAC demonstration		VP413
09/09/1949	Neville Duke	SBAC demonstration. 10G - wings and fuselage wrinkled		VP413
20/09/1949	Neville Duke	Flight test. Panel adrift		VP413
22/09/1949	Neville Duke	Farnborough to Boscombe Down		VP413
15/10/1949	Wimpy Wade	Taxying trials	20	VP422
17/10/1949	Wimpy Wade	First flight	25	VP422
19/10/1949	Wimpy Wade	Test flight	20	VP422
27/10/1949	Wimpy Wade	Cockpit heating	35	VP4??
01/11/1949	Wimpy Wade	General handling, cockpit heating	55	VP422
03/11/1949	Wimpy Wade	Cockpit heating etc	40	VP422
18/11/1949	Neville Duke	Abortive - bogged		VP422
22/11/1949	Bill Humble			VP422

Appendix II

Date	Pilot	Flight Detail	Time (mins)	Aircraft
29/11/1949	Neville Duke	Levels 15,000ft	60	VP422
30/11/1949	Neville Duke	Combat climb and levels 25,000ft	1,35	VP422
02/12/1949	Neville Duke	Climb 12,000 RPM to 35,000ft. Levels 35,000ft	1,30	VP422
02/12/1949	Neville Duke	Demonstration and climb ???? To 35,000ft	1,15	VP422
15/12/1949	Neville Duke	Handling with modified airbrake system		VP422
16/12/1949	Wimpy Wade	Dive brake investigation	35	VP422
19/12/1949	Neville Duke	Cockpit heating 35,000ft	1,40	VP422
20/12/1949	Neville Duke	Cockpit heating 10,000ft	1,10	VP422
21/12/1949	Wimpy Wade	Dive brakes	30	VP422
10/01/1950	Wimpy Wade	Hydraulic ????	20	VP422
12/01/1950	Wimpy Wade	Hydraulic ????	30	VP422
13/01/1950	Neville Duke	Air test	40	VP422
17/01/1950	Wimpy Wade	Dispatch to Boscombe	20	VP422
06/02/1950	Wimpy Wade	Air Test [name Sea Hawk used for first time]	30	VP422
08/02/1950	Wimpy Wade	Air test	15	VP422
17/02/1950	Wimpy Wade	Air test	45	VP413
23/02/1950	Wimpy Wade	To Boscombe	20	VP413
24/03/1950	Neville Duke	Flight test	30	VP422
27/03/1950	Neville Duke	Handling with 2 × 90 drop tanks	1,20	VP422
27/03/1950	Neville Duke	Handling with 2 × 90 drop tanks. Stbd tank [collapse?] 450.	30	VP422
08/06/1950	Wimpy Wade	Air test	40	VP413
09/06/1950	Frank Murphy	Air test and to Boscombe Down	45	VP413
21/07/1950	Wimpy Wade	To Sherburn in Elmet	35	VP413
21/07/1950	Wimpy Wade	Practice for SBAC Challenge Cup Race	55	VP413
21/07/1950	Wimpy Wade	Practice for SBAC Challenge Cup Race	40	VP413
22/07/1950	Wimpy Wade	Practice for SBAC Challenge Cup Race	25	VP413
22/07/1950	Wimpy Wade	Race - last at 584 mph	25	VP413
23/07/1950	Wimpy Wade	Return to Farnborough	40	VP413
02/09/1950	Neville Duke	Flight test and aerobatics		VP413
05/09/1950	Neville Duke	SBAC demonstration		VP413

Date	Pilot	Flight Detail	Time (mins)	Aircraft
06/09/1950	Neville Duke	SBAC demonstration		VP413
07/09/1950	Neville Duke	SBAC demonstration		VP413
08/09/1950	Neville Duke	SBAC demonstration		VP413
09/09/1950	Neville Duke	SBAC demonstration		VP413
10/09/1950	Neville Duke	SBAC demonstration		VP413
14/09/1950	Wimpy Wade	Air test	20	VP413
16/09/1950	Neville Duke	Demonstration		VP413
29/12/1950	Neville Duke	Taxying and landing tests	35	VP413
16/01/1951	Neville Duke	Landing tests	30	VP413
17/01/1951	Neville Duke	Landing tests	40	VP413
19/01/1951	Neville Duke	Landing tests	45	VP413
09/03/1951	Neville Duke	Flight test	20	VP422
12/03/1951	Neville Duke	Farnborough to Ford	15	VP422
13/03/1951	Neville Duke	Air firing 250 kts	30	VP422
13/03/1951	Neville Duke	Air firing 300 kts	30	VP422
14/03/1951	Neville Duke	Air firing 350 kts	25	VP422
14/03/1951	Neville Duke	Air firing 350 kts	25	VP422
19/03/1951	Neville Duke	Air firing 400 kts	20	VP422
19/03/1951	Neville Duke	Air firing 450 kts	25	VP422
19/03/1951	Neville Duke	Ford to Tangmere	10	VP422
20/03/1951	Neville Duke	Air firing 500 kts	25	VP422
20/03/1951	Neville Duke	Air firing 530 kts	25	VP422
21/03/1951	Neville Duke	Air firing 500 - 525 kts	25	VP422
08/05/1951	Neville Duke	Farnborough to Boscombe Down		VP422
18/07/1951	Neville Duke	Boscombe Down to Farnborough	15	VP422
15/08/1951	Neville Duke	Flight test	25	VP422
15/08/1951	Neville Duke	Flight test	15	VP422
28/08/1951	Neville Duke	Handling	30	VP422
18/09/1951	Neville Duke	Flight test	50	VP413
19/09/1951	Neville Duke	Farnborough to Dunsfold	60	VP413
01/10/1951	Neville Duke	Handling	30	VP413
03/10/1951	Neville Duke	Handling	40	VP413
08/10/1951	Bill Bedford	Test flight	35	VP413
09/10/1951	Bill Bedford	Test flight (brakes)	45	VP413
10/10/1951	Frank Murphy	Air brake check	50	VP413
17/10/1951	Neville Duke	Farnborough to Dunsfold	15	VP422

Appendix II 253

Date	Pilot	Flight Detail	Time (mins)	Aircraft
17/10/1951	Neville Duke	Handling	25	VP413
17/10/1951	Bill Bedford	Test flight	45	VP422
18/10/1951	Bill Bedford	Test flight	55	VP413
21/10/1951	Neville Duke	Handling	30	VP413
24/10/1951	Bill Bedford	Test flight	35	VP413
24/10/1951	Bill Bedford	Test flight	40	VP413
12/11/1951	Neville Duke	Flight test	30	VP413
13/11/1951	Neville Duke	Handling air brakes	30	VP413
19/11/1951	Bill Bedford	Air brakes investigation	40	VP413
21/11/1951	Bill Bedford	Air test	20	VP422
22/11/1951	Bill Bedford	Air test	45	VP422
23/11/1951	Bill Bedford	Air test	35	VP422
26/11/1951	Bill Bedford	Air test	40	VP422
27/11/1951	Bill Bedford	Air test	45	VP422
28/11/1951	Bill Bedford	Handling - tanks empty	1,10	VP422
28/11/1951	Bill Bedford	Handling - tanks empty	40	VP422
30/11/1951	Bill Bedford	Performance - tanks empty	60	VP422
09/12/1951	Bill Bedford	Air brake investigation	1,15	VP413
09/12/1951	Bill Bedford	Air brake investigation	55	VP413
12/12/1951	Bill Bedford	Air brakes	60	VP413
17/12/1951	Bill Bedford	Air brakes	1,05	VP413
18/12/1951	Neville Duke	Handling air brakes	50	VP413
28/12/1951	Neville Duke	Flight test drop tanks	1,05	VP422
28/12/1951	Neville Duke	Handling air brakes	35	VP413
31/12/1951	Bill Bedford	Air brakes	40	VP413
04/01/1952	Bill Bedford	Air brakes	10	VP413
05/01/1952	Neville Duke	Air brake investigation	60	VP413
07/01/1952	Neville Duke	Air brake investigation	40	VP413
07/01/1952	Neville Duke	Air brake investigation	25	VP413
22/01/1952	Bill Bedford	Handling with camera installation	45	VP422
25/01/1952	Bill Bedford	Handling with camera installation	60	VP422
01/02/1952	Neville Duke	Handling	50	VP422
01/02/1952	Bill Bedford	Air brake investigation	55	VP413
04/02/1952	Bill Bedford	Air brake investigation	55	VP413
06/02/1952	Bill Bedford	Handling	25	VP422
06/02/1952	Bill Bedford	Handling	15	VP422
06/02/1952	Bill Bedford	Handling	15	VP422

Date	Pilot	Flight Detail	Time (mins)	Aircraft
06/02/1952	Bill Bedford	Handling	25	VP422
12/02/1952	Bill Bedford	Air brake investigation	1,20	VP413
13/02/1952	Bill Bedford	Air brake investigation	1,10	VP413
19/02/1952	Bill Bedford	Air brake investigation	40	VP413
21/02/1952	Neville Duke	Handling	40	VP413
27/02/1952	Bill Bedford	Test flight	40	VP422
29/02/1952	Bill Bedford	Test flight	40	VP422
04/03/1952	Bill Bedford	Delivery to Boscombe. [Last mention of this aircraft in logs]	30	VP422
16/04/1952	Bill Bedford	Test flight	50	VP413
16/04/1952	Bill Bedford	Test flight	35	VP413
14/07/1953	Frank Murphy	Clearance test	25	VP413
17/07/1953	Frank Murphy	Delivery to Farnborough. [Last mention of this aircraft in logs]	35	VP413

Appendix II

P.1052 Flights		VX272 and VX279		
Date	Pilot	Flight Detail	Time (mins)	Aircraft
19/11/1948	Wimpy Wade	1st flight	10	VX272
24/11/1948	Wimpy Wade	Boscombe Down to Farnborough via Langley and general handling	40	VX272
25/11/1948	Wimpy Wade	General handling and stalls	20	VX272
26/11/1948	Wimpy Wade	General handling and stalls	30	VX272
26/11/1948	Neville Duke	First flight and handling	?	VX272
14/01/1949	Wimpy Wade	Faster faster	15	VX272
17/01/1949	Wimpy Wade	Faster faster	35	VX272
18/01/1949	Wimpy Wade	Faster slower	45	VX272
18/01/1949	Wimpy Wade	Faster slower	40	VX272
21/01/1949	Wimpy Wade	Slower faster	45	VX272
27/01/1949	Wimpy Wade	Pressing on	50	VX272
10/02/1949	Wimpy Wade	A chat with Mr. Mach	60	VX272
10/02/1949	Wimpy Wade	A f-ing row with Mr. Mach	1,30	VX272
11/02/1949	Wimpy Wade	A f-ing row with Mr. Mach	35	VX272
16/02/1949	Neville Duke	Trimmed speeds and MN 20,000 ft	?	VX272
16/02/1949	Neville Duke	Trimmed speeds and MN 30,000 ft	?	VX272
17/02/1949	Neville Duke	Combat climb and MN 20,000 and 30,000ft	?	VX272
18/02/1949	Neville Duke	Abortive 30,000 ft	?	VX272
21/02/1949	Neville Duke	Mach no investigation 20,000ft - 30,000 ft	?	VX272
25/02/1949	Neville Duke	Combat climb 40,000ft, 7min 7sec. MN 40,000, 30,000, 20,000ft - 0.88M	?	VX272
02/03/1949	Neville Duke	Photography	40	VX272
02/03/1949	Neville Duke	Demonstration flight	30	VX272
03/03/1949	Neville Duke	Mach no investigation 30,000, 20,000, 15,000, 10,000 ft	?	VX272
18/03/1949	Wimpy Wade	High Mach no. test of rudder	60	VX272
07/04/1949	Neville Duke	Mach no investigation 20,000-30,000ft	?	VX272
11/04/1949	Wimpy Wade	This and that	55	VX272
13/04/1949	Wimpy Wade	Demonstration Langley	20	VX272
13/04/1949	Wimpy Wade	Can't remember (Rudder). [First Flight?]	20	VX279
14/04/1949	Wimpy Wade	Rudder general - big bangs	30	VX279

Date	Pilot	Flight Detail	Time (mins)	Aircraft
21/04/1949	Neville Duke	Mach no investigation B/P U/S	?	VX279
21/04/1949	Neville Duke	Mach no investigation 20,000 - 30,000ft	?	VX279
21/04/1949	Neville Duke	Mach no investigation. trim U/S	?	VX279
22/04/1949	Neville Duke	Photographic with Chas Brown. Landed Boscombe Down	?	VX279
22/04/1949	Neville Duke	Boscombe to Farnborough and Mach no investigation 20,000ft. 0.88M	?	VX279
29/04/1949	Neville Duke	Aerobatics and levels 10,000ft. 0.875M?	?	VX272
29/04/1949	Neville Duke	Handling with modified rudder at high Mach - 5, 10, 20, 30,000ft	?	VX279
30/04/1949	Neville Duke	Farnborough to Woodford	?	VX272
30/04/1949	Neville Duke	Aerobatic demonstration at Woodford Air Display	?	VX272
03/05/1949	Wimpy Wade	More rudder	30	VX279
03/05/1949	Wimpy Wade	Still more rudder	30	VX279
09/05/1949	Wimpy Wade	Working up for Paris, bugger the rudder	30	VX279
09/05/1949	Wimpy Wade	Working up for Paris, bugger the rudder	30	VX279
10/05/1949	Wimpy Wade	Dummy runs for Paris	45	VX279
10/05/1949	Wimpy Wade	Dummy runs for Paris	15	VX279
12/05/1949	Wimpy Wade	Farnborough to London Airport and final check on rudder	15	VX279
13/05/1949	Wimpy Wade	London - Paris 21.40 minutes	30	VX279
13/05/1949	Wimpy Wade	Villacoublay - Bretigny	15	VX279
14/05/1949	Wimpy Wade	Bretigny - Villacoublay via Orly for appreciated demo	35	VX279
15/05/1949	Wimpy Wade	Paris - London	35	VX279
15/05/1949	Wimpy Wade	London - Farnborough plus demo	25	VX279
20/05/1949	Wimpy Wade	Test prior to RAE taking over.	20	VX272
31/05/1949	Wimpy Wade	Clearance test	20	VX272
02/06/1949	Eric Brown	Handling, stalls, dives from 35,000ft at M0.893	?	VX272
02/06/1949	Eric Brown	Dive from 35,500ft at M0.935	?	VX272
08/06/1949	Eric Brown	Handling	?	VX272
09/06/1949	Eric Brown	Levels 20,000ft up to M0.88	?	VX272

Appendix II 257

Date	Pilot	Flight Detail	Time (mins)	Aircraft
14/06/1949	Wimpy Wade	West Raynham and return	40	VX279
14/06/1949	Wimpy Wade	Demonstration	10	VX279
17/06/1949	Wimpy Wade	Rudder tab (electric)	40	VX279
20/06/1949	Wimpy Wade	More electrics	45	VX279
24/06/1949	Eric Brown	Position Error by aneroid method, up to 500kts	?	VX272
28/06/1949	Wimpy Wade	Air test and photographic	60	VX279
28/06/1949	Wimpy Wade	Delivery to A Sqn Boscombe Down	10	VX279
30/06/1949	Eric Brown	Position Error by aneroid method, up to 500kts	?	VX272
11/07/1949	Eric Brown	Stalls and Position Error with 100ft trailing static	?	VX272
12/07/1949	Eric Brown	Stalls and Position Error with 100ft trailing static	?	VX272
18/08/1949	Neville Duke	Air test	?	VX279
19/08/1949	Wimpy Wade	Farnborough to Boscombe and return for "Mr" Tedder	15	VX279
19/08/1949	Wimpy Wade	Farnborough to Boscombe and return for "Mr" Tedder	15	VX279
01/09/1949	Wimpy Wade	vibration investigation for RAE	40	VX272
02/09/1949	Wimpy Wade	Air test prior to SBAC. Landed A&AEE (possible brake problem)	35	VX279
05/09/1949	Wimpy Wade	Return to Farnborough check	30	VX279
06/09/1949	Wimpy Wade	SBAC Show demonstrations	15	VX279
07/09/1949	Wimpy Wade	SBAC Show demonstrations	15	VX279
08/09/1949	Wimpy Wade	SBAC Show demonstrations	15	VX279
09/09/1949	Wimpy Wade	SBAC Show demonstrations	15	VX279
10/09/1949	Wimpy Wade	SBAC Show demonstrations	15	VX279
11/09/1949	Wimpy Wade	SBAC Show demonstrations	15	VX279
24/09/1949	Neville Duke	Farnborough to Yeovilton. Abortive. Scrambled Odiham Vampires	?	VX279
24/09/1949	Neville Duke	Farnborough to Yeovilton. Success	?	VX279
24/09/1949	Neville Duke	Demonstration and return Farnborough	?	VX279
29/09/1949	Lt J. Elliot RN	Test flight. Engine failure. Forced landing at Cove	?	VX272
07/10/1949	Wimpy Wade	This and that	35	VX279
17/10/1949	Wimpy Wade	Test flight	50	VX279
17/10/1949	Neville Duke	Pressure plotting 5,000ft.	?	VX279

Date	Pilot	Flight Detail	Time (mins)	Aircraft
19/10/1949	Wimpy Wade	Test flight	45	VX279
20/10/1949	Wimpy Wade	Test flying	35	VX279
20/10/1949	Neville Duke	Pressure plotting, levels 1,500ft	?	VX279
21/10/1949	Wimpy Wade	pressure plotting	45	VX279
21/10/1949	Wimpy Wade	pressure plotting	45	VX279
24/10/1949	Wimpy Wade	pressure plotting	50	VX279
27/10/1949	Wimpy Wade	pressure plotting	55	VX279
27/10/1949	Wimpy Wade	pressure plotting	55	VX279
28/10/1949	Wimpy Wade	pressure plotting	55	VX279
28/10/1949	Wimpy Wade	pressure plotting	30	VX279
08/12/1949	Wimpy Wade	Unreadable	25	VX279
09/12/1949	Wimpy Wade	Unreadable	30	VX279
13/12/1949	Wimpy Wade	Vibration	30	VX279
29/12/1949	Wimpy Wade	Vibration	20	VX279
31/12/1949	Wimpy Wade	Vibration	10	VX279
04/01/1950	Wimpy Wade	Wiggly wiggly	30	VX279
16/01/1950	Wimpy Wade	Wiggly wiggly	30	VX279
18/01/1950	Neville Duke	Flutter investigation 5,000 - 20,000ft	40	VX279
23/01/1950	Wimpy Wade	Wiggly wiggly	25	VX279
03/02/1950	Neville Duke	Vibration investigation 20 - 10,000ft. Handling with moveable tailplane	?	VX279
07/02/1950	Wimpy Wade	More flutter	30	VX279
14/02/1950	Neville Duke	Vibration investigation	?	VX279
18/02/1950	Wimpy Wade	Vibration? No! [sketch of bullet fitted at fin/tailplane joint]	40	VX279
28?/2/1950	Wimpy Wade	Vibration - No	50	VX279
07/03/1950	Neville Duke	Handling and Mach no investigation with moveable tailplane M0.895	?	VX279
08/03/1950	Wimpy Wade	Vibration test	60	VX279
08/03/1950	Wimpy Wade	Vibration test	40	VX279
09/03/1950	Wimpy Wade	Vibration test	40	VX279
13/03/1950	Wimpy Wade	Vibration test	30	VX279
14/03/1950	Wimpy Wade	Vibration test	35	VX279
15/03/1950	Neville Duke	Vibration investigation. A/C U/S	30	VX279
21/03/1950	Wimpy Wade	Tailplane test	30	VX279
21/03/1950	Wimpy Wade	Tailplane test	10	VX279
24/03/1950	Neville Duke	Vibration investigation	55	VX279

Appendix II

Date	Pilot	Flight Detail	Time (mins)	Aircraft
24/03/1950	Neville Duke	Handling and Mach no investigation	50	VX279
29/03/1950	Neville Duke	Handling, Mach no investigation 0.9. vibro[graph?]	60	VX272
29/03/1950	Neville Duke	Handling	50	VX272
03/04/1950	Wimpy Wade	Handling at high Mach no.	40	VX272
12/04/1950	Wimpy Wade	High Machery	35	VX272
14/04/1950	Wimpy Wade	High Mach no. and airbrake	45	VX272
17/04/1950	Lt J.G. Harrison RN	Wing drop at high Mach investigation. Engine failure. Wheels up landing	?	VX272
19/04/1950	Neville Duke	Farnborough to Boscombe Down, handling	15	VX272
19/04/1950	Neville Duke	Demonstration	?	VX272
19/04/1950	Neville Duke	Boscombe Down to Farnborough and handling with air brake	55	VX272
09/05/1950	Wimpy Wade	Handling with swept tailplane	20	VX279
10/05/1950	Wimpy Wade	Handling with swept tailplane	40	VX279
10/05/1950	Wimpy Wade	Handling with swept tailplane plus rudder chord	40	VX279
23/05/1950	Wimpy Wade	Demonstration	15	VX272
23/05/1950	Wimpy Wade	Air test	30	VX272
17/07/1950	Lt J.G. Harrison RN	[Wing drop at high Mach investigation. Engine failure. Undershot killing contractor]		VX272
04/09/1951	Neville Duke	Handling and forced landing Langley	1,05	VX272
06/09/1951	Neville Duke	Langley to Farnborough	15	VX272
10/09/1951	Neville Duke	Handling	40	VX272
11/09/1951	Neville Duke	SBAC display	10	VX272
12/09/1951	Neville Duke	SBAC display	10	VX272
14/09/1951	Neville Duke	SBAC display	10	VX272
15/09/1951	Neville Duke	SBAC display	10	VX272
16/09/1951	Neville Duke	SBAC display	10	VX272
19/09/1951	Neville Duke	Farnborough to Dunsfold	10	VX272
02/10/1951	Neville Duke	Handling	25	VX272
18/10/1951	Bill Bedford	Test flight	45	VX272
30/10/1951	Bill Bedford	To RAE	10	VX272
10/03/1952	Bill Bedford	Test flight	45	VX272
11/03/1952	Bill Bedford	Test flight	35	VX272

Date	Pilot	Flight Detail	Time (mins)	Aircraft
25/03/1952	Bill Bedford	Test flight	20	VX272
31/03/1952	Bill Bedford	Mach no. and ASI investigation	45	VX272
31/03/1952	Bill Bedford	ASI investigation	30	VX272
01/04/1952	Neville Duke	Handling with bullet fairing	45	VX272
01/04/1952	Bill Bedford	Mach no. investigation	45	VX272
10/04/1952	Bill Bedford	Elevator investigation	55	VX272
15/04/1952	Bill Bedford	Mach no. & ASI investigation & to Farnborough	40	VX272
04/05/1952	Neville Duke	Handling	35	VX272
05/05/1952	Bill Bedford	Farnborough from Dunsfold	30	VX272
03/05/1953	Neville Duke	Flight test	50	VX272
12/05/1953	Neville Duke	Flight test	35	VX272
12/05/1953	Neville Duke	Flight test	40	VX272
20/05/1953	Neville Duke	Flight test	20	VX272
26/05/1953	Frank Murphy	Mach no investigation	20	VX272
27/05/1953	Frank Murphy	Deliver RAE and test	30	VX272
31/08/1953	Sq Ldr W.J. Potocki	[High speed Mach no investigation. Hydraulic failure. Forced landing Odiham]		VX272
25/09/1953	unknown	Engine failure. Forced landing. Cat 5 damage		VX272
26/11/1953	Neville Duke	Flight test	35	VX272
26/11/1953	Bill Bedford	Test flight	50	VX272
01/12/1953	Bill Bedford	Handling	60	VX272
01/12/1953	Bill Bedford	To RAE	20	VX272

Appendix II

P.1081 Flights		VX279	
Date	Pilot	Flight Detail	Time (mins)
19/06/1950	Wimpy Wade	1st flight	30
19/06/1950	Neville Duke	Handling	
20/06/1950	Wimpy Wade	General handling	1,05
20/06/1950	Wimpy Wade	General handling	45
20/06/1950	Wimpy Wade	General handling	40
21/06/1950	Neville Duke	Combat climb 40,000ft. High altitude handling	?
22/06/1950	Wimpy Wade	Farnborough - London Airport. Demonstration Langley (Sopwith)	30
23/06/1950	Wimpy Wade	London Airport - Brussels	25
25/06/1950	Wimpy Wade	Demonstration Antwerp	20
26/06/1950	Wimpy Wade	Brussels - London Airport	25
26/06/1950	Wimpy Wade	London Airport - Farnborough	15
30/06/1950	Wimpy Wade	Modified fairing	40
04/07/1950	Neville Duke	Handling	30
05/07/1950	Wimpy Wade	Air test	20
07/07/1950	Wimpy Wade	RAF display	20
08/07/1950	Wimpy Wade	RAF display	20
18/07/1950	Wimpy Wade	Air test	15
19/07/1950	Wimpy Wade	To Blackbushe	15
19/07/1950	Wimpy Wade	Film demonstration. Photographic epic (ha! ha!). Two wheel landing Odiham	25 + 60
20/07/1950	Wimpy Wade	Return to Farnborough	10
16/08/1950	Neville Duke	Handling up to M0.92	60
18/08/1950	Neville Duke	Performance climb 40,000 ft	1,30
23/08/1950	Neville Duke	Abortive	30,00
23/08/1950	Neville Duke	Climb to 38,000ft. AT calibration	1,05
23/08/1950	Neville Duke	Climb 40,000ft, levels 25,000ft	1,25
24/08/1950	Wimpy Wade	Performance	1,10
24/08/1950	Wimpy Wade	Performance	1,20
25/08/1950	Neville Duke	Levels 5,000ft	60,00
25/08/1950	Neville Duke	Levels 15,000 - 35,000ft	60,00
25/08/1950	Neville Duke	Combat climb 40,000ft and levels	1,15
28/08/1950	Neville Duke	Handling with modified jet pipe nozzle	30
29/08/1950	Neville Duke	Levels 5,000ft and handling	50
01/09/1950	Wimpy Wade	High Machery	55

Date	Pilot	Flight Detail	Time (mins)
05/09/1950	Wimpy Wade	SBAC demonstration	15
06/09/1950	Wimpy Wade	SBAC demonstration	15
07/09/1950	Wimpy Wade	Air test	15
07/09/1950	Wimpy Wade	SBAC demonstration	15
08/09/1950	Wimpy Wade	SBAC demonstration	15
09/09/1950	Wimpy Wade	SBAC demonstration	15
10/09/1950	Wimpy Wade	SBAC demonstration	15
06/10/1950	Wimpy Wade	Handling etc with electric actuator	60
18/10/1950	Neville Duke	Handling to M0.93 with modified tailplane	1,05
24/10/1950	Wimpy Wade	West Malling	20
24/10/1950	Wimpy Wade	MoS? Demonstration and return to Farnborough	30
31/10/1950	Neville Duke	Handling with modified rudder	?
29/12/1950	Neville Duke	Handling	60
12/01/1951	Neville Duke	Handling	60
12/01/1951	Neville Duke	Handling	50
16/01/1951	Neville Duke	Handling	50
07/02/1951	Neville Duke	Handling, modified rudder	50
12/02/1951	Neville Duke	Mach no investigation and handling. Stick force per G, 30 - 5,000ft	1,10
21/02/1951	Neville Duke	Handling up to M0.94	60
22/02/1951	Neville Duke	Handling up to M0.94	1,05
26/02/1951	Neville Duke	Handling	55
03/04/1951	Wimpy Wade	[Flight from Farnborough and fatal crash near Lewes. A/C destroyed]	

| Production Sea Hawk Flights ||||||
Date	Pilot	Flight Detail	Time (mins)	Aircraft
14/11/1951	Neville Duke	1st flight [1st Production aircraft]	50	WF143
15/11/1951	Neville Duke	General handling	40	WF143
21/11/1951	Neville Duke	General handling	50	WF143
28/11/1951	Neville Duke	General handling	40	WF143
30/11/1951	Neville Duke	General handling	55	WF143
06/12/1951	Bill Bedford	Handling	45	WF143
06/12/1951	Bill Bedford	Levels	50	WF143
12/12/1951	Bill Bedford	Handling	55	WF143
12/12/1951	Bill Bedford	Levels	50	WF143
20/12/1951	Neville Duke	General handling	60	WF143
28/12/1951	Neville Duke	General handling	50	WF143
21/02/1952	Neville Duke	Handling	50	WF144
25/02/1952	Neville Duke	Handling	55	WF143
26/02/1952	Neville Duke	Handling	40	WF144
04/03/1952	Neville Duke	Handling	40	WF144
06/03/1952	Bill Bedford	General handling	1,05	WF144
12/03/1952	Neville Duke	Handling	35	WF143
14/03/1952	Bill Bedford	Test flight	40	WF144
15/03/1952	Neville Duke	Handling	1,10	WF144
15/03/1952	Neville Duke	Handling	1,05	WF144
18/03/1952	Bill Bedford	Test flight	45	WF145
20/03/1952	Bill Bedford	Test flight	60	WF143
21/03/1952	Bill Bedford	Test flight	30	WF145
21/03/1952	Neville Duke	Handling	25	WF144
21/03/1952	Neville Duke	Handling	10	WF144
23/03/1952	Neville Duke	Handling	50	WF144
23/03/1952	Neville Duke	1st flight	45	WF145
24/03/1952	Neville Duke	Handling	1,05	WF144
24/03/1952	Bill Bedford	Test flight	1,05	WF143
26/03/1952	Bill Bedford	To and from Farnborough	20	WF145
01/04/1952	Bill Bedford	Aileron investigation	1,10	WF144
02/04/1952	Neville Duke	Handling	1,10	WF145
10/04/1952	Neville Duke	Handling	50	WF14?
17/04/1952	Bill Bedford	Test flight	25	WF143
18/04/1952	Bill Bedford	Test flight	1,10	WF145

Date	Pilot	Flight Detail	Time (mins)	Aircraft
22/04/1952	Neville Duke	Dunsfold to Boscombe	20	WF145
22/04/1952	Bill Bedford	Test flight	55	WF144
24/04/1952	Neville Duke	Handling	60	WF143
24/04/1952	Bill Bedford	Farnborough and return	60	WF144
25/04/1952	Bill Bedford	Aileron assessment	30	WF143
30/04/1952	Bill Bedford	Test flight stick force per G	40	WF143
30/04/1952	Bill Bedford	Test flight stick force per G	45	WF143
01/05/1952	Bill Bedford	Stick force per G	45	WF143
02/05/1952	Bill Bedford	Display for Sec State for Air	10	WF143
07/05/1952	Bill Bedford	Handling with bullet fairing	60	WF143
10/05/1952	Neville Duke	Handling	45	WF143
13/05/1952	Bill Bedford	Geared tab ailerons	45	WF143
15/05/1952	Bill Bedford	First flight	1,10	WF147
16/05/1953	Bill Bedford	Aileron investigation	50	WF143
21/05/1952	Bill Bedford	Test flight	55	WF147
24/05/1952	Neville Duke	Handling	50	WF143
27/05/1952	Neville Duke	Handling	20	WF143
28/05/1952	Bill Bedford	Stick force per G	1,10	WF143
28/05/1952	Bill Bedford	Stick force per G	30	WF143
03/06/1952	Neville Duke	Flight test	45	WF143
05/06/1952	Frank Murphy	Air brake assessment	30	WF143
09/06/1952	Bill Bedford	Stick force per G	50	WF143
10/06/1952	Bill Bedford	Stick force per G	40	WF143
11/06/1952	Bill Bedford	Stick force per G	60	WF143
11/06/1952	Bill Bedford	Stick force per G	35	WF143
12/06/1952	Frank Murphy	Fuel system checks	45	WF147
24/06/1952	Bill Bedford	Test flight	1,05	WF147
25/06/1952	Bill Bedford	Test flight	55	WF143
25/06/1952	Bill Bedford	Test flight	40	WF143
02/07/1952	Bill Bedford	Longitudinal stability	35	WF143
07/07/1952	Bill Bedford	Tank balancing unit	50	WF147
07/07/1952	Bill Bedford	Stick force per G	35	WF143
08/07/1952	Neville Duke	Flight test	25	WF143
08/07/1952	Neville Duke	Flight test	40	WF147
09/07/1952	Neville Duke	Flight test	55	WF143
15/07/1952	Neville Duke	Flight test	40	WF148

Appendix II 265

Date	Pilot	Flight Detail	Time (mins)	Aircraft
16/07/1952	Bill Bedford	Test flight	40	WF147
08/08/1952	Frank Murphy	with 100 octane	60	WF148
11/08/1952	Neville Duke	Flight test	60	WF148
16/08/1952	Neville Duke	Flight test	35	WF147
28/08/1952	Bill Bedford	First flight	50	WF149
28/08/1952	Bill Bedford	Test flight	20	WF147
28/08/1952	Bill Bedford	Test flight	1,05	WF147
28/08/1952	Frank Murphy	With Avtag	10	WF148
29/08/1952	Frank Murphy	With Avtag	60	WF148
29/08/1952	Frank Murphy	Consumption check	25	WF148
29/08/1952	Frank Murphy	Production test	50	WF150
30/08/1952	Frank Murphy	Production test	30	WF150
31/08/1952	Bill Bedford	Test flight & to Farnborough	20	WF147
01/09/1952	Bill Bedford	SBAC display	10	WF147
02/09/1952	Bill Bedford	SBAC display	10	WF147
03/09/1952	Bill Bedford	SBAC display	10	WF147
04/09/1952	Bill Bedford	SBAC display	10	WF147
04/09/1952	Frank Murphy	Dunsfold - Renfrew	60	WF148
05/09/1952	Bill Bedford	SBAC display	10	WF147
06/09/1952	Bill Bedford	SBAC display	10	WF147
07/09/1952	Bill Bedford	SBAC display	10	WF147
08/09/1952	Bill Bedford	Test flight & Farnborough to Dunsfold	20	WF147
08/09/1952	Neville Duke	Flight test	1,05	WF151
09/09/1952	Neville Duke	Flight test	25	WF147
12/09/1952	Frank Murphy	Production test	1,05	WF152
16/09/1952	Bill Bedford	Test flight	60	WF151
17/09/1952	Neville Duke	Flight test	35	WF147
17/09/1952	Bill Bedford	Test flight	45	WF150
18/09/1952	Neville Duke	Dunsfold - Boscombe Down	35	WF144
18/09/1952	Bill Bedford	Test flight	45	WF151
19/09/1952	Bill Bedford	Test and delivery to Manby	40	WF150
19/09/1952	Frank Murphy	Production test	55	WF152
22/09/1952	Frank Murphy	Delivery Ford	15	WF152
25/09/1952	Bill Bedford	Test flight	55	WF151
28/09/1952	Bill Bedford	Test flight	55	WF151

Date	Pilot	Flight Detail	Time (mins)	Aircraft
28/09/1952	Bill Bedford	Test flight	1,10	WF154
29/09/1952	Bill Bedford	Test flight	1,10	WF151
30/09/1952	Bill Bedford	Test flight	15	WF154
02/10/1952	Bill Bedford	Test flight	60	WF151
02/10/1952	Bill Bedford	Test flight	1,05	WF153
02/10/1952	Bill Bedford	Test flight	45	WF154
05/10/1952	Bill Bedford	Test flight	55	WF154
06/10/1952	Bill Bedford	Test flight	50	WF154
06/10/1952	Bill Bedford	Dunsfold to Boscombe Down	15	WF151
07/10/1952	Bill Bedford	Test flight	1,15	WF155
09/10/1952	Bill Bedford	Test flight	60	WF155
11/10/1952	Bill Bedford	Test flight	50	WF153
13/10/1952	Frank Murphy	Fuel pressure investigation	1,05	WF148
13/10/1952	Neville Duke	Test flight	35	WF155
13/10/1952	Bill Bedford	Test flight	55	WF153
14/10/1952	Bill Bedford	Test flight	50	WF153
14/10/1952	Bill Bedford	Test flight	45	WF155
15/10/1952	Neville Duke	Flight test	?	WF155
15/10/1952	Bill Bedford	Test flight	1,05	WF143
16/10/1952	Bill Bedford	Test flight	1,15	WF143
16/10/1952	Frank Murphy	Fuel pressure investigation	35	WF148
17/10/1952	Bill Bedford	Test flight	1,15	WF143
20/10/1952	Bill Bedford	Test flight	20	WF156
20/10/1952	Frank Murphy	Fuel pressure investigation	30	WF148
21/10/1952	Neville Duke	Flight test	60	WF156
25/10/1952	Neville Duke	Dunsfold - Ford	30	WF152?
31/10/1952	Bill Bedford	Test flight	55	WF143
31/10/1952	Bill Bedford	Test flight	1,05	WF143
04/11/1952	Bill Bedford	Test flight	1,05	WF143
04/11/1952	Bill Bedford	Test flight	45	WF143
05/11/1952	Frank Murphy	Delivery Ford	15	WF156
06/11/1952	Frank Murphy	Production Test	25	WF158
07/11/1952	Neville Duke	Flight test	35	WF158
07/11/1952	Bill Bedford	Test flight	1,05	WF143
07/11/1952	Bill Bedford	Test flight	45	WF143
08/11/1952	Neville Duke	Flight test	1,40	WF143
17/11/1952	Bill Bedford	Test flight	40,00	WF154

Appendix II 267

Date	Pilot	Flight Detail	Time (mins)	Aircraft
20/11/1952	Bill Bedford	Test flight	1,15	WF143
20/11/1952	Bill Bedford	Test flight	40,00	WF143
20/11/1952	Bill Bedford	Test flight	30,00	WF147
20/11/1952	Neville Duke	Flight test		WF158
20/11/1952	Neville Duke	Powered ailerons		WF147
20/11/1952	Frank Murphy	Production test	40	WF159
21/11/1952	Bill Bedford	Test flight	1,05	WF143
21/11/1952	Bill Bedford	Test flight	1,10	WF147
25/11/1952	Bill Bedford	Test flight	35	WF158
25/11/1952	Bill Bedford	Test flight	1,15	WF143
29/11/1952	Neville Duke	Flight test		WF158
30/11/1952	Neville Duke	Flight test		WF159
03/12/1952	Frank Murphy	Production test	40	WF158
03/12/1952	Bill Bedford	Test flight	1,20	WF143
04/12/1952	Neville Duke	Flight test	35	WF154
06/12/1954	Bill Bedford	Test flight	60	WF159
06/12/1952	Bill Bedford	Delivery to Ford	15	WF158
11/12/1952	Frank Murphy	Production test	50	WF159
11/12/1952	Bill Bedford	Test flight	50	WF160
11/12/1952	Bill Bedford	Test flight	50	WF159
11/12/1952	Bill Bedford	Test flight	60	WF154
12/12/1952	Bill Bedford	Test flight	1,05	WF146
14/12/1952	Frank Murphy	Production test	40	WF161
14/12/1952	Neville Duke	Flight test	50	WF143
18/12/1952	Frank Murphy	Production test	35	WF160
18/12/1952	Neville Duke	Flight test	20	WF154
19/12/1952	Frank Murphy	Production test (Engine failure. Forced landing Ford, wet airfield, used all runway, 15ft flame at finish)	10	WF159
22/12/1952	Bill Bedford	Test flight	1,05	WF146
23/12/1952	Bill Bedford	Test flight	30	WF146
23/12/1952	Neville Duke	Flight test	45	WF143
24/12/1952	Bill Bedford	Test flight	1,05	WF154
31/12/1952	Neville Duke	Flight test	40	WF154
01/01/1953	Neville Duke	Flight test.	40	WF154
02/01/1953	Neville Duke	Flight test	50	WF157
02/01/1953	Frank Murphy	Production test	35	WF160

Date	Pilot	Flight Detail	Time (mins)	Aircraft
02/01/1953	Bill Bedford	Test flight	60	WF143
02/01/1953	Bill Bedford	Test flight	55	WF145
02/01/1953	Bill Bedford	Test flight	50	WF146
03/01/1953	Bill Bedford	Test flight	50	WF146
03/01/1953	Bill Bedford	Test flight	1,05	WF163
05/01/1953	Bill Bedford	Test flight inverted oil system check. Forced landing Dunsfold		WF154
09/01/1953	Neville Duke	Flight test	35	WF151
10/01/1953	Neville Duke	Return from Ford	35	WF159
12/01/1953	Bill Bedford	Test flight.	60	WF143
12/01/1953	Neville Duke	Drop tanks	60	WF143
12/01/1953	Frank Murphy	Production test	35	WF153
?/1/1953	Neville Duke	Flight test	60	WF153
20/01/1953	Neville Duke	Cabin heating	60	WF146
20/01/1953	Neville Duke	Cabin heating	?	WF146
20/01/1953	Frank Murphy	Production test	30	WF160
20/01/1953	Frank Murphy	Production test	45	WF151
20/01/1953	Frank Murphy	Production test	25	WF160
20/01/1953	Neville Duke	Power ailerons	50	WF147
21/01/1953	Frank Murphy	Delivery to Ford	15	WF151
21/04/1953	Frank Murphy	Production test	35	WF175
22/04/1953	Frank Murphy	Production test	35	WF159
22/01/1953	Neville Duke	Cabin heating	60	WF146
23/04/1953	Frank Murphy	Production test	35	WF176
25/04/1953	Frank Murphy	Production test	30	WF175
25/01/1953	Neville Duke	Cabin heating		WF146
26/01/1953	Neville Duke	Bombs	55	WF146
26/01/1953	Neville Duke	Flight test	35	WF153
27/01/1953	Neville Duke	Flight test	30	WF160
28/01/1953	Neville Duke	Flight test	50	WF145
28/01/1953	Neville Duke	Cabin heating	40	WF146
28/01/1953	Neville Duke	Flight test	30	WF153
29/01/1953	Neville Duke	Flight test	15	WF160
31/01/1953	Neville Duke	Delivery to Ford	20	WF153
02/02/1953	Neville Duke	Flight test	35	WF145
02/02/1953	Neville Duke	Flight test	50	WF159
06/02/1953	Neville Duke	Flight test	45	WF147

Appendix II 269

Date	Pilot	Flight Detail	Time (mins)	Aircraft
12/02/1953	Neville Duke	Flight test	35	WF147
20/02/1953	Neville Duke	Flight test	50	?
25/02/1953	Neville Duke	Flight test	40	?
27/02/1953	Neville Duke	Flight test	30	WM903
27/02/1953	Neville Duke	Flight test	45	WF146?
28/02/1953	Neville Duke	Flight test	45	WF143
28/02/1953	Neville Duke	Flight test	35	WF171
28/02/1953	Neville Duke	Flight test	30	WF171
28/02/1953	Neville Duke	Flight test		?
28/02/1953	Neville Duke	Flight test		WF161
06/03/1953	Neville Duke	Flight test		WF160
06/03/1953	Neville Duke	Flight test	25	WF143
10/03/1953	Neville Duke	Flight test	30	WF171
11/03/1953	Neville Duke	Flight test	50	WF14?
13/03/1953	Neville Duke	Flight test	60	WF14?
20/03/1953	Neville Duke	Flight test	45	WF146
24/03/1953	Neville Duke	Flight test	20	WF146
24/03/1953	Neville Duke	Flight test	45	WF146
24/03/1953	Neville Duke	Flight test	35	WF174
26/03/1953	Neville Duke	Flight test	40	WF172
27/03/1953	Neville Duke	Flight test	25	WF174
27/03/1953	Neville Duke	Flight test	35	WF172
27/03/1953	Neville Duke	Flight test	20	WF147
27/03/1953	Neville Duke	Flight test	45?	WF143
27/03/1953	Neville Duke	Flight test	25	WF143
30/03/1953	Neville Duke	Flight test	30	WF146
30/03/1953	Neville Duke	Flight test	50	WF164
31/03/1953	Neville Duke	Flight test	20	WF169
31/03/1953	Neville Duke	Flight test	15	WF169
31/03/1953	Neville Duke	Flight test	40	WF143
31/03/1953	Neville Duke	Flight test	30	WF143
08/04/1953	Neville Duke	Flight test	15	WF14?
10/04/1953	Neville Duke	Flight test	40	WF14?
?/4/1953	Neville Duke	Flight test	60	WF14?
?/4/1953	Neville Duke	Flight test	30	WF14?
?/4/1953	Neville Duke	Flight test	30	WF14?
17/04/1953	Neville Duke	Flight test	50	WF?

Date	Pilot	Flight Detail	Time (mins)	Aircraft
17/04/1953	Neville Duke	Flight test	15	WF?
19/04/1953	Neville Duke	Flight test	45	?
?/4/1953	Neville Duke	Flight test	15	?
24/04/1953	Neville Duke	Flight test	45	WF?
27/04/1953	Frank Murphy	Production test	30	WF172
29/04/1953	Neville Duke	Flight test	30	?
29/04/1953	Neville Duke	Flight test	25	?
29/04/1953	Frank Murphy	Tremor investigation	10	WF160
29/04/1953	Frank Murphy	Tremor investigation	25	WF160
03/05/1953	Neville Duke	Flight test	60	WF?
07/05/1953	Neville Duke	Flight test	20	WF17?
07/05/1953	Neville Duke	Flight test	25	WF?
07/05/1953	Neville Duke	Flight test	40	WF?
08/05/1953	Neville Duke	Flight test	50	WF14?
12/05/1953	Frank Murphy	Gun heating	1,30	WM901
13/05/1953	Neville Duke	Flight test	35	WF177
14/05/1953	Frank Murphy	Production test	35	WF172
17/05/1953	Frank Murphy	Production test	30	WF177
19/05/1953	Frank Murphy	Gun heating	30	WM901
19/05/1953	Frank Murphy	Gun heating	20	WM901
20/05/1953	Frank Murphy	Gun heating	1,25	WM901
20/05/1953	Frank Murphy	Production test	30	WF172
21/05/1953	Frank Murphy	Production test	30	WF176
22/05/1953	Neville Duke	Flight test		?
22/05/1953	Frank Murphy	Production test	20	WF177
25/05/1953	Frank Murphy	Production test	45	WF177
25/05/1953	Bill Bedford	Test flight	1,15	WF146
25/05/1953	Bill Bedford	Test flight	1,10	WF146
28/05/1953	Frank Murphy	Production test	25	WF175
28/05/1953	Bill Bedford	Test flight	35	WF147
29/05/1953	Bill Bedford	Test flight	45	WF147
29/05/1953	Bill Bedford	Test flight	1,25	WH901
03/06/1953	Frank Murphy	Production test	30	WF175
03/06/1953	Bill Bedford	Test flight	1,3	WH901
04/06/1953	Bill Bedford	Test flight	40	WH901
04/06/1953	Bill Bedford	Test flight	35	WF175
04/06/1953	Frank Murphy	Production test	40	WF175

Date	Pilot	Flight Detail	Time (mins)	Aircraft
04/06/1953	Bill Bedford	Test flight	40	WH901
04/06/1953	Bill Bedford	Test flight	60	WF146
05/06/1953	Neville Duke	Flight test	5	WF175
05/06/1953	Neville Duke	Flight test	30	WF175
08/06/1953	Bill Bedford	Test flight	30	WF175
09/06/1953	Bill Bedford	Test flight	60	WF146
10/06/1953	Bill Bedford	Test flight	50	WH901
10/06/1953	Frank Murphy	Production test	25	WF175
11/06/1953	Frank Murphy	Oil system check	40	WF147
12/06/1953	Frank Murphy	Production test	10	WF177
15/06/1953	Frank Murphy	Production test	45	WF177
16/06/1953	Bill Bedford	Test flight	50	WF177
17/06/1953	Bill Bedford	Test flight	45	WH901
18/06/1953	Bill Bedford	Test flight	30	WH901
18/06/1953	Bill Bedford	Test flight - cabin conditioning	60	WF161
23/06/1953	Bill Bedford	Test flight	1,10	WF146
23/06/1953	Bill Bedford	Test flight	40	WF161
24/06/1953	Bill Bedford	Test flight	1,20	WF161
25/06/1953	Frank Murphy	Production test	35	WF158
26/06/1953	Neville Duke	Flight test	30	WF147
26/06/1953	Neville Duke	Flight test	50	WF147
30/06/1953	Bill Bedford	Test flight	1,3	WF161
30/06/1953	Bill Bedford	Test flight	15	WF143
01/07/1953	Bill Bedford	Test flight	50	WF156
08/07/1953	Frank Murphy	Fuel system checks	50	WF143
10/07/1953	Frank Murphy	IFF invertor cooling	45	WF145
10/07/1953	Frank Murphy	Production test	45	WF170
11/07/1953	Frank Murphy	Production test	35	WF160
13/07/1953	Frank Murphy	Cockpit conditioning	60	WF161
15/07/1953	Neville Duke	Flight test	55	WF143
16/07/1953	Frank Murphy	Production test	30	WF156
05/08/1953	Frank Murphy	Production test	45	WF170
05/08/1953	Bill Bedford	Test flight	1,2	WF161
05/08/1953	Bill Bedford	Test flight	30	WF143
06/08/1953	Frank Murphy	Production test	25	WF170
06/08/1953	Bill Bedford	Test flight	30	WF170
07/08/1953	Frank Murphy	Cockpit heating	1,10	WF161

Date	Pilot	Flight Detail	Time (mins)	Aircraft
10/08/1953	Bill Bedford	Test flight	35,00	WF161
10/08/1953	Bill Bedford	Test flight	1,05	WF145
11/08/1953	Frank Murphy	Production test	20	WF159
11/08/1953	Bill Bedford	Test flight	40	WF152
11/08/1953	Bill Bedford	Test flight	50	WF153
13/08/1953	Bill Bedford	Test flight	50	WF170
13/08/1953	Bill Bedford	Bitteswell and return	45	WF153
14/08/1953	Bill Bedford	Test flight	1,20	WF145
19/08/1953	Bill Bedford	Test flight	60	WF161
20/08/1953	Bill Bedford	Test flight	1,05	WF161
20/08/1953	Bill Bedford	Test flight	45	WF161
21/08/1953	Frank Murphy	Production test	55	WF159
24/08/1953	Neville Duke	Flight test	40	WF159
25/08/1953	Bill Bedford	Test flight - invertor cooling	1,55	WF145
28/08/1953	Bill Bedford	Test flight (ETPS visit)	2,10	WF145
06/09/1953	Frank Murphy	Powered ailerons	35	WF147
08/09/1953	Frank Murphy	SBAC demonstrations	10	WF147
11/09/1953	Frank Murphy	SBAC demonstrations	5	WF147
12/09/1953	Frank Murphy	SBAC demonstrations	10	WF147
13/09/1953	Frank Murphy	SBAC demonstrations	10	WF147
14/09/1953	Frank Murphy	Farnborough to Dunsfold	10	WF147
17/09/1953	Bill Bedford	Test flight	1,20	WF161
22/09/1953	Bill Bedford	Test flight	1,05	WF161
28/09/1953	Bill Bedford	Test flight	60	WF161
29/09/1953	Bill Bedford	Test flight	45	WF143
30/09/1953	Bill Bedford	Test flight	50	WF161
22/10/1953	Neville Duke	Flight test	35	WF147
23/10/1953	Frank Murphy	Elevator tremor	40	WF189
28/10/1953	Frank Murphy	Delivery check	25	WF145
29/10/1953	Bill Bedford	Test flight	55	WF161
02/11/1953	Bill Bedford	Test flight	60	WF147
06/11/1953	Neville Duke	Flight test	20	WF145
12/11/1953	Bill Bedford	Test flight	20	WF143
16/12/1953	Frank Murphy	Spins and to Boscombe Down	40	WF143
04/01/1954	Frank Murphy	Assessment 1st production a/c. Full power ailerons - AWA	25	WF241
29/03/1954	Frank Murphy	Control assessment [AWA built]	40	?

P.1067 Flights		WB188, WB195 and WB202		
Date	Pilot	Flight Detail	Time (mins)	Aircraft
20/07/1951	Neville Duke	1st flight. General handling	50	WB188
24/07/1951	Neville Duke	Handling	60	WB188
25/07/1951	Neville Duke	Handling	55	WB188
10/08/1951	Neville Duke	Flight test. Stalls	60	WB188
10/08/1951	Neville Duke	Handling. Landed Farnborough	40	WB188
16/08/1951	Neville Duke	Handling	40	WB188
17/08/1951	Neville Duke	Handling	45	WB188
23/08/1951	Neville Duke	Handling	45	WB188
24/08/1951	Neville Duke	Handling	25	WB188
31/08/1951	Neville Duke	Handling	45	WB188
03/09/1951	Neville Duke	Handling	45	WB188
05/09/1951	Neville Duke	Handling	40	WB188
06/09/1951	Neville Duke	Handling	35	WB188
07/09/1951	Neville Duke	Handling and to Dunsfold	25	WB188
08/09/1951	Neville Duke	Demonstration USAF	20	WB188
08/09/1951	Neville Duke	Handling and return to Farnborough	35	WB188
11/09/1951	Neville Duke	SBAC display	10	WB188
12/09/1951	Neville Duke	SBAC display	10	WB188
14/09/1951	Neville Duke	SBAC display	10	WB188
15/09/1951	Neville Duke	SBAC display and Biggin Hill	30	WB188
16/09/1951	Neville Duke	SBAC display. 596 kts	10	WB188
21/09/1951	Neville Duke	Flight test and to Dunsfold	35	WB188
08/10/1951	Neville Duke	Performance and handling	35	WB188
09/10/1951	Neville Duke	Performance	40	WB188
09/10/1951	Neville Duke	Performance	45	WB188
11/10/1951	Neville Duke	Performance	55	WB188
11/10/1951	Neville Duke	Performance	45	WB188
12/10/1951	Neville Duke	Performance	35	WB188
12/10/1951	Neville Duke	Performance	50	WB188
13/10/1951	Neville Duke	Performance	30	WB188
15/10/1951	Neville Duke	Performance	50	WB188
17/10/1951	Neville Duke	Performance	50	WB188
18/10/1951	Neville Duke	Performance	25	WB188
19/10/1951	Neville Duke	Performance	35	WB188
19/10/1951	Neville Duke	Performance	35	WB188
21/10/1951	Neville Duke	Performance	35	WB188

Date	Pilot	Flight Detail	Time (mins)	Aircraft
09/01/1952	Neville Duke	General handling	50	WB188
14/01/1952	Neville Duke	General handling	45	WB188
15/01/1952	Neville Duke	General handling	55	WB188
16/01/1952	Neville Duke	General handling	35	WB188
16/01/1952	Neville Duke	General handling	35	WB188
18/01/1952	Neville Duke	General handling	40	WB188
21/01/1952	Neville Duke	General handling	35	WB188
27/01/1952	Neville Duke	General handling	45	WB188
27/01/1952	Neville Duke	General handling	40	WB188
29/01/1952	Neville Duke	General handling	40	WB188
31/01/1952	Neville Duke	General handling	35	WB188
02/02/1952	Neville Duke	Cabin pressure tests	50	WB188
05/02/1952	Neville Duke	Handling with fixed dive recovery flaps	45	WB188
07/02/1952	Neville Duke	Mach no investigation	35	WB188
08/02/1952	Neville Duke	Mach no investigation	45	WB188
13/02/1952	Neville Duke	Mach no investigation	30	WB188
14/02/1952	Neville Duke	Handling with ailerons in manual	35	WB188
16/02/1952	Neville Duke	Cabins pressure tests	45	WB188
16/02/1952	Neville Duke	Cabin pressure tests	40	WB188
20/02/1952	Neville Duke	High altitude handling	45	WB188
20/02/1952	Neville Duke	Mach no investigation up to M0.99	30	WB188
20/02/1952	Neville Duke	Handling with flap on nose wheel door	45	WB188
20/02/1952	Neville Duke	Cabin pressure tests	35	WB188
21/02/1952	Neville Duke	Cabin pressure tests	55	WB188
04/03/1952	Neville Duke	Handling with modified rear f??? [fuselage or fairing]	60	WB188
05/03/1952	Neville Duke	Handling at aft C.G.	55	WB188
10/03/1952	Neville Duke	Mach no and high ASI investigation	60	WB188
10/03/1952	Neville Duke	Mach no up to 599 kts and ???	1,05	WB188
11/03/1952	Neville Duke	Mach no investigation	40	WB188
12/03/1952	Neville Duke	Combat climb to 48,000ft and levels	45	WB188
12/03/1952	Neville Duke	Cockpit heating and pressure	40	WB188
12/03/1952	Bill Bedford	General handling	45	WB188
13/03/1952	Neville Duke	Stalls	1,10	WB188
26/03/1952	Neville Duke	Mach no investigation with modified ???	40	WB188

Appendix II 275

Date	Pilot	Flight Detail	Time (mins)	Aircraft
27/03/1952	Neville Duke	Mach no investigation with modified ???	40	WB188
28/03/1952	Bill Bedford	Handling	35	WB188
02/04/1952	Neville Duke	Mach no investigation with short ??? ???	30	WB188
03/04/1952	Neville Duke	Mach no investigation with spoilers on fin	30	WB188
03/04/1952	Neville Duke	Mach no investigation with fin turbulators?	25	WB188
04/04/1952	Neville Duke	Mach no investigation with fin and tail turbulators?	30	WB188
04/04/1952	Bill Bedford	Test flight	25	WB188
10/04/1952	Neville Duke	Dive recovery flap investigation	30	WB188
22/04/1952	Neville Duke	Mach no investigation with additional ???	30	WB188
24/04/1952	Neville Duke	Mach no investigation with increased dorsal C39???	35	WB188
25/04/1952	Neville Duke	Mach no investigation up to M1.03	35	WB188
29/04/1952	Neville Duke	Stick force per G 45,000ft	55	WB188
29/04/1952	Neville Duke	Manoeuvre boundaries	20	WB188
01/05/1952	Bill Bedford	Stick force per G	40	WB188
01/05/1952	Neville Duke	High altitude handling	30	WB188
02/05/1952	Neville Duke	Demonstration	10	WB188
6?/5/1952	Neville Duke	Demonstration - King of Iraq	15	WB188
05/05/1952	Neville Duke	1st flight	40	WB195
07/05/1952	Neville Duke	General handling	40	WB195
09/05/1952	Neville Duke	General handling	40	WB195
15/05/1952	Neville Duke	General handling	30	WB195
16/05/1952	Neville Duke	Lateral and directional stability	45	WB195
21/05/1952	Bill Bedford	Handling	35	WB195
23/05/1952	Bill Bedford	Air brake investigation	25	WB195
23/05/1952	Bill Bedford	Air brake investigation	25	WB195
24/05/1952	Neville Duke	Stalls	35	WB195
24/05/1952	Neville Duke	Assessment of power controls	25	WB195
04/06/1952	Neville Duke	Handling at high Mach and ASI - 0.96, 600kts		WB195
05/06/1952	Neville Duke	Handling at high Mach and ASI - 0.96, 600kts		WB195
06/06/1952	Neville Duke	handling with reverse bullet		WB188

Date	Pilot	Flight Detail	Time (mins)	Aircraft
06/06/1952	Neville Duke	Demonstration - Mr Findletter		WB195
09/06/1952	Neville Duke	Handling with reverse bullet		WB188
09/06/1952	Bill Bedford	Stick force per G	35	WB188
10/06/1952	Neville Duke	Handling with tail chute removed		WB188
13/06/1952	Neville Duke	Handling with wing fences		WB188
16/06/1952	Neville Duke	Combat climb to 50,000ft and handling	45	WB188
16/06/1952	Bill Bedford	Handling	35	WB188
17/06/1952	Bill Bedford	PEs	45	WB188
17/06/1952	Bill Bedford	PEs	35	WB188
17/06/1952	Bill Bedford	PEs	40	WB188
17/06/1952	Neville Duke	Combat climb to 50,000ft and handling	20	WB188
18/06/1952	Neville Duke	Cabin pressure and Mach no 0.98	50	WB195
19/06/1952	Neville Duke	Cabin pressure and Mach no 0.98	35	WB188
20/06/1952	Neville Duke	Handling	40	WB188
20/06/1952	Neville Duke	Handling	20	WB195
24/06/1952	Neville Duke	High Mach no with reverse bullet. 1st time supersonic	40	WB188
26/06/1952	Neville Duke	Blank	40	WB188
26/06/1952	Bill Bedford	Test flight stick force per G	40	WB188
27/06/1952	Bill Bedford	Test flight stick force per G	45	WB188
27/06/1952	Bill Bedford	Test flight high MNI	45	WB188
30/06/1952	Neville Duke	Mach no investigation up to M1.06	40	WB195
30/06/1952	Neville Duke	Mach no investigation and engine handling	45	WB195
01/07/1952	Neville Duke	?	1,05	WB195
04/07/1952	Bill Bedford	Stick force per G	35	WB188
05/07/1952	Neville Duke	?	40	WB188
07/07/1952	Bill Bedford	Stick force per G	40	WB188
09/07/1952	Neville Duke	?	35	WB195
09/07/1952	Neville Duke	?	15	WB195
09/07/1952	Neville Duke	?	35	WB188
10/07/1952	Neville Duke	Low level cruise 2,000ft, 560 kts	35	WB188
10/07/1952	Neville Duke	Dunsfold - Brussels and M.1	25	WB188
12/07/1952	Neville Duke	Demonstration and M.1	30	WB188
13/07/1952	Neville Duke	Demonstration and M.1	20	WB188

Appendix II

Date	Pilot	Flight Detail	Time (mins)	Aircraft
14/07/1952	Neville Duke	Brussels - Manston	20	WB188
14/07/1952	Neville Duke	Manston - Dunsfold	15	WB188
17/07/1952	Neville Duke	Stick jerking tests	15	WB195
17/07/1952	Neville Duke	Stick jerking tests	15	WB195
17/07/1952	Neville Duke	Stick jerking tests	15	WB195
18/07/1952	Neville Duke	Stick jerking tests	20	WB195
18/07/1952	Neville Duke	Stick jerking tests	20	WB195
08/08/1952	Neville Duke	?	20	WB195
08/08/1952	Neville Duke	?	15	WB195
08/08/1952	Neville Duke	?	15	WB195
01/09/1952	Neville Duke	SBAC display	15	WB195
02/09/1952	Neville Duke	SBAC display landed Dunsfold	40	WB195
02/09/1952	Neville Duke	Flight test	30	WB195
03/09/1952	Neville Duke	Dunsfold to Farnborough	25	WB195
03/09/1952	Neville Duke	SBAC display	25	WB195
04/09/1952	Neville Duke	SBAC display	25	WB195
05/09/1952	Neville Duke	SBAC display	50	WB195
06/09/1952	Neville Duke	SBAC display	40	WB195
07/09/1952	Neville Duke	SBAC display	35	WB195
08/09/1952	Neville Duke	Farnborough to Dunsfold	40	WB195
08/09/1952	Neville Duke	?	25	WB195
11/09/1952	Neville Duke	?	15	WB195
11/09/1952	Neville Duke	?	25	WB195
13/09/1952	Neville Duke	?	35	WB188
15/09/1952	Neville Duke	?	30	WB195
15/09/1952	Neville Duke	?	30	WB195
03/10/1952	Bill Bedford	Test flight	35	WB188
05/10/1952	Bill Bedford	Test flight	30	WB188
05/10/1952	Bill Bedford	Test flight	45	WB188
06/10/1952	Neville Duke	?	50	WB188
10/10/1952	Bill Bedford	Test flight	30	WB188
11/10/1952	Neville Duke	?	35	WB188
11/10/1952	Neville Duke	?	45	WB188
14/10/1952	Neville Duke	?	30	WB195
15/10/1952	Bill Bedford	Measured landings	25	WB188
15/10/1952	Bill Bedford	Measured landings	30	WB188

Date	Pilot	Flight Detail	Time (mins)	Aircraft
15/10/1952	Bill Bedford	Measured landings	30	WB188
16/10/1952	Neville Duke	?	25	WB195
17/10/1952	Neville Duke	?	25	WB195
17/10/1952	Neville Duke	?	30	WB195
17/10/1952	Neville Duke	Dunsfold - Farnborough	25	WB188
18/10/1952	Neville Duke	Demonstration	30	WB188
18/10/1952	Neville Duke	Farnborough - Dunsfold	15	WB188
21/10/1952	Neville Duke	?	50	WB195
22/10/1952	Bill Bedford	Test flight	35	WB188
22/10/1952	Neville Duke	?	50	WB195
22/10/1952	Col Johnson	NATO		WB188
22/10/1952	Maj Davis	NATO		WB188
30/10/1952	Neville Duke	Dunsfold - Tangmere	30	WB188
30/10/1952	Neville Duke	Tangmere - Dunsfold	25	WB188
05/11/1952	Bill Bedford	Test flight	30	WB188
12/11/1952	Neville Duke	Flight test	20	WB188
13/11/1952	Neville Duke	Flight test	25	WB188
13/11/1952	Bill Bedford	Test flight	35	WB188
14/11/1952	Neville Duke	Flight test	20	WB188
20/11/1952	Neville Duke	Flight test		WB188
20/11/1952	Neville Duke	Flight test		WB188
22/11/1952	Neville Duke	Flight test		WB195
25/11/1952	Neville Duke	Flight test		WB195
26/11/1952	Bill Bedford	Landing tests RAE Farnborough	10	WB188
28/11/1952	Bill Bedford	Landing tests RAE Farnborough	5	WB188
28/11/1952	Bill Bedford	Landing tests RAE Farnborough	5	WB188
28/11/1952	Bill Bedford	Landing tests RAE Farnborough	5	WB188
28/11/1952	Bill Bedford	Landing tests RAE Farnborough	5	WB188
28/11/1952	Bill Bedford	Landing tests RAE Farnborough	5	WB188
28/11/1952	Bill Bedford	Landing tests RAE Farnborough	5	WB188
28/11/1952	Bill Bedford	To Dunsfold	30	WB188
30/11/1952	Neville Duke	1st flight. Sapphire Hunter		WB202
03/12/1952	Neville Duke	General handling	40	WB202
03/12/1952	Neville Duke	General handling	45	WB202
03/12/1952	Bill Bedford	Test flight	40	WB195
03/12/1952	Bill Bedford	Test flight	20	WB195

Appendix II 279

Date	Pilot	Flight Detail	Time (mins)	Aircraft
05/12/1952	Neville Duke	Dunsfold - Boscombe Down	30	WB195
12/12/1952	Neville Duke	General handling	45	WB202
14/12/1952	Neville Duke	General handling	25	WB202
18/12/1952	Neville Duke	General handling	55	WB202
20/12/1952	Neville Duke	Boscombe Down - Dunsfold	30	WB195
24/12/1952	Neville Duke	General handling	50	WB202
24/12/1952	Neville Duke	Stick jerking tests	30	WB195
24/12/1952	Neville Duke	Stick jerking tests	15	WB195
24/12/1952	Bill Bedford	Elevator vibration investigation	30	WB195
24/12/1952	Bill Bedford	Elevator vibration investigation	20	WB195
02/01/1953	Neville Duke	Flight test	45	WB202
02/01/1953	Neville Duke	Flight test	20	WB202
12/01/1953	Neville Duke	Flight test, MN 1.02	55	WB202
20/01/1953	Neville Duke	Stick jerking	30	WB195
25/01/1953	Neville Duke	Stick jerking	25	WB195
26/01/1953	Neville Duke	Mach no and demonstration		WB195
27/01/1953	Neville Duke	Flight test	10	WB195
29/01/1953	Neville Duke	Stick jerking	20	WB195
31/01/1953	Neville Duke	Stick jerking	20	WB195
31/01/1953	Neville Duke	Stick jerking	25	WB195
02/02/1953	Neville Duke	Flight test	20	WB195
13/02/1953	Neville Duke	Flight test	20	WB195
16/02/1953	Neville Duke	Flight test	20	WB195
16/02/1953	Neville Duke	Flight test	15	WB195
16/02/1953	Neville Duke	Flight test	15	WB195
16/02/1953	Neville Duke	Flight test	15	WB195
18/02/1953	Neville Duke	Flight test	15	WB195
20/02/1953	Neville Duke	Flight test	20	WB195
23/02/1953	Neville Duke	Flight test	45	?
24/02/1953	Neville Duke	Flight test	15	WB202
03/03/1953	Neville Duke	Flight test	20	WB195
03/03/1953	Neville Duke	Flight test	20	WB195
04/03/1953	Neville Duke	Flight test	50	WB202
04/03/1952	Neville Duke	Flight test	45	WB202
08/03/1953	Neville Duke	Flight test		WB195
08/03/1953	Neville Duke	Flight test	50	WB202

Date	Pilot	Flight Detail	Time (mins)	Aircraft
09/03/1953	Neville Duke	Flight test	45	WB202
09/03/1953	Neville Duke	Flight test	20	WB202
09/03/1953	Neville Duke	Flight test		WB195
10/03/1953	Neville Duke	Flight test	25	WB195
10/03/1953	Neville Duke	Flight test	35	WB202
10/03/1953	Neville Duke	Flight test	25	WB202
12/03/1953	Neville Duke	Flight test		WB195
13/03/1953	Neville Duke	Flight test	15	WB195
16/03/1953	Neville Duke	Flight test	25	WB195
17/03/1953	Neville Duke	Dunsfold to Warton	40	WB202
17/03/1953	Neville Duke	At Warton	35	WB202
18/03/1953	Neville Duke	Warton to Duxford	40	WB202
18/03/1953	Neville Duke	At Duxford. Demo to President Tito	45	WB202
18/03/1953	Neville Duke	Duxford to Dunsfold	20	WB202
20/03/1953	Neville Duke	Flight test	15	WB195
23/03/1953	Neville Duke	Flight test	20	WB195
23/03/1953	Neville Duke	Flight test	20	WB195
23/03/1953	Neville Duke	Flight test	15	WB195
24/03/1953	Neville Duke	Flight test	20	WB195
24/03/1953	Neville Duke	Flight test	20	WB195
25/03/1953	Neville Duke	Flight test	20	WB195
27/03/1953	Neville Duke	Flight test	20	WB195
27/03/1953	Neville Duke	Flight test	20	WB195
31/03/1953	Neville Duke	Flight test	20	WB195
31/03/1953	Neville Duke	Flight test	60	WB195
02/04/1953	Neville Duke	Flight test	50	WB202
02/04/1953	Neville Duke	Flight test	50	WB202
07/04/1953	Neville Duke	Flight test	50	WB202
07/04/1953	Neville Duke	Flight test	20	WB195
07/04/1953	Neville Duke	Flight test	15	WB195
07/04/1953	Neville Duke	Flight test	15	WB195
08/04/1953	Neville Duke	Flight test	15	WB195
08/04/1953	Neville Duke	Flight test	15	WB195
09/04/1953	Neville Duke	Flight test	15	WB195
10/04/1953	Neville Duke	Flight test	15	WB195
10/04/1953	Neville Duke	Flight test	15	WB202

Appendix II 281

Date	Pilot	Flight Detail	Time (mins)	Aircraft
14/04/1953	Neville Duke	Flight test	20	WB202
15/04/1953	Neville Duke	Flight test	30	WB202
15/04/1953	Neville Duke	Flight test	40	WB202
15/04/1953	Neville Duke	Flight test	30	WB202
15/04/1953	Neville Duke	Flight test	30	WB202
?/4/1953	Neville Duke	Flight test	45	WB202
19/04/1953	Neville Duke	Flight test	15	WB202
20/04/1953	Neville Duke	Flight test	25	WB202
20/04/1953	Neville Duke	Flight test	15	WB195
?/4/1953	Neville Duke	Flight test	20	WB195
21/04/1953	Neville Duke	Flight test	15	WB195
21/04/1953	Neville Duke	Flight test	1,1	WB195
23/04/1953	Neville Duke	Flight test	50	WB202
23/04/1953	Neville Duke	Flight test	25	WB195
23/04/1953	Neville Duke	Flight test	25	WB195
23/04/1953	Neville Duke	Flight test	45	WB195
2?/4/1953	Neville Duke	Flight test	20	WB195
26/04/1953	Neville Duke	Flight test	30	WB202
?/4/1953	Neville Duke	Dunsfold to ?	20	WB195
?/4/1953	Neville Duke	Demonstration	20	WB195
?/4/1953	Neville Duke	? To Dunsfold	25	WB195
?/4/1953	Neville Duke	Flight test		WB202
30/04/1953	Neville Duke	Flight test	20	?
03/05/1953	Neville Duke	Flight test	15	WB195
04/05/1953	Neville Duke	Flight test	15	WB195
04/05/1953	Neville Duke	Flight test	15	WB195
04/05/1953	Neville Duke	Flight test	40	WB202
05/05/1953	Neville Duke	Flight test	20	WB195
05/05/1953	Neville Duke	Flight test	15	WB202
?/5/1953	Neville Duke	Flight test	45	WB202
08/05/1953	Neville Duke	Flight test	25	WB195
11/05/1953	Neville Duke	Flight test	15	WB195
12/05/1953	Neville Duke	Flight test	25	WB195
14/05/1953	Neville Duke	Flight test	15	WB202
18/04/1953	Neville Duke	Flight test	25	WB195
18/05/1953	Neville Duke	Flight test	30	WB202

Date	Pilot	Flight Detail	Time (mins)	Aircraft
19/05/1953	Neville Duke	Demonstration. [Duke of Edinburgh at Dunsfold]	35	WB195
19/05/1953	Frank Murphy	Engine handling	35	WB202
19/05/1953	Frank Murphy	Formation	30	WB202
2?/5/1953	Neville Duke	Flight test		WB202
?/5/1953	Neville Duke	Flight test		WB202
21/05/1953	Neville Duke	Flight test	45	WB202
22/05/1953	Neville Duke	Flight test	55	WB202
27/05/1953	Neville Duke	Flight test	45	WB202
27/05/1953	Bill Bedford	Test flight	45	WB202
27/05/1953	Bill Bedford	Test flight	60	WB202
28/05/1953	Neville Duke	Flight test	10	WB202
29/05/1953	Neville Duke	Flight test	15	WB202
29/05/1953	Neville Duke	Flight test	10	WB202
29/05/1953	Neville Duke	Flight test	10	WB202
03/06/1953	Neville Duke	Flight test	25	WB202
04/06/1953	Neville Duke	Flight test	25	WB202
26/06/1953	Neville Duke	Flight test	30	WB202
26/06/1953	Neville Duke	Flight test	25	WB202
26/06/1953	Neville Duke	Flight test	40	WB202
29/06/1953	Neville Duke	Flight test	30	WB202
29/06/1953	Bill Bedford	Test flight	1,40	WB202
01/07/1953	Neville Duke	Flight test. 1st flight with reheat Hunter	40	WB188
02/07/1953	Bill Bedford	Test flight - air brake investigation	40	WB202
03/07/1953	Bill Bedford	Test flight - air brake investigation	10	WB202
03/07/1953	Bill Bedford	Test flight - air brake investigation	45	WB202
03/07/1953	Bill Bedford	Taxying (plus short flight)	10	WB188
07/07/1953	Neville Duke	First Reheat	40	WB188
14/07/1953	Neville Duke	Reheat levels	40	WB188
14/07/1953	Neville Duke	Reheat levels	30	WB188
15/07/1953	Neville Duke	Reheat levels	35	WB188
15/07/1953	Neville Duke	Timed runs (with reheat)	30	WB188
15/07/1953	Neville Duke	Flight test	35	WB202
16/07/1953	Neville Duke	Flight test	40	WB202
06/08/1953	Neville Duke	Flight test	30	WB202

Date	Pilot	Flight Detail	Time (mins)	Aircraft
10/08/1953	Neville Duke	Flight test	20	WB202
10/08/1953	Bill Bedford	Test flight	35	WB202
11/08/1953	Neville Duke	Flight test	30	WB202
12/08/1953	Neville Duke	Flight test	35	WB188
12/08/1953	Bill Bedford	Test flight	30	WB202
17/08/1953	Neville Duke	Flight test	25	WB188
17/08/1953	Neville Duke	Flight test	20	WB188
26/08/1953	Bill Bedford	Test flight - engine air test	40	WB202
30/08/1953	Neville Duke	Speed record runs - Tangmere	20	WB188
30/08/1953	Neville Duke	Speed record runs - Tangmere. 741mph	15	WB188
30/08/1953	Neville Duke	Speed record runs - Tangmere. 704mph	20	WB188
30/08/1953	Neville Duke	Speed record runs - Tangmere. 741mph	15	WB188
31/08/1953	Bill Bedford	Test flight	40	WB202
31/08/1953	Neville Duke	Speed record runs - Tangmere. 703mph	15	WB188
01/09/1953	Neville Duke	Speed record run - Tangmere Forced landing at Dunsfold. Nose and one main wheel. Port u/c leg u/s. Sucked out at 600kts Bognor Pier!	55	WB188
01/09/1953	Bill Bedford	Test flight	40	WB202
06/09/1953	Neville Duke	Flight test	35	WB202
06/09/1953	Bill Bedford	Test flight - to RAE	35	WB202
06/09/1953	Bill Bedford	Test flight	20	WB202
07/09/1953	Neville Duke	Dunsfold to Tangmere	15	WB188
07/09/1953	Neville Duke	726.9mph. First record attempt	15	WB188
07/09/1953	Neville Duke	World speed record 727.6mph	15	WB188
07/09/1953	Neville Duke	727.60mph final attempt	20	WB188
07/09/1953	Bill Bedford	SBAC flying display	25	WB202
08/09/1953	Neville Duke	Flight test Tangmere to Dunsfold via Farnborough	25	WB188
08/09/1953	Neville Duke	Farnborough display - supersonic, from Dunsfold	40	WB188
08/09/1953	Bill Bedford	SBAC display	35	WB202
09/09/1953	Bill Bedford	SBAC display	25	WB202

Date	Pilot	Flight Detail	Time (mins)	Aircraft
10/09/1953	Neville Duke	Farnborough display - supersonic	15	WB188
11/09/1953	Neville Duke	Flight test	20	WB188
11/09/1953	Neville Duke	Farnborough display - supersonic	30	WB188
11/09/1953	Bill Bedford	SBAC display	35	WB202
12/09/1953	Neville Duke	SBAC display - supersonic	30	WB188
12/09/1953	Bill Bedford	SBAC display	30	WB202
13/09/1953	Bill Bedford	SBAC display	30	WB202
13/09/1953	Neville Duke	SBAC display - supersonic	35	WB188
14/09/1953	Neville Duke	Flight test	15	WB202
16/09/1953	Frank Murphy	Photography - excellent (C. Peckham)	55	WB202
18/09/1953	Neville Duke	100km course practice	10	WB188
18/09/1953	Bill Bedford	Test flight	35	WB202
18/09/1953	Bill Bedford	Test flight	30	WB202
19/09/1953	Neville Duke	100km closed circuit record	15	WB188
25/09/1953	Bill Bedford	Test flight	35	WB202
12/10/1953	Bill Bedford	Test flight	10	WB202
14/10/1953	Bill Bedford	Test flight	50	WB202
16/10/1953	Bill Bedford	Test flight	55	WB202
19/10/1953	Bill Bedford	Dunsfold to Le Bourget	40	WB202
19/10/1953	Bill Bedford	Le Bourget to Zurich	55	WB202
20/10/1953	Bill Bedford	Demonstration to Swiss Government	15	WB202
20/10/1953	Bill Bedford	Demonstration to Swiss Government	40	WB202
21/10/1953	Bill Bedford	From Kloten to Emmen - landing tests and thrust measurements	30	WB202
21/10/1953	Bill Bedford	From Kloten to Emmen - landing tests and thrust measurements	20	WB202
22/10/1953	Bill Bedford	Demonstration at Kloten	30	WB202
22/10/1953	Bill Bedford	Zurich to Le Bourget	45	WB202
22/10/1953	Bill Bedford	Le Bourget to Dunsfold	30	WB202
19/11/1953	Neville Duke	Flight test	35	WB188
28/11/1953	Neville Duke	Flight test	40	WB188
28/11/1953	Neville Duke	Flight test	20	WB195
04/12/1953	Neville Duke	Flight test	30	WB195
07/12/1953	Neville Duke	Flight test	30	WB195
11/12/1953	Bill Bedford	Test flight	30	WB195

Appendix II

Date	Pilot	Flight Detail	Time (mins)	Aircraft
11/12/1953	Bill Bedford	Test flight	30	WB195
14/12/1953	Neville Duke	Flight test	25	WB195
16/12/1953	Bill Bedford	Test flight	50	WB202
17/12/1953	Neville Duke	Flight test	20	WB195
19/12/1953	Neville Duke	Flight test	35	WB202
22/12/1953	Bill Bedford	Test flight	15	WB195
31/12/1953	Neville Duke	Flight test	1,05	WB202
31/12/1953	Neville Duke	Flight test	30	WB202
01/01/1954	Neville Duke	Flight test	40	WB202
04/01/1954	Neville Duke	Flight test	45	WB188
06/01/1954	Neville Duke	Flight test	50	WB202
07/01/1954	Neville Duke	Flight test	20	WB202
08/01/1954	Neville Duke	Flight test	50	WB202
08/01/1954	Neville Duke	Flight test	35	WB202
11/01/1954	Neville Duke	Flight test	35	WB202
12/01/1954	Neville Duke	Flight test [last mention of this aircraft in the logs]	30	WB188
12/01/1954	Neville Duke	Flight test	40	WB202
14/01/1954	Neville Duke	Flight test	25	WB202
15/01/1954	Neville Duke	Flight test	25	WB202
15/01/1954	Neville Duke	Flight test	20	WB202
15/01/1954	Neville Duke	Flight test	40	WB195
19/01/1954	Neville Duke	Flight test	45	WB202
19/01/1954	Neville Duke	Flight test	40	WB202
29/01/1954	Neville Duke	Flight test	35	WB202
02/02/1954	Neville Duke	Gun firing	30	WB202
03/02/1954	Neville Duke	Gun firing	20	WB202
03/02/1954	Neville Duke	Gun firing	25	WB202
10/02/1954	Neville Duke	Air test	25	WB195
22/02/1954	Neville Duke	Cabin conditioning	35	WB202
22/02/1954	Neville Duke	Cabin conditioning	35	WB202
24/02/1954	Neville Duke	Cabin conditioning	35	WB202
26/02/1954	Bill Bedford	Test flight - cabin conditioning	60	WB202
26/02/1954	Bill Bedford	Test flight - autostabilisation	35	WB202
01/03/1954	Neville Duke	Air test	30	WB195
03/03/1954	Bill Bedford	Test flight	30	WB202

Date	Pilot	Flight Detail	Time (mins)	Aircraft
04/03/1954	Bill Bedford	Test flight	55	WB202
05/03/1954	Neville Duke	Cabin conditioning	1,05	WB202
19/03/1954	Neville Duke	Mass balance to 120%	40	WB195
19/03/1954	Neville Duke	Mass balance to 120%	30	WB195
23/03/1954	Neville Duke	Spinning	45	WB195
24/03/1954	Neville Duke	Spinning	45	WB195
24/03/1954	Bill Bedford	Test flight - Spinning	55	WB195
26/03/1954	Bill Bedford	Spinning	30	WB195
09/04/1954	Bill Bedford	Test flight	50	WB195
12/04/1954	Bill Bedford	Test flight	45	WB195
27/04/1954	Bill Bedford	Test flight	35	WB195
27/04/1954	Bill Bedford	Test flight	10	WB195
30/04/1954	Bill Bedford	Test flight	30	WB195
03/05/1954	Bill Bedford	Test flight	20	WB195
03/05/1954	Bill Bedford	Test flight	5	WB195
04/05/1954	Bill Bedford	Test flight	20	WB195
05/05/1954	Bill Bedford	Test flight	10	WB195
05/05/1954	Bill Bedford	Test flight	5	WB195
05/05/1954	Bill Bedford	Test flight	5	WB195
08/05/1954	Bill Bedford	Test flight	20	WB195
08/05/1954	Bill Bedford	Test flight	5	WB195
08/05/1954	Bill Bedford	Test flight	5	WB195
08/05/1954	Bill Bedford	Test flight	20	WB195
12/05/1954	Bill Bedford	Test flight	50	WB202
20/05/1954	Neville Duke	Air test	30	WB195
21/05/1954	Neville Duke	Handling	40	WB202
24/05/1954	Neville Duke	External stores	45	WB202
24/05/1954	Neville Duke	External stores	45	WB202
27/05/1954	Bill Bedford	Test flight	25	WB195
27/05/1954	Bill Bedford	Test flight	50	WB195
28/05/1954	Bill Bedford	Test flight	35	WB195
01/06/1954	Bill Bedford	Test flight	60	WB202
03/06/1954	Bill Bedford	Test flight	50	WB195
03/06/1954	Bill Bedford	Test flight	15	WB195
03/06/1954	Bill Bedford	Test flight	15	WB195
21/06/1954	Bill Bedford	Test flight	45	WB202

Date	Pilot	Flight Detail	Time (mins)	Aircraft
21/06/1954	Bill Bedford	Test flight	50	WB202
22/06/1954	Bill Bedford	Test flight	45	WB202
22/06/1954	Bill Bedford	Test flight	45	WB202
23/06/1954	Neville Duke	Position Errors	35	WB202
23/06/1954	Neville Duke	Position Errors	45	WB202
24/06/1954	Bill Bedford	Test flight	30	WB202
29/06/1954	Neville Duke	4-missile photographs	60	WB202
30/06/1954	Bill Bedford	Test flight - performance	45	WB202
30/06/1954	Bill Bedford	Test flight	55	WB202
30/06/1954	Bill Bedford	Test flight - PE s	45	WB202
03/09/1954	Frank Murphy	?	25	WB202
09/09/1954	Bill Bedford	Test flight	40	WB202
10/09/1954	Bill Bedford	Landed SBAC re Russians	10	WB202
10/09/1954	Bill Bedford	From Farnborough. [Last mention of this aircraft in the logs]	10	WB202
20/10/1954	Bill Bedford	Test flight. [Last mention of this aircraft in the logs]	30	WB195

Production Hunter F.1 Flights				
Date	Pilot	Flight Detail	Time (mins)	Aircraft
16/05/1953	Neville Duke	1st flight. [First production Hunter]	40	WT555
17/05/1953	Neville Duke	Flight test	55	WT555
19/05/1953	Neville Duke	Flight test	25	WT555
20/05/1953	Neville Duke	Flight test	30	WT555
27/05/1953	Neville Duke	Flight test	40	WT555
27/05/1953	Neville Duke	Flight test	50	WT555
28/05/1953	Neville Duke	Flight test	1,05	WT555
28/05/1953	Neville Duke	Flight test	20	WT555
04/06/1953	Neville Duke	Flight test	35	WT555
05/06/1953	Frank Murphy	Production test	30	WT555
08/06/1953	Bill Bedford	Test flight	40	WT555
16/06/1953	Frank Murphy	Production test	45	WT556
18/06/1953	Neville Duke	Flight test	1,05	WT555
30/06/1953	Neville Duke	Flight test	35	WT555
01/07/1953	Frank Murphy	Production test	45	WT556
02/07/1953	Neville Duke	Flight test	35	WT555
02/07/1953	Neville Duke	Dunsfold to Paris (bang)	35	WT555
04/07/1953	Neville Duke	Paris Aero Show	10	WT555
05/07/1953	Neville Duke	Paris Aero Show	20	WT555
06/07/1954	Neville Duke	Paris to Dunsfold	45	WT555
10/07/1953	Neville Duke	Flight test	20	WT555
10/07/1953	Neville Duke	Flight test	20	WT555
13/07/1953	Neville Duke	Flight test	20	WT555
13/07/1953	Neville Duke	Flight test	25	WT555
14/07/1953	Neville Duke	Flight test	20	WT555
15/07/1953	Neville Duke	Flight test	30	WT555
16/07/1953	Neville Duke	Dunsfold to Soesterburg	40	WT555
17/07/1953	Frank Murphy	Production test	50	WT557
18/07/1953	Neville Duke	Demonstration. NATO display	45	WT555
18/07/1953	Neville Duke	Soesterburg to Dunsfold	45	WT555
10/08/1953	Frank Murphy	Production test	35	WT556
14/08/1953	Neville Duke	Flight test	45	WT557
14/08/1953	Neville Duke	Flight test	40	WT557
18/08/1953	Bill Bedford	Test flight	30	WT557
18/08/1953	Bill Bedford	Dunsfold - Radlett. Demonstration for Americans	30	WT557

Date	Pilot	Flight Detail	Time (mins)	Aircraft
18/08/1953	Bill Bedford	Radlett - Dunsfold	30	WT557
20/08/1953	Neville Duke	Flight test	35	WT557
24/08/1953	Frank Murphy	Production test	40	WT558
24/08/1953	Bill Bedford	Test flight	40	WT557
25/08/1953	Frank Murphy	Production test. Landed Tangmere	1,10	WT558
25/08/1953	Frank Murphy	Tangmere - Dunsfold	20	WT558
26/08/1953	Neville Duke	Flight test	40	WT557
27/08/1953	Neville Duke	Flight test	40	WT558
28/08/1953	Neville Duke	Flight test	45	WT558
30/08/1953	Bill Bedford	Test flight - to Tangmere	10	WT558
30/08/1953	Bill Bedford	Test flight - from Tangmere	15	WT558
30/08/1953	Bill Bedford	Test flight	30	WT558
31/08/1953	Neville Duke	Flight test	25	WT557
31/08/1953	Neville Duke	Flight test	25	WT558
31/08/1953	Neville Duke	Flight test	1,05	WT558
31/08/1953	Neville Duke	Flight test	1,05	WT558
02/09/1953	Frank Murphy	Production test	25	WT559
03/09/1953	Frank Murphy	Production test	50	WT559
04/09/1953	Bill Bedford	Test flight	50	WT559
06/09/1953	Neville Duke	Flight test	25	WT558
06/09/1953	Neville Duke	Flight test	45	WT557
06/09/1953	Frank Murphy	Air test and SBAC. Delivery and photo	20	WT557
07/09/1953	Frank Murphy	SBAC Demonstration. Landed Dunsfold	15	WT557
08/09/1953	Frank Murphy	Dunsfold - Farnborough	15	WT557
08/09/1953	Neville Duke	Flight test	25	WT559
08/09/1953	Neville Duke	Flight test	50	WT559
08/09/1953	Bill Bedford	Test flight	35	WT559
10/09/1953	Bill Bedford	Test flight - longitudinal stability measurements	30	WT555
11/09/1953	Bill Bedford	Test flight - longitudinal stability measurements	60	WT555
11/09/1953	Neville Duke	Flight test	45	WT555
12/09/1953	Neville Duke	Flight test	30	WT555
14/09/1953	Neville Duke	Flight test	40	WT555
15/09/1953	Neville Duke	100km course practice	60	WT557

Date	Pilot	Flight Detail	Time (mins)	Aircraft
15/09/1953	Neville Duke	100km course practice	30	WT557
16/09/1953	Neville Duke	100km course practice	30	WT557
16/09/1953	Neville Duke	100km course practice	50	WT557
17/09/1953	Neville Duke	100km course practice	25	WT557
19/09/1953	Neville Duke	Flight test (100km course test prior to record run)	20	WT557
22/09/1953	Bill Bedford	Test flight	25	WT559
24/09/1953	Bill Bedford	Test flight	50	WT555
24/09/1953	Bill Bedford	Test flight	45	WT555
25/09/1953	Neville Duke	Flight test	30	WT555
25/09/1953	Bill Bedford	Test flight	30	WT555
28/09/1953	Bill Bedford	Test flight	25	WT555
30/09/1953	Bill Bedford	Test flight	40	WT560
30/09/1953	Neville Duke	Flight test	25	WT555

Index

Aden Cannon, 137, 149, 163, 179, 188, 208, 220
Aircraft – Hawker:
   Fury, 1, 21, 23–4, 27, 33, 43, 66, 238
   Hind, 238
   Hurricane, 1, 18–21, 26, 30, 183, 225
   Hunter, 11–12, 15–16, 32, 38–9, 55, 74, 94, 100, 113, 127, 138, 142, 145, 149, 153, 155–9, 161, 163–5, 167–73, 177–8, 186, 191, 193, 196–7, 199, 201–203, 205, 208, 215, 217, 219, 220–1, 234
   F.1, 16, 160, 162, 166, 174–6, 179–84, 187–8, 195, 204
   F.2, 12, 169, 175, 179, 182
   F.4, 176, 178, 180–2
   F.6, 180, 205
   T.7, 195
   P.1040, 27, 31, 33–4, 36–49, 51–2, 55–6, 58, 60, 66–7, 79, 81, 83, 95, 106, 112, 127–8, 152, 175, 184, 238
   P.1052, 56, 64, 79–84, 86–90, 92–5, 99–100, 111, 127–8, 185, 239
   P.1067, 11, 39, 64, 100, 127, 133, 139, 147–56, 159, 170, 172, 175, 179, 197, 204–205, 240
   P.1072, 48, 51–2, 56–61, 63, 87
   P.1081, 56, 89, 91, 95, 96, 98–101, 103–106, 108–10, 127, 175, 186, 239
   Sea Fury, 21, 66, 238
   Sea Hawk, 31, 34, 36–7, 47, 74–6, 83, 87, 91, 98, 112, 114, 116–26, 139, 142, 145, 159, 170, 175, 183–5, 196, 203, 239
   Tempest, 1, 21–3, 33, 43, 183, 234
   Tornado, 21
   Typhoon, 1, 21–2, 30, 183
Aircraft – Other:
   Avro Lancastrian, 13
   BAC TSR.2, 208, 229–30, 232
   Blackburn Buccaneer, 188
   Boulton Paul Defiant, 19, 21, 36
   Bristol Beaufighter, 149, 179
   De Havilland:
      DH.110, 191
      Mosquito, 26–8
      Vampire, 10, 13, 32, 36, 75, 78, 124, 192, 195
      Vampire NF.10, 193
      Venom, 99, 191–2
      Venom NF.2, 193
      Vixen, 192–3, 196
   English Electric Canberra, 16, 27–8, 133, 229
   English Electric Lightning, 155, 194, 205
   Folland:
      Fo.144, 195
      Gnat, 194–6
      Midge, 194
   Gloster:
      Ace, 190
      GA.1, 190
      GA.2, 190–1
      GA.4, 191
      GA.5, 191
      Javelin, 11, 189, 191, 193, 196
      Meteor, 8, 10–12, 32, 64, 73, 85, 99, 124, 159, 189, 191–2
      Meteor NF.11, 189
      Meteor NF.12, 189
      Meteor NF.14, 189
   Handley Page Victor, 11
   Heinkel He.178, 17
   Lockheed F-104 Starfighter, 124
   McDonnell Douglas F-4 Phantom II, 193
   MiG-15, 14, 99, 197, 199
   Miles M.52, 51, 64
   Myasishchev M-4, 199
   North American P-51 Mustang, 99, 241
   Saunders Roe SR.53, 65
   Supermarine:
      Attacker, 97, 120, 183–6
      Scimitar, 188, 196
      Seafang, 183
      Spiteful, 183
      Spitfire, 26, 183
      Swift, 16, 157, 164, 166, 177, 186–8, 196, 204
      Type 392, 183–4
      Type 508, 188
      Type 510, 185
      Type 525, 188
      Type 529, 188
      Type 535, 186

Type 541, 186
Type 544, 188
Tupolev TU-4, 163
Tupolev Tu-95, 199
Westland Wallace 238
Westland Wyvern, 11
Ansty, 58, 64
Australia, 56, 85, 95, 99–100
Aviation Related Companies:
Arado, 17
Armstrong Whitworth, (Sir W.G.), 219
Avro, (A.V. Roe & Co), 13, 64–5, 205, 208, 229, 232
Blackburn, (Aircraft Ltd), 188, 240
Bristol, (Aeroplane Co.), 1, 16, 21, 23–4, 26, 28, 179, 194, 208, 230
Boulton Paul, (Aircraft), 36, 65
Canadian Car and Foundry, 18
Commonwealth Aircraft Corporation, 100
Dowty, (Group), 37
De Havilland, (Aircraft Co. Ltd), 10, 13, 18, 26, 32, 99, 153, 191–3, 196, 205, 208, 227
English Electric, (Co. Ltd), 27, 133, 194, 205, 230
Fairey, (Aviation Co), 219
Folland, (Aircraft), 194–6
Gloster, (Aircraft Co.), 7–8, 10–12, 18–19, 21, 32, 99, 114, 188–92, 196, 240
Hawker Aircraft Ltd, 1–2, 13, 16, 19, 25–6, 28–9, 31, 55–6, 100, 102, 112–13, 115, 128, 156–7, 170, 196–7, 204, 238
Hawker Siddeley Aviation, 24–5
Hawker Siddeley Group, 11, 25, 55, 114, 195–6, 229–30
Heinkel, (Flugzeugwerke), 17
Junkers, (Flugzeug-und Motorenwerke), 17, 207
Lockheed, (Corporation), 124
Malcolm, R, (& Co.), 39, 47, 104, 106–107
Martin Baker, (Aircraft Co. Ltd.), 39, 45, 47, 104, 106–107, 112, 140, 142, 148, 112, 140, 142, 148
Martinsyde, 24, 104
Messerschmitt, 17, 24, 239
Miles, (Aircraft Ltd.), 49, 61
M.L. Aviation, 39, 102, 104, 107–108, 140
Myasishchev, 199
Saunders Roe, 65, 208
Sopwith, (Aviation Co.), 25, 183
Supermarine, 31, 97, 157, 163, 183–8, 196
Vickers (Aviation Ltd.), 4, 51, 230
Aviation Related Government Establishments and Committees:
A&AEE Boscombe Down, 43, 45, 69, 71–4, 76, 83, 85, 107, 113, 122, 147–8, 153, 157, 164, 173, 175, 177–8, 182, 184–8, 190–1, 193–4, 238
Aeronautical Research Committee, (ARC), 3
Central Fighter Establishment, (CFE), 153, 161, 166, 179–80
Empire Test Pilots School, (ETPS), 237, 240
Fort Halstead, (RARDE), 129
Gas Turbine Technical Advisory Coordinating Committee, (GTTACC), 8
Namou, (CEPE), 117
Reichsluftfahrtministerium, (RLM), 17
Rocket Propulsion Establishment, (RPE), Wescott, 51
Royal Aircraft Establishment (RAE), Farnborough, 3–5, 7–8, 10–11, 24–5, 33, 36–7, 39, 44–6, 48–9, 58–61, 67, 69, 71–6, 79, 83–6, 89, 93–4, 97–104, 111–13, 149, 153–4, 157, 172, 179, 185–6, 191, 193, 197
Royal Aircraft Factory, 3
axial compressor, 3–5, 9, 11, 14, 127

Barnoldswick, 1, 8, 14–15, 30, 35
Bitteswell, 58–61, 63
Blackbushe, 97
Blackpool, 171
Brooklands, 20, 25, 190, 195

Canbury Park Road, 19, 30, 37–8, 41
centrifugal compressor, 5–8, 10, 12–14, 17, 33, 49, 95, 127
Chilbolton, 194, 196
Claremont, 18–19, 27, 30, 33
Coventry, 11, 55, 58, 114, 122, 147

Derby, 1, 15–16, 31, 34–5
Dunsfold, 46, 91, 93–4, 112–13, 117, 119–20, 122–3, 149, 151–3, 156–8, 165–6, 172, 174, 176, 181, 195–6, 204, 233, 240

Engine Manufacturers:
Armstrong Siddeley Motors, 5, 11–12, 14, 48, 51, 55–6, 58, 60, 64, 140, 147, 149, 152, 163, 194, 201
Bristol Engines, 16
BMW, 17
British Thompson Houston, 7
Curtiss-Wright, 11
Daimler Benz, 17
Halford, 10, 36, 190
Metrovick, 4–5, 10–11, 128
Klimov, 13
Napier, 1, 21–2, 26, 28

Power Jets Ltd, 7
Rolls-Royce, 1–2, 5, 8–9, 12–16, 18, 21, 26–7, 29–31, 33–8, 40, 42–4, 49, 55, 64, 95, 97, 100, 127–8, 131, 133, 140, 149, 153, 163–4, 177, 183, 185–6, 190, 193, 201, 204, 208
Rover, 1, 8, 189–90
Engine Types – Reciprocal:
Bristol Centaurus, 1, 21, 23, 26, 28
Napier Sabre, 1, 21–2, 26, 28, 100, 102, 174, 177
Rolls-Royce Griffon, 2, 27
Rolls-Royce Merlin, 1–2, 18, 30
Engine Types – Turbine:
Armstrong Siddeley:
Python, 11
Sa.2, 11, 140
Sapphire, 5, 11–12, 140, 147, 152–3, 163–4, 179, 197, 205
Viper, 194
Bristol Orpheus, 194, 196
De Havilland:
Ghost, 10, 192
Goblin, 10, 36, 192
Gyron, 205, 208, 217, 219, 223, 226–7, 229
Halford H.1, 10, 36, 190
Metrovick Beryl, 11
Power Jets W.2B/23, 8
Rolls-Royce:
AJ.65, 14, 38, 128, 131
Avon, 55, 64, 95, 137, 140, 143–4, 147, 156, 163–4, 168, 177, 180, 193, 197, 206, 207, 213, 215
Avon RA.1, 15
Avon RA.2, 16, 131
Avon RA.3, 16, 133, 149, 158
Avon RA.7, 16, 100, 133, 149, 158, 178, 182, 186–7
Avon RA.7R, 153, 155
Avon RA.14, 151, 154, 201, 205, 208
Avon RA.14R, 153, 204
Avon RA.21, 179
Avon RA.24, 208, 217
Derwent, RB.37, 8–9, 12
Nene, RB.41, 12–14, 26–7, 31, 36, 44, 49–50, 57, 59, 64–5, 76, 94, 95, 111, 113, 118, 126, 183, 185–6, 190
RB.40, 2, 12, 18, 27
RB.106, 211
Tay, RB.44, 14, 64, 95
Welland, RB.23, 8, 10
Engine Types – Rocket:
Armstrong Siddeley:
Alpha, 51
Beta, 51–2
Delta, 52

Screamer, 64–5
Snarler, 51–2, 59–61, 65, 200

flexible deck, 74–6, 78

Guided Missile Projects:
Blue Jay, 204
Blue Sky, 152
De Havilland Firestreak, 153
Fairey Fireflash, 153

Hawker Project Numbers:
P.1005, 26–7, 30–1
P.1011, 26
P.1014, 27
P.1026, 27
P.1031, 27
P.1035, 27, 30–1, 33
P.1039, 27
P.1046, 37, 55, 66
P.1047, 37–8, 55, 66, 79
P.1053, 64
P.1054, 128
P.1057, 128–9, 196
P.1069, 139, 197–8, 200
P.1070, 139
P.1071, 64, 139, 197, 200
P.1077, 205–206
P.1078, 64, 87
P.1080, 99
P.1083, 64, 144, 151, 153–5, 164, 197, 201–205
P.1088, 207, 209
P.1089, 64–5, 208, 210
P.1092, 208, 212–15
P.1093, 208, 214
P.1095, 205
P.1096, 211, 215–16, 218
P.1099, 181, 205
P.1100, 208, 217
P.1102, 208
P.1103, 208, 215, 217, 220, 222–4
P.1104, 217
P.1116, 220, 224
P.1121, 181, 208, 215, 220–1, 225–30
P.1127, 83, 241
P.1129, 208, 229, 230, 232
Hispano cannon, 18, 21, 184
Hucclecote, 11, 18
Hucknall, 1

Karel Doorman HNLMS, 124
Kingston-upon-Thames, 1, 18–19, 23, 25, 27, 29–30, 37, 39, 43, 48, 51, 58, 79, 81, 97, 100–101, 103, 108, 112–14, 117, 137,

148–9, 152–4, 161, 163, 172, 197, 201, 203, 220, 225, 230, 233

Langley, 18, 21–3, 42–4, 58, 93, 112, 151, 162, 172, 238

Mayford, 25

Ministry Specifications/ Operational Requirements:
  E.38/46, 185
  E.41/46, 185
  ER.134T, 211
  F.119D, 203
  F.124T, 64, 208, 210
  F.155T, 217, 219
  F.15/49, 192
  F.28/49, 99
  F.43/46, 55, 128–9, 131, 135, 159
  F.44/46, 129, 131, 159, 191, 193, 196
  F.105P, 186
  F.9/40, 10, 11, 189
  N.7/46, 33, 39–40, 48, 50, 55–6, 66–8, 70–9, 95, 107, 112, 155, 184, 239
  OR.228, 129, 131, 135, 178–9, 186
  OR.329, 217, 225, 227

People – Hawker:
  Bedford, William, 'Bill', 76, 93, 117, 119–20, 122, 158, 180, 240
  Bulman, Paul 'George', 1–2, 20, 30
  Chaplin, Roland 'Roy', 1–2, 19, 25, 55, 108, 140, 148
  Camm, Sir Sydney, 1, 19, 24–5, 44, 55, 104, 208, 234
  Dobson, Sir Roy, 25
  Duke, Neville, 58–9, 71–2, 76, 86, 89, 93, 94, 100, 112–13, 119, 123, 148, 150–1, 156–7, 174, 177, 180–1, 235
  Fozard, John, 29, 205, 208, 211–13
  Hooper, Ralph, 19, 49, 60, 83, 100, 142, 143, 158, 161
  Humble, William 'Bill', 42, 44–5, 238
  Lickley, Sir Robert, 1–2, 18–19, 29, 33–4
  Marsh, Robert, 'Bob', 49, 103, 148, 174
  Merewether, Hugh, 241
  Murphy, Francis 'Frank', 76, 117, 119–20, 123, 178, 180–1, 239
  Sigrist, Fred, 25
  Spriggs, Neville, 1–2, 30, 56
  Stanbury, Vivian, 33–5, 55, 103, 129, 139–40, 156
  Stranks, Donald, 108
  Sutton, F.V.K. 'Fred', 152, 175
  Tuffen, Harold, 104, 142
  Wade, Trevor 'Wimpy', 45–8, 58–9, 63, 67, 72, 75, 78, 84–5, 92, 97, 99–100, 102, 105, 107–108, 111

People – Other:
  Armour, Des 108
  Ascani, Fred, 174
  Bird-Wilson, Harold, 166
  Brown, Eric 'Winkle', 45, 48, 75, 85, 112, 122, 234
  Boyd, Albert, 174
  Churchill, Sir Winston, 159
  Dorey, R.N., 1–2, 31
  Dudley North, John, 36
  Ellor, J.E., 1–2, 29
  Farren, Sir William, 25, 33–4
  Fedden, Sir Roy, 24
  Freeman, Sir Wilfred, 34
  Griffith, A.A., 3–8, 14
  Handasyde, George, 25
  Heathcote, 42–3
  Hives, Ernest 1– 2, 5, 8, 14–16
  Hooker, Sir Stanley, 1–2, 8, 12, 14–16, 30, 234
  Johnson, G.W. 'Jonnie', 117, 153, 174
  Kyle, Sir Wallace, 154–5, 204
  Lappin, W., 1–2, 29
  Liptrot, Roger, 36
  Lithgow, Michael 'Mike', 186
  Lobelle, Marcel, 39, 104, 111
  Martin, H.P., 25,
  Mitchell, R.J., 26, 183
  Ohain, Hans von, 17
  Pepper, Don, 29
  Petter, William 'Teddy', 27, 194–6
  Quill, Jeffrey, 184
  Redshaw, Dr. S.C., 36
  Rowe, N.E., 33
  Sandys, Duncan, 208, 227, 229
  Serby, J.E., 83, 95, 128–9, 131, 133, 142
  Shaw, A.I.R., 76
  Silyn-Roberts, Glynn, 128, 154–5, 204
  Slattery, Sir Matthew, 38
  Smythe, Reginald 'Reg', 57
  Stern, William, 3
  Swinchatt, Roche, 28
  Tennant, Edward 'Teddy', 194–5
  Tizard, Sir Henry, 10
  Tuttle, Sir Geoffrey, 155, 204
  Tweedie, W.L., 6
  Vessey, H.F., 83–4
  Wardle, Alfred, 33
  Waterton, William 'Bill', 240
  Whittle, Sir Frank, 4–12, 17, 51, 64, 234
  Yeager, Charles 'Chuck', 149
  Project Office, (Hawker) 1, 18, 21, 30, 49, 101, 103, 142, 148, 197, 205, 207, 215, 221, 233

RAF Establishments:
  Abingdon, 158, 187
  Biggin Hill, 238–9
  Brawdy, 117, 122, 125–6

Cardington, 93
Central Fighter Establishment, 161, 163, 171, 184, 193
Colerne, 93, 158
Cranwell, 6
Halton, 93, 158, 182
Headley Court, 181
Kemble, 182
Odiham, 93, 99
Shawbury, 238
Tangmere, 74, 158
Thorney Island, 181, 240
Wattisham, 179
West Raynham, 153, 166, 179
Richmond Road, 48, 51, 58, 74, 82, 83, 89, 98, 118, 119, 144, 153–5, 229

Royal Navy Ships:
HMS *Eagle*, 91, 113, 117
HMS *Illustrious*, 69, 72, 77, 184, 186
HMS *Warrior*, 75, 78
RNAS Establishments:
Yeovilton, 24, 93
Ford, 74, 119–20, 123, 178, 181, 239
Lee-on-Solent, 72

Suez, 117

Vikrant INS, 124

Watts, (propeller), 18, 20
Windsor, 24